T0164087

# A Transatlantic Pivot to Asia

*Towards New Trilateral Partnerships*

**Edited by**
**Hans Binnendijk**

Center for Transatlantic Relations
Paul H. Nitze School of Advanced International Studies
Johns Hopkins University

Hans Binnendijk, ed., *A Transatlantic Pivot to Asia: Towards New Trilateral Partnerships*

Washington, DC: Center for Transatlantic Relations, 2014

© Center for Transatlantic Relations, 2014

**Center for Transatlantic Relations**
The Paul H. Nitze School of Advanced International Studies
The Johns Hopkins University
1717 Massachusetts Avenue, N.W. Suite 525
Washington, DC 20036
Tel: (202) 663-5880
Fax: (202) 663-5879
Email: transatlantic@jhu.edu
http://transatlantic.sais-jhu.edu

ISBN  978-0-9890294-7-6

*Cover illustration: Atlas to Walker's Geography, London, 1806*

# Table of Contents

# Preface

The Obama Administration entered office with the belief that the bulk of the 21st century would be written in Asia. U.S. officials across all spectrums of government recognized the need to place greater diplomatic focus on the growing economic dimensions, rising security challenges, and emerging geopolitical realities of the Asia-Pacific. The region presented a complex dichotomy between the fast-pace of development and a rigid historical framework, each alluding to an underlying intense and pervasive state of political flux. In the south, the ASEAN nations were undertaking ambitious steps to achieve greater cohesion and connectivity in a region that was historically marked by decades of conflict. However, persistent maritime disputes threatened to stymie connectivity and enflame resurgent regionalism, including a territorial dispute in the East China Sea that prompted an unprecedented rise in Japanese defense budgets. Moreover, from the uncertainties wrought by North Korea's leadership transition to issues surrounding OPCON transfer in South Korea, it became apparent that the United States required a multi-dimensional engagement strategy to address the fluidity of Asia's security architecture. Consequently, a comprehensive policy was designed to pivot, or rebalance, American economic, diplomatic, and military engagement towards Asia.

In our experience, engagement in Asia requires a certain degree of dexterity best served by close cooperation between the United States and its European allies. Yet, from its outset, this policy of rebalancing was misinterpreted internationally both as an effort to shift attention away from Europe, as well as to hedge and encircle a rising China—neither is true. In fact, the policy set the groundwork for greater U.S.-EU cooperation to creatively engage Asian nations and institutions in ways that enhance regional security, encourage greater economic linkages and growth, and promote the rule of law.

However, despite the fact that European nations share most American values and interests with regard to Asia, the transatlantic partners have yet to coordinate effectively in pursuit of those common objectives. This volume is meant to reinforce the importance of transatlantic cooperation as the United States and Europe engage Asia going forward. Each transatlantic partner brings advantages to the table. The United States provides security to its Asian allies in ways that exceed Europe's current capabilities. In complement, Europe has the economic strength and institutional experience to support large-scale development goals and multilateral forums that promote the rule of law. By mixing hard and soft power, the transatlantic partners together have an opportunity to improve security and provide greater prosperity for the Asia-Pacific region.

As evolving global challenges increase the demands and pressures on American diplomacy, it is critical to identify concrete steps for greater transatlantic cooperation in Asia. The fourteen chapters in this book explore avenues for such cooperation, each containing a set of principal recommendations that governments can convert into a roadmap for future action. We recommend this book to those seeking ways to improve the ever-increasing importance of trilateral U.S.-EU-Asian ties.

KURT CAMPBELL
*Former U.S. Assistant Secretary of State*
*for East Asian and Pacific Affairs*

WIM GEERTS
*Political Director, Netherlands*
*Ministry of Foreign Affairs*

# Acknowledgments

This volume is part of a collaborative project organized by the Center for Transatlantic Relations, directed by Daniel S. Hamilton. It consisted of several workshops and conferences as well as individual contributions by the chapter authors. We have sought to preserve the voice of each author at the expense of some redundancy. The purpose of the volume is both to enlighten and to improve policy. Therefore, each author was asked to provide several policy recommendations.

This project and publication was made possible by a grant from the Foreign Ministry of the Netherlands. The Ministry and the Dutch Embassy in Washington have proven to be exceptional partners in this endeavor. We would like to thank Rudolf Bekink, Marcel de Vink, Peter Mollema, Meline Arakelian, Bartjan Wegter, and in particular Rob Anderson who managed the project for the Ministry and provided excellent coordination. We would also like to thank the American Embassy in The Hague for its support.

A major conference was held in the Netherlands in October, 2013 to refine the concepts presented in this book. We would like to thank Abiodun Williams, Director of The Hague Institute for Global Justice, and his associate Mark Bailey for hosting that conference and for their intellectual support. We also thank Kurt Campbell for keynoting a workshop that helped develop many of the themes presented in this volume.

Many colleagues at CTR contributed in significant ways to this effort. Special thanks go to Dan Hamilton, who helped to design the project, contributed a chapter, and provided a final editorial review. Thanks also go to András Simonyi, Miriam Cunningham, Katrien Maes, Debra Cagan, and in particular to Frederiek Elemans and William Hudec, who helped edit the volume. Finally, thanks to Peggy Irvine and Peter Lindeman for turning the manuscript into final book form.

The authors who contributed to this book express their personal views, which do not necessarily reflect those of any institution or government.

*Hans Binnendijk*

# Executive Summary

The U.S. policy of rebalancing or pivoting to Asia is a core element of America's national security strategy. It is a comprehensive policy with multiple aspects, including security, economics, and diplomacy. It is not intended as an instrument to contain China, but rather as a way to engage more effectively with the rising and sometimes troubled nations of Asia. It has been misinterpreted in Europe as a pivot away from that continent. That is not the case, though it is an effort to change America's profile in the Middle East away from decade-long stabilization operations.

Europe, too, has shifted more attention to Asia, often bilaterally. But Europe's impact on Asia is more limited. Nonetheless, Europe and the United States share common interests and values in Asia. If they coordinate policies and act together, they can magnify their influence on developments there. This volume thus suggests that the American pivot should be "with Europe." This does not mean that Europe would play a role in Asia commensurate with that of the United States, but that Europe would draw on its comparative advantages to pursue common interests and coordinate policies towards Asia with the United States wherever possible. The goal of this effort should be framed as a "new trilateralism" uniting the nations in North America, Europe, and Asia in an effort to solve global problems that affect each of them, to integrate China and others into the existing international system, and to create institutions in Asia that improve settlement of disputes by rule of law.

Russia's annexation of Crimea and ongoing efforts to assert hegemony over its neighborhood do not fundamentally alter these conclusions. It will certainly cause Europe to strengthen its commitment to common defense under the NATO Alliance. But the pivot was never intended to reduce America's commitment to European security or to be limited to security issues alone. The logic of coordinated transatlantic efforts to address the growing problems and opportunities presented in Asia has not changed. The need for greater transatlantic burden sharing in the Middle East has also not changed. Europe will need to maintain a wide aperture on global issues and to avoid returning to a Cold War focus exclusively on military threats from Russia.

The chapters presented in this book were written by individuals from the United States, Europe, and Asia. Most authors have both academic and policymaking backgrounds. The purpose of each chapter is to examine, educate and develop policy recommendations that might give substance to a U.S.-European joint pivot to Asia. The key elements of each chapter are summarized below. Each of these chapters contains specific recommendations for policy change. The recommendations section that follows combines several of those suggestions to design a menu for a new trilateral agenda.

## Chapter 1: Global Trends and the Pivot

The Obama Administration's desire to pivot its attention to Asia flows naturally from global trends. Global power is shifting from the transatlantic nations to Asia. Yet Asia lacks the norms and institutions that have allowed reconciliation and rule of law to thrive in Europe. Europe is relatively united and secure, though Russia's intervention in Ukraine reminds us of the limits of that trend. The desire to terminate two decade-long wars in the Greater Middle East, combined with growing deficits and a weakened economy forced an American reassessment of its priorities. The Middle East will continue to create instabilities that challenge the transatlantic partners and the United States will expect significant support from Europe to share the military burdens involved in managing these challenges in Europe's neighborhood. The world will have formidable actors emerging on the scene, including non-state actors which represent risks and opportunities. International criminal syndicates gain strength at the expense of governments but public-private partnerships can help to solve problems. Multiple new actors and the high velocity information together create a more complex world and can lead to strategic surprises, which in turn creates the need for rapid consultation and decision making. These global trends suggest the need for a new and expanded transatlantic bargain to include:

- Full commitment by all NATO members to Article 5 of the Washington Treaty, especially in light of Russia's annexation of Crimea.

- Transatlantic commitment to completing the U.S.-EU Transatlantic Trade and Investment Partnership (TTIP) and harmonizing it with the Trans-Pacific Partnership (TPP) and EU efforts to forge free trade agreements with Asian-Pacific countries.

- A new trilateralism based on U.S.-European-Asian joint problem solving.

- A European lead in dealing with security in the Balkans and North Africa.

- Shared U.S.-European responsibility for managing instability in the Greater Middle East.

- An American lead, together with its Asian partners, in providing security in Asia.

- Greater European use of its soft power in Asia to improve norms and institutions.

## Chapter 2: The "Pivot to Asia:" Myths and Realities

The strategic pivot to Asia is a core element of President Obama's foreign policy that intends neither to contain China nor to undercut transatlantic relations. It is multi-dimensional, with diplomatic, economic and defense elements to it. Some European policymakers assume that Europe has little to no role to play in this shift in U.S. policy. If one views the pivot narrowly through a defense lens, it is fairly easy to conclude that Europe's militaries, with their declining defense budgets and modernization challenges, will have neither the resources nor the willingness to increase their operational activity in the Asia-Pacific. But that perspective is far too limited in scope and far from what the United States expects or desires. In the minds of many American policymakers, Europe would be wise to follow suit not out of any loyalty to the United States but because Europe too has a vested interest in peace and stability in Asia. It is in Europe's, not just America's, interest to enhance cooperation with Asia, and there are countless ways to advance that agenda both bilaterally and multilaterally.

## Chapter 3: The Pivot and Underlying U.S. Interests in Asia

Although many equate "rebalancing" with strengthening U.S. force posture in the Asia-Pacific, the United States is determined to be as economically and politically vital to the region as it is militarily. While the United States serves a special role vis-à-vis regional security, it is in fact difficult to disentangle security from other interests. Clearly preventing major-power war through deterrence and a robust military presence, backed by a vibrant trading economy, are core U.S. interests. But the military role largely remains one of offshore balancing. As a Pacific rather than an Asian power, the United States retains an element of being a distant guarantor that can reassure allies and partners, persuade others to keep the peace, and concentrate on advancing economic and political development. With staunch allies like Australia, Japan, South Korea, along with growing partnerships with many Southeast Asian states (such as the Philippines and Thailand, both allies, and close partners like Singapore), the United States can build and strengthen a system based on the rule of law, with more democratic governance and institutions. ASEAN is at the center of regional dialogue and cooperation, and the United States can reinforce it as an indispensable framework.

## Chapter 4: European Approaches to Asia

The European Union is not accustomed to thinking about its global role in grand strategic terms, and the larger European countries, by contrast, often pursue a unilateral track. Still, the shift to the East of economic and political power is structural. Europe's strategic interests in Asia are two-fold: economic/security and the relationship with the United States. Its other interests follow from this. Europe's economic well-being is dependent on what happens in the Asia-Pacific. Besides, it is difficult to foresee a situation where transatlantic relations are not negatively impacted if the United States and its Asian partners encounter greater challenges in the Asia-Pacific, and Europe remains impartial. Yet one of the major difficulties the EU and its member states confront is that events in Europe's immediate neighborhood such as the Arab Spring, the Iran crisis, the Syrian civil war, Ukraine and relations with Russia take precedence over developing a larger strategic role in the Asia-Pacific.

## Chapter 5: Asian Institutions and the Pivot

Asian regional institutions are still nascent in developing a strong sense of regional community, even though there have been visible steps and high profile summitry since the Asian crisis of 1997–98. Existing multilateral structures are chiefly preoccupied with economic cooperation and integration. In the field of security, the focus is on dialogue and confidence building, rather than the actual resolution of disputes or the establishment of formal institutions to promote cooperative inter-state behavior. Cultural and civic engagements are also limited. Given the existing diversity of political systems, population sizes, cultures and levels of economic development in Asia, the idea of a regional *Community* has not gained traction. The place of non-Asian actors who have a significant stake and role in the region, especially the United States but also the European Union, is contested. Any attempts by extra-regional players to increase their footprints in the region should thus be sensitive to regional dynamics, unspoken norms, and the needs of Asian regionalism today.

## Chapter 6: Asia's Pivot to the Atlantic: Implications for the United States and Europe

Transatlantic strategies to address Asia's rise should not focus solely on dynamics in the "Asian Hemisphere," they should also consider the implications of Asia's growing engagement in the "Atlantic Hemisphere"—North and South America, Europe, and Africa. While Asia's engagement in the Atlantic is driven primarily by economic considerations, the rise of the Pacific is increasingly influencing pan-Atlantic dynamics in a number of ways, not only in terms of trade but also investment links, resource access, diplomacy, and security. Asian countries act as much as competitors as partners when it comes to their engagement in the Atlantic Hemisphere, often exporting their intra-regional competition with other Asian countries to areas far from Pacific shores. Asian engagement in both the North and South

Atlantic spotlights issues that the United States and Europe have neglected; areas from which they have withdrawn; and future challenges
deserving their attention. Asia's rise is also affecting the Atlantic
Hemisphere in a more global context, particularly with regard to
worldwide norms and standards that should guide countries as they
address contemporary issues. The United States and Europe should
address Asia's rise not only by engaging directly in Asia but by
strengthening the foundations of their own engagement within the
Atlantic space, and by engaging Asian and Atlantic actors in the context of pluralism rather than containment or confrontation.

## Chapter 7: The Impact of the Pivot on the Alliance

The United States will look to European allies and partners to play
a greater role, wherever possible, in the Middle East, in addition to
North Africa and Africa south of the Sahara. What these roles would
be in the Middle East are not yet clear, nor whether the Europeans
would be willing to respond. While greater European involvement
cannot be a complete substitute for continuing US engagement and
for providing reassurances to local partners, it could relieve the
United States of some of its current burdens. In the longer term, the
United States may look to the Europeans to support U.S. actions in
regard to rebalancing, but for the foreseeable future active European
roles in Africa and the Middle East are the outer limits in providing a
substitute for soon-ending allied ISAF deployments.

## Chapter 8: How NATO Can Pivot Towards Asia

Countries like Australia, New Zealand, Japan, Singapore, South
Korea and Malaysia contributed to NATO's mission in Afghanistan.
Through partnerships, European NATO members in particular can
acquire additional means of influence in the region, complementing
the economic ties they have through the European Union. Many Asia-
Pacific countries are particularly interested in military cooperation
with NATO, to learn standardization and procedures, the Alliance
being seen as the "gold standard" of multinational military action. If
NATO intends to take its partnerships seriously, it can hardly limit its
dealings with partners around the globe to a purely Brussels-centered

approach. Instead, common exercises and training missions need to take place in the regions concerned. From this perspective, a coherent partnership policy virtually forces European NATO members to place stronger emphasis on the Asia-Pacific region. Such a logic, however, raises the question of whether European NATO members have the capabilities to operate so far away from their national borders and, if so, which of them is prepared to do so.

## Chapter 9: European Crisis Management in Asia: The Case of Aceh

Many argue that Europe has no role to play in promoting Asian security. This case study of the European Union's monitoring mission in Aceh demonstrates that the EU can be a successful global player in international crisis management. In this case, neither the United States nor Australia could serve this key function. Former Finnish President Martti Ahtisaari served as the EU mediator and Pieter Feith ran the monitoring mission which oversaw implementation in Indonesia. Together they helped end the Aceh insurgency. In closing, Feith wonders if the EU remains willing to play a similar role in the future.

## Chapter 10: Human Rights and the Rule of Law

The United States and Europe share both a strategic objective in furthering human rights and the rule of law in Asia and consolidating the international human rights regime. Many of their methods, especially at the country-level, are also similar, and the two must strive to act in concert, share best practices and identify opportunities for engagement. Care must be taken not to undermine the mutual pursuit of human rights through short-sighted positioning. Successfully engaging Asian countries on human rights and the rule of law will not come through rehashing debates about universalism and relativism nor by setting as a strategic objective the explicit adoption by Asian states of the tenets of the transatlantic values agenda. More effective will be strengthening domestic rule of law institutions and civil society to foster a rule of law culture at the national level and to support effective multilateralism by drawing on the less controversial elements of regional integration in Europe.

## Chapter 11: Asia's Rise and the Transatlantic Economic Response

The United States and European Union have pursued separate but comparable responses to Asia's economic rise. U.S. economic policy toward Asia focuses heavily on the TPP and its prospective enlargement to the major economies of the Asia-Pacific region. Europe had a later start but has pursued parallel bilateral agreements with South Korea and other Asian countries. These efforts have in large measure helped advance regional trade integration, as well as integration between Asia and Europe. The U.S.-EU TTIP negotiations provide the opportunity to align U.S. and EU policies on trade and investment in goods and services and to shift the strategy from competitive regionalism in Asia to cooperative regionalism. The successful negotiation of the TTIP would enhance the already robust transatlantic partnership, bolster the competitiveness of the transatlantic economies, and provide a common platform for engaging Asia in both regional and multilateral economic institutions.

## Chapter 12: Competition for Resources and Consequences for the Environment

Asia's influence on global resource markets, albeit energy or mineral resources, has been increasing substantially. At the same time, the United States and the EU may be heading in different directions. The former is rapidly becoming self-sufficient with regard to energy resources, and efforts are underway to resurrect domestic minerals extraction. The EU is expected to become even more import dependent in the future, and has significantly invested in renewable alternatives, and energy and materials efficiency. Despite these differences the transatlantic partners are searching for ways to facilitate more trade and increase transparency. That does not guarantee effective transatlantic cooperation in the future, but it is a promising outlook. With regard to Asia, China is dominant in the production of rare earth minerals but highly dependent on energy imports. Asia produces the vast majority of greenhouse gasses and many Asian cities are suffering under the effects of pollution. This mix offers the prospect of trilateral cooperation and technology sharing.

## Chapter 13: The New Silk Road

The United States is currently in the midst of its rebalancing to Asia and is partially disengaging from Europe and the Mediterranean. Europe shows little appetite to follow. But strengthening new commercial routes that follow the old Silk Road can contribute to a European pivot to Asia, provide economic growth for some of Asia's poorer areas, and enhance stability in an increasingly unstable part of the world. Southeastern Europe is important to this effort not only because it physically connects Europe with Central Asia and the Levant but also because it can become a trade and investment gateway between east and west. The region needs new engagement from both the EU and the United States. A New Silk Road can help provide that engagement.

## Chapter 14: A New Diplomacy for the Pivot

A new transatlantic diplomacy towards Asia is possible, even overdue. But it needs to build on a clear understanding of the starting positions of the United States and the European Union, as well as their respective interests at stake. Working together for stability in Asia will require a comprehensive concept. Ensuring stable domestic development in all Asian countries, keeping regional hotspots under control, enabling reconciliation between historic enemies, and integrating the emerging economies into institutional structures are important objectives to which the United States and the EU could contribute, both individually and in some areas by jointly working with Asian partners. From the Asian perspective, the United States will continue to be in the lead, with the EU having a comparative advantage where soft power is of the essence.

# Recommendations

The authors of this volume offer an array of recommendations for consideration by governments and other opinion leaders and actors. Each chapter contains recommendations related to its subject matter. Some of those recommendations are consolidated and summarized here to provide a concise menu for further consideration.

## Strategic

**Reassess relative sharing of burdens to account for the American pivot:** The U.S. pivot to Asia is a core element of U.S. national strategy. Faced with budget austerity and growing responsibilities in Asia, the United States will increasingly rely on its European allies to support American efforts across the globe, even as it maintains its commitments in and to Europe. Europe, in turn, has comparative advantages in areas such as institution-building, norm-setting, and promotion of economic and investment links that complement American strength in the security area. And Europe has increasingly vital interests in its own neighborhood. The transatlantic partners need to decide in which regions and with what instruments they can best combine for the common good.

**Develop deeper transatlantic cooperation on Asia:** As part of this reassessment, the United States and Europe should develop a strategic concept and implement a plan based on common interests to better coordinate their policies towards Asia. That needs to be done in close consultation with Asian partners in order to form stronger trilateral relationships. U.S. bilateral summits with European partners, as well as U.S.-EU and NATO summits, should have Asia on the agenda; consolidated working groups covering many of the areas featured in this volume should be established to maintain permanent dialogue and follow through on agreed points of action.

**Achieve the right balance on China:** A "transatlantic pivot to Asia" will fail if nations in the region perceive it simply as a Western effort to contain China. Most Asian nations want to offset China's increasing security influence while maintaining strong economic ties with China. The United States and the EU should develop a realistic analysis of China's rise, its intentions, and its challenges and design transatlantic plans accordingly.

**Don't just turn to the Pacific, harness the Atlantic:** The Atlantic is not only pivoting to the Pacific; the Pacific is turning to the Atlantic. Transatlantic strategies to address Asia's rise should not focus solely on dynamics in the "Asian Hemisphere," they should also consider the implications of Asia's growing engagement in the "Atlantic Hemisphere" — North and South America, Europe, and Africa. The United States and Europe should address Asia's rise not only by engaging directly in Asia but by strengthening the foundations of their own engagement.

## Political and Diplomatic

**Enhance rule of law and human rights:** Europe can play an important role in enhancing rule of law in Asia. In the international domain, enhancing the rule of law includes settling territorial disputes peacefully. Europe should reinforce this message, especially with regard to maritime disputes. The transatlantic partners also need to mainstream human rights in the pivot, maintain a common voice on the issue, focus on domestic rule of law initiatives, and increase the capacity of civil society.

**Negotiate norms for the new global commons:** While the old global commons, including maritime and Arctic issues, has existing rules and norms expressed in the United Nations Law of the Seas Convention, the new global commons is bereft of such norms. In both space and cyber space, new trilateral relationships could usefully develop such norms. Space is "congested, contested, and competitive" and a new international code of conduct like the one proposed by the EU could benefit all nations. In cyberspace there is little agreement on what constitutes prohibited behavior and how it might be punished. The United States, Europe and Asia represent most of the major players in these two domains and together they could create such new norms.

**Promote institution-building and reconciliation:** Europe has built a strong pattern of reconciliation between contending nations through institution-building and a web of agreed norms. Asian institutions are relatively less developed and reconciliation among former enemies is limited. Europe needs to engage with Asian institutions with a view towards strengthening them, based on decades of European experience.

## Economic and Environmental

**Encourage free trade and coordinate development assistance:** Successful completion of transatlantic and transpacific trade talks (TTIP and TPP) will be critical to solidifying enhanced U.S.-European-Asian relations. To ensure the complementarity of transatlantic bilateral and regional initiatives in Asia, the transatlantic partners should consult with each other frequently on progress in trade negotiations with Asian partners. The level of transatlantic development assistance to poorer Asian nations is declining and so close consultations should be held to maximize the positive impact of the declining assistance. Trilateral partners might also coordinate sanctions policies.

**Provide technical solutions to resource and environmental challenges:** Asia is becoming increasingly dependent on energy imports and is suffering from the environmental consequences. A trilateral effort to share technologies to improve this situation is in everyone's interest. For example, nations could cooperate more on the development of technologies to enhance more responsible extraction of unconventional energy resources and to maximize efficient use of resources.

**Take advantage of the Atlantic Energy Renaissance:** Asian countries are so actively engaged seeking energy and other natural resources in the Atlantic Hemisphere in part because the Atlantic basin is recasting the world's energy future. Over the next 20 years the Atlantic is likely to become the energy reservoir of the world and a net exporter of many forms of energy to the Indian Ocean and Pacific Ocean basins. Heightened Atlantic energy links, in turn, could reduce the dependence of many Atlantic basin countries on Eurasian energy sources and take pressure off their intensifying competition with

China and India over energy from some of the world's most unstable regions.

## Security

**Revise and revamp NATO's partnerships:** Many Asian partners seek stronger ties with NATO. Properly done, it is in NATO's interest to pursue these partnerships. NATO should create enhanced partnership mechanisms with capable democratic Asian partners based on twin pillars of greater political consultation and increased military interoperability. NATO also needs to strengthen its own structures to give greater prominence to Asia such as opening liaison offices in key Asian capitals, creating a Senior Civilian Representative for Asia and an Office of Asian Affairs in the International Staff, opening NATO schools and Centers of Excellence to Asian officers, and conducting more military exercises with Asian partners. Poorer Asian nations would benefit from NATO-run security sector reform programs. NATO might also cooperate with Asian partners on such issues as maritime patrols and missile defense.

**Engage in crisis management:** European crisis management in Aceh and its positive involvement in Myanmar demonstrate that being both respected and somewhat removed from the Asian region can be used to powerful effect. Working in cooperation with the United States, Europe can contribute significantly to a more peaceful and democratic Asia. Europe should enhance its crisis management capabilities for Asia.

**Cooperate to manage common security problems:** Whenever possible trilateral partners should work together to perform missions of common interest such as humanitarian assistance and disaster relief, counter-terrorism, counter-piracy, and fighting organized crime.

## Organizational

**Strengthen EU mechanisms to deal with Asia:** The EU should arrange a European strategic dialogue on the "pivot" and seek ways to strengthen European influence in Asia. The EU should better align its

Asia policies among actors in the External Action Service, relevant Directorates-General in the European Commission, and EU member states.

**Design the right institutional entry points:** The principal multilateral institution in Asia is ASEAN, with its many configurations. It is a weak institution that needs to be strengthened. ASEAN+3 adds three key East Asian countries to the mix. On the security side, there is the ASEAN Regional Forum and ASEAN Defense Ministers Meeting (and the ADMM Plus). The United States and Russia now attend the East Asian Summit, and the EU should attend in the future. Transatlantic partners will need to design an approach using variable geometry to connect with Asian partners, starting with ASEAN.

**Engage Asian actors in differentiated dialogues on Atlantic Hemisphere issues:** Use the U.S.-China Strategic and Economic Dialogue and EU-China summit frameworks to elevate consultations on African, Latin American and polar issues, not only to raise concerns but to explore ways to coordinate on such issues as aid, development, technology, technical assistance and alleviating energy poverty. Encourage India's engagement on Atlantic Hemisphere issues, while being careful not to overload expectations. Coordinate more effectively with Japan, Australia, South Korea and other Asian actors on common or complementary approaches to technical assistance, economic development, aid, as well as norms and standards. Incorporate into U.S.-European consultations issues arising from Asian activities in the Atlantic Hemisphere.

**Harness the private sector:** There are multiple public-private partnerships that can enrich the various efforts described above. There is also considerable room for greater Track II initiatives. More initiatives like the IISS Shangri-La Dialogue should be encouraged with broader European participation.

*Part I*

**Background to the Pivot**

## *Chapter 1*

# Global Trends and the Pivot

*Hans Binnendijk*

The purpose of this introductory chapter is to set the global stage for this volume. It presents ten long term global trends that together will significantly affect the future of transatlantic relations and policies toward Asia. The trends also inform the policy recommendations made in this volume.

The decision by the United States to rebalance or pivot its foreign and national security policy focus towards Asia does not take place in a vacuum. It is the result of significant changes in the global strategic environment. That new emerging environment will also help determine how others react to this policy shift and how successfully it can be implemented.

This volume argues that the U.S. pivot is not intended to be a pivot "from Europe," but that it should become a pivot to Asia "with Europe." This does not mean that Europe would play a role in Asia commensurate with that of the United States, but that Europe would draw on its comparative advantages to pursue common interests and coordinate policies towards Asia with the United States wherever possible. If the pivot to Asia is to be a transatlantic pivot, not just a U.S. pivot, then it will be important to evaluate how European partners are affected by these global trends. If it is to be effective, it must seek to solve global problems, which are revealed by global trends. This chapter concludes that this policy needs to be redesigned as a "New Trilateralism" uniting countries in North America, Europe, and Asia in an effort to solve global problems that affect each of them.

These ten trends are derived from a review of multiple global trend studies, with a focus on the U.S. National Intelligence Council's (NIC) *Global Trends 2030*. Each trend will be evaluated for the impact that it could have on transatlantic relations and the pivot to Asia.[1] The trend studies were all completed before Russian occupied and annexed the Crimea, and some of the trends have been adjusted accordingly.

***Trend #1:*** **Most trend studies indicate that the United States is in relative decline, raising questions about the future role of America in the world.**

*Global Trends 2030* assesses that the United States will hold just under 20% of total global power by 2030, a decline from about 25% today.[2] This is less the result of American decline and more the result of the rise of others. By 2030 no one country will be a hegemonic power. Europe and Asia have both relied heavily on the United States to set norms and maintain peace in their regions. U.S. relative decline raises questions among some allies about its continuing global role.[3]

---

[1]This review is based on material originally collected as part of a project for the Center for Naval Analysis and has been adapted for this book. The studies reviewed are: U.S. National Intelligence Council, *Global Trends 2030: Alternative Worlds* (Washington, D.C.: U.S. Government Printing Office, 2012); Delégation aux Affaires Stratégiques. *Strategic Horizons*. (Paris: French Defense Ministry, 2013), http://www.defense.gouv.fr/das/reflexion-strategique/prospective-de-defense/articles-prospective/strategic-horizons; Canadian Department of National Defence, *The Future Security Environment 2008-2030. Part 1: Current and Emerging Trends* (Ottawa, 2009); UK Ministry of Defence, *Strategic Trends Programme: Global Strategic Trends—Out to 2040*, Fourth edition (London: 2010), https://www.gov.uk/government/uploads/system/uploads/attachment_data/file/33717/GST4_v9_Feb10.pdf; U.S. Joint Forces Command, *Joint Operating Environment 2010* (Norfolk, Virginia: Government Printing Office, 2010); European Union Institute for Security Studies, *Global Trends 2030—Citizens in an Interconnected and Polycentric World* (Condé-sur-Noireau, France: Corlet Imprimeur, 2012); *Global Marine Trends 2030* (London: Lloyd's Register, QinetiQ, and University of Strathclyde Glasgow, 2013); North Atlantic Treaty Organization. *Multiple Futures Project: Navigating towards 2030*, 2009; Barry Pavel and Magnus Nordenman, "Global Trends and the Future of NATO: Alliance Security in an Era of Global Competition," (Washington, D.C.: Atlantic Council, October 31, 2013), accessed December 6, 2013, http://www.atlanticcouncil.org/images/publications/Global_Trends_and_the_Future_of_NATO.pdf; Allied Command Transformation, *Strategic Foresight Analysis*, April 8, 2013; Daniel Hamilton and Kurt Volker, eds., *Transatlantic 2020: A Tale of Four Futures* (Washington, D.C.: Center for Transatlantic Relations, 2012).

[2]*Global Trends 2030, op. cit.*, p. 17.

[3]*Ibid.*, p. 101, confirmed by recent simulations.

Specifically, some allies are concerned about a weakened U.S. role as norm-setter and enforcer.

For the first time, the NIC included in its periodic *Global Trends* report a section on the changing geostrategic position of the United States as a potential "game changer." Other trend studies raise similar questions. *Global Trends* states that the relative decline of the U.S. vis-à-vis rising powers is inevitable; whether the United States can work with its partners to reinvent the international system is among the most important future variables.[4]

After a decade of war in Iraq and Afghanistan and a global recession, the United States is showing fatigue and reassessing its global posture and defense requirements. The resistance in the U.S. Congress to authorizing a modest military strike against Syria in 2013 is but a recent example. The pivot to Asia is in part a manifestation of that fatigue with Middle East wars and the subsequent reassessment of the importance of Asia.

The U.S. defense budget is in rapid decline. The 2012 U.S. defense budget was about $681 billion, including supplemental appropriations for Iraq and Afghanistan. With these supplementals gone, the defense budget will be cut to about $500 billion by 2015.[5] The post-2015 U.S. defense budget is still vulnerable to further sequestration reductions. If the defense budget can be sustained at about $500 billion annually, it will still be roughly twice the projected European and Chinese defense budgets, and many of these cuts are offset by reduced operating costs in the Greater Middle East. Nonetheless, theses cuts are sudden and deep and have forced a reassessment of national challenges and priorities.

The U.S. Defense Department's 2012 Strategic Guidance directed that U.S. force structure be rebalanced from a current ratio of 50/50 for Europe and Asia to 40/60 respectively. The most visible result for Europe was the removal of two of the four remaining Brigade Combat Teams; the longer term fate of the remaining two remains unclear.

---

[4]*Ibid.*

[5]See National Defense Budget Estimates for 2014, Office of the Under Secretary of Defense (Comptroller) Page 6; defense spending for European members of NATO in 2011 was about €220 billion or about $300 billion.

The U.S. decision to proceed with negotiations with the European Union on an ambitious Trade and Investment Partnership, or TTIP, is also seen as a rebalancing of U.S. priorities within Europe from an emphasis on military to economic affairs.

While the pivot is intended to be a move away from two wars in the Middle East, this shift in force structure has led to misinterpretation and concern of some in Europe that it is indeed a pivot away from Europe. The TTIP negotiations have not fully compensated for that misinterpretation. Deep political divisions in the Congress and revelations of NSA collection activities in Europe further undercut European confidence in the United States. Even the prospect of U.S. energy independence raises concerns among some that it will encourage U.S. isolationism.[6]

This situation has led one Polish analyst to muse, restating Lord Ismay's famous dictum about NATO, that now "the U.S. is out, Europe is down, and Russia is in."[7] That pithy quote does not reflect the true state of affairs, but it does indicate that the United States needs to restore some confidence in Europe.

> *Recommendation:* **The United States should restate more clearly its narrative about its pivot policy to embrace a pivot "with Europe" not "from Europe."** That new narrative must include a stronger role for Europe, and it needs to be made operational.

*Trend #2:* **Europe over the past decade has seemed peaceful, creating a high degree of European complacency about security issues; Russia's armed occupation and annexation of Crimea may well change that sense of complacency.**

The history of Europe is a history of warfare and division. During the 1990s, Europe experienced turmoil in the Balkans which NATO helped stabilize and it saw the expansion of NATO to the east. Most

---

[6]*Global Trends 2030, op. cit.,* pp. 35–38.

[7]Lord Ismay's original quote was that the purpose of NATO was to keep the U.S. in, Germany down, and Russia out.

trend studies have suggested continued stability in Europe with a focus on recovery from economic recession. They also have concluded that traditional U.S. allies and partners are weakening and turning inward.[8] The NIC's *Global Trends 2030*, using a four-component power forecast, projects that EU member states will lose their current second-place "power position" over the next few years.[9] It remains to be seen how deeply the Ukraine crisis will alter Europe's sense of complacency about security issues.

Europe's sovereign debt crisis created deep divisions within the euro zone, with Germany and other northern nations bankrolling southern nations and requiring austerity as a condition. Unemployment in some southern European nations has been at record levels. A 2013 German Marshall Fund poll concluded that Europeans expressed growing dissatisfaction with the European Union and the euro, and that there is a growing divide in Europe between successful and still troubled economies.[10] There is also growing radical populism in countries like Greece (Golden Dawn), France (National Front), the Netherlands (PVV), Italy (Five Star Movement) and Hungary (current government, and Jobbik party).

There is also considerable European public fatigue with combat operations in the Middle East (generally 60–80% of those polled opposing continuation of ISAF combat operations), though the German Marshall Fund's 2013 poll did reveal that 53% of Europeans would support a continued European contribution to post-2014 training missions in Afghanistan. During the Libya campaign, all NATO nations supported the intervention, but only eight took part in the military operation. The most dramatic example of this fatigue took place in the British parliament, when even members of Prime Minister Cameron's own party refused to sanction a military strike on Syria in response to the Assad regime's use of chemical agents against civilians.

---

[8]*Global Trends 2030*, *op. cit.*, pp. 17, 43–45; UK Ministry of Defence, *op. cit.*, pp. 47–48; *Strategic Horizons*, *op. cit.*, p. 10.

[9]If additional factors such as health, education and governance are included, Europe retains its second-place position for an additional two decades.

[10]German Marshall Fund of the United States, *Transatlantic Trends, Key Findings 2013, Executive Summary*, http://trends.gmfus.org/files/2013/09/Trends-2013-Key-Findings-Report.pdf, p.1.

These trends are complicated by an aging population that could also have a negative impact on economic production and willingness to pursue a global security policy.[11] This complacency is not universal in Europe; France in particular has been willing to use force to stabilize the situation in Libya, Mali and the Central African Republic.

European defense spending has been cut by more than 15% over the past decade, mostly without adequate coordination with other NATO members.[12] Only three European members of NATO meet the 2% of GDP defense spending guideline agreed by the alliance. It remains to be seen if the Ukraine crisis will reverse this trend.

The greatest security concern is about Russia, especially after it occupation and annexation of Crimea. The NIC's *Global Trends* study indicates that Russia's power index is constant over time but anti-Western drift creates isolation and mistrust.[13] Today's Kremlin leaders seek to regain lost strength by confronting the West rather than joining it.

President Putin carries an array of grievances about the West, including NATO enlargement, abrogation of the ABM treaty, regime change operations and so-called interference in Russia's and Ukraine's internal affairs. In response, Russia has followed a policy of domestic repression, foreign intimidation and its own pivot to Asia. Putin is seeking new partnerships with China and other emerging powers as he turns his back to Europe. Russia's defense budget, now at $71 billion annually, is on the rise as Europe's is in decline. The United States and Russia will probably maintain parity in deployed strategic nuclear warheads as part of the new START agreement, though Russia has a ten-fold advantage in European-based non-strategic nuclear weapons. In the longer run, Russia could become politically unstable due to a shrinking population, immigration, and extensive dependency on energy exports.[14]

---

[11]*Global Marine Trends 2030, op. cit.*, p. 16; also see Pavel and Nordenman, *op. cit*, p. 2.

[12]David J. Berteau, Guy Ben-Ari, Joachim Hofbauer, Priscilla Hermann, and Sneha Raghavan, *European Defense Trends 2012: Budgets, Regulatory Frameworks, and the Industrial Base* (Washington, DC: Center for Strategic and International Studies), p.18, http://csis.org/files/publication/121212_Berteau_EuroDefenseTrends2012_Web.pdf.

[13]*Global Trends 2030, op, cit.*, p. 17.

[14]*Global Marine Trends 2030, op. cit.*, p. 17.

Other external security concerns for Europe include violent political transitions in North Africa and the Middle East. These are taking place in Europe's neighborhood and their immediate impact is more pronounced in Europe that in the United States. Other European security concerns include new emerging challenges like cyber security, international terrorism, energy security and contested claims in the High North.

This second trend explains why until recently the United States has felt comfortable reducing its force structure in Europe, but also why pivoting to Asia with Europe will not be easy. The rationale for retaining any U.S. forces in Europe is as a hedge against Russian behavior, as a forward base for operations in the Middle East/North Africa, and as a way to maintain interoperability with European forces. America will expect Europe to pick up some of the slack as it focuses more on Asia.

> *Recommendation:* U.S. policy makers will need to calibrate carefully their expectations about Europe's willingness to pivot with the United States to Asia and to pick up slack in the Middle East, especially given developments in Ukraine. Specific examples of "pivoting with Europe" need to be identified based upon common interests and Europe's natural strengths in the area of "soft power." **The recommendation for European policy makers is to calculate how best to support this shift in U.S. policy**. A transatlantic pivot to Asia must include greater attention to Russia in an effort to reorient it away from its current confrontational policies.

### *Trend #3:* Global power is shifting from the transatlantic nations to the East and South.

*Global Trends 2030* projects that by 2030 Asia will have surpassed North America and Europe combined in terms of global power, based on GDP, population size, military spending, and investment in technology.[15] Some trend studies conclude that this will result in an accelerating de-Westernization of the world.[16] These projections are, of

---

[15]*Global Trends 2030, op. cit.,* p. 16.

[16]*Strategic Horizons, op. cit*; EUISS, *op. cit.,* pp. 139–144; Pavel and Nordenman, *op. cit.,* p. 2.

course, based in part on assumptions about continued economic growth rates that may not materialize.[17] In addition, amassing numbers says little about the ability of a particular region to translate power resources into influence over outcomes. Aggregate numbers about Asian population, military spending etc. belies the fact that Asian countries have few mechanisms to harness this combined potential; in fact Asia's growing military spending reflects intra-Asian divisions and security challenges, whereas both within and between North America and Europe power resources in many instances have been integrated and harnessed to joint purpose.

Nonetheless, China's power index alone as measured by the NIC surpasses that of Europe in the next few decades and surpasses that of the United States by 2045. China's actual defense budget for 2012 was estimated by the U.S. Defense Department to be between $135 billion and $215 billion,[18] with an annual growth of nearly 10% over the past decade. During the next few decades, China will become the world's largest consumer of oil, coal, and steel.

Asia will take center stage in global seaborne trade. Territorial, fishing and seabed disputes could lead to further incidents and interstate conflict, involving countries to which the United States has given security commitments. This may create greater risk of incidents at sea along the Asian coast and the need for a significant U.S. Navy presence.[19] Between 44% and 55% percent of all new shipbuilding will be Chinese.[20] China aggressively supports its maritime claims against most of its neighbors with its insistence on its traditional so-called nine dash line, its renewed claims on the Senkaku Islands, and settlement of these disputes on a bilateral basis, where they have maximum negotiating leverage. Chinese dependence on sea lanes will increase significantly, especially from the Persian Gulf and Latin America. China may seek overseas bases to protect its interests.[21] China's pursuit of energy

---

[17]China's GDP in 2012 was $8.2 trillion, while the United States and the EU each has a GDP of about $16 trillion.

[18]Office of the Secretary of Defense, Annual Report to the Congress on "Military and Security Developments Involving the People's Republic of China, 2013," p. 45, http://www.defense.gov/pubs/2013_china_report_final.pdf.

[19]*Global Maritime Trends, op. cit.*, p. 28; *Global Trends 2030, op. cit.*, p. 66.

[20]*Global Maritime Trends, op. cit.*, pp. 83, 90.

[21]*Ibid.*, pp. 37-40.

security is expected to transform China into a major extra-regional power in the Middle East.[22] These trends will make U.S.-Chinese relations critical to future global security environment.[23]

U.S.-Chinese relations may be in for some difficulty if a new book edited by Nina Hachigian is correct.[24] It presents a debate on an array of bilateral issues between U.S. and Chinese scholars. The basic thesis is that the United States still seeks to engage and integrate China into a liberal U.S.-made world order. That policy worked while China was weak. But as China believes it will surpass the United States in economic power and perhaps global power, Beijing will seek to either change existing rules and institutions or to create a parallel system. Many of the Chinese scholars featured in the book believe they have a right to change the international system because of China's growing strength. U.S. policy towards China may therefore need to change from engagement to managed rivalry. A review of the Hachigian's volume concludes that the United States now needs "strategic hedging," which is consistent with its pivot strategy.[25]

Japan shows signs of emerging from two dormant decades, but it may be held back in the longer term by demographics of aging.[26] *Global Trends 2030* still shows Japan as a declining major power.[27] Nonetheless, Japan has been a "trilateral partner" with Europe and the United States for decades and must remain at the center of any transatlantic pivot to Asia. South Korea, Indonesia and Australia are emerging democratic powers. Vietnam and the Philippines are seeking closer security ties to the United States. The United States has and will maintain defense treaties with Japan, South Korea, Australia, New Zealand, and the Philippines.

*Global Trends 2030* concludes that there are 17 countries in Asia, most of them in Southeast Asia, which have a domestic governance gap. Their economies are growing faster than their ability to adjust

---

[22]ACT, *Security Foresight Analysis*, *op. cit.*, p. 45.

[23]Pavel and Nordenman, *op. cit.*, p. 3.

[24]Nina Hachigian, ed., *Debating China: The U.S.-China Relationship in Ten Conversations* (Oxford: Oxford Press, 2014).

[25]Review by Minxin Pei in *Foreign Affairs*, March-April, 2014.

[26]*Global Trends 2030*, *op. cit.*, pp. 24-25.

[27]*Ibid.*, p. 16-17.

their governments from autocracy to democracy. Countries in this category tend to be unstable.[28]

The complex strategic mix in Asia has the potential for severe political confrontation and possible great power conflict. China is the rising global power challenging the existing superpower, and history demonstrates that wars result from this dynamic. China sees the U.S. pivot to Asia as part of a broader effort at containment, something the United States denies.

North Korea is an enigmatic and dangerous country with nuclear weapons. Defense budgets are increasing everywhere in Asia and in 2012 total defense spending in Asia exceeded total defense spending in Europe.[29] Ocean geography will be redefined in the future with a focus on the Indian Ocean and the South China Sea. These are areas with disputed territory and higher projected volumes of traffic.[30]

There are inadequate institutions and norms of behavior in Asia compared to those that have developed in Europe. In addition, the reconciliation between old enemies that has taken place in Europe has not taken place in Asia to the same degree. These trends will make it difficult to manage the complex strategic mix described above. *Global Trends 2030* concludes that an increasingly multi-polar Asia lacks a well-anchored regional security framework and could constitute one of the largest global security concerns.[31]

The same region, however, offers hope for a more stable and prosperous world if current conflicts can be settled and new norms agreed. Economic growth in Asia can be an engine for global growth. To move towards a more positive vision as Chinese power increases, both Chinese and American officials have referred to the need to develop a "New Type of Major Power Relationship." European partners can help define and participate in this effort.

---

[28]*Ibid.*, p. 51.

[29]Rodion Ebbinghausen, "The New Arms Race in Asia," *Deutsche Welle*, March 18, 2013, http://www.dw.de/the-new-arms-race-in-asia/a-16681158.

[30]*Global Trends 2030, op. cit.*, p. 68.

[31]*Ibid.*, p. ix.

The growth of Asian and specifically Chinese power lies behind the American pivot. It should be seen not as an effort to contain China, but to create relationships in Asia that shift the balance from confrontation to cooperation. European support is needed in this effort.

> ***Recommendation:*** Europe has developed norms and modes of cooperation that allow historical enemies to operate together in relative harmony. Europe is much more likely to participate vigorously in a transatlantic pivot to Asia that is based on a positive vision of improving Asian norms and institutions than one based on containment of China.[32] **European leaders need to develop a plan of engagement to influence Asian norms and strengthen Asian institutions.**

## *Trend #4:* Demographic trends, resource requirements and global warming are neo-Malthusian in nature and suggest even greater future stress in the Greater Middle East as well as in Asia.

Three global factors will converge in the next decade and a half to create additional pressures on already stressed populations in the Greater Middle East and parts of Asia. Those new pressures will create continued political instability and make it difficult for transatlantic partners to neglect the Middle East as they pivot to Asia.

The first Malthusian trend is demographic. As the global population grows from 7.1 billion to about 8.3 billion during this period, the percentage of global population living in urban areas will grow from roughly 50% to about 60%.[33] Much of this urban growth will take place in the Greater Middle East and in Asia (China, Southeast Asia) where most megacities now exist. Youth unemployment in urban areas is already a major cause of political extremism. Asia will see a higher degree of population aging than will the Middle East, which trend analysis indicates could constrain extremism in Asia but not in the Middle East.

---

[32]For example see "Europe's Smart Asian Pivot" by Javier Solana, http://www.project-syndicate.org/commentary/the-eu-s-startegic-advantages-in-asia-by-javier-solana.

[33]*Global Trends 2030, op. cit.*, p. 27.

The second Malthusian trend relates to resource requirements. Growing global requirements for food (more than 35% increase), water (40% increase) and energy (50% increase) between now and 2030 may not be met, especially in the developing world, where population growth will be greatest. Unmet requirements and resource competition could trigger discontent and violence.[34] Growing power in Asia may mean that the Middle East will bear the greatest burden of this competition for resources.

The third Malthusian trend is global warming. Asia is increasingly the principal source of the growth in greenhouse gases that cause global warming. Changing weather patterns would cause a combination of flooding in some areas as oceans rise and drought in other areas. North Africa, South Asia and Middle East would be hit hard with drought.[35] Coastal mega-cities will be more prone to flooding, especially in South Asia and Southeast Asia. Environmental security will be a greater concern. Natural disasters might cause governments to collapse.[36] More humanitarian crises and disaster relief missions can be expected.[37]

The long-term future of the Arab world may hang in the balance as these trends impact the region. Sunni-Shia rivalries are already spilling over national boundaries as conflicts become regional. These three global trends provide a potential perfect Malthusian storm which may accentuate this already spreading conflict. Already U.S. Secretary of State John Kerry is focusing most of his attention on Middle East issues, and most recently on Ukraine, prompting critics to ask whether the pivot to Asia is real. While the United States and Europe may wish to pivot their attention to Asia, trends in the Greater Middle East, and in Europe itself, may not let them.

> **Recommendation:** The United States, Europe, and Asian powers all have a common interest in reducing the negative impact of these three Malthusian trends on the future of

---

[34]*Global Trends 2030*, op. cit., p. 31; EUISS, *op. cit.*, p.16, 46.

[35]*Global Trends 2030*, op. cit., p. iv.

[36]*Global Maritime Trends*, op. cit., pp. 44–45, 103; *Global Trends 2030*, op. cit., p. 52.

[37]UK Ministry of Defence, *op. cit.*, pp. 16, 26; U.S. Joint Forces Command, *op. cit.*, p. 59; Canadian Department of National Defence, *op.cit.*, pp. 39–41.

the Greater Middle East. **A new "trilateral approach" is warranted to mitigate the impact of these negative trends on the stability of the region.**

*Trend #5:* **The rise of emerging powers, non-governmental organizations, and international business creates greater complexity and governance gaps but also opportunities for transatlantic partners.**

Transatlantic partners will increasingly need to address the diffusion of power among states and an increasing number of non-state actors with attributes of states.[38] This will create a multi-polar or even a polycentric world order, which presents new and difficult governance challenges.[39] The international system designed to manage the post-World War II order is heavily stressed by this increased complexity, and will need reform. Global governance is inadequate to deal with emerging powers/actors.[40]

Emerging powers like Brazil, India, Colombia, Turkey, Indonesia, Nigeria, South Africa, Australia, and South Korea present new opportunities for partnership, but the trend studies tend to conclude that most will follow their own path rather than align with transatlantic partners.[41] Some like Turkey, Australia and South Korea are already allied with the United States. New forms of partnership may be needed to shape productive relationships between the transatlantic community and the rest.

We are also witnessing an acceleration of nuclear proliferation by some of these emerging powers and a greater risk of nuclear use, especially in South Asia/ Middle East. Efforts to halt proliferation in Iran,

---

[38]*Global Trends 2030, op. cit.*, pp. 9–13; EUISS, *op. cit.*, pp. 19–20; Pavel and Nordenman, *op. cit.*, p. 2.

[39]*Global Trends 2030, op. cit.*, pp. 60–61; ACT *Multiple Futures*, op. cit., p. 54; EUISS, *op. cit.*, pp. 141–143.

[40]*Ibid.*, pp.156–157; UK Ministry of Defence, *op. cit.*, p. 39.

[41]*Global Trends 2030, op.cit.*, pp. 46–49; Charles Kupchan, *No One's World: The West, the Rising Rest, and the Coming Global Turn* (Oxford: Oxford University Press, 2013).

North Korea, and elsewhere could embroil the United States in major conflict.[42]

The rise of non-governmental actors provides not only complications and new dangers such as international terrorism, but also new opportunities. There are some 1.5 million NGOs in the United States alone.[43] International businesses increasingly want to play a more positive role in sustainable development.[44] These entities can be harnessed to be part of a transatlantic pivot to Asia.

Trend studies conclude that power will shift towards multifaceted and amorphous networks composed of state and non-state actors. Leadership of such networks will be a function of position, enmeshment, diplomatic skill, and constructive demeanor.[45] The transatlantic partners are well suited to take full advantage of this power shift.

Managing this new complex world of the future will require a more flexible set of international arrangements. Emerging powers will seek institutional change that reflects their growing power. New public-private networks will need to be created to deal with their Asian counterparts. These changes will need to be part of a broader pivot to the future. The transatlantic partners would be well served by facing this task together.

> **Recommendation:** In considering how best to "pivot together" to Asia, the transatlantic partners need to form public-private networks with NGOs and international business and harness them where possible for common purpose.

---

[42]*Global Trends 2030, op. cit.*, pp. 60, 63.

[43]U.S. Department of State, Factsheet: "Non-Governmental Organizations in the United States," January 12, 2012, http://www.humanrights.gov/wp-content/uploads/2012/01/FactSheet-NGOsInTheUS.pdf.

[44]See Tim Smedley, "NGOs No Longer Set the Agenda for Development, Say CEOs," *The Guardian*, September 20, 2013, http://www.theguardian.com/global-development-professionals-network/2013/sep/20/ngos-no-longer-set-agenda-development.

[45]*Global Trends 2030, op. cit.*, pp. 19, 104.

*Trend #6:* **Globalization driven by information technology will continue to compress time and space, with multiple consequences for international affairs.**

Information technology will continue to improve dramatically, even if not at the pace of Moore's law.[46] Barriers to entry for most technologies are getting lower. Governments may be at an increasing disadvantage as individuals gain global access. Dependence on the internet will continue to increase. But the underlying technology is vulnerable to attack with massive disruptive impact.

The futures literature draws several conclusions based on continued globalization and developments in technology:

- Complexity among international actors combined with trends in information flows gives rise to a greater prospect of strategic surprise. Most trend studies highlight the increasing importance of game changers, disruptive forces, wild cards or black swans.[47]

- The increase in velocity and mass of information will compress time for decision-making, providing less opportunity for consultation and greater risk of uncoordinated action.[48]

- Big data will provide a powerful tool for individuals, corporations and governments, but with risks to individual privacy.[49]

- There will be an explosion of trade in goods, services, and ideas.[50] Freer movement of goods, information, ideas can strengthen demand for greater political participation, but risks dangers of populism.[51]

---

[46]See *Defense Horizons #30*, National Defense University, 2003.

[47]*Global Trends 2030, op. cit.*, pp. 43,109; ACT, *Strategic Foresight Analysis*, *op. cit.*, p. 126.

[48]Nik Gowing, *Skyful of Lies and Black Swans: The New Tyranny of Shifting Information Power in Crises* (Oxford: Reuters Institute for the Study of Journalism, 2009).

[49]The NSA surveillance case is but the latest example. Also see Pavel and Nordenmann, *op. cit.*, p. ix.

[50]*Strategic Horizons, op. cit.*, p. 16.

[51]EUISS, *op. cit.*, pp. 14–15.

- The relentless 24/7 news cycle means that the battle of the narrative will be increasingly important.[52]

- Closer proximity could mean more common values or it could amplify religious, ethnic and tribal differences.[53]

- Artificial intelligence will play an increasingly large role.[54]

- New techniques such as additive manufacturing (3D printing) and the Internet of Things have the potential to change global work patterns.[55]

- As the world grows ever smaller, there is a greater risk of pandemics and other transnational threats.[56]

Most of these developments would complicate international relations for the transatlantic partners. To compensate for the risk of strategic surprise and the need for rapid decision-making, better mechanisms will be needed to anticipate change and to promote advance consultation. A common narrative of Western values, interests and policies needs to be refined.

> *Recommendation:* **New consultative mechanisms that take advantage of modern technology will be needed** to be established so that transatlantic partners can discuss and coordinate policies toward Asia in an era of rapid communications.

## *Trend #7:* **New areas of potential inter-state conflict are appearing, primarily in the global commons where norms and the rule of law are inadequate.**

Agreed norms and the rule of law are fundamental to avoiding conflict in the international system. As the importance of the global commons has grown, the ability to develop or adapt norms has not kept

---

[52]*Global Trends 2030, op. cit.,* pp 43, 109; ACT, *Strategic Foresight Analysis, op. cit.,* p. 126.

[53]UK Ministry of Defence, *op. cit.,* p. 71, 130; EUISS, *op. cit.,* pp. 39–41, 46–48.

[54]*Global Maritime Trends, op. cit.,* p. 111.

[55]*Global Trends 2030, op. cit.,* p. x.

[56]U.S. Joint Forces Command, op. cit., pp. 33–34; *Global Trends 2030, op. cit.,* p. 14.

up. Four areas require clearer rules of the road, and each will affect the transatlantic partners and Asia.

The first area is contending claims of sovereignty in the ocean area between Vietnam and Japan. According to Allied Command Transformation's *Strategic Foresight Analysis*, energy security will be a major source of maritime disputes, within both 'blue' and 'brown' water environments. Exploitation of the seabed's resources will likely increase the number of disagreements with the potential for conflict and subsequent degradation of trade and investment in those regions. International maritime organizations will be taxed trying to deal with disputes.[57] Meanwhile, incidents at sea continue to create the risk of escalation. Europe has a stake in avoiding conflict over these claims and maintaining open sea lanes.

Second, Arctic warming is taking place at twice the rate of the rest of the planet. If this continues, trans-Arctic shipping may soon be open for several months a year. The melting ice cap also may open up significant undiscovered oil and gas reserves. If disputes in the Arctic over territory, transit, fishing and mineral rights are not settled, incidents may occur and escalate.[58] The eight-member Arctic Council and the Law of the Seas Treaty provide mechanisms to solve disputes, but they may be inadequate. Five of the eight Arctic Council members are also members of NATO; China has permanent observer status.

Third, cyber attacks are becoming more frequent and with greater consequences. International law and norms exist, but they are inadequate for the rapidly expanding set of questionable cyber activities. It is also complex because of the vast array of possible attacks, including hacking for pleasure or profit, cyber espionage, denial of service attacks for political intimidation, attacks of a nation's infrastructure, and attacks on military establishments. Developing clearer norms to prevent cyber attack and potential escalation is in the interest of the transatlantic partners and of Asia.

Fourth, advances in technology and development of commercial delivery systems have facilitated greater access to space by more nations and non-state actors, with the subsequent ability to disrupt

---

[57]ACT, *Strategic Foresight Analysis, op. cit.*, p. 45.

[58]*Global Maritime Trends, op. cit.*, p. 47.

space capabilities.[59] Space has become more "congested, contested, and competitive." The 1967 Outer Space Treaty, now ratified by 102 parties, does prohibit placing nuclear weapons in space, but it does not extend to conventional weapons or anti-satellite weapons. In addition, with new entrants to space, space clutter is an increasing problem. There are an estimated 22,000 objects in orbit larger than four inches; a tipping point may have been reached, which would affect the United States, Europe and Asia alike.[60] The United States has been working with the European Union and other nations to develop an International Code of Conduct for Outer Space Activities, based in part on the 2008 EU Code of Conduct.[61] As more and more nations and private groups launch space satellites, internationally-agreed norms will be needed.

> *Recommendation:* Europe has been at the heart of international institution-building and the rule of law. With The Hague as the seat of international courts, **the Netherlands is well positioned to take a leadership role in using a transatlantic pivot to create new international norms in maritime disputes, the Arctic, cyber attacks and space law.** Development of clearer and more up-to-date international norms in these four areas should be high on the agenda for a transatlantic pivot to Asia.

*Trend #8:* **Some trend analysts foresee additional global economic shocks, with dramatic social consequences.**

The United States and Europe have responded to the 2008 global economic crisis by creating new financial mechanisms and regulations designed to avoid another near financial collapse. *Global Trends 2030* assesses, however, that there is risk of additional global economic shocks and possible further recession, which would affect crisis-prone

---

[59]ACT, *Strategic Foresight Analysis, op. cit.*, p. 37.

[60]Steven Beardsley, "Space Clutter a Growing Concern for Pentagon," *Stars and Stripes*, March 23, 2012.

[61]Micah Zenko, "A Code of Conduct for Outer Space," Innovation Memorandum #10, *Council on Foreign Relations*, November 30, 2011, http://www.cfr.org/space/code-con-duct-outer-space/p26556.

economies and could create considerable political instability.[62] The recovery from 2008 has been slow and economic vulnerabilities remain. For example, Cullen Roche notes that several factors caused the 2008 recession to deepen. They include tight credit, which rendered firms vulnerable; limited scope for monetary policy; constraints on countercyclical fiscal policy; and economic integration, which spread the crisis. None of these factors has gone away.[63]

Trend analyses also conclude that there is a growing asymmetry of wealth and power,[64] both globally and within individual countries, which would complicate the social reaction to additional economic shocks. By 2025 China is expected to contribute one third of global growth. Other areas of the world are stalled economically or in decline.

According to trend studies, the political and social consequences of further economic shocks might include:

- A rise in competing ideologies and world views.[65]

- New social contracts being negotiated in the streets.[66]

- Greater suppression of human rights.[67]

- Vulnerable transition in about 50 nations from authoritarian rule to democracy, enhancing the risk of failed states.[68]

- The growth of populism and illiberal democracies.[69]

---

[62]*Global Trends 2030, op.cit.* pp. 49–50.

[63]"Core Logic: The Housing Price Boom Continues," The Options Industry Council, July 2, 2013.

[64]ACT, *Multiple Futures, op. cit.,* p. 15; EUISS, *op. cit.,* pp. 75–77; UK Ministry of Defence, *op. cit.,* p. 22.

[65]ACT, *Multiple Futures, op. cit.,* p. 16.

[66]Dempsey, *op. cit.*

[67]James Goldgeier and Kurt Volker, "Setting Priorities for American Leadership: A New National Security Strategy for the United States," Project for a United and Strong America, March 2013, http://nationalsecuritystrategy.org/pdf/pusa-report-march-2013.pdf, p.4.

[68]*Global Trends 2030, op. cit.,* p. 51; EUISS, *op. cit.,* p. 155.

[69]Fareed Zakaria, "The Rise of Illiberal Democracy," *Foreign Affairs,* November 1997.

- Further negative trends in U.S. and allied defense spending, creating greater risks for the United States.[70]

In this context, two mega-regional economic deals that the United States is negotiating—the Transatlantic Trade and Investment Partnership (TTIP) with the European Union and the Trans-Pacific Partnership negotiations (TPP) with 11 other APEC countries—take on additional importance. The European Union is also conducting bilateral trade deals with several Asian nations. These agreements should provide more stable trade and investment arrangements among America's major commercial partners. Once these negotiations are completed, additional efforts may be needed to rationalize these two multilateral agreements and to globalize them to the extent possible. An effort might be undertaken now to analyze how transatlantic and transpacific trade agreements might be aligned and codified.

In addition, former Secretary of State Hillary Clinton has suggested developing a "new silk road" to strengthen trade routes and stabilize vulnerable countries in Central Asia.[71] Romania has recently explored in greater detail how this concept might be implemented (see chapter 13). U.S.-EU-Asian collaboration on this effort would be vital to its success.

> *Recommendation:* Economic collaboration is vital to the concept of a transatlantic pivot to Asia. **Completing negotiations on TTIP and aligning it with TPP and EU trade agreements with Canada and Asia-Pacific countries would reduce the risk of another major economic shock.**

---

[70]Stephen Larrabee, Stuart Johnson, et. al, *NATO and the Challenges of Austerity* (Santa Monica, CA: RAND Corporation, 2012); Dempsey, *op. cit.*

[71]See the Bucharest conference on "Anchoring the New Silk Road," September 26-28, 2013, http://www.aspeninstitute.ro/articole/708/Bucharest-Forum-2013.html.

*Trend #9:* **Transnational criminal groups are converging into powerful entities that can out-organize and out-gun some national police forces.**

Trend #5 highlighted the diffusion of power in the modern age and the extent to which non-state actors have grown in strength and scope, sometimes to the detriment of national actors. Some call the dark side of this phenomenon "deviant globalization." This presents such a challenge that it warrants separate mention.

The National Defense University recently published a book called *Convergence* in which former Supreme Allied Commander Europe James Stavridis notes that international criminal organizations have taken maximum advantage of advances in communications and transportation to globalize.[72] Their operations have become complex.

As these organizations globalize, many combine illegal activities to maximize their financial gain. The scope of these activities includes human trafficking from Asia and eastern Europe, illegal arms trade in Africa, narcotics trade from Latin America and South Asia, piracy along both coasts of Africa, international terrorist organizations, international cyber crimes, environmental crimes, counterfeiting, financial crimes, and even illegal transport of weapons of mass destruction. Their operations almost always cross national boundaries.

Many of these illicit activities are not only globalized but there is a convergence of several crimes into one operation. The FARC in Colombia is only one prominent example of an organization that combines terrorism and narcotics with deadly result.

Illicit groups often operate in failing states or in areas where governments are weak such as Pakistan's tribal areas and in parts of Afghanistan. In countries like Mexico they have compromised police forces and elements of the military. In places like North Korea, the state itself is complicit. Perhaps 10% of China's GDP is estimated to come from counterfeit goods.[73] Hubs of illegal activity are created in places like Guatemala. National security forces are often out-manned

---

[72]Michael Miklaucic and Jacqueline Brewer, eds., *Convergence* (Washington, D.C.: National Defense University Press, 2013), p. viii.

[73]*Ibid.*, p.152.

and out-gunned. These groups could fairly easily gain access to precision-guided munitions and biological weapons.

The result is greater international lawlessness and disorder. As terrorist cells and criminal syndicates merge their strengths and increase their ruthlessness, the threat to state sovereignty and to human rights multiplies.

This deviant globalization is international and can only be managed through international norm- setting and international enforcement efforts. The United States, Europe and Asian governments have a common stake in the outcome. They need to act together to meet this expanding challenge.

> *Recommendation:* **An element of the transatlantic pivot to Asia should focus on strengthening international law enforcement operations,** using military forces where appropriate.

## *Trend # 10:* The scope of armed conflict is changing and the NATO alliance needs to adjust further.

Many trend studies tend to concentrate on the future nature of warfare. Below are the most important trends they have identified. They suggest that despite the low level of violence today, the probability and consequences of aggression are increasing.[74] Armed conflict will remain a major element of the strategic landscape but that it will become even more complex. To deal with this prospect, the transatlantic alliance will need to be increasingly engaged, agile, and comprehensive in its efforts to maintain security in its region and beyond. The major global trends in future conflict are highlighted below:

- The NIC points to a rising risk of small-scale interstate conflict in Middle East, Caucasus, South Asia, and East Asia.[75] There will be a greater risk of spillover from regional

---

[74]Dempsey, *op. cit.*

[75]*Ibid.*, pp. 64–65; ACT, *Multiple Futures*, *op. cit.*, p. 6; Canadian Department of Defence, *op. cit.*, pp. 3-4.

conflict.[76] But the NIC concludes, perhaps optimistically, that the risk of interstate warfare among major powers remains low.[77]

- Organized terrorist groups with international reach are franchising and turning to organized crime. They will probably have more firepower (PGMs, biological weapons, radiological devices).[78]

- The greatest concern for American defense planners is what they call "anti-access area denial," which is the result of the growing ability of states like China and Iran to use long-range precision munitions and submarines to deny other navies and air forces access to their littoral.[79]

- Future conflict will present "hybrid warfare" challenges in which the lines between various types of conflict will be blurred[80] with a mix of traditional and irregular war, terrorism, and a greater emphasis on the battle over the narrative. These conflicts will require what NATO calls a "comprehensive approach," which includes both military and civilian assets.

- In the future, nations may face more creative, sophisticated, and injurious asymmetric attacks[81] with a greater risk of use of weapons of mass destruction, including radiological devices, and of cyber warfare.[82]

- Control of space could be critical in the opening days of large conventional war.

- Missile attacks and missile defenses will also become a feature of modern warfare.[83]

---

[76]*Global Trends 2030, op. cit.*, pp. 64–65.

[77]*Ibid.*

[78]*Ibid,.* p. 71; *Strategic Horizons, op. cit.*, p. 21.

[79]*Global Trends 2030, op. cit.*, p. 72.

[80]ACT, *Multiple Futures, op. cit.*, pp 47, 57–58; *Strategic Horizons, op. cit.*, pp. 60, 70.

[81]Canadian Department of Defence, *op. cit.*, pp. 93–94.

[82]*Strategic Horizons, op. cit.*, pp. 56–79.

[83]*Global Trends 2030, op. cit.*, p. 72.

- Militaries will increasingly have a role to play in homeland defense, including emergency and humanitarian operations.[84]

The complexities of modern warfare will mean that alliances and coalitions will become increasingly important to deal with the scope and depth of the problem.[85] The dilemma is that many of America's partners may be less than willing to participate.[86] It will therefore be important to make the transatlantic alliance as flexible an instrument as possible and to create new mechanisms to affiliate NATO's Asian partners.

> *Recommendation:* **The NATO Alliance should create new mechanisms—perhaps "Asian Associates" or "Enhanced Global Partners"—to draw in its principal Asian partners** like Japan, South Korea, and Australia. The focus should be not on membership but on new mechanisms to maximize political consultation and military interoperability.

## Conclusion

The Obama Administration's desire to pivot its attention to Asia follows naturally from the first three trends discussed above. The desire to terminate two decade-long wars in the Greater Middle East, combined with growing deficits and a weakened economy, forced an American reassessment of defense priorities. The pivot was designed as part of an effort to end those wars. It was therefore natural that the United States would turn its attention to Asia. But the pivot strategy has been misinterpreted in Europe and a new narrative is needed. The United States should be seen as pivoting with Europe, not from it.

The fourth trend, however, indicates that this transatlantic pivot strategy may be difficult to implement. The Middle East will continue to create instabilities that challenge the transatlantic partners and take the focus away from Asia. The United States will expect significant

---

[84]*Strategic Horizons, op. cit.*, p. 66.

[85]*Ibid*, p. 10; ACT, *Multiple Futures, op. cit.*, pp. 28–29.

[86]*Global Trends 2030, op. cit.*, p. ix.

support from Europe to share the military burdens involved in managing these challenges in Europe's neighborhood. The danger inherent in the second trend, however, is that Europe will not fulfill America's expectations.

The fifth trend complicates matters, as formidable state and non-state actors emerge. And yet this trend also represents a possible opportunity for the transatlantic partners. By engaging emerging states and creating public-private partnerships with non-state entities, the pivot with Europe to Asia can be strengthened.

The sixth trend further complicates the international scene due to the pace and volume of information available globally. Multiple new actors, together with high velocity information, create a more complex world and can lead to strategic surprises, which in turn creates the need for rapid decision-making. This in turn means that the transatlantic partners will need to develop mechanisms for rapid consultation. Coordinating a transatlantic pivot to Asia will require such consultative mechanisms.

Trends seven, eight and nine expose three major challenges, all of which stretch from Vancouver to Vladivostok. Lack of adequate global norms and rule of law in several areas could lead to potential conflict. The prospect of another global economic recession would increase instability everywhere. And international criminal syndicates gain strength at the expense of governments. These three challenges present areas in which transatlantic partners can collaborate with Asia to solve difficult problems.

The last trend indicates that armed conflict will continue and change in ways that will complicate the transatlantic alliance. Creating new NATO partnerships with key Asian countries will help to manage the military challenges that confront NATO.

These global trends suggest the need for a new and expanded transatlantic bargain to include:

- Full commitment by all NATO members to Article 5 of the Washington Treaty, especially in light of Russia's annexation of Crimea.

- Transatlantic commitment to completing TTIP and aligning it with TPP and EU trade agreements with Canada and Asia-Pacific countries.

- A new Trilateralism based on North American-European-Asian joint problem solving.

- A European lead in dealing with security in the Balkans and North Africa.

- Shared U.S.-European responsibility for managing instability in the Greater Middle East.

- An American lead, together with its Asian partners, in providing security in Asia.

- Greater European use of its soft power in Asia to improve norms and institutions.

# Chapter 2

# The "Pivot to Asia:" Myths and Realities

## *Julianne Smith*

In the fall of 2011, then Secretary of State Hillary Clinton published an article in *Foreign Policy* titled, "America's Pacific Century." In it, Secretary Clinton argued that after nearly ten years in Iraq and Afghanistan, it was time for the United States to shift its emphasis away from the Middle East and make greater investments in Asia in order to "sustain our leadership and advance our values."[1] She then unveiled one of the Obama administration's signature foreign policy initiatives: "the pivot to Asia" or the "strategic pivot." Since then, pundits and policymakers around the globe have been analyzing and debating this new policy, questioning its rationale, overarching aim, staying power, and implications for America's relationships with multiple regions and countries around the world. In Europe, this "rebalancing"—as it is also often called—raised a number of concerns about Europe's place in U.S. foreign policy and has led to a string of false assumptions and conclusions. This chapter aims to counter five core myths about the strategic pivot and outline a way forward for Europe and the United States in light of this significant and very real shift in U.S. foreign policy.

## Myth #1: The Pivot Started with the Defense Review in 2012 and is Therefore Rooted Primarily in Defense Policy.

While some European policymakers took note of Secretary Clinton's piece in *Foreign Policy* in November 2011 and followed her speech on the same subject on the deck of a U.S. warship in Manila

---

[1]Hillary Rodham Clinton, "America's Pacific Century," *Foreign Policy*, October 11, 2011, http://www.foreignpolicy.com/articles/2011/10/11/americas_pacific_century#-sthash.rgJZSeQA.dpbs.

29

Bay later that month, the pivot to Asia didn't make European head-lines until a few months later. It was actually the release of the Depart-ment of Defense's Strategic Review in January 2012 that got Europe's attention. The Strategic Review was a one of a kind, out-of-cycle review that the White House commissioned due to the fact that the United States had reached what the Obama administration called "an inflection point." The United States had withdrawn from Iraq, was in the process of ending the combat mission in Afghanistan, and was also facing unprecedented budget cuts tied to sequestration. As a result, the President asked the Department of Defense (DoD) to examine the global security environment and U.S. interests abroad and then rede-fine U.S. missions, priorities and requirements accordingly.

The end result was an eight-page document that outlined in fairly black and white terms the importance that the administration was now placing on the Asia-Pacific. It stated that "While the U.S. military will continue to contribute to security globally, we will of necessity rebal-ance toward the Asia-Pacific region. Our relationships with Asian allies and key partners are critical to the future stability and growth of the region."[2] This opening paragraph struck a nerve in Europe as it was one of the few times that the United States had put the primary emphasis on its relationship with Asia. For decades, in similar docu-ments from the National Security Strategy to various Quadrennial Defense Reviews, Europe often received first mention as America's preeminent security and trade partner. In the 2012 Strategic Review, however, Europe wasn't even the second region mentioned. It came third after the Middle East. And Europe took note.

Much of the actual text on Europe should have been reassuring, though. It stressed that, "Europe is home to some of America's most stalwart allies and partners, many of whom have sacrificed alongside U.S. forces in Afghanistan, Iraq, and elsewhere. Europe is our princi-pal partner in seeking global and economic security, and will remain so for the foreseeable future."[3] But Europeans didn't find much solace in those two lines, especially as they kept reading. What worried them

---

[2]Department of Defense, "Sustaining U.S. Global Leadership: Priorities for 21st Cen-tury Defense," January 2012, http://www.defense.gov/news/defense_strategic_guid-ance.pdf, p. 2.

[3]*Ibid.*

was a line in italics that came a little later, which foreshadowed significant changes concerning the U.S. footprint in Europe. *"In keeping with this evolving strategic landscape, our posture in Europe must also evolve."*[4] That single sentence did two things. First, it confirmed that the pivot to Asia was far more than a simple slogan. It was an actual policy with real consequences for Europe. Second, it gave many the false impression that the strategic pivot was rooted in U.S. defense policy and had a military bent to it. This is probably the most common myth concerning the strategic pivot.

In truth, though, the Strategic Review was not the launch of the administration's pivot to Asia and, contrary to popular opinion, the rebalancing is not limited to defense and security policy. In fact, the President and Vice President came into office in 2009 convinced that the United States was underinvested in the Asia-Pacific, and therefore made renewing and intensifying the U.S. role in the region a key strategic priority. The two words to note here are "renew" and "intensify," which applied to *existing* U.S. policy in Asia. The United States, after all, had always been a Pacific power, whose interests had been inextricably linked with Asia's economic, security and political order. The U.S. government, therefore, did not set out to launch a new policy towards Asia in 2009, nor did it opt to "return" to the region because, as Kurt Campbell pointed out in his article for Chatham House in August of 2013, "the United States had never left."[5]

Why the special emphasis then? What was the strategic basis for the President's decision to turn towards the Asia-Pacific as soon as he came into office? First, the President and his foreign policy team realized early on in the administration that "the lion's share of the political and economic history of the 21$^{st}$ century will be written in the Asia-Pacific region."[6] Second, some of the countries in the region had been demanding heightened U.S. engagement. Third, the core characteristics of the region describe a corner of the world that is dynamic, constantly evolving, and increasingly influential. For example, Asia is

---

[4]*Ibid.*, p. 3.

[5]Kurt Campbell and Brian Andrews, "Explaining the US 'Pivot' to Asia," *Chatham House*, August 2013, http://www.chathamhouse.org/sites/default/files/public/Research/Americas/0813pp_pivottoasia.pdf, p. 2.

[6]*Ibid.*, p. 2.

home to half the world's population and some of the world's largest militaries. It is also home to some of the biggest emerging powers (such as China, India, and Indonesia) as well as old friends and allies (such as Japan, the Republic of Korea, and Australia). On the economic front, the region has seen unprecedented growth in recent years, thanks in no small part to the role the United States has played in helping underwrite regional peace and security. As a result of such growth, Asia has become the engine of the global economy and home to some of the world's most dynamic trade and energy routes. APEC's 21 economies have a combined GDP of $39 trillion (56% of world economic output). Six APEC economies are among the top ten U.S. export markets and U.S. exports to APEC economies are up 175% since 1994 (and 15% since 2010). In short, Asia's ever increasing impact on world affairs and the world economy was indisputable. Recognizing that fact, the President consciously began to turn his attention to that region as soon as he arrived at the White House. Secretary of State Hillary Clinton followed suit, scheduling her first trip abroad not to Europe or the Middle East, as was tradition, but Asia. In February of 2009, she travelled to Japan, Indonesia, Korea, and China. While the phrase had not been coined yet, the strategic pivot was well underway.

What evolved in the months following that trip was the development of a multifaceted, whole-of-government Asia policy that relied on all of the elements of U.S. national power and required the full participation of the President's cabinet. Cooperation among principals was exceptional, with not a single cabinet member objecting to the shift in emphasis and each principal developing his or her own elements of the policy. The overarching policy broke down into three baskets: diplomatic, economic, and defense.

### The Diplomatic Elements of the Strategic Pivot

During the first term, the State Department, in cooperation with other U.S. Government (USG) agencies, focused on four lines of effort in regards to the strategic pivot. The first priority was to deepen and modernize existing alliances, the bedrock of America's work in the Asia-Pacific. History had shown the benefits of America's longstanding bilateral relationships with Japan, South Korea and Australia: increased stability and greater strategic confidence among the major regional players, both of which have enabled the region and the U.S. to shift their focus from security to economic ties. Secretary Clinton set out to strengthen those traditional relationships and enhance those that were less mature. She took a special interest, for example, in U.S.-Filipino ties, committing her agency to a series of high-level meetings and exchanges aimed at bringing more depth and substance to that relationship.

The Secretary's second priority was to broaden U.S. engagement with the emerging partners in Asia. One of the most important (but not the only) priorities on that list was China. Since her first trip to China in February 2009, Secretary Clinton and other high-level officials have worked tirelessly towards positive and constructive relations with China. The overarching goals have been to build trust, identify areas of common interest and encourage China's active efforts in global problem-solving. While the administration decided to significantly increase the amount of bilateral engagement with China, U.S. officials at all levels were urged to stay focused on practical results and remain true to U.S. principles and interests. The end result has been an unprecedented amount of dialogue that has led to the creation of a number of new policy initiatives, including the recent U.S.-China agreement to cut their use of hydro fluorocarbons.[7] To be sure, deep disagreements remain on a wide array of issues, but the two countries have learned the value of keeping the channels of communication open even when they fail to see eye to eye. As one example, the Strategic and Economic Dialogue—which was launched in the spring of 2009 by President Obama and Chinese President Hu—has managed to maintain its rigorous schedule of high-level and mid-level engagements even in the face of increased tensions over events in the South China Sea, U.S. arm sales to Taiwan, and the U.S. Embassy's decision to take in legal activist Chen Guangcheng.

Of course, China hasn't been the only emerging power that has seen heightened U.S. engagement in recent years. The United States has extended a hand to India as well, recognizing its important place in South and East Asia as the world's largest and oldest democracy.

---

[7]"U.S., China Agree to Reduce Use of Hydrofluorocarbons," *Reuters*, June 8, 2013, http://www.reuters.com/article/2013/06/08/us-usa-china-environment-idUSBRE 9570EX20130608.

Obama's very first state dinner was with India's Prime Minister Singh in the fall of 2009, yet another signal of the importance the administration was placing on the region.

In addition to focusing on specific bilateral relationships, Secretary Clinton made sure to put special emphasis on the emerging multilateral architecture in Asia. Unlike Europe, Asia lacks institutions that have decades of operational experience. Many of the region's institutions are quite young and remain largely political forums that struggle to produce tangible and actionable results. Understanding the potential impact that such institutions could have on regional stability and integration, the United States developed a robust strategy for cooperating with them. From its decision to open the first non-member permanent mission at ASEAN to the President's decision to be the first U.S. President to attend the East Asian Summit, to the launch of the Lower Mekong Initiative, the United States has sent a strong signal to the Asia-Pacific about both the value it places on such institutions and its long-term commitment to those institution's development and growth.

Finally, in all of the State Department's diplomatic efforts listed above, the United States has maintained its support for universal values, particularly the protection of human rights and democracy. The United States has deliberately deepened engagement with partners in Asia that disagree with the United States on such issues, urging them to "embrace reforms that would improve governance, protect human rights, and advance political freedoms."[8] It has done so in Vietnam as well as in Burma, where U.S. officials have worked closely with Burmese leaders to secure the release of political prisoners.

### The Economic Elements of the Strategic Pivot

In addition to its diplomatic agenda, the Obama administration has put a strong emphasis on enhancing economic ties with its partners in Asia (while recognizing the leading role that the business community plays in that regard). Multiple U.S. agencies have had a hand in shaping the economic agenda, including the Treasury Department, the Commerce Department, and the State Department. The cornerstone

---

[8]Clinton, *op. cit.*

of U.S. economic engagement has been the Trans-Pacific Partnership (TPP), a trade agreement that will, once finalized, enhance trade and investment among the TPP partner countries, promote innovation, economic growth and development, and support the creation and retention of jobs. Including the United States, there are twelve countries—both developed and developing—currently participating in negotiations. Since a number of countries in Southeast Asia are not included in that list, the U.S. has worked with ASEAN to launch an "Expanded Economic Engagement" initiative to help move those countries towards eventual TPP membership should they so desire.[9] More broadly, the Obama administration has worked to reinvigorate the Asia-Pacific Economic Forum (APEC), which has long suffered from an image of inaction and fruitless dialogue. It has urged APEC to develop a stronger business presence, build capacity and enhance regulatory regimes, and agree to a set of common ground rules concerning imports and national subsidies.[10] As Secretary Clinton stated in her 2011 *Foreign Policy* article, the United States "is committed to cementing APEC as the Asia-Pacific's premier regional economic institution."[11]

### The Defense Elements of the Strategic Pivot

As stated earlier in this piece, the strategic pivot is best known, particularly in Europe, for its accompanying global posture changes. In response to demand signals from Southeast Asia for more training and interaction with the U.S. military and in an effort to more broadly distribute U.S military presence across the region, the Department of Defense decided to deploy 1500 Marines in northern Australia and a U.S. littoral ship in Singapore. This enhanced presence in Southeast Asia was intended to move the United States away from its heavier presence in Northeast Asia that developed during the Cold War. The Obama administration believes that the changes it has made in the defense arena have made the U.S. better positioned to support humanitarian missions, work with a greater number of allies and part-

---

[9]Campbell and Andrews, *op. cit.*, pp. 5–6.

[10]Howard Schneider, "Obama Hopes to Resurrect Influence of Asia-Pacific Economic Cooperation Forum," *Washington Post*, May 29, 2011, http://articles.washingtonpost.com/2011-05-29/business/35264880_1_apec-obama-administration-dorothy-dwoskin.

[11]Clinton, *op. cit.*

ners, and ultimately provide a more robust bulwark against threats or efforts to undermine regional peace and stability.

## Myth #2: The Pivot's Main Focus is China or Containing China.

Despite a long list of speeches and articles by high-ranking officials from the Obama administration stating the contrary, a number of outside observers—many in China but also in Europe—continue to believe that the strategic pivot was designed with only one country in mind: China. Some take it a step further by stating that the policy's overarching goal is to contain China. While China is a key component and driver of the strategy, both of these assumptions are false. As Jeff Bader, former Senior Director for Asia on the National Security Staff during Obama's first term, reminds us in his book, *Obama and China's Rise*, some of the strategic judgments behind the strategic pivot were indeed tied to China:

> The major strategic development in the region and arguably the whole world is the emergence of China as a major power that by most measures appears poised to become the second most influential country on the globe within a generation.
>
> America's relationship with China could be shaped to maximize the chances that China's rise will become a stabilizing and constructive force rather than a threat to peace and equilibrium.[12]

Those two judgments clearly stress China's critical place in U.S. foreign policy and help explain why the Obama administration was so intent on turning America's attention towards Asia. China's centrality in U.S. Asia policy is simply indisputable. But the administration's countless engagements and new initiatives across the *entire* Asia-Pacific region also support a policy that stretches far beyond U.S.-Sino ties. Secretary Clinton alone traveled to virtually every corner of the region—including the remote Pacific Islands—in an effort to

---

[12]Jeffrey A. Bader, *Obama and China's Rise: An Insider's Account of America's Asia Strategy* (Washington, D.C.: Brookings Institution, 2012), p. 7.

broaden and deepen America's engagement with a wide array of countries large and small. The breadth of that engagement also demonstrates just how multifaceted the strategic pivot has been. From climate change to trade to gender equality to the freedom of navigation, the administration has rigorously pursued a comprehensive Asia strategy that includes but is not driven by a rising China.

As for the claims that the administration has its sights on containing China, one should take another look at Jeff Bader's list of key strategic judgments that served as the foundation for the strategic pivot. There, Bader outlines the pillars of the administration's China strategy:

> (1) a welcoming approach to China's emergence, influence, and legitimate expanded role; (2) a resolve to see that its rise is consistent with international norms and law; and (3) an endeavor to shape the Asia-Pacific environment to ensure that China's rise is stabilizing rather than disruptive.[13]

The administration has translated those strategic pillars into policy in many ways. First, it has deliberately increased the level of engagement under the assumption that greater engagement breads greater trust, which tends to bread greater stability. Second, it has increased the prominence of political and security issues in the bilateral relationship, moving away from President Bush's core focus on the economic side of the relationship.[14] Third, the administration has stressed repeatedly that its enhanced military presence in Asia benefits the *entire* region, including China. As Defense Secretary Panetta said in Beijing in September of 2012, "Our rebalance to the Asia-Pacific region is not an attempt to contain China. It is an attempt to engage China and expand its role in the Pacific."[15] While China continues to view many of the defense-related aspects of the strategic pivot with skepticism and angst, it has also expressed a strong desire to enhance mil-to-mil engagement between the United States and China.

---

[13]*Ibid.*

[14]Bader, *op. cit.*, p. 22.

[15]Chris Carroll, "In Beijing, Panetta Says US Strategy Not Aimed at Containing China," *Stars and Stripes*, September 19, 2012, http://www.stripes.com/news/pacific/in-beijing-panetta-says-us-strategy-not-aimed-at-containing-china-1.189917.

Regardless of how they may interpret U.S. policy in the region, there is a clear Chinese appreciation of the potential benefits of bringing our two militaries together, particularly in regards to counter piracy cooperation, nuclear proliferation, and natural disaster response.

Most recently, the United States and China have introduced a new slogan aimed at both capturing the nature of their evolving relationship and serving as a guiding light for their work moving forward: "A New Model of Major Power Relations." This slogan tries to counter power transition theory, which predicts that war is more likely when a rising power is approaching parity with a declining power. Because so many Chinese analysts and academics view the United States to be a declining power, they assume that the United States will do anything to halt China's rise, including turning to the use of force. In an effort to avoid that trajectory and give China greater political cover for engaging with the United States, then Vice President Xi Jinping used his February 2012 speech in Washington to call for a "new type of great power relations," a new cooperative approach that would help the two countries avoid what some viewed as an inevitable path to conflict. In the speech, Xi described that "new type of relationship" as based on four key factors: (1) increasing mutual understanding and mutual trust; (2) respecting each other's core interests and major concerns; (3) deepening mutually beneficial cooperation; (4) enhancing coordination and cooperation in international affairs and on global issues. Months later, Secretary Clinton began using the term and in their meeting in California in June of this year, both President Obama and President Xi adopted the term and began the process of putting policy behind the phrase.

Moving forward, the real question, therefore, is not whether the United States is trying to contain China but how the two countries will find ways to deliver on their clearly articulated intent to move away from conflict and towards closer and pragmatic cooperation even in the face of disagreement.

## Myth #3: The Pivot is Purely Rhetorical.

Among the skeptics of the strategic pivot, there is still a small group of outside observers who genuinely believes that the entire policy is merely rhetorical and lacks real substance. To be sure, the casual observer would no doubt have picked up on a number of catchy slogans and phrases that the administration has launched in recent years. Countless U.S. government officials have also given numerous speeches on the subject, which have been rich in platitudes and high ambitions. But even the most modest research effort (or a simple Google search for that matter) will easily unveil plenty of examples of concrete, actionable policies in Asia that have taken root since President Obama came into office. From the very real changes in U.S. force posture to the string of free trade agreements finalized or currently under negotiation to the significant role the United States played in Burma's transformative reform processes, it is hard to reach the conclusion that nothing has been achieved.

Another question people often ask is whether the strategic pivot is sustainable. Can the United States continue its heavy emphasis on Asia given the administration's pressing concerns in the Middle East? Will Secretary Kerry dedicate as much time to this policy as Secretary Clinton did in light of his own personal interest in brokering Middle East peace? And finally, knowing that the administration seized on a number of high-impact, low-cost opportunities during the first term, will it now have to work harder to identify new "wins" in Asia? Knowing the President's personal interest and commitment to this major foreign policy initiative and the amount of time he has personally invested in it, it is probably unlikely that the strategic pivot will fade from the priority list. And even if top officials finds themselves occupied with other regions and occasionally canceling or shortening trips to the region (as the President did in October of 2013 due to the government shutdown), dozens of mid-level officials at the State Department and the Defense Department continue to dedicate 100% of their time to this policy. Obviously, they will have to recalibrate the policy from time to time as events in the region change course but the overarching aim and structure of the strategic pivot will not alter.

## Myth #4: The Strategic Pivot Produces Winners and Losers. Europe is a Loser.

Unfortunately, the use of the term "pivot" has left some with the impression that the United States is pivoting *away* from something. Europeans sometimes assume that that something is Europe. But as I stated in a speech I gave in Latvia in September of 2012, "the rebalancing means neither leaving Europe to Europeans nor going it alone in Asia."[16] Yes, the transatlantic relationship has evolved quite significantly over the last two decades and U.S. force presence in Europe is evolving. But as various Obama administration officials (including the President) have stated time and again, Europe is the cornerstone of U.S. engagement with the world. And that engagement will continue to serve as a catalyst for global cooperation. The United States has every intention of working closely with Europeans not only on European matters but on the full range of shared global challenges, including Asia (assuming Europe is both interested and able).

In terms of the force posture changes underway in Europe, too many Europeans look at those changes as a net loss and are unfamiliar with the broader policy decision that led to that change. What grabbed European headlines was the news that the United States would be removing two Brigade Combat Teams (BCTs) from Europe. Few know, however, that the U.S. Army is actually removing eight BCTs from the active duty force as it becomes smaller and leaner in the coming years. Two of those BCTs will come from Europe and six will come from the United States. In other words, Europe is not the only place experiencing a loss. Multiple U.S. bases in the United States will feel the impact of those reductions. And contrary to what some have stated, the BCTs formerly based in Europe will not be deployed to Asia.

While U.S. force posture in Europe is evolving, it is inaccurate to say it is declining. Yes, the U.S. will no longer have heavy brigades designed for repelling large-scale ground attacks stationed in Europe. But the United States will ensure that it can meet all of its Article 5 commitments, and it is also enhancing its presence in a number of different areas, particularly in regards to Special Forces. Furthermore, recognizing the need for Europe and the United States to maintain their high level of interoperability and institutionalize lessons learned from operations in Afghanistan and elsewhere, the United States

---

[16]Julianne Smith, "Panel Discussion: Europe in the Shadow of the U.S. Election Debate: Are We Losing to the Greater Middle East and Asia?" Riga Conference 2012, Latvia, September 15, 2012, http://iipdigital.usembassy.gov/st/english/texttrans/2012/09/20120915136081.html#axzz2fonInCo4.

announced in early 2012 that it would regularly rotate a U.S.-based battalion task force to Europe. The United States will also be making its first-ever commitment to the NATO Response Force, a concept the U.S. helped create but has never actually participated in.

Finally, the United States remains committed to defending against the growing threat of ballistic missile attack as embodied by the European Phased Adaptive Approach, which is the U.S. contribution to NATO ballistic missile defense (BMD). In addition to the radar already deployed and operational in Turkey and the BMD-capable Aegis ship in the eastern Mediterranean, this will include putting assets in Poland and Romania, and the home porting of missile defense-capable Aegis destroyers in Spain.

Of course, the transatlantic relationship isn't defined strictly by defense relationships. In addition to continuing our critical work together in that area, the United States expects our relationship to continue to expand and thrive in countless other political and economic areas. No two other regions share such a long list of shared values. Rebalancing is not at Europe's expense, but rather improves our ability to address 21st century threats and our collective security together.

## Myth #5: Transatlantic Cooperation on Asia is Either a Nonstarter or Limited.

Regardless of what one actually thinks of the strategic pivot, a number of European policymakers assume that Europe has little to no role to play in this shift in U.S. policy. This is particularly true among those that believe falsely that the strategic pivot is strictly defense-oriented. If one views the pivot narrowly through a defense lens, it is fairly easy to conclude that Europe's militaries, with their declining defense budgets and modernization challenges, will have neither the resources nor the willingness to increase their operational activity in the Asia-Pacific. But that perspective is far too limited in scope and far from what the United States expects or desires. As stated earlier in this chapter, the United States has taken a "whole-of-government" approach with the strategic pivot, developing new policies on countless issues across multiple U.S. government agencies. In the minds of many American policymakers, Europe would be wise to follow suit not out of any loyalty to the United States but because Europe too has a vested interest in peace and stability in Asia. It is in Europe's, not just America's, interest to enhance cooperation with Asia, and there are countless ways to advance that agenda both bilaterally and multilaterally.

Europeans sometimes mention another obstacle to enhancing their cooperation in Asia: the financial crisis. While numerous economic indicators look better than they did a few years ago, the reverberations of the eurozone crisis continue to loom large and occupy the minds of European leaders. Most of the countries in southern Europe are still teetering between recovery and crisis, limiting the bandwidth some individual European countries and EU leaders feel they can dedicate to new initiatives in the Asia Pacific. That said, compared to 2010 and 2011, when the EU's foreign policy arm had a much lower profile globally, Lady Ashton's office has seen a noticeable uptick in Asian engagement.

Fortunately, a handful of European countries and a small group of European leaders inside the EU have started to embrace the strategic pivot and worked to create some low cost, high impact initiatives in or on Asia. Some European countries, especially those with longstanding relationships in Asia, have also conducted an informal review of their current policies in the region and sought opportunities to deepen or expand such policies. What one now finds, therefore, is a smattering of national and multinational initiatives on Asia starting to take root. Some of those initiatives like EU-U.S. Dialogue on Asia have been designed specifically to enhance transatlantic cooperation in Asia. Others, like the Netherlands' enhanced work in Indonesia and Burma, are primarily bilateral in nature. While many of these initiatives are admirable and show real promise, the policies are largely uncoordinated and ad hoc, limiting their impact and effectiveness. In other words, national efforts across the EU are not part of a wider narrative or collective story outlining broader strategic objectives.

## Recommendations for the European Union

Catherine Ashton, the EU's foreign policy chief, is near the end of her tenure. Given her relatively consistent engagement in the region over the last 18 months, including her important joint statement on the Asia-Pacific region with Secretary Clinton in Cambodia in July of last year, Lady Ashton should seize on her last few months in office to strengthen the EU's work in Asia. The European Union issued a set of "Guidelines on the EU's Foreign and Security Policy in East Asia" in June of 2012, which is a lengthy and quite substantive document outlining the importance of East Asia for the European Union.[17] It serves as a useful orientation for those in or outside the EU looking to better understand EU priorities and policies. But it also reveals the heavy emphasis that the EU continues to place on the economic and trade relationships in Asia as well as the EU's lack of a more coherent and focused common foreign and security policy in the region. To the authors' credit, the document does list several concrete recommendations for enhancing the EU's political and security role in East Asia, including making full use of existing strategic partnerships, deepening the EU's relationship with ASEAN, and developing exchanges on regional issues with other important players like Russia, India and Australia. That list is a good start and some of the recommendations have already been implemented. Lady Ashton would be wise, however, to also focus her efforts on helping EU members deploy their combined weight more effectively.

First, as American interlocutors have mentioned before, it would be helpful if Lady Ashton's office could bring greater purpose and focus to the wide array of development assistance policies that individual member states are already pursuing in Asia. That effort might start with an audit of how and where member states invest their resources. Could those resources be better spent if they collectively focused on a limited set of high priority areas? For example, should member states put special emphasis on social and economic reform? Improved governance or sustainable development? Of course, the EU's role is not to dictate how members should allocate national resources and there are genuine limits on what Brussels to can do to influence the decision making of a mid-career official working in Bangkok or Naypyidaw. But the EU might be a little more vocal about its preferences in order to help steer those countries that are

---

[17]Council of the European Union, "Guidelines on the EU's Foreign and Security Policy in East Asia," June 15, 2012, http://eeas.europa.eu/asia/docs/guidelines_eu_foreign_sec_pol_east_asia_en.pdf.

currently looking at making adjustments to existing Asia policies or launching new ones.

Second, the EU might want to consider a similar role on trade policy. Some countries like Germany have significant and quite unique trade policies with China. Other member states are only beginning to navigate those waters. Again, the question is whether **the EU might be able to play a more active coordinating role and provide a proper narrative for the various trade initiatives and sanctions policies across the European continent.** As for the EU itself, it is already negotiating Free Trade Agreements with Singapore, Malaysia, Japan and India (among others) and has completed negotiations with South Korea. It should expand that list to keep pace with the U.S. efforts on the Trans-Pacific Partnership and other regional trade agreements.

Third, beyond specific development or trade policies, **the EU may want to foster a broader conversation about the EU's strategic priorities in Asia.** As stated earlier, there are countless ways for the EU member states to enhance their role in Asia. Given the limited resources and, at least in some EU member states, the limited political will to do anything large scale, the EU may want to survey member's interest in certain regional and functional issue areas. To date, the EU's work in Asia has been largely divided into three broad areas: rule of law and governance, climate, and non-traditional security issues like cyber and maritime security. These categories are both logical fits and a tribute to the EU's interest in stretching beyond its core competencies. But they still don't provide useful guidance for some of the medium and small member states interested in dipping their toe into Pacific waters. For the Asia hand at the Swedish or Czech Foreign Ministry, for example, how should he or she pair Sweden or the Czech Republic's interests in Asia with the EU's efforts? Surveying members' interests, expertise, and geographic preferences as well as Asian partners' interests in seeking assistance could be time well spent, although one needs to be clear-eyed about the limited resources to do so. The EU may also want to consider sharing lessons learned from individual members. For example, former Norwegian Foreign Minister Espen Barth Eide took a strong interest in Burma and actively enhanced Norway's political and economic support for that developing country. What lessons might former Foreign Minister Eide share from his work with the Burmese? If the EU finds it lacks the time and resources to do so, a European think tank could alternatively play that role.

## Recommendations for the European Union and the United States

While countless transatlantic forums and institutions exist for Europe and the United States to work together on everything from trade to Iran to climate change, there are sadly few venues for transatlantic dialogue on Asia. Other than its operational partnerships with a handful of Asian countries in current missions, NATO has yet to express a strong interest in playing a stronger role in the region or even fostering greater transatlantic dialogue on Asia. The OECD and the OSCE are in the same boat, preferring to stay focused on their core missions in their respective neighborhoods. The only forum that has shown some promise in this regard is the EU-U.S. channel. In fact, in that June 2012 "Guidelines for East Asia" document mentioned previously, **the EU actually states, "Given the great importance of transatlantic relations, the EU has a strong interest in partnership and cooperation with the U.S. on foreign and security policy challenges related to East Asia."[18] More should be done to seize on this stated interest and build on the meetings that have taken place to date.**

One of the biggest challenges for Europe and the United States is how to talk to Asia, particularly China, about cyber threats. China is often viewed as part of the problem (although recent NSA revelations have put the United States in that category as well). As a result, EU-U.S.-China dialogue on this issue is nonexistent. But if Europe, the United States and China have any hopes of establishing international norms and standards in regards to this rapidly evolving threat, they will need to find a way to foster some form of a high-level dialogue. Space is another area that could benefit from a U.S.-EU-China exchange of ideas. **Bringing Asia, particularly China, into these two dialogues might be a useful way to encourage Asian partners to assume a more active role in global problem-solving.**

---

[18]Council of the European Union, *op. cit.*, p. 8.

However useful transatlantic dialogue and cooperation on and with Asia might be, it is worth reminding ourselves that going it alone in the Asia-Pacific regions is also an acceptable path. In fact, it may occasionally be preferable depending on the situation. While the collective weight of transatlantic cooperation can be a tremendous asset in shaping the international landscape, there are also circumstances in which one side of the Atlantic has a comparative advantage that is strongest when used unilaterally. Sometimes it is just a case of one side being able to do something the other side cannot. One of the better examples of this can be found in Burma where the EU has taken the lead on police training, something the United States is unable to provide at the moment due to limits on providing security sector assistance (other than de-mining).

Even in cases where Europe and the United States do choose to stand shoulder-to-shoulder, they don't always need to—as one EU official told me—"over-advertise it." Private and off-the-record conversations with partners in Asia are sometimes far more effective than joint public lecturing, especially when it comes to human rights issues. In other words, **transatlantic cooperation in and on Asia can take many forms and neither side should fall prey to the "one size fits all" approach when dealing with the region.**

### Recommendation: Use Informal and Unofficial Channels of Cooperation

**Above and beyond the EU-U.S. channels mentioned above, Europe and the United States should chart new ways to cooperate on Asia outside of formal government channels. Each side of the Atlantic enjoys a rich think tank and NGO tradition that stands ready to provide services for which governments often lack the time and resources.** One idea might be to encourage the think tank community to organize a Dialogue on Asia that would convene high-level experts from the U.S., Europe, and Asia to address a series of global challenges. Smaller versions of this dialogue already exist but nothing on the scale of the German Marshall Fund's Brussels Forum or the Munich Security Conference has been organized to date. Asian issues (TPP and the South China Sea) now regularly appear on the agendas of the big transatlantic conferences but they remain footnotes in the broader transatlantic dialogue. Furthermore, Asian experts are not regular attendees at such events. Hosting an annual, high-level gathering specifically targeted at Asia (and with Asian participants) would therefore breathe fresh life into decades of transatlantic dialogue that has started to grow stale. More importantly, such a dialogue might help counter Chinese complaints that Western solutions are often presented as final well before Asian counterparts have had a chance to provide input into the process. Hosting more frequent exchanges between American, European and Asian experts and policymakers would give all three partners a seat at the table and a stronger voice in mapping solutions to common challenges.

## Conclusion

Regardless of what one thinks of the strategic pivot, it is a policy that stands to shape the future of transatlantic work for years to come. Events in the Asia Pacific region are simply too important for either the United States or Europe to ignore. The next U.S. president may choose to rename the policy or recalibrate it based on current events but Asia will remain a cornerstone of U.S. foreign policy. Similarly, however far away Asia may feel to European policymakers at times, it is also hard to imagine a declining interest in Asia among European policymakers in the coming years.

In order to channel effectively their collective resources at enhancing prosperity and security across the Asia-Pacific region, the United States and Europe should double their efforts to hold action-oriented dialogues and exchanges. The first priority of these dialogues should be to work through many of the myths and misperceptions outlined in this chapter in order to bring clarity to U.S. and European objectives in the region. Concerted effort should also be made to trade lessons learned and seize on the comparative advantages of the two sides of the Atlantic in addressing the economic and security needs of the region. Furthermore, if impossible through formal government channels, a group of European and American think tanks should host a regular Track II Dialogue on Asia that includes senior level experts from all three continents.

Europe and the United States have a remarkable track record of working together to address global challenges. The challenge in years to come will be to take that collective experience and apply it in the Asia Pacific in ways that will positively impact the people in the region and serve our common interests.

*Part II*

The Actors

# Chapter 3

# The Pivot and Underlying U.S. Interests in Asia

*Patrick M. Cronin and Alexander Sullivan*

The U.S. pivot or rebalance to Asia is a strategic imperative. Notwithstanding competing interests in other regions of the world, it remains in America's vital interest to use the past few years as a springboard for widening and deepening our strategic engagement in what is likely to remain the most important region of the 21$^{st}$ century. This chapter examines the recent U.S. policy of rebalancing to Asia; looks at the underlying pivot policy and the evolution of America's expanded interests in the Asia-Pacific region; considers the principal near-term and long-term security challenges to the region; and offers some general observations about how the United States and Europe can together help create a stable balance in this increasingly important region of the world.

## The Pivot: A Search for Strategic Balance

America's 'pivot' to Asia is in a fundamental sense a search for strategic balance in a dynamic and shifting international security environment. Every government searches for strategic balance. After all, strategy involves aligning policy objectives with available means. When the environment in which one is crafting a strategy is in constant flux, there is a persistent need for recalibration. As the United States prepares to hand responsibility for Afghanistan's security to Afghans later in 2014, officials in Washington, D.C. continue to search for a new strategic balance, one that responsibly weighs short-term against long-term risk, aligns finite resources with objectives that promise the greatest strategic upside, and assesses the proper weight to place on military power as opposed to diplomacy, development, and other levers of power.

The search for strategic balance and coherence is hardly new. The Obama administration entered office in 2009 determined to address a heavy "inheritance" of two protracted ground wars, a global counter-terrorism campaign, Iranian and North Korean nuclear proliferation, and mounting debt and deepening economic recession. The 2010 Quadrennial Defense Review (QDR) kept the focus on winning the current wars, but also signaled growing concern about the potential long-term decline in America's military preeminence, as the diffusion of modern technology complicated the ability of the U.S. armed forces to operate forward in defense of allies and partners.[1]

Less than two years later, the administration adjusted its strategic course. With combat operations concluded in Iraq and winding down in Afghanistan, the Department of Defense issued new strategic guidance in January 2012 that called for minimizing the cost of stabilization operations in the Middle East and Southwest Asia in favor of enhancing engagement in the Asia-Pacific region.[2] Anticipating how to reduce defense budget by nearly $500 billion over the next decade, to comply with the Budget Control Act of 2011, the guidance switched defense priorities from waging counterinsurgency to countering anti-access capabilities. Ground forces would be reduced, while preserving and building agile and mobile forces to help defend the global commons. Future defense procurement "winners" would include technologies for intelligence, surveillance and reconnaissance (ISR), robotic and autonomous unmanned sensors and systems, and cyberspace, as well as Special Operations Forces (SOF).

This combination of cutting defense spending and changing the technological and geographical focus of defense remains a major balancing act today. The United States is attempting to pivot to the Asia-Pacific region at a time of great tumult and uncertainty. Near-term budgetary constraints are real, even as the long-term direction of Asia and China remains murky and distant. Let us begin by examining the deep historical roots of America's commitment to the Asia–Pacific region.

---

[1] *Quadrennial Defense Review Report* (Washington, D.C.: Department of Defense, February 2010), http://www.defense.gov/qdr/.

[2] *Sustaining U.S. Global Leadership: Priorities for 21st Century Defense* (Washington, D.C.: Department of Defense, January 2012), http://www.defense.gov/news/Defense_Strategic_Guidance.pdf.

## The Evolution of American Interests in Asia

The U.S. interest in safeguarding Asian-Pacific security is neither new nor transient. Indeed, U.S. interest in the Asia-Pacific has developed over the course of two centuries and, as the region figures to be the geographical locus of power throughout this century, it continues to grow today. After the 1784 voyage of the *Empress of China* that inaugurated U.S. Pacific maritime trade, the United States over the course of the nineteenth century built robust economic ties with Asia and gradually established outposts from Hawaii to Manila. These toeholds gave it inchoate security interests and made America a resident, and therefore permanent, Pacific power.[3] President Theodore Roosevelt's deployment of the "Great White Fleet" of modern battleships to the Asia-Pacific in 1908–09 symbolized U.S. determination to play a strong security role in the region.

After the defeat of Imperial Japan in 1945, the United States assumed a heavy burden as the chief guarantor of peace and security in the region. America's strategic approach to the Asia-Pacific region mirrored maritime Britain's focus on preserving a continental balance of power. Especially following the conclusion of the four-decade civil wars in China in 1949, the United States formalized a strategy designed to deny any single power from dominating the vast Eurasian mainland. In identifying stability and prosperity throughout most of the Asia-Pacific region as a vital U.S. interest, the United States helped catalyze the region's subsequent impressive economic and political development. But it was strategic self-interest that anchored U.S. policy.[4]

In recent years, U.S. interests in the region have deepened and widened. Although denied clear victories in limited wars in Korea and

---

[3]Rhys Richards, "Re-Viewing Early American Trade with China, 1784–1833," *Mains'l Haul: A Journal of Pacific Maritime History*, Vol. 39, No. 2 (Spring 2003), 14–19; Michael H. Hunt and Steven I. Levine, *Arc of Empire: America's Wars in Asia from the Philippines to Vietnam* (Chapel Hill: University of North Carolina Press, 2012), pp. 39–40.

[4]As historian S. C. M. Paine observes, "The United States has emulated the British maritime strategy of keeping the sea lanes open to trade so that the home economy can produce uninterrupted by warfare, of relying on its economic moat to insulate itself from foreign threats, and of fighting wars far from home, at times and places of its choosing." S. C. M. Paine, *The Wars for Asia, 1911–1949* (New York: Cambridge University Press, 2012), 23.

Vietnam (wars fought within the context of a bipolar superpower contest), successive U.S. administrations have pursued a lengthening roster of economic, diplomatic, and military interests in the Asia-Pacific region. Those interests have expanded further since the end of the Cold War, as China, India and other Asian countries have experienced sustained and rapid growth. In addition to seeking to preserve a balance of power and freedom of navigation within a changing regional security environment, the United States supports higher standards for expanded trans-Pacific trade, the peaceful resolution of disputes, trust and reciprocity with other great powers, and an inclusive regional architecture undergirded by international law and norms.

U.S. interests and linkages in the Asia-Pacific are likely to deepen even further in the decades ahead. Just as much of the world is increasingly looking to enhance its relations with Asian-Pacific nations, there is a broad U.S. understanding that the region is of paramount importance.[5] One major poll recently showed that a majority of Americans now believe Asia is more important to America's future than is Europe.[6] The Asia-Pacific region possesses about half of the world's population, more than half of global trade and economic output, and has recently overtaken Europe with respect to overall defense spending.[7] As Asian economies drive the global economy throughout the twenty-first century, these nations appear poised to enhance their clout in world affairs.

Against this historical backdrop (of which this is but a cursory treatment), the Obama administration has declared its determination to prioritize the comprehensive engagement of the Asia-Pacific region. This strategic approach to the region, something is now often reduced to a single word, "rebalancing." Irrespective of the name, the United States requires growing trade, active but effective diplomacy, and sufficient

---

[5]Patrick M. Cronin, "As the World Rebalances in the Asian-Pacific Century, So Must the United States," *Global Asia*, Vol. 7, No. 4 (Winter 2012), pp. 8–13.

[6]This is a gradual trend that has been apparent since the end of the Cold War. *Foreign Policy in the New Millennium: Results of the 2012 Chicago Council Survey of American Public Opinion and U.S. Foreign Policy* (Chicago: Chicago Council on Global Affairs, 2012), pp. 33–34.

[7]Myra Macdonald, "Asia's Defense Spending Overtakes Europe's: IISS," *Reuters*, March 14, 2013, http://www.reuters.com/article/2013/03/14/us-security-military-iiss-idUSB RE92D0EL20130314.

military investment and presence to promote and preserve a peaceful and prosperous region. "Our strategic 'rebalance' to the Asia-Pacific region," Joseph Yun, Acting Assistant Secretary of State for East Asian and Pacific Affairs, has testified, "therefore reflects a deep recognition that the United States must substantially increase its political, economic, development, and defense investments in the Asia-Pacific given the region's fundamental importance to our future prosperity and security." He added that, "We are bound to Asia through our geography, history, alliances, economies, and people-to-people ties, which will continue to grow in importance over the next decade."[8]

As with most complex overarching policies, rebalancing has grown and changed over time. Let us dissect briefly the origins, subsequent developments, and likely future trajectories of the rebalance to Asia.

### Rebalancing

There remains some debate even in U.S. policy circles precisely what is meant by the policy of rebalancing to Asia. Before "rebalancing" became synonymous for U.S. policy to the Asia-Pacific region, it was more broadly a description of a global phenomenon.[9] For decades past and future, the steady shift in power from West to East, from the Atlantic to the Pacific and Indian Oceans, requires a global recognition of rising economic, political, technological, and military power of a dynamic Asia-Pacific region. Japan, South Korea, Singapore and Taiwan were at the vanguard of this trend a few decades ago as the Asian tigers. Today the swift economic and military rise of China exemplifies the region's ascent, with an unprecedented expansion of wealth and a growing middle class.[10] Despite widely varying forecasts about the future, few analysts doubt that in the future China will overtake the United States as the world's largest economy—a position the United States has held since the late nineteenth century. Many forecast that China and

---

[8]Joseph Yun, "The Rebalance to Asia: Why South Asia Matters," Statement before the House Committee on Foreign Affairs Subcommittee on Asia and the Pacific, February 26, 2013.

[9]I have amplified this argument about a global rebalancing to Asia in Patrick M. Cronin, "As the World Rebalances in the Asian-Pacific Century, So Must the United States," *Global Asia* (Vol. 7, No. 4, Winter 2012, December 2012).

[10]Linda Yueh, "The Rise of the Global Middle Class," *BBC News*, June 18, 2013, http://www.bbc.com/news/business-22956470.

other Asian-Pacific countries will increasingly determine peace and prosperity in the twenty-first century, as the education, wealth, and capability of this region ascends even further in the decades ahead. Military capabilities are following these largely economic trends.

While the Obama administration and its predecessors have responded to long-term global trends, the current U.S. government has also sought to address two short-term developments. One immediate driver was the unsustainability of waging two protracted ground wars in the Middle East and South Asia. Whether because of growing exhaustion or a growing recognition of the diminishing returns of protracted stabilization operations or both, the Obama administration decided U.S. interests would be better served by ending major combat operations and shifting more attention to a rising Asia-Pacific region. The pivot was meant to help the United States shift emphasis from war to peace and prosperity, from the wolf at the door to future opportunities and challenges.

A second immediate development accelerated this shift: namely, growing Chinese assertiveness since roughly 2009, particularly in China's near seas. An increasingly confident China opted not to "hide and bide" capability so much as to probe how to flex newfound muscle in the South and East China Seas, targeting Vietnamese, Japanese and even U.S. Navy vessels for harassment.[11]

The perception of growing Chinese maritime assertiveness was reinforced by Chinese diplomacy in 2010. A tough, rising China stirred widespread concern in the region. Speaking at the Association of Southeast Asian Nations (ASEAN) Regional Forum in Hanoi, U.S. Secretary of State Hillary Clinton sought to reassure allies and partners in the region that "unimpeded commerce" and the peaceful resolution of maritime disputes were "pivotal to regional stability." Then PRC Foreign Minister Yang Jiechi responded ominously to the comment, saying, "China is a big country and other countries are small countries, and that's just a fact."[12]

---

[11]For details, see the sections on the East and South China Seas in Patrick M. Cronin et al., "Tailored Coercion: Competition and Risk in Maritime Asia" (Washington, D.C.: Center for a New American Security, March 2014).

[12]John Pomfret, "U.S. Takes a Tougher Tone with China," *The Washington Post*, July 30, 2010, http://www.washingtonpost.com/wp-dyn/content/article/2010/07/29/AR2010 072906416.html.

The rhetorical rebalance to Asia reached its apogee in November 2011. Between hosting the Asian-Pacific Economic Cooperation (APEC) summit and being the first U.S. president to attend the East Asia Summit in Indonesia, President Obama traveled to Australia. Despite drawing down two wars, the President pledged increased focus on the region during a speech to Parliament in Canberra. "As President," he said, "I have, therefore, made a deliberate and strategic decision—as a Pacific nation, the United States will play a larger and long-term role in shaping this region and its future." The fullest articulation of U.S. rebalancing policy remains a single article in *Foreign Policy* magazine, published in November 2011, entitled, "America's Pacific Century." In that article, Secretary Clinton enumerated U.S. interests and America's determination to retain comprehensive power focused on long-term strategic priorities in a rising Indo-Pacific region. Then U.S. Assistant Secretary of State Kurt Campbell implemented the policy not by following through on a rigid template but rather by constantly recalibrating opportunities for advancing U.S. interests with a rising Asia-Pacific region.

Between the summitry and the policy narrative, the Obama administration's concerted move to rebalance U.S. strategic priorities to the Asia-Pacific engendered a reaction. China has pushed back on the notion of the United States strengthening its regional posture. Many Chinese commentators and officials have sought to portray rebalancing as tantamount to containment. Riding a growing tide of public nationalism, moreover, Chinese leaders have exerted unrelenting pressure on Japan and the Philippines, especially after the latter brought an arbitration case concerning China's South China Sea claims to the International Tribunal on the Law of the Sea. This pressure has not abated despite a Chinese charm offensive begun in October 2013, meant to calm the rest of the region's fears. Virtually all countries in the region, including the United States, have a strong interest in preserving growing economic ties with China and need China's cooperation on an array of important global issues. Even so, this pushback has helped to catalyze a rebalancing of rebalancing.

### Rebalancing the Rebalance

Despite some initial confusion over what was meant by rebalancing, the concept remains in flux. Even before the budgetary turning of the screw started to squeeze strategic decision-making, the pushback on rebalancing from China and others forced the administration to clarify precisely what it was pivoting from and to and why. A full governmental explication—and even more, a detailed resourcing plan—is still called for. But rebalancing should be about shifting from war to peace, although taking care not to exit so swiftly from current conflicts, e.g. Afghanistan, that it might jeopardize future stability in those areas and with perceptions of American resoluteness. This point has been reemphasized by Susan Rice, President Obama's second-term National Security Advisor, who stated that "matter how many hotspots emerge elsewhere," the shift to Asia would retain priority.[13]

Rebalancing is also about providing a strategic challenge to China but not containing China. Long-term U.S. presence should help to counter any Chinese tendency toward reemerging as an aggressive regional hegemon; but stepped-up dialogue and cooperation with China should seek to provide sufficient strategic reassurance to dampen unnecessary military arms racing and competition. The second-term Obama administration has sought to strike this balance through sustained dialogue combined with tough statements of principle, in an adaptive way basically consonant with the approach under Hillary Clinton and Kurt Campbell.[14] America should be rebalancing to Asia *with* Europe and the rest of the world, not away from Europe and the rest of the world.

The United States should pivot within Asia, as well, away from an almost exclusive concentration on Northeast Asia and toward a much wider network of contacts, especially the Association of Southeast Asian Nation (ASEAN) member states. Part of this rebalancing should include moving from mostly bilateralism to greater multilateralism, especially by embracing ASEAN-centered institutions; unfortunately, this will require patience, given that the region's multilateral security architecture badly lags behind the challenges of the region. Rebalancing also means building a bridge between the confluence of two

---

[13]Susan Rice, "America's Future in Asia," Georgetown University, Washington, D.C., November 20, 2013, http://www.whitehouse.gov/the-press-office/2013/11/21/remarks-prepared-delivery-national-security-advisor-susan-e-rice.

[14]Patrick M. Cronin, "America's China Paradigm is Back on Track," *War on the Rocks*, February 21, 2014, http://warontherocks.com/2014/02/americas-china-paradigm-is-back-on-track/.

oceans—the Indian and the Pacific—by strengthening ties between India, East Asia, and Oceania and embracing the reform-minded new government of the geographical swing state of Myanmar (Burma). In the medium term, engaging Asia powers will involve shaping their behavior as they begin to act outside the immediate region, such as several nations' naval deployment to fight piracy in the Gulf of Aden. Finally, rebalancing means economic and diplomatic power, and not just military might. In these and other ways, the resistance the United States sometimes receives toward its rebalancing policy enables U.S. officials an opportunity to provide greater strategic clarity about America's long-term aims in the region.

Comprehensive power is vital, especially in the context of those who would reduce America's involvement and influence in the region to military forces and defense budgets. Even so, military power will remain the main insurance policy. Military presence in general and near-term military readiness in particular need should be maintained to the greatest extent possible while not robbing funds intended for future modernization.[15] This need not break the bank, because mostly involves retaining and adapting American's strong extant military force. At the same time, allies and partners can and should do more to share burdens. We need to widen the scope for engagement if we are to realize the ideas embedded in the phrase "geographically distributed, operationally resilient and politically sustainable."

Although many equate "rebalancing" with strengthening U.S. force posture in the Asia-Pacific, the United States is determined to be as economically and politically vital to the region as it is militarily. This is why completing negotiations on and implementing the Trans-Pacific Partnership (TPP)—an ambitious high-standard free trade

---

[15]The Pentagon's decision in its 2014 QDR process to make drastic cuts to ground forces' end strength represents, in part, this commitment to safeguard present readiness to the greatest degree possible, by fielding a numerically smaller force that preserves existing standards of equipment and training. In the case of the Army, this will involve a return to a "tiered readiness" system familiar from the Cold War years. Acute short-term gaps are expected to moderate, with increasing room for modernization, over a five-to-ten year term—though this will depend on the evolution of the defense budget from FY2016–2019. United States Department of Defense, *Quadrennial Defense Review 2014* (March 2014), vii-x; Sydney J. Freedberg Jr., "Tiered Readiness Returns In Army 2015 Budget; Not All Brigades Ready to Fight," *Breaking Defense*, March 4, 2014.

agreement that would encompass 12 countries and, if successful, over 40 percent of global GDP—will be the most important plank in the second-term rebalancing agenda. President Obama will have to expend political capital to shepherd TPP through a fractious Congress, but its passage will both benefit the U.S. and global economy and blunt the criticism of those who reduce the pivot to its military dimension.[16]

Because of the United States' special role vis-à-vis regional security, it is in fact difficult to disentangle security from other interests. Clearly preventing major-power war through deterrence and a robust military presence, backed by a vibrant trading economy, are core U.S. interests. But the military role largely remains one of offshore balancing. As a Pacific rather than an Asian power, the United States retains an element of being a distant guarantor that can reassure allies and partners, persuade others to keep the peace, and concentrate on advancing economic and political development. With staunch allies like Australia, Japan, Korea, along with growing partnerships with many Southeast Asian states (such as the Philippines and Thailand, both allies, and close partners like Singapore), the United States can build and strengthen a system based on the rule of law, with more democratic governance and institutions. ASEAN is at the center of regional dialogue and cooperation, and the United States can reinforce it as an indispensable framework.

Although ASEAN continues to be a stronger economic body than a security institution, for instance, as revealed by the failure to advance a binding Code of Conduct in the South China Sea, its inclusive approach to security dialogue remains indispensable. Both the ASEAN Regional Forum and the annual East Asia Summit processes make it difficult for any single power to use coercion without triggering other powers to balance against it. Results-based institutions, and not simply dialogue forums, are needed to address an array of traditional and non-traditional security challenges, from maritime disputes and weapons proliferation to piracy and humanitarian disaster. At the same time, the United States will also continue to provide a voice for

---

[16]Murray Hiebert et al., "How Important is TPP to Our Asia Policy?" in eds. Craig Cohen et al., *Global Forecast 2014*, (Washington, D.C.: Center for Strategic and International Studies, 2013), pp. 42–44.

those seeking individual human justice and by spotlighting the onerous cost of corruption.

Notwithstanding America's interests and general determination to retain its influence in the region, there is substantial skepticism about its ability to do so far into this century. Indeed, a temporary omnibus budget deal notwithstanding, the climate in Washington of political stalemate and fiscal austerity that led to the October 2013 shutdown of the government—and thus the cancelation of a presidential trip to Asia—is likely to persist.

## Guiding Principles for Achieving Strategic Balance

Looking ahead, U.S. policymakers working on recalibrating America's rebalancing policy to Asia will or should be guided by several key overlapping principles.

*The first principle undergirding our policy should be this: the long-term shift in economic, political and military power to the Indo-Pacific region gives urgency to our short- and mid-term decisions.* The urgency is because we have a limited window of opportunity for maximizing our current position to shape the future in a manner congruent with our interests and values. The rapid growth of economic and military power in Asia writ large will, over the long term, dilute America's relative preponderance and thus capacity to influence outcomes. In making strategic investment tradeoffs both between Asia and elsewhere on the globe and within Asia itself, we must recognize that inattention will result in the United States getting left behind.

*The second guiding principle is that countering coercive diplomacy, averting crises and de-escalating them when they occur, and countering growing anti-access and area denial capabilities are at the core of our military mission in the Asia-Pacific region, if we are to preserve and adapt a rules-based, inclusive international system.* With respect to U.S. interests and those of our allies and partners, gradual diminution through coercive salami slicing and prospective losses in future high-end military conflicts are equally distasteful. This requires delicately balancing present and future capabilities in defense planning, so as to maintain effective presence in the short run without selling out future capability—or inviting the perception that one is shortchanging either.

*The third principle to guide our policy is to recognize that this enterprise is bigger than any one country, even the United States of America.* We will increasingly have to work with allies and partners. Multilateral security institutions in the Asia-Pacific region are growing by baby steps; ASEAN provides critical legitimacy for an inclusive venue, but that legitimacy is not yet matched by effectiveness. Thus, the United States must continue to work from the inside out, first building on our strong network of alliances, and then advancing meaningful partnerships with like-minded states and others as the region's institutions continue to mature. And as capabilities continue to grow in Asia, there should be even more new opportunities for collaboration and burden-sharing in the years ahead.

*In supporting regional cooperation, we should increasingly draw on what we have called the "emerging Asian power web," the constellations of intra-Asian security relations that are being built at a quickening pace.* These burgeoning coalitions remain far from latent war communities that define alliances, but they are the building blocks for helping Asian nations better defend themselves against the arbitrary use of force. Japan's recent effort to build maritime capacity in the Philippines and elsewhere improves the credible defense of Southeast Asian partners at a time of crucial uncertainty. At the same time, to the extent that many of the nodes on this web are longstanding U.S. partners, these relationships provide the basis for greater interoperability with U.S. forces.

*A fifth guiding principle is for the United States to constantly put forward its positive vision for an inclusive, rules-based region to advance peace, freedom and prosperity for all.* We must not allow others in the region to drive the general strategic narrative by legitimizing their expanded rights while reducing our permanent Pacific presence, by building up their military capabilities while seeking to eclipse ours, or by mobilizing and influencing some key actors in order to marginalize our allies and partners.

*Sixth and finally, our policy of rebalancing should be guided by a quest to preserve and extend the various forms of U.S. power—economic, diplomatic and military—and harness them to ensure continued U.S. influence in the region.* The biggest immediate threat may well be the potential for miscalculation that comes from errant assumptions that the United States cannot or will not play a strong role in the Asia-Pacific region in the years ahead. We don't want an ally or a potential adversary to think that the United States would shirk from defending liberty and fulfilling its commitments in a moment of crisis. Nor can we allow regional leaders to doubt long-term U.S. economic vitality or political leadership. Allowing these misperceptions could undercut not only American interests, but broader shared goals that countries have spent years advancing, including nonproliferation and international rule of law.

These principles should be applied to tomorrow's security challenges and opportunities, a few of which will be explored below.

## Present and Emergent Security Challenges in Asia

Prediction of world affairs is impossible. The world before September 11, 2001 and the world a dozen years later seem very different strategic environments. Yet despite the difficulty in forecasting relatively near-term events, many strategic thinkers are preoccupied with the trajectory of global and regional power as they analyze trends and seek to peer out towards the middle of the twenty-first century.

Asian countries are faced with a number of trends that will impact their security in complex ways, including demographic graying in some places and youth booms in others, environmental and resource strains resulting from rapid urbanization, the potentially destabilizing effects of new technologies, and increased vulnerability to natural disasters that are growing more frequent because of climate change. All of these trends will have unknown effects on political stability in individual countries and possibly across the region.[17] But the security dynamic that most engages Asia-Pacific strategists is the relative power decline of the United States and the simultaneous re-emergence of China as a regional heavyweight.

Australia's Defence White Paper 2009 was not the only report to extrapolate the future on the basis of recent events, but its expression of doubt about American staying power in the Asia-Pacific was emblematic of a growing wave of regional concern. Ostensibly writing

---

[17]For a slightly more detailed discussion, see Alexander Sullivan, "Charting the Contours of Asia's Megatrends," (Washington, D.C.: Center for a New American Security, January 2014) pp. 2–8.

about "the very long term," the paper questioned whether a diverted and relatively declining United States would continue to play "the strategic role that it has undertaken" over the past six or seven decades.[18] The report appeared on solid ground when it forecast that the United States would have "to seek active assistance from regional allies and partners, in crises, or more generally in the maintenance of stable regional security arrangements."[19]

Since China's reemergence is likely but not inevitable and American relative decline appears likely, the outlook for regional institutions and leadership remains murky. In addition to constraints that may impede an Asian century, strategic competition and rising nationalism will continue to require investment and leadership. Countries are not bandwagoning with China, but many governments appear to see their future economic relations with China at odds with their strong security ties with the United States, and are accordingly hedging on all sides. Even if the United States remains *primus inter pares*, there is no guarantee that postwar institutions will not experience further fragmentation In the absence of vibrant multilateral institutions or a single power capable of mobilizing others around a common agenda, burgeoning intra-Asian security ties, built on top of longstanding economic and diplomatic ties, are creating a complex web of relationships in the Asia-Pacific. For the moment, this "Asia Power Web" is supplementing rather than replacing the postwar American "hub-and-spokes security model." This web is not an alliance and not likely to become one; but it is a trend that complicates simple solutions for maintaining national interests and regional order in future decades.[20]

Against these uncertainties and potential volatility, the Asia-Pacific region is beset with at least three somewhat intertwined hard security challenges: avoiding conflict with an authoritarian North Korean regime bent on expanding its nuclear and long-range missile programs, escalating tensions and competing claims in the East and South

---

[18]*Defending Australia in the Asia-Pacific Century: Force 2030* (Canberra: Australian Department of Defence, 2009), p. 32.

[19]*Ibid.*, p. 33.

[20]Patrick M. Cronin, Richard Fontaine, Zachary M. Hosford, Oriana Skylar Mastro, Ely Ratner and Alexander Sullivan, *The Emerging Asia Power Web—The Rise of Bilateral Intra-Asian Security Ties*, (Center for a New American Security, June 2013), pp. 28–34.

China Seas, and the larger geostrategic challenge of managing a more assertive and rising China. While governments have to be concerned with far more than these security challenges, they pose some of the starkest threats to the dynamism of the Asia-Pacific region.

### The Korean Peninsula

Because China poses the starkest long-term geostrategic challenge, many analysts in the United States and the Asia-Pacific region are quick to dismiss the threat posed by North Korea. But to do so would be a mistake. Due to a number of converging trends—the continuing advance of conventional and unconventional DPRK capabilities, increased economic and political instability inside North Korea, unexamined assumptions in the counter-provocation and escalation strategy within South Korea and the U.S.-ROK alliance, a U.S. military de-emphasizing readiness in favor of long-term retooling, and the still-uncertain role of China in any contingency—the short-run risk of major conflict on the Korean Peninsula is growing and may be higher than at any time in the past two decades.[21]

With the successful launch of a long-range, three-stage *Unha-3* rocket in December 2012 and a successful third nuclear test in February 2013, the regime of Kim Jong-un now possesses the technological building blocks of a nuclear intercontinental ballistic missile (ICBM).[22] Even more troubling, North Korea may be exploring the

---

[21]For an expanded treatment of this argument, see Patrick M. Cronin, "If Deterrence Fails: Rethinking War on the Korean Peninsula" (Center for a New American Security, March 2014).

[22]The resumption of plutonium production and expansion of uranium enrichment at Yongbyon nuclear facility means that North Korea may well be on the way to possessing two dozen or more nuclear weapons by 2016. Moreover, North Korea remains well armed with medium-range missiles and expanding mobile and fixed missile launch facilities and presumably remains hard at work trying to realize a long-range missile capability. When it does, it will create a far more immediate threat to the United States than it does at present. Reports that South Korea is developing a system for a 'kill chain' preemptive strike against an imminent North Korea missile attack or nuclear provocation suggests how a crisis could suddenly escalate to war. James R. Clapper, Director of National Intelligence, "Worldwide Threat Assessment of the U.S. Intelligence Community," Statement to the Senate Select Committee on Intelligence, January 29, 2014, p. 6; David Albright and Christina Walrond, "North Korea's Estimates Stocks of Plutonium and Weapons-Grade Uranium" (Institute for Science and Inter-

use of tactical nuclear weapons to attack South Korea.[23] This is all in addition to its growing cyber capabilities and the world's largest special forces, both capable of creating mayhem south of the De-Militarized Zone through terror, sabotage and other hard-to-attribute asymmetric attacks.

This panoply is in the hands of a 31-year-old Kim family dynast whose authority could be increasingly shaky. While developments inside North Korea remain murky as always, the first two years of Kim Jong-un's reign suggest at least the possibility of an increasingly unstable political and economic situation.[24] South Korean President Park Geun-hye's ambitious "jackpot" goal of achieving unification in the next five years tacitly acknowledges the potential for discontinuous change in the medium term.[25]

Meanwhile, those in South Korea and the United States tasked with deterring North Korean intransigence and responding to its cyclical provocations are laboring under both budgetary constraints and unexamined assumptions. Following Pyongyang's violent provocations of 2010 and the political shock of the resulting loss of life, the current South Korean response emphasizes instantaneous, disproportionate response to any use of force. However, too little attention has been paid to second and third moves, which are likely to include North Korean reprisal through terror and sabotage. At the same time, the U.S. Department of Defense is preparing to absorb declining budgets by slashing force structure in favor of future modernization. This is creating the specter of a readiness crisis precisely at the time

national Security, August 16, 2012), p. 4; Joe Boyle, "South Korea's Strange Cyberwar admission," *BBC News*, March 2, 2014; Song Sang-ho, "Around 70% of N. Korean Missiles Target S. Korea," *The Korea Herald*, March 4, 2013.

[23]This is based on Patrick Cronin's interviews with senior Korean officials in Seoul in January 2014. See Cronin, "If Deterrence Fails," *op. cit.*

[24]When the young ruler publicly and gruesomely executed his regent-uncle Jang Song Taek in December 2013, he eliminated the primary interlocutor with China, the DPRK's only economic patron, and the overseer of the North's black-market efforts to obtain hard currency. Even if Jang's killing indicates power consolidation rather than insecurity, the lagging effects of reduced trade may further imperil the North's failed economy and undermine political stability.

[25]Seo Ji-Eun, "Unification may be jackpot: Park," *Korea Joong Ang Daily*, January 7, 2014.

when military readiness is needed to reinforce deterrence. Finally, the role of China remains ill-understood—although Beijing is unlikely to remain quiescent should a broad, nuclear-activated crisis start to unfold on its borders.

Working in concert with President Park, the United States needs to fashion a comprehensive strategy that includes defense improvements but goes far beyond military measures alone. A new strategy should be designed to preserve peace, to curb proliferation, and to ultimately to convince Kim to denuclearize. Deterrence should be strengthened through the deployment of new theater missile defense systems (including PAC-3 and SM-6 missiles) and creating a more integrated ISR (intelligence, surveillance and reconnaissance) network. Counter-provocation strategies need further attention and must be exercised to ensure better readiness. Informational, social, legal, and economic measures are all needed as part of a comprehensive approach to penalize provocations without unduly risking war. Further improvements will have to be made to South Korean military forces, including building enhanced capabilities for offensive operations, even if the reversion of wartime operational control (OPCON) in 2015 is delayed as Seoul desires.

From the U.S. perspective, careful management of the North Korean issue is a prerequisite to advancing regional peace and prosperity, not least because if Korea or Japan doubts the effectiveness of U.S. deterrence, they may be tempted to explore independent nuclear programs of their own. In addition to improved cooperation from China, Europe and other like-minded countries will be important, whether it is because of influence on the United Nations Security Council or as a potential partner in debating future strategic moves. And the outcome of sudden change on the Korean Peninsula could also have a profound effect on the future position of the United States in the Asia-Pacific region and the resulting Sino-American dynamic as well.

### The South and East China Seas

The Korean Peninsula is far from the only part of the region experiencing rising tensions. The East and South China Seas also appear to be settling into a long-term state of heightened confrontation. While that confrontation appears manageable, which is to say not likely to trigger a full-scale war, it seems likely to impose both significant security burdens and risks for the foreseeable future. Resolution will likely elude the region given the variety of actors involved and the growth in domestic nationalism fired by sovereignty disputes.

The waters of maritime Asia are a critical conduit for global trade, and are thus indispensible if Asia is to fulfill the economic promise that many observe over the next century. But the South and East China Seas are also the sovereign home to adjacent states. Because of the vagaries and complexities of history and international law, the precise ownership of territorial waters, specific land features, and underwater and seabed resources defies easy adjudication. No single state or institution can impose a resolution.

Too many commentators appear to expect states to move from problem to grand bargain, for instance through an almost magical binding code of conduct in the South China Sea. Had a binding code of conduct been acceptable to all, it would have been fashioned far earlier in the process between ASEAN and China, currently entering its third decade. And although fishery and joint oil and gas exploration agreements between China and Japan point to possible cooperation, such agreements have faded in the face of heightened tensions over the Senkaku/Diaoyu Islands.

Absent resolution, the United States and the region are seeking shared mechanisms to mitigate the risks of miscalculation and conflict. Unfortunately, tensions have outpaced cooperation. National leaders have engaged in provocative actions that foreclose the possibility of serious dialogue, such as Japanese Prime Minister Shinzo Abe's December 2013 trip to the controversial Yasukuni Shrine. China, meanwhile, is engaging in a persistent strategy of "tailored coercion" against rival claimants to disputed territories, including Japan, the Philippines, and Vietnam.[26] This concept combines classic coercive diplomacy with economic and political inducements to isolate target countries from the rest of the region and, ideally, allies such as the

---

[26]For a brief overview of this concept, see Patrick M. Cronin, "China's Tailored Coercion," *War on the Rocks*, November 25, 2013, http://warontherocks.com/2013/11/chinas-tailored-coercion/. A fuller discussion with policy implications can be found in: Patrick M. Cronin et al., "Tailored Coercion: Competition and Risk in Maritime Asia" (Center for a New American Security, March 2014).

United States. It also involves persistent pressure through constabulary forces, such as the near-daily patrols of the waters around the Senkaku/Diaoyus by the China Coast Guard, which seeks to assert administrative control but keep things below the military threshold. In late 2013, China expanded its East China Sea dispute with Japan to the skies, proclaiming an East China Sea Air Defense Identification Zone, which the United States viewed as peremptory and "neither recognizes nor accepts."[27] Finally, China has sought to frustrate multilateral stands against unilateral changes to the status quo, as it did by interfering with ASEAN's 2012 summit in Cambodia and scuttling a joint communiqué that would have included language on a shared approach to the South China Sea.[28]

For its part, China should expect the United States to respect sovereign disputes, rather than to impose an arbitrary solution. And major U.S. foreign policy pronouncements pertaining to either the East or South China Sea, have carefully distinguished between administrative control and sovereignty. But China should not expect the United States to stay aloof. The United States will continue forcefully to insist on China peacefully resolving disputes, whether with a treaty ally like Japan or the Philippines or a growing trading partner like Vietnam. And Chinese officials would be prudent not to test the commitment of the United States. Statements from senior administration officials, including Secretary of State John Kerry and Assistant Secretary of State for East Asian and Pacific Affairs Daniel Russel, have emphasized a tougher approach to protecting allies against Chinese tailored coercion.[29]

Restraint and measured steps are called for, even as both China and the United States expand their relations with countries in the region and with ASEAN as a whole. The establishment of national security councils in both China and Japan could either encourage restraint by

---

[27]John Kerry, U.S. Secretary of State, "Remarks With Japanese Foreign Minister Fumio Kishida After Their Meeting," Washington, D.C., Benjamin Franklin Room, February 7, 2014, http://www.state.gov/secretary/remarks/2014/02/221459.htm.

[28]Donald K. Emmerson, "ASEAN Stumbles in Phnom Penh," *Asia Times Online*, July 17, 2013, http://www.atimes.com/atimes/Southeast_Asia/NG17Ae02.html.

[29]Patrick M. Cronin, "America's China Paradigm is Back on Track," *War on the Rocks*, February 21, 2014.

solidifying top-level control, or could merely lead to more-coordination pursuit of nationalist aims.[30]

The challenge for U.S. policymakers, with allies and partners, is how to construct a maritime strategy that takes a firm stance against coercion by any actor, while neither precipitating conflict nor compromising on its values of freedom of navigation and open lawful access to the maritime commons. To do this, the United States should simultaneously remain strong—economically and militarily. This raises the third and related challenge of managing a rising China.

### Managing the Rise of China

Disputes in the South and East China Seas are symptomatic of a larger, long-term geostrategic challenge posed by a rapidly rising China. To be sure, a China that quickly stopped rising could pose an equally complex array of problems, in particular as the PLA continues to gain power and Chinese nationalism remains the most accessible outlet to curry popular legitimacy within China's authoritarian system.

But assuming yet further growth, China appears to be in the midst of reassessing its strategy after decades of near-continuous policy aimed at a patient approach and a peaceful rise. China's newfound power provides a rationale for expanding core interests—expanding from traditional concerns such as Taiwan, Tibet and Xinjiang to its near seas and Sea Lines of Communication (SLOCs). The visible displays of nationalism over the South and East China Seas also suggest that China may well become more assertive and difficult to manage when it comes to defending its interests and creating new, anti-access, area-denial military capabilities. In short, the new leadership in Beijing is likely to continue to pressure Japan from asserting itself while simultaneously pushing U.S. military power farther from its shores and out beyond the first island chain. It is also likely to continue promoting greater Chinese influence, not only through the acquisition of a fleet-in-being but also by non-military steps such as reducing China's and the world's dependence on the dollar as the global reserve currency. The failure to realize heightened popular Chinese expecta-

---

[30]Kurt Campbell, "Watch the Rise of Asia's National Security Councils," *Financial Times*, January 9, 2014.

tions could well trigger an escalatory spiral of tensions with the United States and neighbors.

Australian strategist Hugh White has crystallized the issue well in his book *The China Choice*, when he wonders how long in the future past policies will persist: "For forty years, both the US-China relationship and the Asian strategic order have been built on Chinese acceptance of America's superior power."[31] But that expedient policy may be ending, he notes, and he points out that China does not need to overtake America to pose a very serious challenge. He concludes that the United States has one of three basic options: resist China's challenge to preserve status quo; step back from dominant role; or remain in Asia on new basis, allowing China a larger role.[32]

China, under new leader Xi Jinping, has attempted to address these strategic dynamics in its new model for Sino-U.S. relations, the so-called "new type of major country relations." While gaining limited acceptance from U.S. officials—including President Obama at his April 2013 summit with Xi Jinping at Sunnylands, and new National Security Advisor Susan Rice—the term is as yet ill-defined. To the extent that China interprets the concept as a recognition that the U.S. will acquiesce in Chinese revisionism on an expanding menu of core interests, the term is unlikely to persist in the bilateral relationship. It will have more staying power if it becomes a framework for the two countries to frankly address difficult issues and find pragmatic areas for cooperation.[33]

There is, however, a fourth option: one of cooperation from strength. First of all, the straight-line projections that have induced many to posit an inevitable Chinese ascendancy may falter, as China undertake several years of a tightrope balance between needed structural reforms and maintaining economic and employment growth, with a consistent specter of short-term debt crises.[34] Secondly, it

---

[31]Hugh White, *The China Choice: Why America Should Share Power* (Collingwood, Victoria: Black Inc. 2012), p. 3.

[32]*Ibid.*, p. 5.

[33]Ely Ratner, "(Re)Defining the New Type of Major-Country Relationship' Between the United States and China," *PacNet* 2014 No. 4 (Pacific Forum CSIS, January 13, 2014).

[34]Michael Pettis, "Hello 2014: Don't Be Afraid of Slower Chinese Growth," *Financial Times*, December 27, 2013.

should be possible to remain militarily and economically strong and yet still expand cooperation on critical areas like North Korea and climate change—as Secretary of State John Kerry re-emphasized on his February visit to Beijing.[35] While Chinese concerns that relations are increasingly zero-sum in nature should not be ignored, there is no fundamental reason why a United States that remains powerful should automatically feed China's security dilemma and inexorably lead to conflict. In fact, we would argue that a weak United States, rather than a strong United States, is a more likely source of miscalculation and instability in the Asia-Pacific region.

## Conclusions and Recommendations

This final section will offer some general observations about why and how to rebalance or pivot to Asia with Europe. It will focus on ideas for the U.S. and Europe to deal with existing hard security issues, managing a rising China, and building an inclusive, rules-based architecture.

- **U.S. rebalancing is based on strengthening rules and norms, and Europe must play a role in safeguarding them wherever they are under pressure.** As Assistant Secretary of State for East Asian and Pacific Affairs Daniel Russel put it, "The common thread running through our strategic rebalancing is a determination to ensure that the Asia-Pacific remains an open, inclusive, and prosperous region guided by widely accepted rules and standards and a respect for international law."[36] These norms include freedom of navigation, unimpeded lawful use of the global commons, and a variety of international treaties and agreements that are in the interests of all to preserve. Europe's role in shaping these ideas, its clout at the UN, and its commitment to normative gover-

---

[35]Secretary of State John Kerry, "Solo Press Availability in Beijing, China," JW Marriott Hotel, Beijing, China, February 14, 2014, http://www.state.gov/secretary/remarks/2014/02/221658.htm.

[36]Daniel Russel, Assistant Secretary of State, Bureau of East Asian and Pacific Affairs, "Maritime Disputes in East Asia," Statement to the Subcommittee on Asia and the Pacific, House Foreign Affairs Committee, February 5, 2014, p. 1, http://www.state.gov/p/eap/rls/rm/2014/02/221293.htm.

nance give it an important political role in calling for adherence to common standards. In many cases, Europe can be a stronger voice on these issues than the United States, which must account for alliance commitments and other direct interests in the region. Where Chinese interests are concerned, close coordination among European states will be necessary, or Beijing will exert bilateral pressure to stymie the EU's collective voice.

- **The U.S., NATO and individual European countries should promote interoperability with Asian militaries, especially as the latter start contributing to security challenges outside Asia.** Asian countries are developing their militaries not only to meet new challenges within Asia, but also to operate outside the region in response to expanding global interests and broader threats. The experience of NATO has been that developing true interoperability takes long-term, diligent effort. As the NATO mission in Afghanistan draws down, the next evolution of that alliance should be to promote interoperability with growing partners in Asia, in view of future cooperation to meet still unforeseen challenges in the Middle East and elsewhere. The NATO-Japan Joint Political Declaration of April 2013 was an important step in this direction.

- **As the United States endeavors to emphasize economic opportunity in Asia, the EU should encourage the growth of its own free trade with the region.** The United States believes that opportunities for trade and growth should trump sources of tension and instability, and nowhere is near-term opportunity greater than in Asia. This is one reason why we are in discussion with both Europe and Asia on separate massive 21$^{st}$-century free trade agreements. In this spirit, the European Union—for its own economic and strategic interest—should continue negotiations on an FTA with Japan and revive similar negotiations with ASEAN (moribund since 2008), as well as search for new opportunities for closer trade links with Asia. This is in addition to advancing the free trade agenda through TPP and the Transatlantic Trade and Investment Partnership.

The United States needs Europe's support in its rebalance to Asia as it does in so many other areas. Discussions of progress on Asian security and economic issues should be made a permanent agenda item in future U.S.-EU summits and at lower-echelon coordinating bodies. America has placed a long-term strategic bet that that the opportunities and challenges associated with Asia's historic re-emergence will define the coming century in important ways, and thus deserve a commensurate commitment of U.S. attention and power. Europe should join the United States to play a meaningful role in securing Asia's peaceful and prosperous future, and share in the benefits that will accrue.

# Chapter 4

# European Approaches to Asia

*Rem Korteweg*

European nations have left their mark on the history of the Asia-Pacific, yet today's Europe hardly seems to matter in the strategic calculations of Asian powers. Current dynamics in Asia are producing a shift in international relations, impacting European interests, requiring the EU and its member states to take a more strategic approach to the region. The rise of China represents a structural change in the international balance of power. Its economic development offers vast opportunities, yet it also creates security risks upsetting the strategic balance in Asia. The expansion of Beijing's economic influence, its military build-up and its increasingly assertive foreign policy—particularly its territorial claims in adjacent maritime zones—are heightening regional security concerns. The Asia-Pacific holds the keys to global economic growth, but the region could become the theatre of interstate conflict. As the United States shifts its focus towards Asia—in what has become known as the Asia "pivot" or "rebalance"—questions are raised across Europe to what extent European governments and the EU have a role to play as a strategic actor in Asia to promote peace, security and the international rule of law.

The issue is two-sided. On the one hand, how can Europe protect and promote its interests in the Asia-Pacific? Europe's economy relies on continued Asian growth and a growing consumer market for European exports. This requires stability across the region. In addition, several EU member states have territorial interests in the region, giving them an additional stake in peace in the region. As Asia's strategic landscape changes, it will influence Eurasian geopolitics, further necessitating Europe's attention. On the other hand, what does the rise of Asia mean for transatlantic relations? President Obama has made the Asian "rebalance" one of the main strategic issues of his foreign policy agenda. If Europe fails to play a role to promote Asian security, Washington may see less value in the transatlantic relation-ship. Europeans are right to be concerned about a growing transat-lantic divide; cooperation with the United States remains central to European security policies and transatlantic cooperation favours global security and the promotion of liberal democratic and economic values. In a recent survey however, American respondents said Asia was just as important as Europe.[1]

European strategic interests are at stake in the Asia-Pacific, but events such as the Arab Spring, developments in Ukraine, the euro-zone crisis, and fatigue from military deployments to Iraq and Afghanistan, have led to growing European retrenchment, or a regional focus at best.[2] In Brussels, the Asia-Pacific is considered important, but not urgent. In a security environment characterized by decreasing European defense expenditures and a perceived U.S. with-drawal from European security affairs, the transatlantic partners must identify new grounds for strategic cooperation, lest the relationship evolve towards complacency or even irrelevance. The Asia-Pacific offers an area for transatlantic strategic cooperation and requires Europe and the United States to work towards common approaches to promote common interests.

A European reflection on the changing strategic environment in the Asia-Pacific is overdue. Brussels-based institutions as well as national capitals have deepened their engagement—particularly their economic relations—with countries in Asia in recent years, and there are elements that taken together could potentially constitute a Euro-pean strategy in the Asia-Pacific balancing against revisionist behavior. This chapter addresses the different approaches by European powers in the Asia-Pacific. It also assesses how Asian powers deal with

---

[1]German Marshall Fund of the United States, *Transatlantic Trends, Key Findings 2013* (Washington, D.C., 2013), p. 16. Another survey, performed by the Pew Research Cen-ter, claimed the opposite and said Americans believe Europe to be more important than Asia (Pew Research Center, "America's Place in the World 2013," (Washington, D.C., December 2013), 37. That same survey did point out that young Americans—between 18 and 29 years old—believe Asia (52%) to be more important than Europe (37%) to U.S. interests.

[2]Doug Stokes and Richard G. Whitman, "Transatlantic Triage? European and UK Grand Strategy After the US Rebalance to Asia," *International Affairs* 89.5 (2013), pp. 1087–1107.

Europe, and it suggests what elements a European strategy towards the Asia-Pacific region could contain.

## European Policy Confusion

The Asia-Pacific is characterized by increasing economic prosperity and decreasing political trust. In this context, the United States plays a special role. Washington has a substantial military presence in the region and security treaties with a number of Asian states, including Japan, South Korea, Australia, Thailand, and the Philippines. But as tensions rise in the region, the United States confronts a strategic dilemma: it must reassure its allies about its security commitments to avoid its partners from pursuing unilateral actions contrary to US interests, but it also cannot be over-protective perhaps allowing its allies to act recklessly. The United States has an interest in maintaining control over the behavior of its Asian partners, and thus is very engaged in the region. Besides, the relationship between China and the United States is crucial to the global economy and security, and is too important to let derail over misperceptions and miscalculations. This makes Washington's relations with Asia complex and prone to error. Europe however faces a different dilemma.

There is no coherent European strategic approach to Asia. European states have a multitude of Asia policies; they are unconnected and mostly focused on trade and bilateral relations, while the European Union is struggling to formulate a policy that goes beyond the lowest common denominator.

Brussels and Washington have acknowledged the need for transatlantic cooperation in the Asia-Pacific, and various member-states—like the UK and the Netherlands—are supporters of a strategic dialogue with the United States on Asia. At the EU-U.S. summit in 2011 it was agreed that "the EU and the United States have a strategic interest in enhancing co-operation on political, economic, security and human rights issues in the Asia-Pacific region to advance peace, stability and prosperity."[3] In 2012, the European Union said it sees the

---

[3]Office of the Press Secretary, "Joint Statement: US-EU Summit," The White House (Washington, D.C., November 28, 2011), http://www.whitehouse.gov/the-press-office/2011/11/28/joint-statement-us-eu-summit.

United States as a crucial partner to promote stability and security in Asia and it wants to "develop its strategic dialogue on East Asia with the US."[4] At the Association of South East Asian Nations' (ASEAN) Regional Forum in 2012, High Representative Catherine Ashton signed a declaration of intent with then-Secretary of State Hillary Clinton. The declaration recognizes the need for transatlantic cooperation on Asian strategic issues. The transatlantic partners noted the centrality of ASEAN, and the need to work towards a Code of Conduct between ASEAN and China on the South China Sea. Washington and Brussels also agreed to cooperate on security issues such as maritime security, and counter-proliferation. Unfortunately, since 2012, the declaration has not been given a follow-up.

In the summer of 2013, EU officials complained that the idea of a "pivot" together with the U.S. was effectively "dead." For several months there was a policy vacuum in Washington due to changes in senior U.S. foreign policy leadership and competing policy priorities, such as events in the Middle East. It was not clear what the United States would want from Europe: participation in "coalitions of the willing," diplomatic support for U.S. efforts in the region, or a transatlantic division of labor based on a common strategy? Meanwhile British and other officials worried that without U.S. willingness to "pivot together" with Europe, amidst issues competing for attention in the European neighborhood, European governments would find it difficult to sustain a focus on Asia at all.

European governments are gyrating between four different schools of thought about what the U.S. "rebalance" to Asia means. First, there is a school of "global Atlanticists" that sees a need to pivot together with the United States to maintain the relevance of the transatlantic security partnership, among other reasons. Part of the U.S. "pivot" involves boosting the Pentagon's ties in the region, but—aware of Europe's limited military prowess—European policymakers prefer an approach to Asia that is diplomatic and economic, rather than based on military assets. These approaches however, could be coordinated. A second school of "global Europeanists" sees a role for Europe in Asia,

---

[4]European External Action Service, "Guidelines on the EU's Foreign and Security Policy in East Asia," 10313/2 (Brussels, June 15, 2012), http://eeas.europa.eu/asia/docs/guidelines_eu_foreign_sec_pol_east_asia_en.pdf, p. 8.

but any complementarity with the United States is considered a bonus, not an objective. This school exhibits discomfort in the prospect of being seen as America's junior partner in Asia and is reluctant to become entangled in the emerging great power rivalry between Beijing and Washington. Europe's unique selling point in Asia, the school's advocates point out, is that it is Western, but not the United States. In practice, Europe's approach to Asia is a mix between the schools mentioned above.

But two more schools complicate the picture, drawing European attention away from Asia. A third school of "regional Europeanists" feels the U.S. "pivot" is accompanied by a growing reluctance in Washington to focus on security issues in the European neighborhood, such as the Arab Spring, the Sahel and its relations with Russia. Given Europe's limited resources, it should prioritize its immediate neighborhood. In theory this opens the possibility of a transatlantic division of labor, where the U.S. looks west towards the Asia-Pacific, and Europe looks towards its southern and eastern flanks. Critics of this school however, argue that a division of labor risks further transatlantic estrangement. A fourth school of "regional Atlanticists" acknowledges the security challenges in Europe's neighborhood, but fears that European powers are unable to fill the void created by decreased U.S. interest in European security issues. They see the U.S. "rebalance" as an unfortunate and undesirable development.

Threat perceptions regarding Asia (particularly China) differ between Europe and the United States. This helps explain different ideas about the Asia-Pacific on both sides of the Atlantic and differences in their approach. Europeans do not see China as a geopolitical rival and are comfortable prioritizing trade promotion with Beijing. Instead they are also concerned about an overwhelmingly confrontational approach of the United States, which they feel could pose a threat to regional stability. According to the 2013 Transatlantic Trends survey, 46% of Europeans see China as an economic threat, while that figure jumps to 62% in the United States. Among Europeans, 37% see China as a military threat, and 49% of Americans do.[5] Europeans do not feel they are engaged in a great-power struggle with China, and

---

[5]German Marshall Fund, "Transatlantic Trends 2013," http://trends.gmfus.org/files/2013/09/TT-TOPLINE-DATA.pdf.

therefore have difficulty seeing events in the Asia-Pacific through a grand strategic lens. This complicates the development of a common transatlantic approach to the region.

Amidst this policy confusion about the U.S. "rebalance," the ability of Europe to play a strategic role in Asia—and contribute to security, stability and a reduction of regional tensions—can be captured through the analogy of supply and demand. On the supply side, the potential for coherent and strategic European engagement in Asian affairs is a matter of debate. Does Europe have a commonly agreed set of objectives it wants to reach and the means to achieve them? On the demand side, how do Asian states perceive the European Union and its member states in their evolving strategic environment? Europe may want to play a role, but whether it can do so depends on its Asian partners. And what does the United States—as Europe's premier ally and a Pacific superpower in its own right—expect from Europe on Asian security?

## Four Pillars of Europe's Asia Policy

Europe's strategic engagement in the Asia-Pacific is an aggregate of the separate activities undertaken by its member states, primarily the UK, France, Germany, and the EU. Their approaches to the Asia-Pacific are distinct and separate, but if coordinated, could be complementary.

The UK has an Asia policy aimed at building stronger diplomatic, economic, defense and security relations with Asian powers, including in coordination with the United States. The UK focuses on cooperation with old allies, such as Japan, Australia and the Commonwealth; important trade partners such as China; as well as deepening ties to ASEAN. France's approach is similar, but Paris sees its role in the Asia-Pacific as distinctly separate from the United States. In his speech in Jakarta in August 2013, French foreign minister Laurent Fabius said France is focused on pursuing a more economic and diplomatic pivot to Asia than the United States.[6] Germany takes a different,

---

[6]Laurent Fabius, "Speech by Laurent Fabius at the ASEAN Headquarters Jakarta," Embassy of France to Laos, August 2, 2013, http://www.ambafrance-my.org/IMF/pdf/Speech-by_Laurent_Fabius.pdf.

mercantilist approach. Its policy is primarily, and almost exclusively, shaped by trade, reasoning that strong trade relations equal political influence. The European Union attempts to formulate a middle ground between the three policies, but finds itself often overtaken by the unilateral pursuit of German, British or French agendas.

Alongside the EU-3—Germany, France, and UK—other member states, like the Netherlands, Sweden, Italy and Poland, have extensive relations in Asia. Many member states pursue bilateral relations with countries that the EU considers its strategic partners; China, Japan, South Korea and India. Specific, niche interests may be a reason for this; for instance Sweden focuses on human rights in Asia, while the Netherlands aims to develop stronger relations with Jakarta, building on its historical and cultural ties to the archipelago.

Yet these smaller EU member states look to Brussels to act as a policy multiplier. The Hague, for instance, is a proponent of deepening EU-China relations through the EU-China summit. The Netherlands looks to the EU to discuss trade issues, remove trade barriers and improve market access in China; but also to address rule of law and human rights issues, climate change, and sustainable energy and natural resources use. Through the EU, countries like the Netherlands are able to amplify their political voice.

Among Brussels institutions there are policy differences as well. The European Commission and the European External Action Service (EEAS) do not pursue a harmonized policy towards Asia, in particular towards China. While the trade commissioner, Karel de Gucht, is willing to be tough with Beijing and confronts China on trade issues. EEAS chief Catherine Ashton is much more reluctant to do so. This interagency dissonance leads to confusion among Asian counterparts or, in the worst case, creates vulnerabilities that can be exploited. It is worsened due to the competition between member states and the Commission. Interagency problems are not unique to the Brussels institutions; in terms of responding to the U.S. "rebalance," national bureaucrats wonder whether Asia hands or transatlantic policymakers are in the lead.

## Europe's Strategic Interests in Asia

Europe's primary interest in the Asia-Pacific is economic. Due to the nature of the fast-paced global economy and its interdependent supply chains, trade disruptions—as a result of escalating conflicts over territorial and maritime security issues or an escalating Korean or Taiwan Straits crisis—would have negative economic and financial consequences. They would expose Europe's ailing economy to substantial risks. European economies have a stake in the unfettered global flow of goods: half the world's tonnage of merchant shipping passes through the South and East China seas. These maritime zones are one of the main flashpoints in the Asia-Pacific. Freedom of navigation and a peaceful resolution of territorial disputes are a crucial European security interest.

Other interests figure as well. Asia's growth creates opportunities for European exports and investments, but Europe is equally concerned that Asian governments do not share Western trade norms. Trade irritants such as restricted market access, state subsidies or other forms of protectionism and non-tariff barriers are an issue of concern that impact on Europe's economic well-being. A further negative side-effect of Asia's growth is the increased demand for energy and natural resources, which creates the risk of resource competition or unsustainable exploitation of resource-rich countries.[7] Europe, as a resource-poor continent with a strong tradition of protecting human rights, has an interest to develop a stable and sustainable global system of resource governance that incorporates Asian states. Finally, cooperation with Asian governments is necessary to deal with transnational issues that have an Asian dimension, such as cyber security, climate change and countering proliferation of dangerous weapons.

At the grand strategic level, Europe should have an interest in avoiding the rise of China as a regional hegemon. The prospect of the Asia-Pacific dominated by a single power is a strategic risk to Europe's economies and regional peace. It is unlikely that all Asian powers would fall in line and kowtow to Chinese dominance. Japan, Taiwan

---

[7]See Bernice Lee et al., *Resources Futures: A Chatham House Report* (London: The Royal Institute of International Affairs, December 2012), http://www.chathamhouse.org/sites/default/files/public/Research/Energy,%20Environment%20and%20Development/1212r_resourcesfutures.pdf.

and countries with overlapping claims in the South China Sea would be negatively affected. Countries like Vietnam and the Philippines are already reaching out to others, mainly the United States, to balance against what they perceive as Chinese expansionism. The United States is also unlikely to accept a dramatic shift in its influence in the region. Chinese revisionism would be accompanied by unpredictability, turbulence, the increased risk of miscalculations and ultimately the threat of war. Chinese regional hegemony could also lead to increased challenges to European interests across Central Asia and the Middle East. Instead, a balance of power in the Asia-Pacific is desirable, whereby the powers keep each other in check and reduce the risk of unilateral revisionist behavior. This requires greater regional integration to balance China's rise, as well as China's incorporation in regional multilateral frameworks. The European Union and its member states have a strategic interest in strengthening multilateral institutions, such as the Association of South East Asian Nations (ASEAN). The EU's guidelines on East Asia spell out the EU's strategic objective for the Asia-Pacific:

> The EU's long-term aims should be to support the development of increasing regional integration and the emergence of strong regional institutions based on clear recognition of shared interests.[8]

Brussels sees China not just as a regional, but as a global power that should bear commensurate responsibility for promoting a peaceful and stable international system through "the promotion of effective multilateralism and the resolution of international and regional issues."[9]

## Do Trade and Geopolitics Mix?

Europe engages with the Asia-Pacific through trade. In 2012, Asia's share of EU global goods trade was 27.9%—while Europe's trade with the United States almost made up a quarter—and European exports to

---

[8]"Guidelines on the EU's Foreign and Security Policy in East Asia," *op. cit.*, p. 15.

[9]*Ibid.*, p. 7.

Asia's major economies are growing. In 2010 nearly a quarter of investment in Europe originated from Asia. Given the size of the Chinese market, Europe's focus on Asia has been China-centric. China is the EU's largest source of imports and the second largest destination of its exports. As a result, many European member states have made a beeline to Beijing, vying for stronger trade and investment relations.

Germany, the EU's largest trading economy, plays a central role in Europe's trade relationship with Asia. In 2012, German exports to China totaled €66 billion, or 46% of the EU's total exports to China, while imports from China totaled €77 billion, equivalent to 26% of the EU's total imports from the country. The German Foreign Office states that "China is Germany's most important economic partner in Asia and Germany is China's leading trading partner in Europe." Globally, China is Germany's third most important trading partner. As a result, commentators have described strong German-Chinese ties as a new privileged relationship.[10]

For Berlin, the relationship has translated into political access in Beijing. Since 2011, Germany and China have annual intergovernmental consultations involving between 10 and 14 ministers from both sides. Germany also has an annual rule of law dialogue with China. According to an EEAS official in Brussels, however, Berlin wants to make its foreign policy subject to trade interests and does not want to leverage its political access for strategic purposes.

The strong ties between Berlin and Beijing have translated into German-Chinese cooperation on trade issues of common interest. For instance, in 2013 Berlin was reticent to support the European Commission's proposed anti-dumping measures against Chinese solar panels. While trade is a competence that resides with the European Commission, German pressure contributed to Brussels reversing its course and negotiating a deal with Beijing.

Under the stewardship of Chancellor Angela Merkel, Germany has increased its bilateral ties across the region and beyond China. Even though trade is the main pretext, it potentially opens the opportunity

---

[10]Hans Kundnani and Jonas Parello-Plesner, "China and Germany: Why the Emerging Special Relationship Matters for Europe," *European Council on Foreign Relations*, May 2012, http://ecfr.eu/page/-/ECFR55_CHINA_GERMANY_BRIEF_AW.pdf.

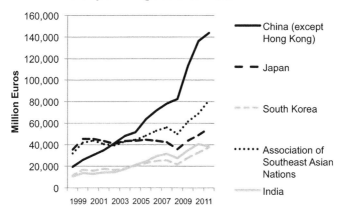

**EU export of goods to Asia**

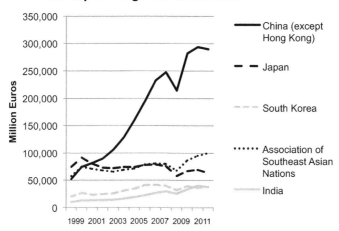

**EU import of goods from Asia**

*Source: Eurostat.*

for a more geopolitical approach. For instance, Chancellor Merkel visited Mongolia in October 2011—the first visit to the country by an EU head of government—in order to promote diplomatic relations and investment in the natural resources sector. The Mongolian president reciprocated during a visit to Berlin in March 2012. The visit was of geopolitical significance as Mongolia—squeezed by its Russian and Chinese neighbors—is pursuing a diversification policy in its diplomatic relations and is building relations with third countries.

Mongolia is hedging its foreign policy and has reached out to Germany, as well as the EU. High Representative Catherine Ashton signed a partnership and cooperation agreement with Mongolia in April 2013; a first step towards negotiating a free-trade agreement. The EU explicitly mentioned the Central Asian country as a priority for deeper cooperation. The UK is now also pursuing commercial opportunities in Mongolia's mining sector. The trade ties are important as Mongolia, amongst others, extracts rare earth minerals, a market which is dominated by China. Access to Mongolian resources reduces Europe's dependency on China, and increases its resource security. If Europe wanted to, it could leverage its trade ties, in an area China considers its sphere of influence, for geopolitical effect.

Besides China, Europe is promoting trade with ASEAN. The ASEAN group of countries is the fifth largest global trading partner of the EU and the EU is the second largest trade destination of ASEAN. In Asia, ASEAN is Europe's second largest trade partner. Investment is an increasingly large part of the relationship as European governments hope to attract interest from South East Asia's sovereign wealth funds.

Brussels has been building a network of free trade agreements in the region. While much attention has been paid to U.S.-led efforts to negotiate a regional free trade framework in the Asia-Pacific—the Trans-Pacific Partnership—the EU is pursuing an impressive range of bilateral trade deals of its own. Free trade agreements with India, Japan, Malaysia, Thailand and Vietnam are under negotiation and Brussels is considering opening discussions with Indonesia and Brunei. Given positive political reforms in Myanmar in recent years, an ASEAN-wide FTA with the EU may be in the cards. In addition, since 2009, the EU is negotiating (or has concluded) political agreements with eleven countries in the Asia-Pacific: Thailand, Vietnam, Singapore, the Philippines, New Zealand, Indonesia, Australia, Japan, South Korea, Brunei and Malaysia. These agreements precede or accompany free trade deals and are testament to deeper diplomatic relations. In addition, the EU has concluded a partnership and cooperation agreement with Mongolia and is discussing opening negotiations with China to deepen investment relations. The EU estimates that the effect of free trade agreements with ASEAN, India, Japan and an investment agreement with China would contribute 0.43% to EU

GDP, 72 billion euros in additional EU exports and generate 1.2 million jobs across the EU.[11]

In order to promote trade, European countries have been expanding their diplomatic presence in Asia, including China. France, Germany and the UK have consulates in Shanghai, Guangzhou and Hong Kong. Additionally, Germany has a consulate in Chengdu, the UK in Chongqing and France in Wuhan, Chengdu and Shenyang. The UK is in discussions to open a fifth consulate general in China, although it remains to be decided where. Other EU states are also increasing their diplomatic presence; in 2013, the Netherlands opened a third consulate general in China in Chongqing.

Beyond China, the UK has an assertive diplomatic policy towards Asia. Even though the UK Foreign Office's budget was cut by 10% in 2013, the UK will open eight new diplomatic posts in Asia by 2015, and some 140 more UK diplomats will be deployed to the region (60 in China, 30 in India and 50 across South East Asia, the Korean peninsula and Mongolia). One of the reasons for this expansion is that the United Kingdom—as well as many other European countries—shares Germany's enthusiasm for Asia's trade potential. William Hague, the British foreign minister, has set a target to "double bilateral trade with China, India, Vietnam, Indonesia, Malaysia and South Korea" by 2017.[12]

Trade however, is not only a soft power instrument. It is also a tool of influence. Stronger trade relations with Asia will allow Europe to increase its voice in the region. For two reasons, negotiations about a Transatlantic Trade and Investment Partnership (TTIP) are crucial for the development of a transatlantic agenda towards Asia. If Europe fails to negotiate a free trade agreement with the United States, while TPP is still under negotiation, it will reinforce America's shift towards Asia. TTIP would maintain the relevance of transatlantic cooperation and strengthen the hand of both Europe and the United States when negotiating TPP or bilateral trade agreements in Asia. Secondly, although the EU and the United States are economic competitors, a

---

[11]European External Action Service, "The EU in Asia: Facts and Figures Concerning the EU's Engagement in the Asia-Pacific," http://eeas.europa.eu/asia/docs/2012_ eu_in_asia_year_facts_figures_en.pdf.

[12]William Hague, "IISS-Fullerton Lecture" (Singapore, April 26, 2012), https://www.iiss. org/en/events/events/archive/2012-4a49/april-1f83/william-hague-fc0b.

framework of TPP, TTIP and Europe's network of bilateral free trade negotiations with Asian economies could together form a comprehensive transatlantic push to set the terms of global trade. This has geo-economic consequences, since non-members of the agreements would be required to adapt to these standards and norms. TTIP thereby becomes an instrument of political influence in Asia.

## The EU's Policy towards the Asia-Pacific

Four of the EU's ten strategic partnerships are with Asian countries; China, India, Japan and South Korea. While the strategic nature of that partnership mostly revolves around trade discussions, there is an ambition to broaden it. The European Union has increased its focus on Asian security in recent years and wants to play a stabilizing role in the region. In June 2012 the European Council adopted the "Guidelines on the EU's Foreign and Security Policy in East Asia." The document outlined three specific security issues that impact the EU's interests: North Korea's nuclear program, tensions over the Taiwan Straits and the South China Sea. In addition, the EU said that the strategic balance in the region is shifting—due to the rise of China—which poses challenges compounded by competition over energy and natural resources. This power shift and the increasing global presence of Asian economies push Brussels to engage with Asian powers on global economic and security issues, such as the Iran sanctions regime, dealing with climate change or developing sustainable business practices in Africa. The EU concluded that it "needs, and seeks to promote, multilateral solutions to global challenges" together with Asian powers, in line with its 2003 EU security strategy.

The EU is clear that its interests in Asia are primarily derived from its economic relations. Its trade-centric perspective, along with Europe's post-war experience of regional integration, is considered a unique selling point to promote security in the Asia-Pacific.[13] David O'Sullivan, the Chief Operating Officer in the EEAS, formulated the EU's posture in Asia as follows:

---

[13]"Guidelines on the EU's Foreign and Security Policy in East Asia," *op. cit.*, p. 8.

Now, it is true that we as EU don't have a leading role on the headline, hard security issues, given the absence of military assets or bases in the region. But in a way this is perhaps also an asset. The [Asia-Pacific] region perhaps doesn't need another hard security player; our added value is different. We are seen as engaged but not threatening; active but without a geopolitical agenda. Perhaps the greatest value of the EU is to act as a principled champion of rules-based, co-operative security.[14]

The EU's self-perception is based on the premise that it is an exemplary power; its lack of military "hard power" enables it to effectively promote cooperative multilateral solutions, build trust, strengthen ASEAN, promote military-to-military contacts and share the lessons of its post-war reconciliation without antagonizing others. The EU feels it can succeed since its posture is non-threatening. "Our rhetoric is rarely stirring; we don't do shock and awe. But that's also the point," says O'Sullivan.[15]

Other European leaders reinforce the idea that the EU has a distinct approach to international affairs. In February 2013, Germany's then-foreign minister, Guido Westerwelle, said that "Europe's lifestyle, the freedoms and living standard enjoyed by its people have worldwide appeal. In a world ever more diverse and fragile, this internal cohesion becomes a major asset."[16] The comprehensive approach—the pursuit of foreign policy objectives with different elements of civilian and military power deployed in an integrated fashion—is considered a uniquely European asset. The problem with this self-congratulatory posture, however, is that it is not reciprocated by Asian governments. For all its merits, the European Union is still not considered a serious security actor in the region.

---

[14]David O'Sullivan, "Priorities for Diplomacy in East Asia," GRIPS Forum (speech, Tokyo, February 12, 2013), http://eeas.europa.eu/asia/docs/20130205_grips_speech_final_en.pdf.

[15]*Ibid.*

[16]Guido Westerwelle, "IISS-Fullerton Lecture" (speech, Singapore, February 8, 2013), https://www.iiss.org/en/events/events/archive/2013-5126/february-677e/fullerton-lecture-guido-westerwelle-6dfd.

Before 2012, Asian governments complained that the EU and its member states were absent from the region. This message did not go unheeded. The EU has annual summits with its four strategic partners in Asia and Presidents Van Rompuy and Barroso visited the region in 2013. Catherine Ashton attended the ASEAN Regional Forum (ARF) in 2012 and 2013, and she participated in the Shangri-La Dialogue for the second time in June 2013.

One of the clearest expressions of Europe's ambitions in Asia is its desire to be part of the myriad institutions that have been set up over the years. The European Union is a member of the Asia-Europe meeting (ASEM)—a somewhat disappointing gathering of 32 heads of state—and the ARF, where it discusses several security issues. But the EU now aspires to join the East Asia Summit (EAS). The EAS is the only forum where the major powers—including China, Japan, India, the United States and Russia—and South East Asian nations meet to discuss regional security issues. Initially conceived as an economic forum, the Summit includes discussions on energy, climate change, disaster relief, education, trade and finance. Security issues that follow from these are on the agenda and include maritime security, energy security and territorial disputes. Since 2007, the EU has lobbied countries in the region to join the East Asia Summit, but to no avail. Japan, for instance, insists that– after U.S. and Russian membership in 2011—the EAS should first consolidate before admitting others.

## Europe's Security Relations with Asia

France and the UK are the European powers that are militarily involved in the region. By virtue of their seats on the United Nations Security Council, their foreign policy addresses peace and security in the Asia-Pacific, such as North Korea's nuclear program and rising tensions over territorial claims. Paris and London aspire to increase their role in regional security affairs, and both have a permanent military presence in the Asia-Pacific, albeit of limited size.

Brunei is host to a British garrison of roughly 900 troops. In Singapore, the Royal Navy operates a large fuel depot and berthing wharf. The Royal Navy's HMS Daring was deployed to South East Asia in the second half of 2013 to build military-to-military relations, make port calls and contribute to maritime security. The frigate also assisted in humanitarian relief operations following Typhoon Haiyan in the Philippines. The UK has plans to have a similar naval presence in the region on a regular basis.

Besides, the UK is the only European state that has a security treaty with Asian countries. The Five Power Defense Arrangement dates back to 1971 and was agreed between the UK, Singapore, Australia, New Zealand and Malaysia. Although it does not impose a collective defense obligation on any of the parties, it is a formal mechanism for discussing security issues and for improving military cooperation and training. The five militaries take part in yearly naval and air force exercises to improve interoperability. Through the Defense Arrangement the UK has a voice in defense issues in South East Asia, even though there seems to be little appetite among the five powers to extend its range of activities.

France's territories in the Southern Pacific and in the Indian Ocean led Jean-Yves Le Drian, the French defense minister, to declare in June 2013 that "France is a power of the Indian Ocean and of the Pacific Ocean."[17] The French 2013 defense White Book noted that France is a political and maritime power in the Pacific and has an interest in the freedom of navigation in the Indian Ocean. Paris has military forces deployed in New Caledonia and French Polynesia. Both deployments involve roughly 1000 to 1500 troops and include infantry forces, a frigate, surveillance and transport aircraft. Due to its territorial presence in the region, France now wants to join regional security frameworks, including the ASEAN Defense Ministers Meeting Plus (ADMM+).

ADMM+ is a forum of defense ministers to discuss South East Asian security issues. Participants include the ASEAN countries, as well as members of the East Asia Summit (China, United States, Russia, Japan, India, South Korea, Australia, and New Zealand). Maritime security, counter-terrorism, disaster relief and humanitarian assistance are on the agenda. Territorial claims are not. In 2013, France declared its interest in becoming a member. In Brussels there has been discus-

---

[17]Jean-Yves Le Drian, "Address to the Shangri-La Dialogue" (speech, Singapore, June 2, 2013).

sion whether the EU should join, but some member states—including the United Kingdom—are opposed to the EU playing a role in Asian defense issues.

Both Paris and London have a range of security dialogues in the region. France has a 2+2 security dialogue with Japan—a joint meeting of defense and foreign ministers—as does the UK. In October 2013, the UK and Japan signed an agreement on intelligence-sharing, anti-terrorism efforts and maritime security. Japan and the UK also cooperate on military interoperability. Since 2012, China and Britain have a "defense strategic dialogue," and France has a similar dialogue dating back to 2002. Vietnam and the UK announced a "strategic dialogue" in 2013 where military issues, such as joint training, are discussed. British and Indian defense ministers meet annually. The UK played an important role to push for the start and end of sanctions in Myanmar/Burma. London will now appoint a defense attaché to the country, and it has announced the possibility of training its police and riot forces. The UK has increased its cooperation with Australia on cyber security, and has signed a new "Defence and Security Cooperation Treaty." As part of deepening its ties, Australia and the UK have agreed to share confidential diplomatic cables.

Any role for the EU's Common Security and Defense Policy (CSDP) in Asia should be approached with realistic expectations. European navies will not patrol the East China Sea. But EU countries could be involved in training, security sector reform, anti-piracy efforts in the Malacca Straits, disaster management, co-operation on cyber security, counter-proliferation or counter terrorism activities. NATO similarly has an important role to play in many of these issues, and ad hoc decisions will probably determine whether any contribution would take place under NATO, EU or national flags. NATO has shown an interest in reaching out to partners in East Asia, particularly South Korea and Japan. In 2007, Japanese Prime Minister Shinzo Abe addressed the North Atlantic Council and in April 2013, NATO Secretary General Anders Fogh Rasmussen visited Japan and South Korea. Japan and NATO signed a Joint Political Declaration announcing cooperation on emerging security challenges including cyber defense, counterterrorism and non-proliferation.[18] Rasmussen,

---

[18]For more on NATO's role in Asia, see chapter 8 in this volume.

however, has made clear that NATO does not have plans for military training in the region; the agreement initially refers to information exchange. In the field of cyber security, the UK, Hungary and South Korea have hosted international conferences to discuss the issue. In 2015, the fourth iteration will be hosted by the Netherlands.

In terms of conflict prevention and humanitarian relief, the European Union has been active in South East Asia, particularly in Indonesia (in Aceh), Timor Leste, Mindanao and most recently with hurricane relief in the Philippines. In the area of development aid, the EU and its member states are the largest donors globally, totaling some 53.15 billion euros in 2012, more than double U.S. aid, a lot of which is directed at South and South East Asia.

European relationships with Asia are based around trade, and this includes defense sales.[19] While Europe's military presence in the region is limited, the scale of defense-industrial involvement shows broader involvement. France, the UK and Germany, among others, compete over defense sales. As security tensions increase in the region, military budgets rise. France and the UK are eyeing contracts in Japan, as the Japanese government liberalizes some of its defense procurement restrictions. London signed a defense agreement with Tokyo in July 2013, and in January 2014 France and Japan agreed to work together on various military technologies. France's dialogue with Japan also includes discussions on France's export policy of dual-use capabilities: a key Japanese concern. Germany and India signed an "Agreement concerning Bilateral Defense Cooperation" in 2006. This agreement encompassed the exchange and training of military personnel and cooperation in the field of defense technology. India has aging German-built submarines and is renegotiating replacements. Germany has sold Type-214 submarines to South Korea and is rumored to have supplied diesel engines for sophisticated Chinese submarines. France has similarly sold submarines to India and Malaysia, and is negotiating with Delhi for the sale of 126 Rafale fighter aircraft. London has negotiated the sale of AgustaWestland helicopters with South Korea. Along with Italy, Germany and Spain, it has been promoting

---

[19]David Lague, "The Chinese Military Machine's Secret to Success: European Engineering," *Reuters*, December 19, 2013, http://www.reuters.com/investigates/china-military/#article/part5.

the Eurofighter Typhoon jet in places like Indonesia, Malaysia and South Korea. The UK also hopes to sell air defense missiles to Jakarta. Smaller European defense technology producers have joined the competition. The Netherlands has negotiated the sale of two, and up to four, corvettes to Vietnam, and Poland is increasing its defense relations with Hanoi. According to SIPRI, a Swedish think tank, one-fifth of Asia's arms come from Europe, and particularly the militaries of South Korea, Indonesia, Malaysia, Singapore and Thailand rely on European military technologies. The defense-industrial relationship between Europe and Asia suggests that European powers have some influence over the direction of Asian security policies. At the least, it allows European states to discuss security issues with their Asian counterparts.

## Deeper Cooperation with ASEAN

ASEAN could be the basis for a multilateral security community that balances unilateral behavior of other regional powers. Both the EU and member-state governments believe that ASEAN could become the main organization that promotes cooperative security in the Asia-Pacific. Across Europe there is a strong belief that ASEAN would benefit from European support to move it towards greater economic and political integration. Documents published by the EU with titles such as "EU-ASEAN: Natural Partners," reflect these views.[20] The EU has signed the Treaty of Amity and Cooperation with ASEAN, which France and the UK have joined as states, demonstrating the link between the two organizations. In a sign of increased cooperation, in February 2014, ASEAN and EU ambassadors met for the first time.

The shifting regional balance of power is positioning ASEAN in a more central strategic role. As tensions mount between regional powers, smaller states seek security in collective action and the international rule of law. Some of ASEAN's members are now starting to embrace the protection that international law and regional coopera-

---

[20]European External Action Service, "EU-ASEAN: Natural Partners," (Jakarta: EU Delegation, June 2013), http://eeas.europa.eu/asean/docs/eu_asean_natural_partners_en.pdf.

tion brings: Vietnam, Malaysia and Singapore are showing interest in international and regional institutions like ASEAN that have a stabilizing influence.

European leaders like to point to the similarities between the EU and ASEAN as institutions for regional integration. Germany's then-foreign minister Westerwelle said that the EU should "take a more strategic role and bring Europe's expertise into the emerging security architecture. We need to consider further upgrading EU-ASEAN relations."

The EU aspires to play a role in security issues that concern ASEAN members. There are regular EU-ASEAN meetings, which are mostly about trade, but Brussels wants to expand them to include security issues, such as maritime security, cyber security and illegal fishing. At the ASEAN Regional Forum in 2012, for instance, the EU chaired a session on Myanmar/Burma. Brussels has also suggested hosting joint meetings of the EU political-security committee and its ASEAN counterparts to discuss disaster relief, crisis management, counter-terrorism and counter-piracy in the Malacca Straits.

While the EU officially does not have an opinion on the territorial issues in the South and East China Seas, there are things it can do. Brussels has offered ASEAN its advice on dealing with territorial disputes, but the organization has yet to respond. As was made clear during the 2012 ASEAN summit—when no final communiqué could be agreed—the regional body is divided when it comes to territorial issues in the South China Sea.

Alongside the EU, Berlin, Paris and London are similarly intensifying their focus on South East Asia and reaching out to ASEAN. Germany acknowledges the stabilizing role that a stronger ASEAN could play, arguing that the organization is an Asian variant of the embryonic European Union. Then-Foreign Minister Westerwelle has said that regional economic integration, stronger trade relations and respect for the international rule of law created prosperity and security in Europe, and ASEAN could replicate that example.

In 2013 the UK opened an embassy (or "British Interests Office") in Myanmar/Burma—as did the EU—and a British embassy was recently opened in Laos. Trade may be the dominant motivation, but a stronger diplomatic network enables discussing a broader range of topics. At the opening of the embassy in Vientiane, Foreign Secretary William Hague said, "With this new Embassy, Britain becomes one of only three European countries to be represented in all ten states of ASEAN, at a pivotal moment in the organization's history, as it works towards becoming the fourth largest single market in the world. We will now be able to have constant discussions about foreign policy and security issues in your region, and on global issues such as climate change."[21]

Among ASEAN members, the UK is particularly strengthening its diplomatic relations with Indonesia. Aside from Indonesia's growing economy, its leadership role in ASEAN, its market potential, its historical status as a non-aligned power and its prospects as a regional political power, London believes Jakarta could help build bridges in the Asia-Pacific between those countries leaning towards China (such as Laos and Cambodia) and those leaning towards the United States (such as Singapore and the Philippines), and thereby have a stabilizing influence in the region. In addition, since Indonesia is one of the few South East Asian states that has no disputes with China over islets in the South China Sea, there is a limited risk of antagonizing China.

However, Europe should manage its expectations regarding ASEAN. It remains to be seen whether the group of countries can overcome its internal division and become a coherent multilateral organization promoting cooperative security for the broader region. ASEAN's members have yet to show that they are willing to work together on the tough issues their region confronts. In addition, outside powers—like the United States, the EU and Japan—are funding the organization. They should be careful not to want ASEAN's success more than its members do.

## Asian Demand for European Strategic Involvement

How do Asian states respond to possible European involvement in strategic issues in the Asia-Pacific? And why might countries in the

---

[21]William Hague, "Opening of Britain's New Embassy in Vientiane, Laos" (speech, Vientiane, Laos, November 5, 2012), Foreign and Commonwealth Office, https://www.gov.uk/government/speeches/with-this-new-embassy-britain-becomes-one-of-only-three-european-countries-to-be-represented-in-all-ten-states-of-asean.

Asia-Pacific want European involvement in their security affairs? As tensions rise in the Asia-Pacific, particularly around the South and East China seas, governments are reaching out to Europe for diplomatic support. Europe is particularly becoming the target of Chinese and Japanese strategic diplomatic competition.

East Asian states benefit from the EU's Single Market but they prefer to deal with European states at the national level. This is especially the case with Beijing. In 2013 China pressured Germany, and less so France, in order to frustrate the European Commission's anti-dumping case against Chinese manufacturers of solar panels. To underline the point, at the height of tensions over the case, Prime Minister Li Keqiang's first visit to Europe in 2013 was to Bern and Berlin, and he side-stepped Brussels. At the G20 summit in St Petersburg, in September 2013, the EU felt snubbed when China cancelled a bilateral meeting with EU president Herman van Rompuy while Xi Jinping's bilateral meeting with Germany's Angela Merkel did take place.[22]

China appears to be playing EU states off against each other. Since Prime Minister Cameron's meeting with the Dalai Lama in May 2012, the UK government did not have high-level meetings with Beijing for more than a year, and only after Whitehall decided no longer to have official meetings with the religious leader, even though France and Germany—which have had meetings with the Dalai Lama in the past—remained welcome.[23] China is also cultivating ties with other groupings of European states. In 2012, then-premier Wen Jiabao initiated a dialogue with sixteen central and eastern European states to improve trade and investment relations. As part of his visit, organized by the Polish government, the Chinese premier announced a $10 billion soft loan for infrastructure and green technology projects, the creation of a common investment fund, and more student exchanges. Poland is important for Chinese trade as it is the European entry point for the "silk railroad," a railway that runs from China across Central Asia to Europe. In January 2013 the first delivery of rail containers from Chongqing arrived in Łódź Olechów station. The "silk

---

[22]On March 31, 2014 Xi Jinping visited the EU in Brussels for the first time as president.

[23]"Chinese Roll Out Red Carpet for Hollande," *Financial Times*, April 24, 2013, http://www.ft.com/cms/s/0/03182260-acef-11e2-b27f-00144feabdc0.html#axzz2sVXbe4Ay.

railroad" can carry freight from China to Europe quicker than by ship. In August 2013, during the visit of the Serbian prime minister to Beijing, president Xi Jinping and Premier Li Keqiang underlined the importance of central and eastern Europe to China and pledged to further strengthen economic ties. In November 2013, Li Keqiang met his sixteen central and eastern European counterparts again. The two sides agreed on an annual heads of government meeting, a common ministerial on economic cooperation and trade, further investment in railway links between Central Europe and China, and deeper cultural, academic and people-to-people exchanges. China agreed to help Hungary and Serbia upgrade their railway links, and assist to build a high-speed railway. Beijing was pursuing 'checkbook diplomacy' among a cluster of EU member states. This strengthens China's position in EU internal debates, and weakens EU cohesion.

Beijing also reached out to six southern European countries to start a dialogue on agricultural cooperation. In February 2013, China's Vice President, Hui Liangyu, met with food and agriculture ministers from Greece, Malta, Spain, Portugal, Italy and Cyprus, to discuss EU food exports to China, and cooperation on agricultural technology. In Brussels and Western Europe these Chinese overtures raised eyebrows; they are seen as part of a divide-and-rule approach to Europe. UK officials say China may be trying to drive a wedge between those Europeans that are willing to address human rights issues with the Chinese, and those that are exclusively interested in a pragmatic, trade-driven relationship.

The question is why China chooses to pursue a policy of European division? One explanation may be based on power politics: China is concerned that a strong, cohesive Europe could form a threat to its norms, restrict its economic behavior and generally be better able to balance its rise. Given the poor state of European economies, Beijing has both an opportunity and an interest to fragment the EU. A more generous explanation is that Beijing is disappointed in the ability of the EU to deliver coherent policy responses and therefore is looking towards bilateral relations with member states as an alternative. A third explanation is that as part of a power struggle in Asia, Asian powers compete for European diplomatic support for their respective positions; instead of swaying the entire EU-28, Beijing and others could carve up Europe instead.

In a sign that Europe may indeed become the target of intra-Asian competition, Japan set up a dialogue with the Visegrad-4 countries (Poland, Czech Republic, Hungary and Slovakia). At the meeting of prime ministers in June 2013, organized by the Polish government, Prime Minister Abe underlined shared values and support for a market-based economy, as well as cooperation to promote nuclear energy.

Tokyo is concerned about European indifference. It fears that European navel-gazing and its economic vulnerability focuses European leaders on short-term economic benefits rather than the strategic picture in Asia. To the Japanese government, the prominence of European economic and financial concerns gives an advantage to Beijing and its deep pockets. Instead, rather than competing on funds and projects, Japan is appealing to Europe's shared democratic values and hopes to improve Europe's understanding of dynamics in the region. For its part, Tokyo is also reaching out to ASEAN, India and Russia to balance against the perceived threat from China.

Japanese officials make the case that the United States has limited resources and express concern about Washington's willingness to back Tokyo at all times. Thus it is appealing to European powers for support, diplomatic and otherwise. On security issues, Japan looks to Europe for three things. Firstly, it wants the European Union to maintain the Chinese arms embargo. Secondly, it wishes to increase dialogue and information exchange about non-proliferation and cyber security, amongst others by reaching out to NATO. Thirdly, Japan seeks access to European defense technology—mostly British, French and German—in order to boost its defense capabilities and develop its defense industry.

Japan also wants European diplomatic support and its help to influence third parties. For instance, the EU and Japan have agreed to cooperate on strengthening ASEAN, and Tokyo hopes European help will enable it to persuade Canada to reconsider its economic reorientation towards China. The EU and Japan have a yearly summit, yet it still mostly revolves around trade relations.[24]

---

[24]See report of the 16th EU-Japan Conference, November 25, 2013, http://www.eu-japan.eu/sites/eu-japan.eu/files/FINAL-SeminarReport_20131125.pdf.

South Korea, contrary to Japan and China, does favor working with the EU. Relations between Brussels and Seoul have deepened in recent years. The EU's first free trade agreement in the Asia-Pacific was signed with South Korea, and Brussels and Seoul have a joint committee on science and technology to promote common research and innovation initiatives. Among EU officials, South Korea is viewed as more receptive to regional initiatives for mediation, trust-building, and conflict resolution than other Asian countries. Given the EU's good relations with South Korea and its deepening ties with Japan, Brussels could attempt to promote further reconciliation between the two East Asian nations.

## Neutrality No More

Even though Europe continues to emphasize trade promotion, it is becoming increasingly difficult for European states to ignore—and remain impartial to—the region's strategic issues, particularly the territorial disputes in the South and East China seas. Europe will find it increasingly difficult to avoid becoming diplomatically involved in these emerging tensions. Not only because its economic interests are at stake, but also because the affected Asian states will not let Europe be neutral anymore. For them, regional maritime tensions are issues of vital national interest, and they will force Europe to take sides.

During his first visit to Beijing in late December 2013—after having been snubbed for hosting the Dalai Lama—the British prime minister did not discuss security concerns with senior Chinese leadership. His visit however, came shortly after Beijing's unilateral declaration of an air defense identification zone (ADIZ) that overlaps the Japanese-administered Senkaku islands. China's move led to indignation among the U.S., Japanese and South Korean leadership and increased tensions in the region. David Cameron however, was accompanied by nearly 100 business leaders and he stuck to his agenda of trade promotion. It raised eyebrows in Tokyo. Despite being quiet on the matter to his hosts, shortly after Cameron's visit, the UK's top naval commander visited Japan's minister of defense, where the recent Chinese move was discussed. It caused outrage in Beijing. Similarly, Japan frowned upon—what it perceived as—a muffled EU response to China's ADIZ; Brussels expressed "concern" and called "on all sides to exercise caution and restraint." Tokyo felt that Brussels shied away from criticizing China. A month later the tables were turned, when China was disappointed by the EU's weak statement on Abe's controversial visit to the Yasukuni shrine. The EU "took note" of the visit, and said the "action is not conducive to lowering tensions in the region." In Tokyo, officials were pleased.

European member states and the EU have continuously underlined their neutrality regarding the territorial claims in the East and South China Sea. Yet, regarding the latter they may also be forced into a difficult position. The international maritime tribunal in Hamburg is working on an arbitration case brought forward by the Philippines over islets in the South China Sea. A ruling would force Europe to decide between neutrality and backing international legal opinion that possibly annoys China.

The EU and its member states are walking a diplomatic tightrope. As tensions flare, it will become more difficult for European states to maintain a position of impartiality among the heated tempers in the Asia-Pacific. If it wants to be an honest broker in the region, perhaps Europe should accept that its declarations will never be considered satisfactory by either side. However, an honest broker who is indifferent has little influence and if Europe wants to be taken seriously on security issues, it may have to start picking sides.

## The Eurasian Transition Zone

As Asia's emerging powers expand their influence westward, a zone of overlapping interests with Europe will grow. Such is the case in Central Asia, but also the Indian Ocean, the Middle East and the Arctic. Central Asia is a region where Asian countries increasingly provide development assistance, have economic interests or contribute to stabilization operations, such as in Afghanistan. It is an area with a range of security challenges but on which countries like China—and increasingly Europe as well—rely for their energy resources. Besides, the development of the Shanghai Cooperation Organization, a regional organization that includes resource-rich Central Asian nations, could both be a challenge or a partner for European activities in the region.

China's well-publicized presence in Africa and the Middle East is growing and Beijing continues to invest massively in port and infrastructure projects across the continent to gain access to critical resources to feed its economy. In 2013 China deployed nearly 100 infantry troops to the UN mission in Mali. It was the first expeditionary deployment of Chinese combat forces and it signaled a greater willingness to become involved in African security issues. In Africa, Japan has a naval base in Djibouti for anti-piracy operations and Tokyo is one of the continent's largest development aid donors.[25] In January 2014, Prime Minister Abe announced an $83.4 million aid package to help with the refugee crisis in the Sahel. Japan and Europe share concerns about terrorism, state failure and resource security in northern Africa. The attack on the Il-Amenas gas facility in southern Algeria in January 2013 cost the lives of 10 Japanese citizens. At a Japanese-African conference in 2013, Abe announced nearly $1 billion in antiterrorism assistance to the continent, including training of security personnel.

As Asian powers expand their influence in the Middle East and Central Asia, and as the United States signals increasing hesitation to become involved, Europe may find that cooperation with Asian partners is an issue of growing interest.

It is along two oceans that many East Asian and European interests intersect, or could even collide. The Indian Ocean is the maritime conduit between Europe and Asia. Not only is it a conveyor belt for global manufacturing, it is also the access route to the resource riches of the Middle East and Africa. France and the UK have a permanent military presence along—or in—the Indian Ocean. France has forward deployed military assets in Djibouti, Abu Dhabi, and La Reunion, while the UK has a military base in Diego Garcia. European and Asian militaries cooperate in the Indian Ocean. The navies of Brunei, China, India, Indonesia, Japan, Malaysia, South Korea, Singapore, Taiwan, and Thailand contribute to the EU-led counter-piracy coalition in the Gulf of Aden. As China and India seek to secure their lines of communication, they are expanding their naval presence with

---

[25]Mohamed Osman Farah, "Japan Opens Military Base in Djibouti to Help Combat Piracy," *Bloomberg*, July 8, 2011, http://www.bloomberg.com/news/2011-07-08/japan-opens-military-base-in-djibouti-to-help-combat-piracy.html.

fueling stations and ports dotting the Indian Ocean rim to protect their sea lines of communication. The Arctic Ocean offers a similar area where European and Asian interest overlap, as Asia's hungry economies eye the opportunities of more accessible Arctic natural resources and transit routes.

Overlapping interests in Central Asia and the Arctic are bringing Russia closer to East Asia's powers. Moscow could become a major energy exporter to China or Japan, offering support to deal with the security issues in CentralAsia, but also providing welcome diplomatic backing to either East Asian country. Greater Russo-Asian cooperation has consequences for the geopolitics of Euro-Russian relations. It provides all the more reason for a broader security dialogue between Europe and Asian partners. The Eurasian transitional zone is set to become increasingly important to Euro-Asian relations, creating the necessity for greater cooperation and understanding.

## A European Strategy of Soft Balancing?

The European Union and its member states are actors in the Asia-Pacific, but a coherent strategy to promote security and peace is lacking. This reduces Europe's relevance and credibility in the region. Disagreements among European states about the role that security and defense policy play, and the desired level of transatlantic coordination, form the main obstacles. A further difficulty is that the EU and its member states confront an uncertain security environment in their immediate neighborhood. Developments such as fallout from the Arab Spring, the Iran crisis, the Syrian civil war and difficult relations with Russia, including but not limited to differences over Ukraine, are complicating the pursuit of a coherent policy for the Asia-Pacific.

But Europe cannot be strategically ambivalent about Asia. The eastward shift of economic and political power is structural. Europe's economic interests dictate it, its Asian partners demand it and the importance of the transatlantic relationship warrants it.

Most EU member states have bilateral relations with Asian powers to promote trade, not deal with security. The exceptions are the UK and France. Some European states are developing their defence industrial ties with regional partners. At the EU level, EU officials are

**Chart 1. European Approaches to the Asia-Pacific Region**

| | Coordination with US | Military role in Asia-Pacific | Defense sales | Security role | Focus on trade promotion | Focus on ASEAN | Relations with China |
|---|---|---|---|---|---|---|---|
| European Union | Desired | No | | ARF, humanitarian relief and crisis management, lessons learned | Yes | Yes, free trade agreement envisioned | Trade-centric, China focuses on national level |
| France | | Yes, through territorial presence | Yes | ADMM+, bilateral 2+2 dialogues | Yes | Yes | Trade-centric |
| United Kingdom | Desired | Five Power Defence Agreement, maritime security, territorial presence | Yes | Bilateral 2+2 dialogues | Yes | Yes | Trade-centric, but troubled |
| Germany | | No | Yes | | Yes | Yes | Cabinet level meetings, trade-centric |

increasingly present in the region, and the European Commission is negotiating free trade agreements across the Asia-Pacific. Europe's deepening ties with the Asia-Pacific suggest greater ambition in the region.

Europe needs to align its views and spell out what its objectives are for engaging with the Asia-Pacific. Foremost, this requires coordination between the EU and the three largest member states. Chart 1 captures the central elements of the four main pillars of Europe's approach to the Asia-Pacific. It shows where major differences lies. It also shows the potential for intra-European coordination, including the strengthening of ASEAN as a regional multilateral security organization, the pursuit of free trade agreements to promote Western trade norms, and leveraging the export of defense technology.

Europe's strategic objectives in Asia are two-fold: economic security and a strong relationship with the United States. Other interests follow from this. Europe's economic well-being is dependent on what happens in the Asia-Pacific. It has a vital interest in the region's peaceful and stable development. Besides, it is difficult to foresee a situation where transatlantic relations are not negatively impacted if the United States and its Asian partners encounter greater challenges in the Asia-Pacific, and Europe remains on the sidelines.

The Asia-Pacific is at risk of becoming caught in a dangerous security dilemma. It could draw the United States in. Without a concerted approach to the region Asian countries will slowly diplomatically divide Europe, currying favors among different EU member states. And without a concerted effort to develop a transatlantic agenda towards Asia, European relations with the United States will suffer.

The European Union is not accustomed to thinking about its global role in grand strategic terms, and the larger European countries, by contrast, have often pursued unilateral trade-centric approaches to Asia. Yet Europe's Asia-Pacific strategy should focus on reducing revisionist tendencies in the region. The EU and its member states agree on strengthening ASEAN; the organization could become a multilateral cooperative security framework for the region that could balance unilateral tendencies. The EU and its member states, through their variety of channels based on trade, defense-industrial ties, territorial presence and participation in security dialogues, should emphasize trust-building between China and its neighbors and underline the importance of the international rule of law and multilateral solutions. The EU and its member states should also make clear to Beijing that revising the status quo in the region through bullying or the use of force is unacceptable. Europe's engagement would equally make it possible to soften an overly confrontational approach from Washington. Together this could form the beginning of a soft balancing strategy aimed at maintaining a balance of power in East Asia. The challenge is that the EU and its member states must realize that an impartial, trade-centric and disconnected approach to the Asia-Pacific is no longer in their common interest.

## Recommendations

1. **Developing a common agenda with the United States towards the Asia-Pacific is necessary to build a coherent transatlantic partnership for the "Asian century."** This must start with the formulation of shared interests while acknowledging that Europeans and Americans may favor different means to pursue them. Europe's embryonic soft balancing strategy should form the basis for cooperation with the United States. The United States and Europe should have

regular high-level discussions about the Asia-Pacific. A permanent dialogue to develop common approaches to the Asia-Pacific should be set up between the United States and the EU, and include the UK, France, and Germany and possibly others. Nigel Sheinwald, then the UK's ambassador to Washington, said in late 2011 that the Asia-Pacific "should be a standing issue on the agenda for EU-US summits." He is right. The transatlantic discussions should focus on strengthening ASEAN, building a complementary network of trade ties, maritime security and freedom of navigation, confidence-building with Asian partners, and energy and resources security. The common declaration at the ASEAN Regional Forum in 2012 should be given a follow-up.

2. **The EU High Representative should arrange a strategic dialogue on the "pivot" in Europe.** The internal strategic reflection should focus on the question how to deal with the rise of China. This does not exclusively mean issues in the Asia-Pacific, but also China's increasing influence in the space between the Arctic and the Indian Oceans. The EU should align its Asia policies in the External Action Service and DG Trade. A European approach to the region will not be based on the larger EU member states deferring to Brussels, instead it should be considered a common effort between the EU institutions and the EU-3.

3. **The EU and its member states should use anti-piracy operations in the Indian Ocean as a vehicle to build military-to-military relations with Asian powers like China, South Korea, India and others.**

4. **Brussels and relevant EU member states should focus on Arctic governance as a way to engage with China, Japan, Korea and the United States on common security issues.**

5. **A strong ASEAN is a shared transatlantic objective.** Europe should continue to focus on strengthening ASEAN as a regional economic, political and security actor. The EU should share its lessons in maritime demarcation and dealing with conflicts regarding fishing grounds and other resources. Europe could facilitate expert-level discussions on maritime

and territorial disputes. Individual European member-states could offer this in dialogues like ADMM+. EU navies should follow the UK's example and undertake port visits in South East Asia and engage in military-to-military contacts to build trust and transparency. A tripartite dialogue between the EU, the United States and ASEAN countries should be considered. The EU does not have a dedicated ambassador to ASEAN. If ASEAN's political clout increases, the EU should accredit an ambassador exclusively to the regional organization.

6. **A transatlantic approach to Asia will only be realized if the United States and Europe both commit to its success.** The EU's pursuit of free trade agreements with Asian partners is separate from, albeit complementary to, U.S. trade efforts in the region. TTIP, TPP and the EU's bilateral agreements with Asian partners could together strengthen shared Western norms of trade, and are an element in a soft balancing strategy in the Asia-Pacific. If Washington is serious about its Asia "rebalance," it should push for a successful conclusion of TTIP. Europe should remain focused on concluding bilateral agreements with Asian states and ASEAN.

## Chapter Five

# Asian Institutions and the Pivot

*Reuben Wong and Simon Tay*[1]

How is Asian regionalism to progress in the context of wider Asia-Pacific and global linkages? This chapter argues that Asian regional institutions are still nascent in developing a strong sense of regional community, even though there have been visible steps and high-profile summitry since the Asian crisis of 1997–98. Existing multilateral structures are chiefly preoccupied with economic cooperation and integration. In the field of security, the focus is on dialogue and confidence-building, rather than the actual resolution of disputes or the establishment of formal institutions to promote cooperative inter-state behavior. Cultural and civic engagements are also limited. Given the existing diversity of political systems, population sizes, cultures and levels of economic development in Asia, the idea of a regional *Community* (with a capital 'C') has not gained traction. The place of non-Asian actors who have a significant stake and role in the region, especially the United States but also the European Union, is contested. Any attempts by extra-regional players to increase their footprints in the region should thus be sensitive to regional dynamics, unspoken norms, and the needs of Asian regionalism today.

Even though pan-Asian institutions have grown in the last fifteen years, there is no guarantee that they will endure and develop. For most of the Cold War period, one could argue that multilateral institutions in East Asia were weak and derivative of relationships that Asian states had with the United States, the Soviet Union and China.[2] The

---

[1]The authors are grateful to Loke Hoe Yeong and Daniel Stephen for research assistance.

[2]See Michael Yahuda, "China and Europe: The Significance of a Secondary Relationship," in Thomas W. Robinson and David Shambaugh, eds., *Chinese Foreign Policy: Theory and Practice* (Oxford: Clarendon Press and New York: Oxford University Press,

constraints of a bipolar structure precluded Japan and the two Koreas from initiating regional institutions on their own; each was limited by ties to its respective superpower patron. The task of region-building fell by default to the non-communist states in Southeast Asia. Several multilateral institutions in the Southeast Asia region came and went— the Southeast Asia Treaty Organization (SEATO, 1954–77), the Associ- ation of South East Asia (ASA, 1961–67) and the Greater Malaysian Confederation (or MAPHILINDO, 1963).[3] Of the very few which sur- vive today, the stand-out organization is the Association of Southeast Asian Nations (ASEAN), which has broadened to include all ten coun- tries of the region, and deepened its ambitions of integration.

ASEAN was established in 1967 by Indonesia, Malaysia, the Philip- pines, Singapore and Thailand. ASEAN cut its teeth as a diplomatic bloc and playmaker when it helped to resolve the Cambodian conflict (1978–91). Throughout the post-Cold War era of the 1990s and into the 21st century, an expanded ASEAN was in the driver's seat in the frenetic growth in international and regional organizations in Asia.[4] Initially formed with a declared social and economic focus in the 1967 Bangkok Declaration, security dialogue and confidence-building were secondary concerns. ASEAN did not even have a permanent Secre- tariat until 1975 or an organizational Charter until 2007.[5] ASEAN was

---

1994), pp. 266–282; and Michael Yahuda, *The International Politics of the Asia-Pacific, 1945–1995*, (London and New York: Routledge, 1996).

[3]For the impact of the Cold War on regionalism in Asia, see Donald Weatherbee, "The Cold War in Southeast Asia," in Donald Weatherbee, *International Relations in Southeast Asia* (Rowman & Littlefield, 2005), 57–87. See also Leszek Buszynski, *SEATO: The Failure of an Alliance Strategy* (Singapore: Singapore University Press, 1983).

[4]For discussions of ASEAN's 'centrality' in Asian institution-building, see Amitav Acharya, *The Quest for Identity: International Relations of Southeast Asia*, (Singapore: Oxford University Press, 2000); Khong Yuen Foong and Helen Nesadurai, "Hanging together, institutional design and cooperation in Southeast Asia: AFTA and the ARF," in Amitav Acharya and AI Johnston, eds., *Crafting Cooperation: Regional International Institutions in Comparative Perspective*, (Cambridge: Cambridge University Press, 2007), pp. 32–82; *Reinventing ASEAN*, eds. Simon Tay, Jesus P. Estanislao and Hadi Soesastro (Singapore: Institute of Southeast Asian Studies, 2001); and Reuben Wong, "Asian Integration—Scope and Limits," *ISPI Analysis*, 2010, http://www.ispionline.it/it/docu- ments/Analysis_14_2010.pdf, p. 14.

[5]Reuben Wong, "Model Power or Reference Point? The EU and the ASEAN Char- ter," *Cambridge Review of International Affairs*, 25.4 (2012), pp. 669–682.

not meant to be a regional security organization; its member states, emerging out of European colonialism into independent statehood, were happy to leave the job of ensuring security (both *intramuros* and extra-regional) to the United States as a benign hegemon.[6]

Once the Cold War ended and the need to incorporate the Asian communist states into peaceful cooperative structures arose, however, ASEAN stepped up to the task at hand. Trusted by states on both sides of the capitalist/communist divide, and supported by Northeast Asian states divided by rivalries and mutual suspicions, ASEAN quickly became, by default, the hub of regional organizations in Southeast and Northeast Asia. Amid fears of U.S. military withdrawal from the region and China's rise, the Association built on its reputation, following the successful resolution of the Cambodian conflict in 1991, to carve out a central role in the Asia-Pacific Economic Cooperation (APEC, 1989), the ASEAN Regional Forum (ARF, established 1994), Asia-Europe Meeting (ASEM, 1996), ASEAN plus Three (APT, 1997), East Asia Summit (EAS, 2005), ASEAN Defense Ministers' Meeting (ADMM, 2006), and "ADMM plus" (2010).

Much of this recent pan-Asian institutionalism has been driven by the financial crisis that engulfed the region in 1997–98, and by the practical need to "enmesh" the rising powers in an inclusive, cooperative framework of norms and rules.[7] Are these burgeoning structures a sign of Asia's budding regional order—one that is characterized by the rise of indigenous great powers (especially China and India)—alongside that of U.S.-led alliance systems? Do these activities add up to a peaceful and stable region-wide order in the world's most economically dynamic region? The next section maps the interests and concerns of the main intra-Asian and extra-regional actors in Asia. The chapter then concludes with recommendations on how Asians can work with the United States and Europe—as non-regional countries

---

[6]A good statement of this idea is made by Peter J. Katzenstein, *A World of Regions: Asia and Europe in the American Imperium* (Ithaca, NY: Cornell University Press, 2005); The United States has formal military agreements with Japan, South Korea, Taiwan, Thailand and the Philippines (notwithstanding 1991 and SOFA), and less formal arrangements with Australia, Indonesia, Malaysia and Singapore in what is known as the 'hub-and spokes' system centered on the United States.

[7]Evelyn Goh, "Great Powers and Hierarchical Order in Southeast Asia: Analyzing Regional Security Strategies." *International Security* 32.3 (2008), pp. 113–157.

with interest and stakes in the region—to develop a more stable and cooperative order in Asia.

## Mapping Multilateralism in Asia

Although China and Japan boast the largest economies in Asia, and China and India host the largest populations in the world, the three Asian giants still have unresolved conflicts and historical tensions among them. Aside from a brief period of Sino-Indian amity that resulted in the Non-Aligned Movement in the 1950s, China and India went to war over disputed borders in 1962 and have not been able to work together to build meaningful regional institutions except through ASEAN. Similarly, China and Japan enjoyed a short "honeymoon" after diplomatic relations were normalized in the 1970s, but disputed islands, history and unforgiven wartime atrocities continue to bedevil closer cooperation. There have been religions that have crossed and linked Asians, as well as intellectual hopes—especially in the late colonial period.[8] But neither large states nor big pan-Asian ideas have been able to play a "natural" leadership role in the region; instead this leadership vacuum has been filled by ASEAN since 1991.

### ASEAN

When ASEAN was set up in 1967, the idea of regional reconciliation was critical to accommodate the overlapping territorial claims between newly independent post-colonial states. The informal agreement to respect sovereignty and non-interference in the domestic affairs of neighboring states as fundamental principles of the Association—or the "ASEAN Way"—thus began as a pragmatic approach to "accommodate" and manage these basic tensions, which were viewed as flashpoints for inter-state conflict. It was usefully employed between four of the five founding states in particular—Indonesia, Singapore, Malaysia and the Philippines.[9] Sukarno's Indonesia had just ended a low-level state of military confrontation

---

[8]Simon S.C. Tay, *Asia Alone: The Dangerous Post Crisis Divide from America* (Wiley, 2010), especially chapter 2, "Two Crises, One Asia."

[9]Michael Antolik, *ASEAN: The Diplomacy of Accommodation* (Armonk, NY: ME Sharpe, 1990).

with Malaysia and Singapore (*Konfrontasi*, 1963–66); Singapore had separated from Malaysia in 1965; and the Philippines and Malaysia had—and still have –outstanding territorial disputes over Sabah.

The communist victory and Vietnamese reunification in 1975 at the end of the Second Indochinese War galvanized the ASEAN-5 to work more closely together and with allies like the U.S., for a common response to potential communist aggression. Vietnam was then invited to sign a Treaty of Amity and Cooperation (TAC) with ASEAN. When Vietnam invaded Cambodia in 1979, ASEAN was initially divided on whether to accept this as a *fait accompli*. But strong representations by Thailand and Singapore moved the Association towards working at the UN and at every available international forum to deny recognition to the regime installed by Hanoi.

After the Cold War, ASEAN has been at the forefront building multilateral institutions and mechanisms such as the ASEAN Regional Forum (ARF), Asia-Pacific Economic Cooperation (APEC), Asia-Europe Meeting (ASEM), East Asia Summit (EAS), Asian Defense Ministers' Meeting (ADMM) and ADMM+, in which eight non-Asian countries participate. The focus of ADMM+ is humanitarian assistance and disaster relief (HADR);[10] hosted by ASEAN states, the military exercises of ADMM+ provide precious arenas in which countries like the U.S., China, India and Japan actively work together.

Over the course of 2008-2009, an ASEAN Charter was passed and ratified by national parliaments in Southeast Asia, thereby giving the Association of Southeast Asian Nations legal personality for the first time in its then 40-year history. ASEAN centrality is asserted in a number of wider, pan-Asian processes and summits and, at least in word, accepted by the much larger powers that participate. Yet, the ability of ASEAN to strongly lead or drive these processes is extenuated.[11]

---

[10]Brunei Ministry of Defence, "2nd ASEAN Militaries' HADR Exercise," June 16, 2013, http://www.mindef.gov.bn/ADMM2013/index.php/admm-plus/157-2nd-asean-militaries-hadr-exercise; Singapore Ministry of Defence, "SAF and Other Militaries Conclude the ADMM-Plus HADR/MM Exercise," June 20, 2013, http://www.min-def.gov.sg/imindef/press_room/official_releases/nr/2013/jun/20jun13_nr.html#.-UpHUExzCTms.

[11]Tay (2010), *op. cit.*, especially chapter 3, "Leading Asia's Rise."

## ASEAN+3

The core of "East Asia" today is generally accepted to consist of the 10 Southeast Asian members of ASEAN, and the three Northeast Asian states of China, Japan and South Korea. These 13 states, sometimes referred to as "ASEAN+3" or "ASEAN Plus Three" (APT) held their first annual summit in Kuala Lumpur in 1997. They first organized themselves as "ASEAN + 3" thanks to the Asia-Europe Meeting which was inaugurated in 1996.

The nexus of an East Asian community thus already exists in the form of ASEAN+3, institutionalized as a collective response to the 1997-8 Asian financial crisis. This framework brings together the high technology, capital and political weight of three Northeast Asian states with the natural resources and diplomatic organization of the 10 ASEAN countries. It has helped to promote regional dialogue and the common interest, including plans for a region-wide free trade agreement (FTA) to replace the patchwork of bilateral and ASEAN FTAs with China, Japan and South Korea. It has also reduced intramural tensions, including episodes of friction between China and Japan, and tensions in the South China Sea.

The three richest countries of Northeast Asia—China, Japan and South Korea—quietly made history by holding regular trilateral summits, beginning in Fukuoka on December 13, 2008. There have been recurring efforts to negotiate a free trade agreement between these three states, which do enjoy a great deal of interdependence; whether as a trio, or bilaterally. But there is too much mutual suspicion between them, and the lack of external existential threats requiring any coordinated response has inhibited this trilateral relationship from proceeding further.

For ASEAN+3 as a whole, cooperation has been spurred in response to regional crises—the public health concerns of SARS in 2002–03 and the financial and currency fluctuations that triggered the Asian crisis of 1997–98. These events led to the incremental development of the Chiang Mai Initiative Multilateralization (CMIM), a multi-currency swap arrangement. As at 2012, CMIM's foreign exchange reserves pool stood at some $240 billion, with the bulk of the guarantees from China and Japan. Moreover, there is the AMRO (Asian Macro-economic Research Office), an independent surveillance unit established by the

ASEAN+3 countries to monitor regional economies in order to assist in the early detection of risks, and make policy recommendations for remedial actions and effective decision-making in the CMIM.

Yet despite these considerable steps, ASEAN+3 is neither the sole nor the dominant framework of what constitutes the "region," if one understands the region as a social and cognitive construct rooted in political practice.[12] What is happening in East Asia is that the borders and membership of "East Asia" are being contested by ASEAN, China, Japan, Australia, the United States and a whole host of states, NGOs, and scholars, and this contestation has led to a proliferation of other groupings and summit meetings.

### East Asian Summit (EAS)

At the end of 2005, the ASEAN+3 invited India, Australia and New Zealand to join them in the inaugural "East Asia Summit", held in Kuala Lumpur. This surprising step deviated from the earlier expectation that ASEAN+3 would be transformed into a deeper community.[13] In part, this was because Japan and a number of smaller Southeast Asian states—of which the most assertive was Singapore, despite its close ties to China—were uncomfortable with the increasing dominance of China in ASEAN+3. As such, the political logic was that a larger framework involving India and Australia would "balance" China's weight in the region. Australia's membership in the EAS was also seen in Canberra as a vindication of several governments' sustained attempts to integrate Australia more closely in the region's political economy (which was ironically undermined by the failed attempt by the Rudd government to foster a new Asia Pacific community). Despite being formal and loyal allies of the United States, Australia has become increasingly wary of having to choose sides between the United States and a rising China.[14] The same dilemma has been

---

[12]Katzenstein, *op. cit.*, p. 11.

[13]For a more detailed examination of the steps and process for the creation of the East Asia Summit, see Tay (2010), *op. cit.*, pp. 66–71.

[14]See Hugh White, *Power Shift: Australia's Future Between Washington and Beijing*, No. 39 (Collingwood, Victoria: Black Inc., 2010), and his article "Power Shift: Rethinking Australia's Place in the Asian Century," *Australian Journal of International Affairs*, 65.1 (2011), pp. 81–93.

felt by many other small to medium-sized states in Asia, and their strategy has been to "hedge" and secure close ties to *both* Washington and Beijing.[15]

### Security Institutions

The U.S.-centered alliances in Northeast and Southeast Asia have been in place for many decades. But for many years, there were no wider regional institutional structures for security as Asians, including ASEAN, eschewed NATO-like structures.

The longest established security dialogue is the ASEAN Regional Forum (ARF), created in 1994. The ARF meets annually to discuss security issues but does not make binding or enforceable decisions, especially with regard to the South China Sea disputes. It has some-times struggled to even discuss the most contentious issues, such as the Korean Peninsula, cross-Strait issues and military build-ups. This has led some to perhaps unfairly dismiss the ARF as a "talk shop." This may underrate the contribution of this process, current and potential, to increase dialogue and understanding and build confidence amongst Asian powers—including China, Japan and India—which, as noted earlier, have tangled and unsettled histories. There have been instances moreover when the ARF has been an important venue to openly discuss differences, such as the 2010 ARF when then U.S. Sec-retary of State Hillary Clinton raised the South China Sea issue with China.

A more recent security meeting among Asians is the "ASEAN Defense Ministers-Plus 8" (ADMM+8). These talks are held among defense ministers (rather than the foreign ministers who meet in the ARF) in July/August each year and have shown notable progress in mutual exercises in search and rescue and humanitarian assistance, as building blocks for understanding and trust.[16]

---

[15]Something dubbed "The Power of &" by Tay in Tay (2010), *op. cit.* See also Kuik Cheng-Chwee, "The Essence of Hedging: Malaysia and Singapore's Response to a Ris-ing China," *Contemporary Southeast Asia: A Journal of International and Strategic Affairs*, 30.2 (2008), pp. 159–185.

[16]Brian Harding, "Don't Underestimate the ADMM+," *PacNet* #65R, August 19, 2013, https://csis.org/files/publication/Pac1365R.pdf.

The members of the Five-Power Defense Arrangements (FPDA)—the UK, Australia, New Zealand, Malaysia and Singapore—have been holding regular joint military exercises since the FPDA was established in 1971. Essentially a series of bilateral defense relationships, the FPDA provides for defense cooperation and for an Integrated Air Defense System for peninsular Malaysia and Singapore. There is otherwise no permanent European military presence in the region except for small French bases in the South Pacific and in the Indian Ocean.[17] This scanty European security presence makes many Asians skeptical of the utility of a greater role for the EU in regional security discussions beyond the ARF, where the EU is already present.

## External Actors in Asian Multilateralism

Within the multilateral structures in Asia, there has been a role for extra-regional actors as well. Asian multilateralism has an inclusive nature that allows for states with different political, economic and cultural backgrounds to work together. The United States and Russia are both members of the EAS, APEC and the ARF, and Russia has recently joined ASEM (in 2010). The EU is a full member in the ARF and ASEM, and has been an active dialogue partner of ASEAN since 1980.

### The United States

Many Asian states—except China, North Korea, and Myanmar—are already closely tied to the United States in a "hub and spokes" system of bilateral military alliances, intense economic relationships and other exchanges. According to Peter Katzenstein, world politics has been built around regions that have been hugely influenced by the post-war American "*imperium.*"[18] Asia—together with Europe—is one of two major *imperiums* underwritten by the United States. Yuen Foong Khong has characterized the U.S.-led order of alliances as a "tributary system"—after the China-centered international relations of ancient times—in which the United States offers its Asian allies military protection as well as economic access to its markets. Since the

---

[17]Paul Stares and Nicolas Régaud, "Europe's Role in Asia-Pacific Security," *Survival* 39.4 (1997), pp. 117–139.

[18]Katzenstein, *op. cit.*

United States never left Asia after it had captured power (from the Spanish in the Philippines in 1898), and it filled or attempted to fill many spaces left by the Europeans after decolonization, the notion of pivot or rebalancing really misses the point. The United States is seen by some as the *sine qua non* hub around which Asian countries are grouped, and as a provider of markets, security and stability. The "tributary system" of the United States is far more effective than China's ever was, because of its overwhelming power.[19]

In recent years, there has been a flurry of activities to build trust and closer cooperation, often with the active participation of the United States, since its "pivot to Asia" strategy was announced in the second year of Obama's presidency. Julianne Smith's chapter in this volume goes into some detail about the economic and long-term strategic imperatives behind this strategic shift, and how it has often been misunderstood as a guise to "contain" China.

The mega-free trade agreement that is the Trans-Pacific Partnership (TPP) has been one of the clearest policy manifestations of the Obama administration's orientation towards Asia. TPP was first mooted by four small Pacific countries (Chile, New Zealand, Singapore and Brunei) in 2005, but it took a significant political turn when the United States joined in 2008, and when Japan joined in 2013.

Security cooperation between the United States and Asia has also taken place, as seen in the U.S.-Japan-India-China-ASEAN disaster relief exercise held in Brunei in June 2013. For the United States at this juncture, the question is whether the "pivot" can be sustained. What role will the TPP play vis-à-vis the other mega-FTAs in Asia, especially the Regional Comprehensive Economic Partnership (RCEP)? What emphasis will the United States give to military ties, whether with traditional allies or with newer partners? And how much of this is divisive for Asian regionalism—if the perception is that these are efforts at containing China? Can the United States balance economic and security ties with a variety of others areas, including climate change and human trafficking?

---

[19]See Khong Yuen Foong, "The American Tributary System," *The Chinese Journal of International Politics*, 6.1 (2013), pp. 1–47.

### The European Union

The United States is seen by most Asian countries as part of the regional infrastructure. This, however, does not hold for the European Union/Europe. But this is a relatively recent, post-1945 development, as European empires (e.g. the Dutch until 1949, the French until 1954) were obviously very present in Asia for centuries before the decolonization period (the British withdrawal over 1947–71). As Rem Korteweg's chapter in this volume indicates, most European scholars and think tanks recognize that Europe (or at least the "Big Three" of France, the UK and Germany) has important economic, political and even military stakes in the continued stability and economic prosperity of Asia.[20]

But there are important normative EU- and national-level dilemmas and institutional constraints that militate against coherent action if Europe is to "pivot" to Asia.[21] With the Asia-Europe Meeting (ASEM), which began with a summit in Bangkok in 1996, and the hope for an ASEAN-EU FTA, channels exist for the EU to utilize. But despite time and goodwill, these have not developed as strongly as might be anticipated and EU interest has sometimes seemed to wane, as with ASEM. It bears re-emphasis to dispel the perception of European crisis and preoccupation with domestic and near-abroad crises in the Middle East and North Africa.[22] New areas of engagement may also be explored where Asian regionalism is still deficient, for instance, in values and community engagement. For ASEAN, besides the FTA for which negotiations have been suspended since 2009, ties with the EU can also be developed on global issues. Now that the ASEAN chairman is being invited to the G20, this is an area where the group could cooperate and learn from EU experience in representing diverse member governments on global issues.

---

[20]Paul Stares and Nicolas Régaud, *op. cit.*, pp. 117–139; Doug Stokes and Richard G. Whitman, "Transatlantic Triage? European and UK 'Grand Strategy' after the US Rebalance to Asia," *International Affairs* 89.5 (2013), pp. 1096.

[21]*Ibid.*, pp. 1087–1107.

[22]Richard G. Whitman and Ana E. Juncos, "The Arab Spring, the Eurozone Crisis and the Neighbourhood: a Region in Flux," *Journal of Common Market Studies Annual Review of the European Union in 2011*, 50 (2012), pp. 147–61.

If the EU does not organize itself better, it will not have any impact on the regional rules and structures taking shape in Asia, nor will the EU be regarded any longer as being important to stakeholders in the region. It is already seen in some Asian capitals as a peripheral player. This is demonstrated, among other indicators, by the increasing lack of interest among Asian students to study Europe, and very low political expectations of what the EU could do in Asia aside from trade and aid.[23]

The present time is an exciting one for strengthening and stream-lining a whole host of recently established regional multilateral insti-tutions in Asia. There is much that the United States and EU can do to contribute to continued economic growth, peace and stability in the region. But they need to do so in close partnership and consultation with the critical actors in Asia, in line with accepted regional norms and dynamics, and at a rate that states and regional organization in East Asia are willing to proceed.

## Recommendations for Deepening Asian Multilateralism

More time is needed for the current key institutions in the region—in particular ARF, ASEAN and EAS—to further develop habits of cooperation. There are promising signs that these habits are develop-ing, even in traditional security areas—such as in ARF disaster relief missions, maritime security cooperation, anti-piracy and counter-terrorism—with useful support from external actors like the United States and the EU. The key is to focus on the substantial relationships and to develop them to be deeper and multi-dimensional. This is a more sustainable path for regionalism than over-focusing on the ques-tion of the institutions and "who's in and who's out." Otherwise, like former Australian Prime Minister Kevin Rudd's failed proposal for an Asia-Pacific community (APc) to be established by 2020, the form can sometimes engender more debate than the substance.

Here are three policy recommendations for advancing deeper and more effective multilateralism in Asia.

---

[23]Reuben Wong, "Still in Deficit: Perceptions of the EU's Capabilities among Foreign Policy Elites in Singapore, Indonesia and Vietnam," *EU External Affairs Review*, 2 (2012), pp. 34–45.

*Focus More on Southeast Asia*

**The United States should continue and develop the Obama administration's "pivot to Asia" strategy to a further stage, with the Trans-Pacific Partnership (TPP) and through efforts to engage the other ASEAN and Asian countries currently outside the TPP, such as South Korea and the Philippines.**

If the EU is to rebalance its resources and attention in Asia, then it needs to focus more on ASEAN, and not fixate so much on China and, to a lesser extent, India as the emerging drivers of the world economy. ASEAN is a region with a population of over 650 million people in 10 economies, which are rapidly developing. To take the example of one member state, Indonesia—the largest ASEAN country—has a huge population of 238 million and a fast-growing economy that is expected to overtake that of Germany, the largest EU member state, by 2030.

The EU has already signed an FTA with Singapore in December 2012. It should conclude FTA negotiations with Thailand, Malaysia and Vietnam. Over time, the EU should seriously explore the possibility of concluding a region-wide FTA between the EU and ASEAN, the negotiations for which were suspended back in 2009. This would complement U.S. efforts in the TPP, and boost the share of EU trade in the region.

Besides trade agreements, the EU should look to increase its contribution to the ASEAN Regional Forum (ARF) and to the Asia-Europe Meeting (ASEM). There is a relative lack of interest and a low level of participation in ASEM especially, on the part of EU leaders. The attendance rate of EU leaders at ASEM summits has not been encouraging, even when they were held in Europe; and no British prime minister has attended the last six ASEM summits.[24]

The EU also has soft power resources that it has used to good effect, for instance in conflict-resolution activities in Aceh, Indonesia, after the 2004 Indian Ocean earthquake and tsunami and in human development activities across developing Asia. These soft power resources could be channeled towards working more closely with the

---

[24]Lai Suet-Yi and Loke Hoe Yeong, "ASEM: Crystal-Gazing Beyond 51 Members," *ASEM Outlook Insights* (Singapore: Asia-Europe Foundation, 2013), p. 6.

United States and Asian partners to build greater human security in the region.

*The United States and the EU should cooperate with Asian partners trilaterally.*

A joint U.S.-EU pivot to the region might be seen as threatening and may not be welcomed by some countries in the region.[25] Instead, the United States and the EU should work on a trilateral cooperation with Asian partners to increase their economic and strategic engagement in the region. ASEAN would be the natural partner for such a trilateral cooperation, just as it has been the natural catalyst for cooperation with Northeast Asian countries under ASEAN+3.

Much of significance that the United States has done over the past 60 years has been in partnership with Europe; their relations with Asia have been the exception to that rule, and that should change. Myanmar is a good example of where U.S.-European cooperation had made a considerable difference. Progress needs to be made on a U.S.-European strategic approach to Asia, though there are roadblocks. There are concerns in Europe about being entangled in a policy of the containment of China. The euro crisis has also deflected interest in this aim, as has the character of the decision-making process within the European External Action Service (EEAS)—the United States did more with Europe in the days of the Quint, a grouping comprising the UK, France, Germany, Italy and the United States.[26]

The United States and Europe could better coordinate aid programs to less affluent Asian countries to maximize the impact of declining aid. They can also better coordinate macroeconomic policies and trade policies with regard to Asia. Europe's experience with institution building should be used as an example in Asia. The transatlantic partners can coordinate cyber policy in dealing with Asia. Of the global warming problem, 90% comes from Asia—particularly China, India and Indonesia, so common transatlantic approaches on these and other emerging issues are important and will be valued.

---

[25]Miguel Otero-Iglesias, "The Geopolitics of the TTIP as Seen from Beijing," *EUSA Review* 26.3 (2013), pp. 7–8.

[26]Catherine Gégout, "The Quint: Acknowledging the Existence of a Big Four—U.S. Directoire at the Heart of the European Union's Foreign Policy Decision-Making Process," *JCMS: Journal of Common Market Studies* 40 (2002), pp. 331–344.

The EU should adopt a more pan-Asian rather than bilateral approach to building relations too, and especially with ASEAN. In this sense, the push led by the United Kingdom to upgrade trade ties with China bilaterally, as advocated by British Prime Minister David Cameron on his high level visit to China in early December 2013, is self-defeating.

### ASEAN is the most acceptable player in Asia, which can engage everyone, but its processes need to be streamlined.

ASEAN has been the key catalyst for processes of regionalism in Asia, as most clearly witnessed in the genesis of ASEAN+3. This is due to its inherent nature as a "non-threatening" organization—the "ASEAN Way" is after all predicated on the non-interference of states in the domestic, "sovereign" affairs of other states. Moreover, countries like China, Japan and South Korea would rather trust ASEAN than each other or an external actor like the United States to be in the driver's seat of Asian regionalism,

However, the Jakarta-based ASEAN Secretariat is short on funding, and the ASEAN member states give it a very short leash. It is thus hard for third parties to take ASEAN seriously as an organization if the ASEAN member states themselves do not entrust or strengthen the Secretariat in relevant areas, such as in giving it a clear mandate to negotiate free trade agreements, or in taking members to task for slowness or failure to implement ASEAN agreements. In this regard, programs to strengthen ASEAN, whether from member states or from third parties, should be encouraged.

The ASEAN Secretariat operates on a very lean budget of some $15 million a year, with a staff of just 260. A much larger amount than that is being furnished by foreign governments, institutes and agencies—some of these are housed in the Secretariat building itself, and many are European (primarily the German *Stiftungen*), or Japanese. In comparison the European Commission is a gargantuan organization with a staff of over 25,000—though this comparison is perhaps unfair given the vastly different type and scale of mandate between the European Commission and the ASEAN Secretariat.[27] The existing

---

[27]See Kavi Chongkittavorn, "ASEAN Secretariat Must Be Empowered," *The Nation*, May 21, 2012, http://www.nationmultimedia.com/opinion/Asean-Secretariat-must-be-empowered-30182419.html (accessed November 25, 2013).

manpower of ASEAN itself reflects the scant regard ASEAN countries accord ASEAN as an active, purposeful organization.

Proposals for growing the ASEAN Secretariat's budget are unlikely to be greeted with enthusiasm, however. A non-paper circulated by Singapore's Ministry of Foreign Affairs to its ASEAN counterparts for discussion in 2013 on the review of ASEAN institutions recognized the need to strengthen the capacity of the ASEAN Secretariat.[28] But it also sought to streamline ASEAN processes, ostensibly to guard against bureaucratic bloat.

In Southeast Asia, crises have provided conditions for considering creative solutions involving forms of governance beyond the traditional "ASEAN Way" of non-interference and sovereignty. ASEAN only *began* considering delegating powers to central institutions— mainly the Secretariat—with the advent of the ASEAN Free Trade Agreement (AFTA) in 1991, although the pace and extent of such delegations has increased over the years with agreements on the Chiang Mai Initiative (1998), trans-boundary haze pollution (2002), the ASEAN Charter (2007) and AICHR (2009).[29] Even legal integration is being discussed now, with a large-scale project involving 80 scholars since 2010, and which is financed by the Attorney General's Chambers of Singapore.[30]

---

[28]Channel NewsAsia, "Singapore Calls for Review of ASEAN's Processes and Institutions," April 11, 2013, http://www.channelnewsasia.com/news/singapore/s-pore-calls-for-review/635584.html; Grace Hai Yien Fu, for the Minister for Foreign Affairs, *Parliamentary Debates (Hansard)*, Singapore, May 13, 2013.

[29]See Tan Hsien-Li, *The ASEAN Intergovernmental Commission on Human Rights: Institutionalising Human Rights in Southeast Asia* (Cambridge: Cambridge University Press, 2011).

[30]"ASEAN Integration through Law: The ASEAN Way in a Comparative Context," Project, Plenary 1: General Architecture of ASEAN, July 4, 2013 (Singapore: Centre for International Law, 2013), pp. 5-6. See also Michael Ewing-Chow and Tan Hsien-Li, "The Role of the Rule of Law in ASEAN Integration," EUI Working papers RSCAS 16, 2013.

# Chapter 6

# Asia's Pivot to the Atlantic: Implications for the United States and Europe

*Daniel S. Hamilton*

As Atlantic powers consider how to pivot together to Asia, they would do well to understand how Asian powers are pivoting to the Atlantic. Transatlantic strategies to address Asia's rise should not focus solely on dynamics in the "Asian Hemisphere," they should also consider the implications of Asia's growing engagement in the "Atlantic Hemisphere"—North and South America, Europe, and Africa.[1]

This chapter looks at Asia's pivot to the Atlantic. It compares and contrasts the diverse motivations driving particular Asian countries to engage in the Atlantic Hemisphere. It explores the impact of these trends on Europe and North America, as well as on their own respective relations with Latin American and African countries; the extent to which North Atlantic partners have shared or differing interests with regard to Asian activities in the Atlantic Hemisphere, and how they should address growing Asian influence. The chapter addresses the economic, energy, security and diplomatic dimensions of these chang-

---

[1]Kishore Mahbubani's assertion that there is an "Asian Hemisphere" means by definition that there is also an Atlantic Hemisphere. Following Mahbubani's assertion and definition, I define the Atlantic Hemisphere as the four continents of the Atlantic—North and South America/Caribbean, Europe, and Africa. This chapter explores the Asian Hemisphere's engagement in the Atlantic Hemisphere, and implications for the United States and Europe, as well as other Atlantic actors. See Kishore Mahbubani, *The New Asian Hemisphere: The Irresistible Shift of Global Power to the East* (New York: PublicAffairs, 2008). Unless otherwise stated, "Asia" refers to all of the region, which according to the aggregated data of the WTO classification includes the following countries: Afghanistan, Australia, Bangladesh, Bhutan, Brunei, Cambodia, China, Fiji, Hong Kong, India, Indonesia, Japan, (South) Korea, Laos, Macao, Malaysia, Maldives, Mongolia, Myanmar, Nepal, New Zealand, Pakistan, Papua New Guinea, Philippines, Samoa, Singapore, the Solomon Islands, Sri Lanka, Taiwan, Thailand, Tonga, Vanuatu and Vietnam.

ing connections, and offers recommendations for U.S. and European decision makers and opinion leaders.

This review underscores that economic considerations are the primary, although not exclusive, drivers behind Asia's engagement in the Atlantic Hemisphere. It also suggests caution and a sense of perspective in the face of breathless talk about Asia's global rise, since Asian engagement in the Atlantic Hemisphere is quite uneven. Some connections are thick, others quite thin. The review also shows that there is no coherent strategy behind Asia's turn to the Atlantic; Asian countries act as much as competitors as partners when it comes to their engagement in the Atlantic Hemisphere. Yet if Asian countries have no coherent South Atlantic policy, neither do the United States or Europe. Asia's Atlantic engagement spotlights issues that the United States and Europe have neglected; areas from which they have withdrawn; and future challenges deserving their attention. Asia's rise is also affecting the Atlantic Hemisphere in a more global context, particularly with regard to worldwide norms and standards that should guide countries as they address contemporary issues. That debate should influence how the United States and its European partners engage South Atlantic countries, as well as those in Asia. The chapter concludes that the United States and Europe should address Asia's rise not only by engaging directly in Asia, but by strengthening the foundations of their own engagement, in the context of pluralism rather than containment or confrontation.

## Atlantic-Pacific Dynamics

The rise of the Pacific is increasingly influencing pan-Atlantic dynamics in a number of ways. First, trade between Atlantic and non-Atlantic markets has boomed. China in particular has become an important trading partner for all Atlantic continents, and China's trade with Africa and Latin America has grown faster than with North America and Europe. Yet the trade of both southern Atlantic continents with most Asian countries, not only China but India, South Korea, Singapore and Malaysia, resembles traditional colonial patterns. For instance, about 90% of Brazilian exports to China consists of commodities, while 90% of Brazilian imports from China consists of manufactured goods. The pattern is similar throughout Africa and

Latin America. South-North Atlantic trade, in contrast, is far more complementary; Brazil's merchandise trade with the United States is evenly balanced between commodities and manufactured goods. Such imbalances in trade with Asia are provoking questions on both southern continents about the value of becoming locked into colonial-style trading relationships at a time when countries on each continent are working to diversify their respective economies, and when both Europe and the U.S. have lost ground in their respective economic ties in the South Atlantic.

Second, booming Atlantic-Pacific sea trade has created new port facilities throughout the Atlantic Basin, especially along its southern shores, and more are coming. The Panama Canal is marking its 100th birthday in 2014 by doubling its capacity, expanding ocean-to-ocean connections and altering global shipping patterns—and China controls the leases at both ends of the Canal. Large new deepwater port facilities are being developed in Santos, Suape, and Açu in Brazil; at Lobito in Angola; and at Walvis Bay in Namibia. Spain's Algeciras and Morocco's massive Tanger-Med complex are growing in importance, and port cities along the Gulf of Mexico and the U.S. east coast are scrambling to revamp their infrastructure to berth megaships coming from and going to the Pacific and other Atlantic destinations.[2]

Third, melting ice in the Arctic Ocean is opening new and shorter shipping routes from East Asia to and from Eastern North America and Europe. The U.S. government estimates that cargo transport via the Northern Sea Route alone will increase from 1.8 million tons in 2010 to 64 million tons by 2020. This is already changing commercial shipping patterns and has boosted both Atlantic and Pacific attention to Arctic issues. In 2012, 46 vessels carried more than 1.2 million tons of cargo through the Northern Sea Route, up 53% compared with 2011. In 2010, only four vessels used the route. Chinese analysts predict that by 2020 up to 15% of China's foreign trade will be transported through the Northern Sea Route. South Korea's Vice Minister for Foreign Affairs has estimated that travel time and distance between the shipping hubs of Busan and Rotterdam will reduced by

---

[2] *A New Atlantic Community: Generating Growth, Human Development and Security in the Atlantic Hemisphere*, by the Eminent Persons of the Atlantic Basin Initiative (Washington, D.C.: Center for Transatlantic Relations, 2014).

about 30%, referring to the new route as the "Silk Road of the Twenty-First Century."[3]

These changing Atlantic-Pacific trade patterns have captured the headlines and the attention of pundits and policymakers, yet they paint only a partial picture, since Asia's presence in the Atlantic Hemisphere is perhaps as significant in terms of its growing foreign direct investment, or FDI. While more Asian FDI flows within Asia than to any individual Atlantic continent, Asian FDI in the Atlantic Hemisphere is actually greater than in the Asian Hemisphere.[4] Asian companies are increasingly seeking resources in South and Central America and Africa, while profiting from open investment regimes in North Atlantic countries.

## Asia's Changing Presence in the North Atlantic

First some perspective. Figure 1 shows that Asia's overall FDI in North America at the end of 2012 of $484 billion was 62% of North America's own cross-border FDI and a quarter of EU FDI in North America. Asian FDI in the EU is about one-fifth of North American FDI in the EU and about 78% of investment from South and Central America., including from offshore Caribbean havens.

Japanese companies are the major source of Asian FDI in North America and Europe. In the 1980s and 1990s Japanese firms boosted

---

[3]Trude Petterson, "China Starts Commercial Use of Northern Sea Route," *Barents Observer*, March 14, 2014; Page Wilson, "Asia Eyes the Arctic," *The Diplomat*, August 26, 2013.

[4]Daniel S. Hamilton and Joseph P. Quinlan, "Commercial Ties in the Atlantic Basin: The Evolving Role of Services and Investment," in *Atlantic Rising: Changing Commercial Dynamics in the Atlantic Basin*, ed. Daniel S. Hamilton (Washington, D.C.: Center for Transatlantic Relations, 2014). The World Bank defines foreign direct investment as the net inflows of investment to acquire a lasting management interest (10 percent or more of voting stock) in an enterprise operating in an economy other than that of the investor. It is "the sum of equity capital, reinvestment of earnings, other long-term capital, and short-term capital as shown in the balance of payments." According to the OECD, "lasting interest" implies "the existence of a long-term relationship between the direct investor and the enterprise and significant degree of influence by the direct investor on the management of the enterprise." See also http://epthinktank.eu/2013/04/25/chinese-investment-in-europe/.

## Figure 1. Foreign Direct Investment: Inward, 2012

(Billions of $)

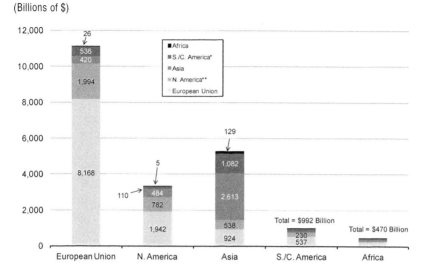

*Includes Caribbean.
**U.S., Canada, Mexico
Source: International Monetary Fund: *Coordinated Direct Investment Survey.*

their investment presence in North Atlantic economies, partially in response to a stronger yen and to sidestep bilateral trade disputes, but also to tap technological know-how and innovation and to access more effectively the large and prosperous markets of the West. While this attracted considerable political attention at the time, such investments have since become almost routine; on the whole Japanese companies are relatively well-integrated into the European and North American economies.

Japanese investments to Europe and the United States subsided for a time, but have surged again in the wake of the financial crisis in the West and as other factors, such as an appreciating yen, a stagnant domestic market and a domestic energy crisis, prompted Japanese companies to again look for investment opportunities abroad.[5]

Many South Korean firms have followed suit, motivated by possibilities to acquire or improve technology and innovation and to posi-

---

[5]McKinsey Global Institute, "A Yen for Global Growth: The Japanese Experience in Cross-Border M&A," August 2012.

tion themselves strategically within NAFTA and the European Single Market.[6] The Korea-U.S. and Korean-EU free trade agreements have further stimulated commercial links between Korea and the two sides of the North Atlantic. North America now attracts about 22% ($54.4 billion), and Europe 17% ($41.4 billion), of overall South Korean global FDI of $242.4 billion.[7]

### Coming to America

Asia's FDI position in the United States, on a historical-cost basis at year-end 2012, totaled $427.7 billion, or 16% of overall FDI in the United States of $2.65 trillion and about 23% of European FDI in the United States of $1.88 trillion.[8] Japan accounted for about 72% of all Asian FDI in the United States. Japanese FDI of about $308 billion was second only to that of the UK ($486.8 billion). Japanese companies continue to invest in the U.S. economy; Softbank Corporation's 2013 acquisition of Sprint Nextel Corporation was the largest Japanese acquisition of a U.S. company in more than 30 years. About 34% of Japan's FDI in the United States is in wholesale trade; Japanese companies account for 79% of Asian FDI in this sector. 30% of Japan's FDI in the U.S. is in manufacturing ($93.4 billion); Japanese companies account for about 76% of Asian FDI in U.S. in this area. Banking and finance accounted for 22% ($66.4 billion) of Japan's FDI in the United States; Japanese FDI accounted for 80% of Asian FDI in the U.S. banking and finance sectors.

Australian companies represent the next largest Asian investors ($42.7 billion) in the United States; their investments are comparable to Swedish investments in America. They are followed by firms from Singapore ($26.2 billion) and South Korea ($24.5 billion), each comparable to Irish investments in America. 60% ($15.8 billion) of Singa-

---

[6]Jung Min Kim and Dong Kee Rhe, "Trends and Determinants of South Korean Outward Foreign Direct Investment," *The Copenhagen Journal of Asian Studies* 27(1) 2009, pp. 126–154; also P. Gammeltoft, "Emerging Multinationals: Outward FDI from the BRICS Countries," *International Journal of Technology and Globalisation* 4(1), 2008, pp. 5–22.

[7]Korean Exim Bank, "Foreign Investments Statistics," http://211.171.208.92/ odisas_eng.html.

[8]Hamilton and Quinlan, *op. cit.*

pore's FDI in the United States is in manufacturing; 69% ($16.9 billion) of South Korea's FDI in the United States is in wholesale trade.[9]

### Asia in Europe

Total Asian FDI in the EU is about one-fifth of North American FDI in the EU of $2 trillion, but it continues to diversify and expand.[10] Japanese foreign direct investment in Europe has grown dramatically over the past few decades, extending into many sectors of the European economy. The stock of Japanese FDI in the European Union totaled €144.2 billion in 2011, about 4% of overall non-EU FDI in the EU, comparable to Canadian FDI in the EU. The main EU country recipients of Japanese FDI are France, Germany, the Netherlands and the United Kingdom. Japanese investment can be significant for some smaller European countries. For example, Japan is second only to Germany as the most important source of foreign direct investment in the Czech Republic, accounting for 16.5% of total foreign direct investment in the country.[11]

Other major Asian sources of FDI in the EU at the end of 2011 included Singapore (€67.3 billion), Hong Kong/China (€63.9/€15.0 billion), Australia (€34.3 billion), and South Korea (€33.1 billion). In 2011, the highest annual growth among these partners was achieved by Hong Kong (54%) and Singapore (12%).[12] Media hype about Chi-

---

[9]Jeffrey H. Lowe, "Direct Investment Positions for 2009–2011: Detailed Historical-Cost Positions and Related Financial and Income Flows," *Survey of Current Business*, September 2012, p. 80; James K. Jackson, "Foreign Direct Investment in the United States: An Economic Analysis," *Congressional Research Service Report*, December 11, 2013.

[10]At the end of 2011, the United States held 35% of total EU inward stocks from the rest of the world. Despite the rise of other markets, Europe continues to account for 56% of U.S. foreign direct investment worldwide. U.S. investment in Europe is nearly four times larger than U.S. investment in all of Asia and 13 times more than U.S. investment in the BRICs. See Hamilton and Quinlan, *op. cit.*; and Daniel S. Hamilton and Joseph P. Quinlan, *The Transatlantic Economy 2014* (Washington, D.C.: Center for Transatlantic Relations, 2014).

[11]Hamilton and Quinlan, *Ibid.*; European Commission; JETRO; Ivan Deseatnicov, *Japanese Outward Foreign Direct Investments: A Study of Determinants and Incentives* (Tokyo: Waseda University, February 2013), p. 44; "Czech Republic is center for Japanese investment in Central Europe," http://www.worldeyereports.com/reports/2014/2014_czechrepublic/2014_czechrepublic01.aspx.

[12]Eurostat.

nese investments need to be kept in perspective; even though China's stocks in the EU grew almost three-fold in 2011, the country was still not among the top ten investors in the EU.

India's presence in the EU is more visible in terms of people than in investment; the largest foreign-born population in the UK is from India. Indian investment in the EU has grown considerably over the past decade, but these amounts are from miniscule levels, and even such rapid growth has barely made a ripple in the EU's overall FDI picture. Nonetheless, while China's outward investment has gone mainly to developing nations and to the natural resource and energy sectors, about two-thirds of India's outward FDI investment has been directed at developed nations, and in such sectors as manufacturing and services.

### China in the North Atlantic

As companies from such Asian countries as Japan, Singapore and South Korea have built out their investment presence on both sides of the North Atlantic, they have elicited episodic concerns in the United States and Europe, but on the whole are relatively well-integrated. Chinese foreign direct investment, in contrast, has more recently become the subject of much greater attention in both Europe and the United States; for some a source of hope, for others a source of anxiety.

Since 2000, China has encouraged its companies to develop operations overseas with preferential long-term government loans in order to "go global." Whereas the first phase of China's "going out" (*zou chuqu*) strategy was to seek opportunities in the field of energy and resources, particularly in Asia, Africa and Latin America, changes in Chinese economic priorities at home and Chinese corporate strategies abroad, together with a stronger Chinese currency, have ushered in a new, second phase of the "going out" strategy, which is more focused than before on developed markets as a means to help Chinese companies move up the value chain, look for opportunities in high and green technologies, tap additional talent and resources, better serve customers in overseas markets, learn the ropes of regulation in advanced economies, and buy into established brand names and business know-how and supply chains. As prominent destinations of this second wave of Chinese investments, North America and Europe can expect to receive a substantial share of the $1-2 trillion in direct investment that

China is expected to place around the world over the coming decade. Signs are that Beijing will liberalize the outward FDI policy environment for its companies at an accelerated pace. [13]

Despite considerable media and political hype, Chinese outward foreign direct investment in the United States and in Europe is still minute, accounting for less than 1% of total FDI stock on either side of the North Atlantic. Nonetheless, it is growing quickly, and in fact Europe has been the fastest growing destination for Chinese investment since 2008. Chinese FDI into Europe and North America in 2010 amounted to nearly 14% of total Chinese FDI flows, compared with just over 2% two years earlier. [14]

Direct investment by Chinese firms in the United States has grown quickly since 2009 and doubled in 2013 to $14 billion, half of which was due to the $7.1 billion takeover of prominent Virginia-based pork producer Smithfield Foods by China's biggest meat producer, Shuanghui International. Prominent commercial real estate deals worth $1.8 billion included the Sheraton Gateway in Los Angeles, the GM building and Chase Manhattan Plaza in New York, and the David Stott and former Free Press buildings in Detroit. China has also targeted natural resources; its largest overseas energy acquisition was the $15.1 billion takeover of Canadian oil and gas producer Nexen by state-owned CNOOC in 2012. Beyond the Nexen deal, Chinese companies have invested an additional $17 billion into other oil and gas deals in the United States and Canada since 2010. Financial services, entertainment and IT services are attracting greater Chinese interest. Chinese acquisition of IBM's personal computers unit; the $2.6 billion acquisition of AMC, the second largest U.S. movie theater chain, by Dalian Wanda; and the announced $4.2 billion takeover of Interna-

---

[13]Daniel H. Rosen and Thilo Hanemann, "China's Reform Era and Outward Investment," Rhodium Group, December 2, 2013; Thilo Hanemann, "Chinese FDI in the United States and Europe: Implications and Opportunities for Transatlantic Cooperation," German Marshall Fund of the United States, June 2011; Thilo Hanemann and Cassie Gao, "Chinese FDI in the US: 2013 Recap and 2014 Outlook," Rhodium Group, January 7, 2014.

[14]"The Second Wave," *The Economist*, October 26, 2013; Ting Xu, Thieß Petersen and Tianlong Wang, "Cash in Hand: Chinese Foreign Direct Investment in the U.S. and Germany, " Bertelsmann Foundation, 2012.

tional Lease Finance Corp (ILFC) are emblematic of the potential for Chinese investment in these and other industries. [15]

These investments are turning into jobs. According to the Rhodium Group, Chinese-owned companies provided more than 70,000 full-time jobs in the United States by the end of 2013, a more than 8-fold increase compared to 2007. Still, that figure represents only about 90% of jobs provided by Spanish companies (85,000) and only 44% of jobs provided by Irish companies (175,000) in the United States.[16]

Chinese investors are encountering a less-than-hospitable environment in the United States. The failed $18.5 billion bid for Unocal by the China National Offshore Oil Cooperation (CNOOC) in 2005 made Chinese investors cautious about U.S. investments, particularly in sensitive infrastructure. The Dubai Ports World controversy in 2006 did not involve China, but it did highlight ongoing U.S concerns about the impact of foreign investment on U.S. national security. An October 2012 U.S. House of Representatives intelligence committee report said U.S. firms should avoid doing business with Chinese telecommunications companies Huawei and ZTE because they posed a national security threat, and the U.S. National Security Agency's clandestine "Shotgiant" operation hacked Huawei servers and monitored communications among executives.[17]

---

[15]Hanemann and Gao, op. cit.; David Wertime, "Hard Target," Foreign Policy, February 27, 2014; Sophie Meunier and Justin Knapp, "Coming to America: Top Ten Factors Driving Chinese Foreign Direct Investment," Huffington Post, July 31, 2012; Thilo Hanemann, "Chinese Investment: Europe vs. the United States," Rhodium Group, February 25, 2013.

[16]Chinese investors are also ramping up community outreach and philanthropic efforts; for example, Dalian Wanda Group, the new owner of the AMC movie theater chain, donated $20 million to the U.S. Academy of Motion Picture Arts & Sciences. See Hanemann and Gao, op.cit.; Hamilton and Quinlan, Transatlantic Economy 2014, op. cit.; Thilo Hanemann, "Chinese FDI in the United States: Q4 2011 Update," The Rhodium Group, 2012; Thilo Hanemann A. & Lysenko, "The Employment Impacts of Chinese Investment in the United States," The Rhodium Group, 2012; T. Moran & L. Oldenski, Foreign Direct Investment in the United States: Benefits, Suspicions, and Risks with Special Attention to FDI from China (Washington, D.C.: Peterson Institute for International Economics, 2013).

[17]David E. Sanger and Nicole Perlroth, "NSA Breached Chinese Servers Seen as Security Threat," New York Times, March 22, 2014, http://www.nytimes.com/2014/03/23/world/asia/nsa-breached-chinese-servers-seen-as-spy-peril.html?partner=rss&emc=rss&smid=tw-nytimes&_r=1.

Although there is some concern among European governments and publics about the security implications of Chinese investments, the overall environment is more hospitable. As a result, Chinese investment trends in Europe are more dynamic than in the United States. Chinese telecommunications equipment firms, for example, have spent more than three times as much in Europe than in the United States.

Although Chinese investment still represents less than 1% of the FDI stock in the EU, it is growing very fast. Annual flows to the EU grew from less than $1 billion annually before 2008 to an average of $3 billion in 2009 and 2010, before tripling again in 2011, reaching flows of $7.8 billion in 2012, and still growing in 2013. According to recent estimates, Europe could receive about a quarter of anticipated Chinese global FDI of $1-2 trillion by 2020.[18]

Over the past number of years, the eurozone crisis and attendant recession has offered Chinese firms an opportunity to purchase advanced manufacturing assets, talent and know-how; modernize technology, and acquire stakes in utilities and transportation infrastructure. Chinese companies have gained footholds in the automotive industry, as exemplified by Geely's acquisition of Volvo, Shanghai Automotive Industry Corporation's purchase of Rover; and China's stake in Saab. Great Wall Motors is setting up local production in Bulgaria and BYD automobiles in Hungary. Chinese companies have made investments and purchases in utilities (e.g. stakes in Portugal's EDP and UK's Thames Water); industrial machinery (e.g. Sany's acquisition of Putzmeister in Germany); information and communication technology (e.g. Huawei in Hungary, China Unicom in the UK); financial services (e.g. ICBC in the UK); and transportation infrastructure projects such as airports (e.g. Germany's Parchim and London's Heathrow), railways (e.g. in Slovenia and Hungary), and ports (e.g. Rijeka in Croatia, as well as Chinese shipping company Cosco's expansion of the port of Naples, Italy and its €3.4 billion long-term lease to run the two main container terminals at Piraeus port outside Athens—one of Europe's largest gateways for Chinese goods). Chinese firms also spent more than $7 billion on firms in the oil and gas industry, including local exploration and production joint ventures

---

[18]Thilo Hanneman, "How Europe Should Respond to Growing Chinese Investment," The Rhodium Group, September 2012; Thilo Hanneman and D.H. Rosen, "China Invests in Europe: Patterns, Impacts and Policy Implications," The Rhodium Group, 2012.

(Sinopec-Talisman), local refining assets (Petrochina-INEOS) and EU-headquartered firms with global upstream assets (Sinopec-Emerald Energy). Sensitive to potential hostility to outright takeovers, Chinese companies have also shifted tack and shown a growing willingness to take minority stakes, which now make up 58% of Chinese deals.[19] Since 2012 Europe has become the top destination for Chinese non-resource deals; by certain estimates 95% of China's new industry and services investment deals have gone to Europe.[20]

While China did not appear as the white knight rescuing fragile European governments who found themselves on the precipice of the European financial crisis, it did offer help at the margins. China purchased $625 million in Spanish debt and has pledged to buy Greek bonds when the government starts selling again. China has provided billions of dollars in state financing for key public works projects in Greece and Italy that support Chinese state-owned companies and Chinese workers, including a $5 billion fund to help finance the purchase of Chinese ships by Greek shipping companies.[21]

---

[19]While sensational deals often grab the headlines, they do not always work out. For example, Europe was shocked when Chinese consortium Covec won a bid to build a stretch of a major highway in Poland in 2009, but little attention was paid when the company pulled out of the deal in 2011, citing soaring costs. See also Central and Eastern Europe Development Institute, *Partners or Rivals? Chinese Investment in Central and Eastern Europe*, 2012; J. Clegg, & H., Voss, *Chinese Overseas Direct Investment in the European Union* (London: Europe China Research and Advice Network, 2012); F. Godement, & J. Parello-Plesner, *The Scramble for Europe* (London: European Council on Foreign Relations, 2011); Thilo Hanemann, "Building a Global Portfolio: What China Owns Abroad," The Rhodium Group, 2012; Hanneman and Rosen 2012, *op. cit.*; Thilo Hanneman, "The EU-China Investment Relationship: From a One-Way to a Two-Way Street," The Rhodium Group, January 28, 2013.

[20]A Capital Dragon Index, 2012.

[21]Irish authorities are trying to parlay their position as a major center for U.S. FDI into a competitive advantage with regard to Chinese investments as well. Officials and business leaders have opened talks with Chinese promoters to develop a 240-hectare industrial park near Athlone, in central Ireland, to create a "Europe China Trading Hub" where Chinese manufacturers could operate inside the EU free of quotas and costly tariffs, and U.S. companies could have easy access to the Chinese market without costly and time-consuming visa applications and travel. Irish Prime Minister Brian Cowen has announced that Ireland could become the "gateway" for Chinese investment into Europe. For more on the Athlone project, see http://www.independent.ie/business/irish/337acre-chinatown-hub-comes-to-athlone-26848974.html.

These investments have also created jobs. Employment numbers generated by Chinese FDI are not available for Europe, but are likely higher than the 70,000 jobs directly supported by Chinese FDI in the United States. Huawei alone employs roughly 7,000 Europeans throughout the EU. Overall these numbers are not high, but in the context of Europe's continued economic turbulence and high unemployment, such investment can be significant at the margin for some countries and some sectors of the economy.

Chinese companies now have investments in all 28 EU member states. Between 2000 and 2011, the older member states known as the EU-15 attracted more than 85% of Chinese FDI. But new EU member states in central and eastern Europe have since become more attractive, in part due to their role in the extended supply chains supplying the EU Single Market, their location as the western gateway for the "Iron Silk Road" rail project being promoted by China,[22] and to Chinese perceptions that the political climate in parts of this region is more conducive to Chinese investments than in western Europe. Moreover, more Chinese FDI in the newer EU member states has been in greenfield investment than in merger and acquisitions, the opposite of the pattern in the EU-15.[23] China has also established a special diplomatic venue for economic and political cooperation with 16 EU and non-EU countries in central and eastern Europe, replete with annual summits, and between 2011 and 2013 pledged $61 billion in investments and loans to the region.[24]

China has singled out EU members Romania and Hungary for special attention. Chinese Premier Li Keqiang pledged $10 billion in investments and loans to Romania at the end of 2013, and in early 2014 he and Hungarian Prime Minister Viktor Orban announced that they had agreed on the financing of a Budapest to Belgrade rail project.[25]

---

[22]See the chapter by Mircea Geoana in this volume.

[23]Central and Eastern Europe Development Institute, *op. cit.*; Sophie Meunier, "Political Impact of Chinese Foreign Direct Investment in the European Union on Transatlantic Relations," Draft Paper for the European Parliament, May 2012.

[24]"Wen Announces $10 Billion Line of Credit," *Deutsche Welle*, April 26, 2012; "The Bucharest Guidelines for Cooperation between China and Central and Eastern European Countries," http://gov.ro/en/news/the-bucharest-guidelines-for-cooperation-between-china-and-central-and-eastern-european-countries.

[25]James Kynge, "Ukraine a Setback in China's Eastern Europe Strategy," *Financial*

China has also paid particular attention to Ukraine, having forged a "strategic partnership" that included Ukrainian engine production for Chinese fighter jets and Beijing granting Kyiv access to $3 billion in loans to irrigate its southern farmlands in return for annual exports of about 3 million tons of corn to China. Although Beijing has employed similar loans-for-oil deals with other countries, the arrangement with the Ukraine was a first for China. Keen on meeting surging food demand at home, and now having relaxed its previous policies stressing self-sufficiency in grain, China is closely eyeing the rich agricultural potential of Ukraine, one of the world's leading grain exporters, and is interested in directly leasing Ukrainian farmland or enticing local producers into loan-for-crop deals. Russia's 2014 annexation of Crimea, however, crippled a $3 billion agreement with Chinese entrepreneur Wang Jing for the first phase of a deep water port construction project there, and the change of government in Kyiv called into question another $8 billion in Chinese investments promised to now-deposed Ukrainian President Viktor Yanukovych at the end of 2013.[26]

### Asia as Creditor

China's investment mix in the United States and Europe differs in one other aspect. In the United States, Chinese FDI has come under considerable scrutiny, yet China has invested massively in U.S. bonds and in fact is America's largest foreign creditor. In Europe the situation is reversed; China has generally eschewed European sovereign debt purchases in favor of investments in tangible assets.

In terms of portfolio assets, Figure 2 shows that as of 2012, the EU held triple the value of North American portfolio assets than North Americans held of each other's assets in 2001, and about double in 2012. Asia's share was roughly equal to North America's own share in

---

*Times*, February 27, 2014, http://blogs.ft.com/beyond-brics/2014/02/27/ukraine-a-set-back-in-chinas-eastern-europe-strategy/?#axzz2wpPv1aJy.

[26]Kynge, *Ibid.*; Kateryna Choursina, "Ukraine close to $3 billion China loan for irrigation project," *Bloomberg*, October 1, 2013, http://www.bloomberg.com/news/2013-10-01/ukraine-close-to-3-billion-china-loan-for-irrigation-project.html; "China Looks to Ukraine as Demand for Food Rises," *Financial Times*, November 5, 2013, http://www.ft.com/intl/cms/s/0/a9c0db18-4554-11e3-b98b-00144feabdc0.html?siteedition=intl#axzz2wpQpOePY.

**Figure 2. Regional Composition of North American Portfolio Assets, 2012***

(Billions of $)

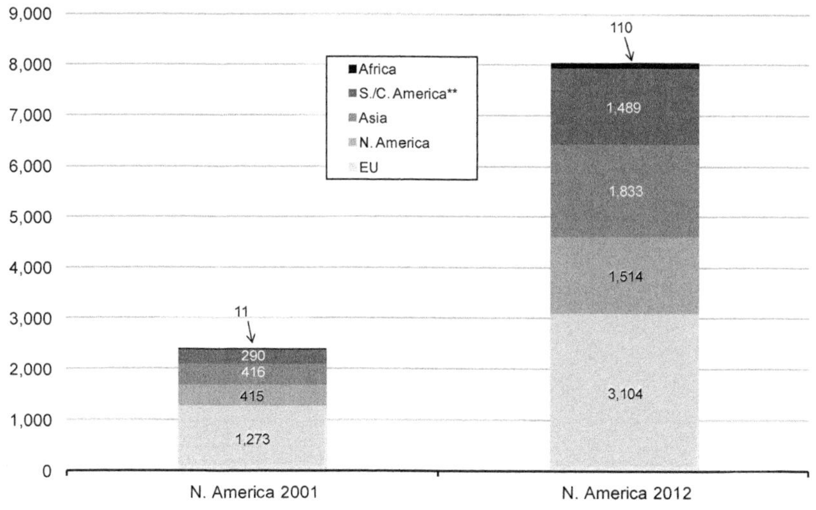

*U.S., Canada, Mexico
**Includes Caribbean.
Source: International Monetary Fund: *Coordinated Direct Investment Survey.*

2001; by 2012 Asia's share had grown relative to North America's share, but still less than the EU's share.

The U.S. is considerably dependent on Asian creditors, particularly China and Japan. As America's debt burden soared in the wake of the financial crisis and wars in Iraq and Afghanistan, China and Japan became the second and third largest owners of U.S. Treasuries after only the Federal Reserve. Together they account for over 42% of the $5.8 trillion in U.S. Treasuries held by overseas investors (China $1.3 trillion; Japan $1.2 trillion in January 2014). Their holdings are dropping toward the lowest level in a decade; however, as U.S. investors have shown greater willingness to finance a greater share of America's $12 in marketable debt securities. In the past two years, Japan has added fewer Treasuries on a percentage basis than at any time since 2007, and China has slowed its accumulation to about 3.1% annually since 2010. That compares with an average yearly increase of 34% over the previous decade. The reduction in buying is one signal that

**Figure 3. Regional Composition of EU Portfolio Assets, 2012**

(Billions of $)

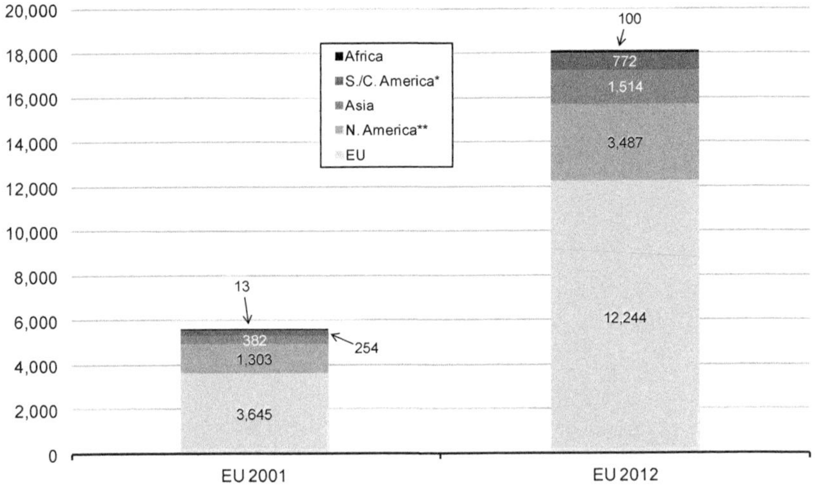

*U.S., Canada, Mexico
**Includes Caribbean.
Source: International Monetary Fund: *Coordinated Direct Investment Survey.*

the People's Bank of China believes it is no longer in Chinese interest to accumulate such massive foreign exchange reserves, estimated at $3.8 trillion, more than triple those of any other nation and bigger than Germany's gross domestic product.[27]

Figure 3 indicates that EU portfolio holders account for about two-thirds of portfolio assets within the EU. North America accounted for $3.487 trillion, about 2.3 times Asia's holdings of $1.514 trillion in the EU in 2012, but Asia's relative share is growing, as in 2001 North America had accounted for 3.4 times as much as Asian holdings.

---

[27]http://finance.yahoo.com/news/foreign-demand-u-treasuries-slides-152103025.html;_ylt=A0LEVwkzGDBThAMAgYBXNyoA;_ylu=X3oDMTB0Yjkwb3 VoBHNlYwNzYwRjb2xvA2JmMQR2dGlkA1ZJUDM3MF8x; Daniel Kruger, "Foreign Grip on Treasuries loosens as U.S. Investors Buy," *Bloomberg*, March 24, 2014, http://www.bloomberg.com/news/2014-03-23/foreign-grip-loosens-on-treasuries-as-u-s-buyers-bolster-demand.html.

China's portfolio mix in Europe is far more modest than in the United States. Estimates are that China holds €5.6 billion in the European rescue fund known as the European Financial Stability Fund (EFSF), and that across European countries overall China holds up to 7% of Europe's debt. China's reticence reflects its relative risk aversion in light of the eurozone crisis and Europe's recent economic volatility.[28]

## Asia in Africa

Asian countries have substantially bolstered their presence in Africa in recent years. Asian actors share some common interests in the development of commercial, energy and resource opportunities, but the nature and depth of their respective interests differ, the depth of their engagement varies, and some compete with each other, as well as with Western and indigenous players, economically, politically and even militarily across the continent and its adjoining waters.[29]

Asian investments in Africa, particularly from China, have been the subject of considerable attention in recent years. Despite these growing numbers, one must be careful to compare. As is clear from Figure 1, the EU is the largest source of FDI in Africa, accounting for twice Asian FDI in Africa. Asian FDI, however, was 2.3 times North American FDI in Africa. In fact, South and Central American FDI in Africa is approaching the levels invested by North America in Africa—a sign of diminished U.S. attention to the African continent. Africa, however, remains reliant on foreign investment—the EU, Asia and North America all invested more in Africa than African companies invested in Africa.

Asia's rise in Africa is more apparent if one looks at portfolio assets. As Figure 5 indicates, Asia and the EU were roughly equal as portfolio asset holders in Africa, each accounting for roughly 3 times more assets than North America held in Africa. The trend is quite striking.

---

[28]Parello-Plesner 2012, *op. cit.*; Hamilton and Quinlan, *The Transatlantic Economy 2014*, *op.cit.*

[29]Adriana Erthal Abdenur and Danilo Marcondes de Souza Neto, "La creciente influencia de China en el Atlantico Sur," *Revista CIDOB d'Afers Internacionals*, No. 102–103, 2013, pp. 169–197.

**Figure 4. South/Central America and Foreign Direct Investment: Inward, 2012**

(Billions of $)

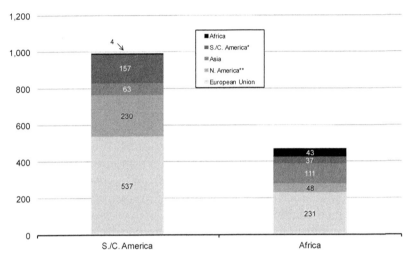

*Includes Caribbean.
**U.S., Canada, Mexico
Source: International Monetary Fund: *Coordinated Direct Investment Survey.*

Whereas in 2001 Asian portfolio assets in Africa were practically non-existent, they have risen dramatically. EU portfolio assets in Africa also rose 4 times in this period, but in 2001 the EU accounted for the vast majority of African portfolio assets; now its share is roughly equal to that of Asia. South and Central American portfolio assets in Africa have also grown to about half of North American assets held in Africa.[30] In sum, between 2001 and 2012 the EU's share of total portfolio assets in Africa fell from 71.8% to 40.7%, and North America's share fell from 15.8% to 11.4%.

*Japan in Africa*

As other Asian countries step up their engagement in Africa, Japan has been scaling back. Formerly the world's top donor to developing countries, Japan now ranks fifth. In 2013 Tokyo pledged to Africa $32

---

[30]This includes money flowing from Caribbean havens, and so could originally be from Asian, U.S., European or other sources.

## Figure 5. Regional Composition of South/Central America and Africa Portfolio Assets, 2012

(Billions of $)

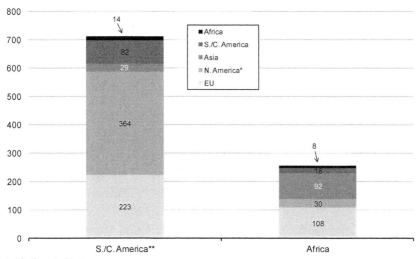

*U.S., Canada, Mexico
**Includes Caribbean.
Source: International Monetary Fund: *Coordinated Direct Investment Survey.*

billion in public and private funding, including $14 billion in official development assistance and $6.5 billion to support build infrastructure projects. Africa's share of Japan's official development assistance has increased, but the absolute amounts going to Africa have declined, and Japanese foreign aid is still tied to spending with Japanese companies or other Japanese organizations. Japan's trade with Africa in 2012 of $25 billion was only about 40% of India's trade with Africa, and its rather paltry FDI in Africa of $460 million in 2011 was only about 14% of China's $3.17 billion—and the gap is likely to widen further. Tokyo has declared its intent to is buy rare earths in Africa to end its dependence on China, the world's leading supplier of these minerals, yet has done relatively little to develop such industries.[31] Japan had been courting Africa in the last couple of decades as part of Japan's

---

[31]JETRO; Javier Blas, "Abe Leads Fresh Push for Africa Riches," *Financial Times*, January 13, 2014; "Japan Competing with China for Asia Trade," *Asia News*, May 31, 2013, http://www.asianews.it/news-en/Japan-competing-with-China-for-Africa-trade-28073.html.

effort to become a permanent member of the United Nations Security Council. But as the impetus towards its bid has faded in recent years, so too has Japanese engagement.

### South Korea in Africa

South Korea is also primarily interested in Africa's resources, although it does seek African support within UN and other international bodies. Africa is still a marginal economic partner for South Korea, accounting for only 2% of total Korean FDI and 1.85% percent of Korea's total trade in 2011. As with most other Asian economies, the foundation of Korea's commercial engagement with Africa is to access commodities, especially crude oil, in exchange for manufactured products. Seoul has also sought to promote the Korean model of state intervention as a guide to promote rapid and sustained economic development among African economies. It has focused on capacity-building in Africa's agricultural sector modeled on *Saemaul Undong*, an agricultural movement in South Korea initiated by the South Korean government in the 1970s, which eventually led to the eradication of rural poverty in South Korea; joined with 15 African states to advance a three-year 'Green Growth Initiative' emphasizing low-carbon growth, and has pledged to boost development aid to Africa to $1 billion.[32]

### India in Africa

There is a long history of Indian communities in parts of Africa and the large Indian diaspora in countries like Kenya, Tanzania and Mauritius has facilitated closer economic relations. India has a common colonial experience with many African countries and has long ties with those that are members of the British Commonwealth. Indian energy and economic interests in Africa are substantial. India's annual trade with Africa jumped from $3 billion in 2000 to about $64 billion today, and is expected to exceed $90 billion by 2015. This is less than a third of Sino-African trade, but with similar growth rates, and India now

---

[32]Forty Korean investments in Africa have so far been limited to a few sectors dominated by mining sector, and with over half in Madagascar. See also Soyeun Kim, "Korea in Africa: A Missing Piece of the Puzzle?" http://www.lse.ac.uk/IDEAS/publications/reports/pdf/SR016/SR-016-Kim.pdf.

ranks as Africa's fourth largest trade partner, after the EU, China and the United States. India's dependency on foreign oil, which stood at around 75% in 2010 and is projected to rise to 90% by 2025, compels the country both to diversify its sources from the volatile Middle East and to seek new energy sources, including in Africa. India now gets a fifth of its energy imports from Africa, particularly Nigeria. India's mainly imports commodities, particularly oil, from Africa, whereas over two-thirds of its exports consist of manufactured goods such as pharmaceuticals, machinery and transport equipment.[33]

This pattern has drawn criticism that India, like China, is engaged in "neo-colonial" relationships with some African countries, even as it has been a leader in the fight against colonialism. Yet in contrast to China's model of state-led, investment-driven growth and "non-inter-ference" in internal affairs, India's model is based on support for democratic governments, private sector-driven investment, and consumer-driven growth. Indian companies also tend to hire local laborers for their projects in Africa, while many Chinese companies import Chinese laborers.

Indian investment in Africa has increased markedly in recent years, especially in agriculture, energy, infrastructure, telecoms and mining, exceeding $35 billion in 2011. Throughout the first decade of the new century roughly two-thirds of India's African investments flowed to Mauritius, a critical offshore financial center for Indian firms. The stock of Indian FDI in Mauritius is estimated in excess of 20% of the country's GDP, helping it to emerge as one of the strongest in sub-Saharan Africa.[34]

India, like China, has instituted a duty-free tariff preference scheme for exports from poorer African countries, and has offered soft loans—but it does not attach conditions as China does. Africa is the largest regional recipient of India's Exim Bank's total line of credits. In part because India is unable to match Chinese aid levels, it has focused

---

[33]Joseph P. Quinlan, "Growing Economic Linkages with Latin America and Africa: Key Drivers and Trends," in *China and India: New Actors in the Southern Atlantic*, Emiliano Alessandri et. al. (Washington, D.C.: German Marshall Fund of the United States, December 2012).

[34]Sudha Ramachandran, "India's African 'Safari,'" *The Diplomat*, December 2012; Quinlan, *op. cit.*

instead on capacity building in Africa. It is setting up scores of institutions in areas as diverse as food processing, agriculture, textiles, weather forecasting and rural development, and helping to build a pan-African e-network linking schools and hospitals across Africa with institutions in India.[35]

Like other Asian countries, India seeks African support in international forums, especially for its aspiration to become a permanent member of the UN Security Council. It has 26 embassies in Africa; China has 49. It has engaged in periodic India-Africa summits, as well as in different forms of regionalism, of which the BRICS framework is today perhaps the most prominent, although India, Brazil and South Africa created in 2004 the India-Brazil-South Africa (IBSA) Dialogue, which includes regular summits among the leaders of these significant democracies. As India engages more extensively with Africa and other continents, internal debates are raging about the country's foreign policy priorities, with some strongly focused on economic and security needs, others who favor the ideology of a Global South, and those who emphasize coordination with other democracies, across the South but also with North America and Europe.[36]

As the third largest contributor of UN peacekeepers in the world, India has a long history of UN peacekeeping in Africa. Current UN Indian deployments include the United Nations Operation in Côte d'Ivoire, the UN Mission in South Sudan and the UN Organization Stabilization Mission in the Democratic Republic of Congo. It has supported the African Union Mission in Somalia and the African-led International Support Mission to Mali. The Indian navy has also contributed to anti-piracy operations in the Gulf of Aden since 2008. With an eye to Chinese naval activities in the Indian Ocean, India has developed close security relationships with Africa's Indian Ocean islands and several African countries bordering the Indian Ocean, including Mauritius, the Seychelles, Madagascar, Tanzania, Mozambique and especially South Africa.

---

[35]Ramachandran, *op. cit.*; Daniel Large, "India's African Engagement," London School of Economics, http://www.lse.ac.uk/IDEAS/publications/reports/pdf/SR016/SR-016-Large.pdf.

[36]Dhruva Jaishankar, "India in the Southern Atlantic: An Overview," and Emiliano Alessandri and Dhruva Jaishankar, "Introduction: New Players in the Atlantic Basin," in Alessandri et. al, *op. cit*;

## Malaysia in Africa

For all of the hype regarding China's activities in Africa, according to UNCTAD Malaysia had more cumulative FDI stock in Africa than did China at the end of 2011.[37] Malaysia was the third biggest investor in Africa behind France and the United States, pushing China and India into fourth and fifth positions. France and the United States also lead in terms of historical stock of investments in Africa, with Britain in third place and Malaysia in fourth, followed by South Africa, China and India. While official FDI figures significantly underestimate actual Chinese investment for a number of reasons,[38] Malaysian investment in Africa is considerable. Malaysia's portfolio of global FDI increased by more than five times over the past decade to reach $106 billion by the end of 2011. Of that, $19.3 billion was in Africa, which is equivalent to 24% of its total FDI. Trade between Africa and Malaysia has grown steadily at 22% per year in the past decade. The countries with the largest record of Malaysian investments are South Africa, Kenya and Nigeria. Malaysia has invested in agribusiness mostly in East and West Africa, but like India has focused its finance FDI on Mauritius.[39]

---

[37]Global Investment Monitor, "The Rise of BRICS FDI and Africa," UNCTAD, March 25, 2013.

[38]According to David Shinn, "The official FDI figure for China in Africa significantly understates the actual amount for a variety of reasons. 1. It only represents FDI that is officially reported to the government of China. Some private Chinese investors do not report FDI flows. China's official numbers miss FDI that passes through Hong Kong, the Cayman Islands and the British Virgin Islands and goes to many countries, including some in Africa. 2. Chinese FDI statistics do not include investment in the financial sector. For example, China's $5.5 billion purchase of 20% of Standard Bank of South Africa is presumably not reflected in the cumulative figures for FDI to Africa. 3. China has also made several large investments in companies located in countries outside Africa that have significant holdings in Africa. These investments would not appear in the cumulative figure for Africa." http://davidshinn.blogspot.com/2013/03/foreign-direct-investment-in-africa.html

[39]"Malaysia, Not China, is Asia's Top Investor in Africa," *Reuters*, March 25, 2013, http://www.reuters.com/article/2013/03/25/malaysia-africa-idUSL5N0CH2QY 20130325; http://www.trademarksa.org/news/huge-investment-potential-malaysian-companies-resource-rich-africa; "In Africa, Malysia Now Top Developing Country Investor," *Malay Mail Online*, June 27, 2013, http://www.themalaymailonline.com/malaysia/article/in-africa-malaysia-now-top-developing-country-investor.

### Dubai and Mauritius as Hubs for Asian Capital in Africa

Dubai and Mauritius have become key operational hubs for foreign businesses expanding their operations across Africa. In 2013, Dubai's trade with Africa was worth $30 billion, and outward FDI from Dubai to Africa in the past 10 years was worth $56 billion, much of it from Asian sources. $8 billion flowed into continental Africa from Mauritius, which continues to be among the most competitive, stable, and successful African economies. According to the World Bank, Mauritius is one of the world's most open economies to foreign ownership and one of the highest recipients of FDI per head of population. Its financial services sector accounts for 13% of the country's GDP. Money is also flowing the other way; Mauritius ranks among the top 10 largest sources of FDI into China.[40]

### China in Africa

Foreign direct investment plays a key role in Beijing's "going out" strategy to secure strategic assets and natural resources to support China's transformation. China's hunger for global commodities has been stunning. It is now the second largest consumer of oil after the United States, and presently consumes 25% of the world's soybeans, 20% of the world's corn and 16% of the world's wheat. The mainland also accounts for nearly 25% of world rubber consumption. Name the commodity and there is a good chance China is among the largest consumers in the world.[41]

Nowhere is China's explosive growth more visible than in Africa, whether measured in terms of trade, investment, or Chinese workers building railways, roads and other African infrastructure. There are now around 1 million Chinese people in Africa, a figure which has grown from 100,000 early in the last decade.

In Africa, China is seeking to procure natural resources and agricultural products; expand and diversify its exports; and enlist the support of African countries for Chinese foreign policy priorities.

---

[40]Malcolm Moller and Anjana Ramburuth, "Mauritius Positioned to Cash in on China-Africa FDI," *FDI Intelligence*, August 14, 2013; *Financial Times*, August 2013.

[41]Quinlan, *op. cit.*; Hamilton and Quinlan, "Commercial Ties..." *op. cit.*

Africa accounts for about one-third of China's overall oil imports, and about 85% of Africa's exports to China comes from the oil-rich countries of Angola, Equatorial Guinea, Nigeria, the Democratic Republic of Congo and Sudan. Africa also provides China with 30% of its tobacco, 25% of its pearls and precious metals, 20% of its cocoa, 10% of its ores, and 5% of its iron and steel. China has also become the world's top consumer of fish, and Chinese fishing companies now regularly ply the waters of the South Atlantic. China is helping West African countries conduct "frontier exploration" in the Gulf of Guinea and has committed billions to upgrade Africa's rail network and information technology infrastructure to the benefit of ZTE and Huawei. Beijing has offered bundled aid packages, development loans and other preferential financing arrangements to facilitate the flow of resources back to China. Chinese imports from Africa, which tallied just $5.4 billion in 2000, exceeded $105 billion in 2012.[42]

Chinese companies are also seeking to take advantage of Africa's fast-growing markets. Despite many challenges, on several indicators Africa is better positioned than the Asian Tigers before their explosive growth in the 1980s and 1990s, according to Credit Suisse and the IMF. China's exports to Africa soared from just $4.2 billion in 2000 to nearly $75 billion in 2012. South Africa, Nigeria and Egypt ranked as the three largest African export markets for China; South Africa alone accounted for nearly one-fifth of total exports. China has borrowed a page from its own economic development by establishing and planning numerous special economic zones in several African nations. Just as the establishment of such zones in China helped fuel export-led growth and kick start the industrialization of the mainland beginning in the late 1970s, the same effect is expected in such African nations as Ethiopia, Mauritius, Nigeria, and Zambia. The Forum on China-Africa Cooperation (FOCAC), launched in October 2000, has provided an

---

[42]See also Christopher Alessi and Stephanie Hanson, "Expanding China-Africa Oil Ties," Council on Foreign Relations, February 8, 2012, http://www.cfr.org/china/expanding-china-africa-oil-ties/p9557; Alessandri, et. al, *op. cit.*; Shelley Zhao, "The China-Angola Partnership: A Case Study of China's Oil Relations in Africa," *China Briefing Magazine*, May 25, 2011.

additional framework for cooperation extending to food security, health care, training and student scholarships.[43]

China now ranks as Africa's largest trading partner; total trade hit $198.5 billion in 2012. By comparison, U.S.-Africa trade volume was $108.9 billon. Research from Standard Chartered estimates that trade between China and Africa will hit $385 billion by 2015 The stock of outward Chinese FDI to Africa has also soared, from $491 million in 2003 to over $21.7 billion in 2012, more than a twenty-five fold increase. About 10 percent of China's new FDI has been flowing to Africa. The main recipients are South Africa, Nigeria, Zambia, Algeria, DRC and Sudan.[44]

Overall, Africans have embraced China's economic surge. Yet feelings of resentment are also growing, fed by shoddy construction, environmental damage and predatory practices, and there is concern that Africa could be locked into a commodities-for-manufacturing pattern in its economic ties to China. More countries are reviewing contracts with a critical eye, and some governments have raised their concerns in public. Nigeria's central bank governor has criticized the Chinese for exuding "a whiff of colonialism," and South African president Jacob Zuma, who has long cultivated Chinese contacts, has warned that the unbalanced nature of Africa's burgeoning trade ties with china is "unsustainable" in the long term.[45]

Africa's 54 countries constitute well over one-quarter of UN members. The continent has three non-permanent seats on the UN Security Council and is well represented in many international organizations, including the World Trade Organization. Beijing seeks to cultivate African countries, both bilaterally and in international

---

[43]Deborah Brautigam, "Africa's Eastern Promise: What the West Can Learn From Chinese Investment in Africa," *Foreign Affairs*, January 5, 2010; Quinlan, *op. cit.*

[44]Keith Proctor, "China and Africa What the U.S. Doesn't Understand," *CNN Money*, July 2, 2013, http://management.fortune.cnn.com/2013/07/02/china-africa-us; Hamilton and Quinlan, "Commercial..." *op. cit.*

[45]Dambisa Moyo, "Beijing, A Boom For Africa," *The New York Times*, June 28, 2012, p. A27; http://www.thisisafricaonline.com/Policy/China-Africa-engagement-Has-it-peaked? ct=true; "More than minerals," *The Economist*, March 23, 2013, http://www.economist.com/ news/middle-east-and-africa/21574012-chinese-trade-africa-keeps-growing-fears-neo-colonialism-are-overdone-more/print.

forums, to support Chinese foreign policy priorities. Other Asian—and Western—countries, of course, do the same. In China's case, priority issues include Tibet, Taiwan and human rights. China has deployed about 3,000 peacekeepers under UN missions in Africa, joined international anti-piracy efforts off of East Africa, and displaced Russia as the largest supplier of arms to sub-Saharan Africa.[46]

China has been a staunch defender of the principle of non-interference in political affairs, yet it has also sought to advance its model of authoritarian capitalism as an alternative to Western models. There are internal debates in Beijing about the relative importance of each approach. As China engages more deeply in Africa, the policy of non-interference has become challenging, given the temptation to favor certain domestic actors promising advantageous resource deals, or dilemmas caused by the divisions and tragedies generated by conflict in some African states. And as some of Africa's "strongmen" have left the scene, Beijing now faces a new generation of African leaders, some of whom are influenced more by notions of democratic accountability and the rule of law, and who may regard China's "non-interference" policy with caution.[47]

## Asia's Evolving Presence in Latin America and the Caribbean

Asia's rise has been an important factor prompting the leaders of Colombia, Peru, Chile, Costa Rica, Mexico, and possibly soon Panama, to form the Pacific Alliance, an initiative committed to build down barriers to the movement of goods, capital and people among member countries. The Pacific Alliance seeks economic integration oriented toward Asia-Pacific markets, and could become a platform for other Latin American nations with a Pacific shore to join the Trans-Pacific Partnership (TPP).[48] Being part of the Pacific Alliance is potentially significant, because a country like Costa Rica might other-

---

[46]Abdenur, *op. cit.*; Proctor, *op. cit.*; Brautigam, *op. cit.*; Taiwan now has diplomatic relations with only four African countries: Swaziland, Burkina Faso, Gambia and São Tomé and Principe.

[47]"China's Image Problem in Africa," *The Diplomat*, October 25, 2012, http://thediplomat.com/2012/10/non-interference-a-double-edged-sword-for-china-in-africa/2/.

[48]http://www.worldpolicy.org/blog/2013/06/24/us-and-china-fight-latin-america.

wise be an unlikely candidate for the TPP. But the Pacific Alliance's focus on economic integration also draws a page from the experiences of the European Union and NAFTA.

Asian investment, especially from China, has been far larger in Africa than in Latin America and the Caribbean (LAC). In 2012 Asian FDI in the region was less than half Asian FDI in Africa, although for countries like Japan and South Korea, LAC is a more important FDI destination than Africa. Like Africa, LAC countries have become more important to Asia as both as a source of raw materials and a new market for manufactured goods. And as with Africa, the underlying question is whether and how Asian and LAC countries might build out their relationships in ways that go beyond such basic commodities-for-manufacturing arrangements.

Moreover, as with Africa, headlines about rising Asian investments in this region must be put in perspective. In terms of portfolio investments, North America increased its portfolio holdings in South and Central America four-fold between 2001 and 2011, accounting for over half of the region's assets. As Figure 5 makes clear, the EU was the only other major asset holder. The region's own holdings are modest, and both Asia and Africa are non-players.

The story with regard to foreign direct investment is shown in Figure 4. The EU is the largest source of FDI in South and Central America. EU FDI in South and Central America of $537 billion in 2012 was 2.3 times the level of North American investment in the region ($230 billion), 3.4 times greater than South and Central American FDI flows within the region itself, and 8.5 times greater than Asian FDI flows to South and Central America. The eurozone accounts for 40% of all FDI in Latin America, the EU is the biggest foreign investor in Brazil, and São Paulo hosts the largest concentration of German corporate investment outside Germany.

Despite all the hype about China, Figure 6 shows that Japan is actually the leading Asian investor in the region, with $26.5 billion, and South Korean investments of $5.1 billion were almost 3 times more than Chinese investment in the region of $1.8 billion.[49]

---

[49] *The Economist*, October 26, 2013.

*Japan and LAC*

Ties between Japan and the region have diversified from an initial focus on minerals and agriculture to encompass a broad panorama of trade, direct investment, and government-to-government cooperation that has shaped the development of sectors from automobiles and alternative energies to computer software and natural disaster preparedness, while helping to launch some key LAC export sectors. Trade between Japan and the region reached nearly $65 billion in 2012. During this most recent period, bilateral trade grew at an annual average of 13%, a growth rate that puts LAC-Japan trade below the region's total trade growth (14%) and well short of its dynamic trade with China (32%), but still ahead of mature markets such as the United States (9%) and European Union (12%). LAC exports to Japan were the most dynamic component of trade, growing at an average of 18% each year versus 11% growth for LAC imports from Japan. Japan's share of LAC's total trade is only 3%, having declined from around 7% in 1990. Likewise, LAC accounts for less than 5% of Japan's overall trade, a figure that has not changed considerably over the past two decades.[50]

Seen in isolation, Japan's trade patterns resemble the same commodities-for-manufacturing exchange that has characterized the region's overall trade boom with Asia. Yet trade numbers tell only a small part of the Japan-LAC story. As Figure 6 indicates, Japan is by far the biggest Asian investor and in fact one of the most important overall sources of FDI for the region. What's more, its FDI is spread nearly equally across the primary, manufacturing, and services sectors. Even though initial Japanese investment in LAC was driven by the search for natural resources, Japan's FDI has diversified and grown, and in recent years Japan has accounted for 5-6% of LAC's annual FDI inflows between 2008 and 2012—and in some countries as much as 10%. LAC's share of Japan's total outward FDI stock averaged 6.9% a year from 2010 to 2012, up from 3% percent in 2005.[51] This stands in sharp contrast to FDI from China, which, in addition to

---

[50]Inter-American Development Bank, *Japan and Latin America and the Caribbean: Building a Sustainable Trans-Pacific Relationship*, November 2013.

[51]*Ibid;* In the 1960s Latin America absorbed a quarter of Japanese FDI.

**Figure 6. Asian FDI in Latin America and the Caribbean**

(Billions of $)

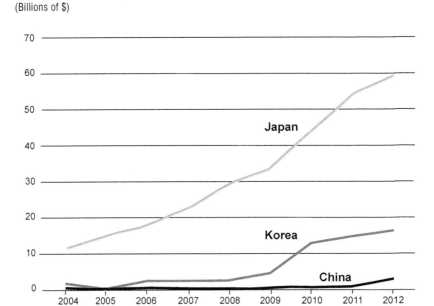

*Data for China's outward investment in LAC for 2012 is a projection.
Source: Japan JETRO, Korea ExIm Bank, and China Ministry of Commerce; Totals do not include tax havens.

being much smaller in absolute terms, appears to be heavily concentrated in the primary sector.

In many cases, Japanese firms have become major exporters from their LAC production bases, highlighting how the economic relationship is deeper and more diversified than indicated by simple bilateral trade flows. Japanese exports are less likely to be in direct competition with LAC exporters, given Japan's export profile, which is weighted more towards high-technology, capital intensive products. This stands in contrast to Chinese exports, which often pose a direct competitive threat for LAC exporters, especially in destinations such as the United States. Japanese technical assistance was critical in transforming Brazil's *cerrado* region into the country's agricultural heartland, whose production places Brazil among the world's leaders in exports of soybeans, maize and other grains. Japanese technical assistance and financing also helped develop Chile's competitive salmon industry.[52]

Strong consumption growth among LAC's burgeoning middle classes has attracted Japanese companies. Japan's free trade agreements with Mexico (2005), Chile (2007), and Peru (2012) have not only reduced tariffs and other trade barriers but have also encouraged direct investment and established mechanisms for governmental cooperation on a broad array of policy issues, although significant barriers on certain tariff lines remain. These countries are also all involved in the Trans-Pacific Partnership negotiations; a comprehensive TPP agreement would ideally harmonize the rules of origin and other regulations in these bilateral agreements as well as deepen liberalization in the sectors where barriers remain.

The Japan Bank for International Cooperation's LAC portfolio of nearly $500 million supports rural economic infrastructure, environmental protection and natural disaster mitigation. Its loan and equity financing to LAC has reached nearly $200 billion. The Japanese government has also worked with LAC countries to advance cooperation in areas such as environmental management, health, renewable energy, and infrastructure. Japan has a long history of engagement in the region and strong cultural ties through the presence of Japanese communities in Brazil, Peru, Paraguay, and elsewhere. Sao Paulo alone is home to the largest Japanese population outside of Japan.[53]

### South Korea and LAC

South Korea has also been strengthening its presence in LAC, although from a low base. Bilateral trade of $2.5 billion is relatively small, accounting for just 2.5% of LAC trade, but it is booming, averaging 16% annual growth over the past two decades. Trade is geographically concentrated, with Brazil, Chile, Peru and Argentina accounting for most exports, but in terms of product mix bears closer resemblance

---

[52]Inter-American Development Bank, *op. cit.*; Kevin P. Gallagher and Roberto Porzecanski, *The Dragon in the Room: China and Future of Latin American Manufacturing* (Stanford: Stanford University Press, 2010); Mauricio Moreira, "Fear of China: Is There a Future for Manufacturing in Latin America?" *World Development* Vol. 35, No. 3, 2007.

[53]Inter-American Development Bank, *op. cit.*

to diversified patterns of exports to the EU and the United States than do LAC exports to China; manufacturing accounts for about double the share of the region's exports to South Korea than the region's exports to China. Korea's FDI share is relatively modest, accounting just over 1% of total LAC inflows and 8% of Korea's outward FDI flows in 2010— yet about 6 times more than Korean FDI into Africa.[54] Like their Japanese counterparts, South Korean companies have upgraded their investments in the region, focusing on manufacturing assets. And as with Africa, Seoul is offering its own model of development as a more relevant source of policy learning than that of China.

### India and LAC

Indian-Latin American ties are in their infancy, but likely to accelerate as India seeks to tap into Latin America's abundant fresh water supplies and agricultural/energy resources. Between 2002 and 2010, Latin America accounted for roughly 4% percent of India's FDI outflows versus Africa's 12% percent share. Moreover, a large share of Indian investment in the region — around 70% — is invested in tax haven nations like the Cayman Islands and the British Virgin Islands. Indian exports of $13.4 billion to LAC in 2011 were 43% of India's exports to Africa, and Indian imports of $16.4 billion were also less than half of the $39 billion India imported from Africa in 2011. Brazil is the largest market in Latin America for Indian goods, while oil-rich Venezuela is the largest regional supplier to India, underscoring the importance of energy imports for India's economy.[55] Nevertheless, India's priorities will almost certainly remain closer to home than the seemingly distant Southern Atlantic.

### China in LAC

Despite these broader and sometimes more extensive Asian activities in LAC, China's meteoric rise and its profound impact on South and Central America has eclipsed attention paid to the region's other Asian partners. China's soaring energy and agricultural needs account for China's rising investment profile in Brazil, Peru and Venezuela, the top destinations for Chinese foreign direct investment, and China is

---

[54]Korean Exim Bank, http://211.171.208.92/odisas_eng.html.

[55]Quinlan, *op. cit,*; Jaishankar, *op. cit.*

also engaged in substantial investment in the offshore centers of the Cayman Islands and the British Virgin Islands.[56]

The last decade has seen sharp spikes in Chinese investment in Brazil (where China's FDI stock rose from just $52 million in 2003 to $1.1 billion in 2011), Peru (from $126 million in 2003 to $802 million in 2011) and Venezuela (from just $19.4 million in 2003 to $802 million in 2011). Chinese FDI stock in Panama, particularly in transportation, totaled $331 million, larger than China's investment position in Mexico ($264 million). In 2013 two Chinese state oil companies, PetroChina and CNOOC, participated (with a 10% stake) in the winning consortium, led by Petrobras and including Dutch Shell and France's Total, for the right to develop, during a 35-year concession, the pre-salt oil in Brazil's Libra Field. PetroChina announced acquisition of $2.6 billion in Peruvian oil and gas fields from its partner Petrobras. In 2012 Chinese oil companies bought Occidental Petroleum's operations in Argentina for $2.45 billion. In sum, while LAC is not yet a priority region for Chinese investments, it is becoming an increasingly important part of China's energy diversification strategy.[57]

Since 2005, China has promised upwards of $87 billion in loan commitments to LAC countries. China's announced loan commitments of $37 billion in 2010 were more than those of the World Bank, Inter-American Development Bank, and U.S. Export-Import Bank combined.[58] These impressive numbers have grabbed the headlines, but closer examination reveals that most Chinese investment flowing to LAC has not materialized. The China-Brazil Business Council found that only one-third of announced Chinese investments in Brazil between 2007 and 2012 actually appeared; around $44 billion in publicized investments never were realized.[59]

---

[56]Quinlan, *op. cit.*; Hamilton and Quinlan, "Commercial..." *op. cit.*

[57]Cornelius Fleishhaker, "Libra Out of Balance—International Oil Companies Indifferent to Brazilian Pre-Salt Oil," No Se Mancha, October 22, 2013, http://semancha.com/2013/10/22/libra/; http://www.reuters.com/article/2013/11/13/us-petrochina-petrobras-acquisition-idUSBRE9AC0CU20131113.

[58]"China-Latin America Finance Database," July 22, 2013, http://www.chinaandlatinamerica.com/2013/07/china-latin-america-finance-database.html.

[59]China-Brazil Business Council, *Investments in Brazil from 2007–2012: A Review of Recent Trends*, June 2013; http://www.businessinsider.com/chinese-investors-have-soured-on-brazil-projects-are-melting-away-2013-11; Theodore Kahn, "Chinese

According to official statistics from China's Ministry of Commerce, Chinese FDI in Latin America has been only $5.7 billion since 2006—far less than the breathless totals bandied about in the media. This figure does not account for investment routed through Hong Kong, the Caribbean, or other tax havens. But it clearly shows that Chinese investment has been a major disappointment, especially in light of wildly inflated investment announcements.

In addition to the quantity of flows, the composition of Chinese investment has given LAC leaders additional reasons for concern. Chinese companies have been more than willing to make resource investments but not those that would increase capital stock or create value-added activities. 85% of China's investments in the region since 2005 have been in oil, mining, or agriculture. In short, China's overall engagement with the region remains a one-dimensional affair: the commodities-for-manufacturing pattern dominates trade, and Chinese investments reinforce that trend.[60]

Within this overall narrative, however, three subthemes are worth noting. The first has to do with Chinese ties to Venezuela. In exchange for guaranteed supplies of oil, China loaned Venezuela an estimated $46.5 billion between 2005 and 2012, 55% of all loans it issued to nations in South America. Chinese support was critical for a Venezuela unable to access international capital markets after defaulting on its debts. Yet leadership changes in both countries and deteriorating conditions in Venezuela have resulted in a dramatic decline in such Chinese largesse.[61]

The second area of note is an ambitious $40 billion project, ostensibly to be financed largely with funds from China, to build a new canal

---

Investment in Latin America: Much Ado about Next to Nothing," No Se Mancha, http://semancha.com/2013/11/20/chinese-investment-in-latin-america-much-ado-about-next-to-nothing/.

[60]See the Heritage Foundation's China Investment Tracker. There are significant statistical problems regarding the total FDI coming into and leaving China, since a significant amount of such funds flow through Hong Kong, the Cayman Islands and the British Virgin Islands. Nonetheless, even with significant error there appears to be a substantial difference between announced investments and investment commitments and actual investment numbers.

[61]Inter-American Dialogue, *op. cit.*; http://www.americasreport.com/2013/09/04 china's-pivot-to-latin-america; http://www.chinaandlatinamerica.com, *op. cit.*

linking the Atlantic and Pacific across Nicaragua. The Nicaraguan Canal would have a larger draft, length, and depth than the Panama and Suez canals, and the Nicaraguan National Assembly granted a Hong Kong-based company permission to build and control the canal for nearly 100 years. It remains questionable whether this effort will go forward, due to ongoing differences between the Nicaraguan government and Chinese billionaire and HKND Group CEO Wang Ping—but it bears watching.[62]

The third subtheme of note is China's presence in the Caribbean, including sizeable flows to tax havens in the Cayman Islands and the British Virgin Islands, from whence funds can be and are being channeled to many other destinations. Much of China's post-WWII involvement in the Caribbean was tied to its diplomatic competition with Taiwan. Now Chinese state banks have established themselves as the leading lenders in the region, and Chinese FDI stock in the region totaled almost $500 million in 2011. Beijing has signed a series of bilateral investment treaties with Cuba, Jamaica, Belize, Barbados, Trinidad and Tobago, Guyana and the Bahamas, and Chinese companies have initiated ventures in more than dozen Caribbean countries. Cuba, Guyana, Suriname, and Jamaica stand out as the most important destinations for investment. In 2011, the Chinese national oil company CNPC began a $6 billion expansion of Cuba's Cienfuegos oil refinery. Chinese state-owned enterprises have also established stakes in Trinidad and Tobago's offshore oil industry. Activity by the Chinese government and its firms in global resource sectors reflects an effort to secure access to raw materials, including bauxite in Guyana, sugar in Jamaica, and palm oil production in Suriname; and lucrative infrastructure development projects, from harbor construction in Jamaica and shipbuilding in Guyana to rebuilding the main road to Kingston Jamaica airport. Chinese banks are financing the Punta Perla tourism complex in the Dominican Republic and the Baha Mar resort in the Bahamas, which alone has employed some 5,000 Chinese construction workers. The China Harbour Engineering Company is also nearing agreement to build a $1.5 billion transshipment port and logistics hub in Jamaica's Goat Islands, to take

---

[62]*Ibid.*

advantage of the expansion of the Panama Canal and growing Atlantic-Pacific maritime trade passing through the region.[63]

## Asia at the Poles

Asian countries have also exhibited heightened interest and engagement in the Arctic, in particular due to the implications of shorter trading routes between Atlantic and Pacific; the impact of Arctic warming on Asia-Pacific weather, circulation patterns and sea levels; and the potential for access to fishing and new resource finds. The U.S. Geological Survey has estimated that the Arctic contains 30% of the world's undiscovered reserves of natural gas, 20% of its undiscovered natural gas liquids, and 13% of its undiscovered oil—and that 84% of the Arctic's estimated resources are located offshore.[64]

The Arctic Council has now expanded to include as permanent observers China, Japan, South Korea, and India, all of which maintain their own Arctic research stations, as well as Singapore, and both members and observers are engaged in a far wider set of activities than was the case some years ago. South Korea has already invested in Canadian Arctic energy resources in the Mackenzie Delta.

As Arctic geopolitics evolve, one relevant development is the potential for Greenland's independence. Since its 2008 referendum Greenland is now largely self-governing except in some important areas, including defense and foreign policy. Momentum towards full independence continues, however, and seems limited only by the reality that Denmark still provides about half of Greenland's budget. An independent Greenland would recast the map of the North Atlantic as

---

[63]Kevin P. Gallagher, Amos Irwin, Katherine Koleski, "The New Banks in Town: Chinese Finance in Latin America," Inter-American Dialogue, March 2012; Robin Wrigglesworth, "Chequebook Diplomacy," *Financial Times*, December 18, 2013; http://jamaica-gleaner.com/gleaner/20130913/business/business5.html; http://www.jamaicaobserver.com/columns/The-Chinese-Goat-Islands-offer-is-non-negotiable_16158194.

[64]U.S. Department of Energy, Energy Information Administration, "Arctic Oil and Natural Gas Potential," October 2009; U.S. Department of the Interior, U.S. Geological Survey, "Circum-Arctic Resource Appraisal: Estimates of Undiscovered Oil and Gas North of the Arctic Circle," May 2008; http://thediplomat.com/2013/11/understanding-chinas-arctic-policies/.

well as the Arctic. Denmark would no longer be an Arctic Ocean littoral state, the Arctic Council would gain a non-EU, non-NATO
member state, the U.S. air base at Thule would be at question, and
Greenland authorities would be focused on ensuring that their economy could support the burdens associated with independence. Some
advocating independence look to the development of mineral and
hydrocarbon extraction industries as a way to a more self-sustaining
economy. In this regard, Chinese investment in Greenland is of some
note. Chinese companies are already active in Greenland, particularly
in copper exploration and mining.[65] Some analysts claim that Beijing
is concerned that Greenland's increasing presence in the field of rare-
earth minerals could compete with China's near-monopoly on some
rare earths. South Korea has been particularly keen to develop Greenland's rare-earth riches; state-owned Korea Resources Corporation
and Greenland agreed in September 2012 to pursue joint ventures
with respect to rare earth elements, tungsten and cobalt.[66]

Iceland is another northern territory that has garnered Chinese
attention. In 2010, China provided Iceland with a $500 million-plus
currency swap to support the struggling Iceland bank system; in April
2013 Iceland became the first European country to sign a free trade
agreement with China; and the country has been the subject of other
Chinese entreaties.[67]

---

[65]There have been uncorroborated reports of a $2 billion project for iron-ore produc-
tion by a joint British-Chinese undertaking; "Prospects Fade for Huge Greenland Iron
Mine," April 23, 2013, http://www.nunatsiaqonline.ca/stories/article/65674prospects_
fade_for_huge_greenland_iron_mine; "Denmark Gives Access to Arctic Minerals, Rare
Earths to China," *International Business Times*, Australia, January 19, 2012,
http://au.ibtimes.com/articles/284118/20120119/denmark-gives-access-arctic-miner-
als-rare-earths.htm#.UzcPckZOXQ5.

[66]"China Concerned about Greenland Rare Earth Activity," *Ice News*, July 27, 2013,
http://www.icenews.is/2013/07/27/china-concerned-about-greenland-rare-earth-activ-
ity/; "Asia Eyes the Arctic," *The Diplomat*, August 26, 2013, http://thediplomat.com/
2013/08/asia-eyes-the-arctic/.

[67]http://www.mfa.is/media/fta-kina/China_fact_sheet_enska_15042013_Final.pdf.
After considerable debate Iceland rejected a controversial proposal from Chinese busi-
nessman and former CCP International Department division head Huang Nubo for
the purchase of 300 square kilometers of land for an "ecotourism center," replete with
golf course, in a desolate strip of territory in the northeast of the country. Iceland's
minister of the interior, upon rejecting the deal, said "it never seemed a very convincing plan...One has to look at this from a geopolitical perspective and ask about motiva-

At the other end of the globe, Japan has captured more than 10,000 whales off Antarctica since 1988 via a program of "biological research" that was ordered banned by the International Court of Justice at the end of March 2014.[68] China has demonstrated greater interest in Antarctica, having established at least three scientific bases on the continent, stepped up its domestic base of expertise, and indicated interest in potential resources.

## Conclusions and Recommendations

As Europeans and Americans consider how to address Asia's rise, they should not only consider how to work jointly or in complementary fashion in the "Asian Hemisphere," they should incorporate into their deliberations an understanding of how Asian countries are pivoting to the "Atlantic Hemisphere." In this regard, five aspects are worth considering. In each area the transatlantic partners also need to be aware of issues where their own respective interests are common, where they are complementary, and where they differ.

First, this review has underscored the primarily economic drivers behind Asian engagement in the Atlantic Hemisphere, which in the South Atlantic is focused largely on acquisition of and access to fossil fuels, minerals, and agricultural commodities, and in the North Atlantic on access to significant consumer markets, technological know-how and innovation. Economic engagement has offered Asian countries a basis for greater political interaction in some contexts, but Asian political influence is on the whole less significant than Asian economic influence.[69]

This chapter has also demonstrated that there is no coherent strategy behind Asia's turn to the Atlantic; Asian countries act as much as

---

tions." See Andrew Higgins, "Teeing Off at Edge of the Arctic—A Chinese Plan Baffles Iceland," *New York Times*, March 22, 2013. Also Christian Le Miere and Jeffrey Mazo, *Arctic Opening—Insecurity and Opportunity* (London: IISS, 2013).

[68]Australia, a former whaling country, brought the suit against Japan in 2010, accusing the country of using a loophole to get around a 1986 worldwide moratorium on commercial whaling. See Hiroko Tabuchi and Marlise Simons, "U.N. Court Orders Japan to Halt Whaling Off Antarctica," *New York Times*, March 31, 2014.

[69]See Alessandri, et. al, *op. cit.*, p. 7.

competitors as partners when it comes to their engagement in the Atlantic Hemisphere. Individual Asian countries often export their intra-regional competition with other Asian countries to areas far from Pacific shores, seeking to eke out marginal advantage or curry favor from third parties in support of their respective political and economic priorities. The nature and aims of their respective engagement, as well as their approaches to human rights, democratic governance, civil society and the rule of law, vary considerably. Moreover, many Asian countries are learning as they engage. As Elizabeth Economy and Michael Levi have observed, "China is not pursuing its resource quest with reckless abandon; instead, it is adjusting its strategy and tactics as it learns from experience, moderating its global impact in the process."[70] This offers opportunities for engagement.

Third, if Asian countries have no coherent South Atlantic policy, neither do the United States or Europe. Yet the peoples of the North and South Atlantic are engaging and interacting with each other, as well as with Asia, in a whole host of new ways. Globalization has generated more connections among the four continents of the Atlantic Basin, and with the world, than perhaps ever before. Yet there is no framework for Atlantic countries to address the issues they face together, even though there are many such efforts in the Asia-Pacific region. Asian engagement in both the North and South Atlantic spotlights issues that the United States and Europe have neglected; areas from which they have withdrawn; and future challenges deserving their attention.

Fourth, Asia's rise is also affecting the Atlantic Hemisphere in a more global context, particularly with regard to worldwide norms and standards that should guide countries as they address contemporary issues. That debate should influence how the United States and its European partners engage South Atlantic countries, as well as those in Asia.

Finally, this review has also shown that breathless talk about Asia's global rise must be put in perspective. Asian engagement in the Atlantic Hemisphere is uneven. Some connections are thick, others quite thin. On most indicators most Asian actors in the Atlantic lag significantly behind the United States and Europe in terms of their

---

[70]Elizabeth C. Economy and Michael Levi, *By All Means Necessary—How China's Resource Quest is Changing the World* (Oxford: Oxford University Press, 2014), p. 8.

overall presence, with some exceptions. Africa has been a greater ben-
eficiary of Asian activities than Latin America, yet throughout the
South Atlantic there is rising concern about the nature and terms of
Asian, and particularly Chinese, engagement. Few mechanisms are in
place in the Atlantic Hemisphere, however, for established and emerging powers to hash out the terms of their interaction.[71]

With these themes in mind, the United States and European states,
either individually or collectively, should consider the following
measures:

- **To act together abroad, get your act together at home.**
  Without U.S. fiscal solvency, economic growth, and job creation,
  without a better-functioning domestic political process, Washington is unlikely to be the type of consistent, outward looking
  partner that Europeans need and want. Similarly, Europe's protracted economic and financial crisis threatens to drain U.S. confidence in Europe and its institutions and derail American support for major transatlantic policy initiatives, including a
  "transatlantic pivot to Asia." The single most important effort
  each partner could make to improve its ability to act together
  with its transatlantic partner abroad—in Asia, in the Atlantic,
  around the world—is to get its act together at home. This is particularly important as the United States and Europe engage with
  Asian countries that offer different models of economic and soci-
  etal development, because the normative appeal and continued
  relevance of the U.S. and European models for others depends
  heavily on how well they work for their own people.

- **Don't just turn to the Pacific, harness the Atlantic.** The rise
  of developing Asia has captured the world's attention, and rightly
  so. Yet this review of Asian activities in the Atlantic Hemisphere
  underscores that globalization, by its very nature, is not about
  one region of the world, it is about how different regions of the
  world are connecting. And for all the talk of the Pacific, it is
  important to recognize that the Atlantic Basin is a central arena
  of globalization. The well-being of people across this vast region
  is increasingly influenced by interrelated flows of goods, services,

---

[71]Alessandri et al, *op. cit.*, pp. 1–5.

and energy, people, money and weapons, technology, toxins and terror, drugs and disease. Yet there is no framework for Atlantic countries to address the issues they face together, even though there are many such efforts in the Asia-Pacific region.

The United States and Europe should address Asia's rise not only by engaging directly in Asia but by strengthening the foundations of their own engagement. The Asian Hemisphere is the hemisphere of contested norms and principles among and between open and closed societies. The Atlantic Hemisphere, in contrast, is—admittedly with fits and starts—coalescing around basic aspirations regarding domestic governance. Across the Atlantic space there is growing commitment to promote liberty, improve the efficiency of markets, and to respect human dignity.[72] And the Atlantic Hemisphere offers diverse models of practice that can be relevant to broader global debates about effective and responsive governance.

Of course, across the full Atlantic space achievement does not always match aspiration. Setbacks abound and challenges remain. Yet a shared and growing commitment to democracy, good governance and a culture of lawfulness also positions the Atlantic Hemisphere as the test bed for how established and emerging powers can formulate shared approaches to ensure the legitimacy and effectiveness of the international rules-based order. Whether emerging powers choose to challenge the current international order and its rules or promote themselves within it depends significantly on how established democracies engage with rising democracies. The stronger the bonds among core democratic market economies, the better their chances of being able to include rising partners as responsible stakeholders in the international system. The more united, integrated, interconnected and dynamic the Atlantic Hemisphere, the greater the likelihood that emerging powers will rise within this order and

---

[72]All countries in North America, the European Union and Latin America—with the exception of Cuba—are now rated partly free or better by Freedom House. Africa, too, has experienced greater democracy. In 1990 Freedom House recorded just 3 African countries with multiparty political systems, universal suffrage, regular fraud-free elections and secret ballots. Today close to 60 percent of African countries are now rated partly free or better by Freedom House.

adhere to its rules. The looser or weaker those bonds, the greater the likelihood that rising powers will challenge this order. In this sense more effective 21st century global governance, including how Asian states relate to such debates about governance—is likely to depend on a more effective—and thus redefined—Atlantic Community.

In short, stronger ties among North and South Atlantic countries are not only important in their own right; they can offer a framework to address Asian engagement on issues of pan-Atlantic concern while strengthening the foundations of Atlantic engagement in the Asian Hemisphere. The reverse is also true: without active U.S. and European engagement as pan-Atlantic, not just transatlantic powers, exclusionary mechanisms could emerge; new privileged partnerships or resource arrangements could be built; and restrictive trade deals or discriminatory financial arrangements could threaten U.S. and European interests. An Atlantic Basin Initiative[73] of one hundred Eminent Persons across the four continents of the Atlantic has called for a new Atlantic Community that erases the invisible line that has separated the North and South Atlantic for so long and gives shape to these emerging trends, not as an exclusive bloc but as an open global region. North America and Europe should embrace it.

- **Address Asia's Atlantic turn in the context of pluralism, not containment or confrontation.** This does not mean excluding or neglecting competition or hard geopolitical considerations, but it underscores the importance of placing such considerations within the broader framework of interdependence. Asian countries are already Atlantic actors and in many cases are important sources of jobs, growth and economic development. A number are important allies and partners for North Atlantic countries. Yet there is concern, particularly in the South Atlantic, about dependencies and various operating methods. The United States and Europe should not seek to isolate or prevent China and other Asian powers from operating in the Atlantic Hemisphere, they should work with them and Atlantic actors to tackle issues arising from their activities, for instance how to move beyond

---

[73]*A New Atlantic Community, op. cit.*

traditional commodities-for-manufacturing patterns to make trade more balanced and sustainable; how to manage volatility in commodity and resource markets; and how to ensure that growth does not come at the expense of regional development or local manufacturing industries.[74]

- **Take advantage of the Atlantic Energy Renaissance.** Asian countries are so actively engaged seeking energy and other natural resources in the Atlantic Hemisphere in part because the Atlantic basin is recasting the world's energy future. An Atlantic Energy Renaissance is setting the global pace for energy innovation and redrawing global maps for oil, gas, and renewables as new players and technologies emerge, new conventional and unconventional sources come online, energy services boom, and opportunities appear all along the energy supply chain and across the entire Atlantic space. Together these developments are shifting the center of gravity for global energy supply from the Middle East to the Atlantic Hemisphere. Over the next 20 years the Atlantic is likely to become the energy reservoir of the world and a net exporter of many forms of energy to the Indian Ocean and Pacific Ocean basins. Already 21% of China's oil imports come from the Atlantic basin. Furthermore, nearly an identical share (around 35%) of all world oil imports now comes from the Atlantic basin (including the Mediterranean) as from the Middle East. Heightened Atlantic energy links, in turn, could reduce the dependence of many Atlantic basin countries on Eurasian energy sources and take pressure off their intensifying competition with China and India over energy from some of the world's most unstable regions.[75]

  - **Create a private-public Atlantic Energy Forum** to facilitate and develop Atlantic basin energy trade and investment.

---

[74]See Alessandri, et. al, *op. cit.*, p. 66.

[75]See Amy Myers Jafee, "The Americas, Not the Middle East, Will Be the World Capital of Energy," *Foreign Policy*, Sept/Oct 2011; Paul Isbell, *Energy and the Atlantic: The Shifting Energy Landscape of the Atlantic Basin* (Washington, D.C.: German Marshall Fund of the United States, 2012).

- **Create an Atlantic Action Alliance for Renewables Deployment and the Reduction of Energy Poverty** that would develop a mechanism for putting actual and potential renewables entrepreneurs into contact with finance mechanisms, regulatory officials and policymakers, technical assistance programs and facilities, so as to stimulate more rapid development. The Alliance's goals would be to offer advice for policy, locate potential niches, identify investment projects and financial resources, provide a link between small-and-medium sized enterprises and existing and evolving global support networks, and to contribute, where possible, to remove barriers to sustainable development. Asian renewables companies could be included in this effort.

- **Start an African Energy Initiative** with key African actors to spark the energy transformation of Africa, which is still characterized by deep pockets of energy poverty.[76] Expanding energy accessibility can reduce poverty and infant mortality, improve education, advance environmental sustainability, and accelerate economic growth and prosperity. Such efforts would reposition the United States and Europe as important African actors, while including relevant Asian actors within a norms-based framework.

- **Engage African, Latin American and Asian leaders, through various mechanisms, to promote basic norms of openness, transparency and accountability.**

  - **Advance a common approach to open investment principles.** This should proceed along different tracks. The United States and the EU should incorporate into a final TTIP framework a common stance regarding principles of open investment, building on their previous statements in

---

[76]*Energy for All: Financing Access for the Poor* (Paris: International Energy AgencyD, 2011); Blake Clayton, "The Biggest Energy Problem that Rarely Makes Headlines," *Forbes*, November 9, 2012, http://www.forbes.com/sites/blakeclayton/2012/11/09/the-biggest-energy-problem-that-rarely-makes-headlines/; International Energy Agency, *World Energy Outlook 2010*, Paris, 2010. The IEA estimates the cost of putting in place universal access to modern energy by 2030 at 48 billion dollars per year—only 3 percent of what experts expect to be invested in energy projects globally over the next sixteen years.

this area, and act together to advance those principles when engaging third parties. This is particularly important in the context of separate U.S. and EU negotiations now underway with China on bilateral investment treaties. They should also ensure that differences of approach to national security reviews of investment do not undermine or offer opportunities to exploit such differences.

- **Gain greater support for the Extractive Industry Transparency Initiative,** a global coalition of governments, companies and civil society working together to promote openness and accountable management of revenues from natural resources. Countries abiding by the EITI Standard agree to full annual disclosure of taxes and other payments made by oil, gas and mining companies to governments. While over 40 countries participate and the Initiative is gaining ground, many countries have yet to join.

- **Define agreed standard operating principles by state-owned enterprises.** The increased importance of such enterprises—in financial services, telecommunications, steel, chemicals and energy, and other natural resources—requires new rules so that private businesses can compete fairly with state capitalism. The rules need not push privatization or roll back state enterprises, but they should require transparency, commercial behavior, declarations of subsidies, nondiscrimination and open procurement.

- **Engage Asian actors in differentiated dialogues on Atlantic Hemisphere issues.**

  - **Engage China directly.** Take up China's call for a "new type of big power relationship" by using the U.S.-China Strategic and Economic Dialogue and EU-China summit frameworks to elevate consultations on African, Latin American and polar issues, not only to raise concerns but to explore ways to coordinate on such issues as aid, development, technology, technical assistance and alleviating energy poverty.[77]

---

[77]Vera Songwe, Yun Sun and Julius Agbor, "Obama-Xi Summit: Four Reasons Africa Deserves Attention at the Talks," The Brookings Institution, June 7, 2013,

- **Encourage India's engagement** on Atlantic Hemisphere issues, while being careful not to overload expectations or to tout India's development model bluntly as an alternative to that of China. Identify practical areas for mutual support, for instance electoral best practices and foreign assistance.[78]

- **Coordinate more effectively with Japan, Australia, South Korea and other Asian actors** on common or complementary approaches to technical assistance, economic development, aid, as well as norms and standards.

- **Incorporate into U.S.-European consultations issues arising from Asian activities in the Atlantic Hemisphere.** U.S. and EU officials each engage with Latin American and African counterparts on issues related to Asia's rise, yet do little to consult each other on such issues, particularly with regard to Asian activities in the South Atlantic.

- **Ensure that the Transatlantic Trade and Investment Partnership, or TTIP, is part of an open architecture of international trade, and open to accession or association by third countries.** TTIP promises a boost to North Atlantic economies. But unless properly designed as part of an "open architecture," the partnership could hurt the trade prospects of other countries. President Obama and EU leaders should declare publicly that TTIP is indeed part of the open architecture of international trade. As the negotiations proceed, in time officials should outline future modalities for accession, association, or complementary economic agreements with other countries. The United States and the European Union have common interest in demonstrating that TTIP is about trade creation, not trade diversion.

- **Harmonize trade preference arrangements for low-income African countries.** North American countries and the EU should harmonize their current hodgepodge of trade preference mechanisms for low-income African countries. Latin America

---

http://www.brookings.edu/blogs/up-front/posts/2013/06/07-obama-xi-summit-africa-songwe-sun-agbor; Alessandri, et. al, *op. cit.*, pp. 1-5.

[78]Jaishankar, *op. cit.*

could conceivably join in offering the same market access, building on preferences already given by some countries in Latin America, and on interests they have expressed within the WTO to improve market access for poorer developing countries. Such efforts should harmonize country and product coverage as well as rules of origin of current preferential arrangements, taking the best and most effective provisions of each respective program, making them compatible and updating the rules to the current trading environment.[79]

- **Work with emerging donors towards a new architecture for aid.** The international landscape for development aid has changed. Once-poort countries in Asia and the South Atlantic have became economic powerhouses and started their own foreign aid programs. New donors like Brazil fully understand and respect the importance of developing country ownership of assistance programs. They have a clear competitive advantage in sharing their own development experiences with emphasis on the "how-to" aspects of implementing development projects. South Korea offers relevant lessons for South Atlantic countries, and its contributions could be enhanced through more effective coordination with other new donors, as well as the United States and the EU. India has now emerged as a new aid provider, and has worked on various projects with both Americans and Europeans. Enhanced coordinated offers the prospect for more effective and transparent efforts for the benefit of recipient countries. A new aid architecture should arise in which "new" donors primarily focus on transfer of knowledge, while "traditional" donors focus on continued transfer of financial resources to poor countries that need external concessional resources. Donors old and new should implement commitments made in the Busan Partnership Document; participate actively in the Global Partnership for Effective Development Cooperation; and participate in the International Aid Transparency Initiative.[80]

---

[79]Eveline Herfkens, "Harmonized Trade Preferences for Low Income African Countries: A Transatlantic Initiative," in *Atlantic Rising*, Daniel S. Hamilton, *op. cit.*; Also K.Y. Amaoko, Daniel Hamilton and Eveline Herfkens, "A Transatlantic Deal for Africa," *New York Times*, May 8, 2013, http://www.nytimes.com/2013/05/08/opinion/
[80]*A New Atlantic Community*, *op. cit.*

- **Encourage Asian countries to enhance their contributions to the regional development banks of the Atlantic Hemisphere.** The African Development Bank, the Inter-American Development Bank, and the CAF Development Bank of Latin America—as part of a general effort to encourage these countries to be responsible actors in the development of the South Atlantic.

- **Be open to good practice coming from Asia.** The APEC-Asia-Pacific Infrastructure Partnership is a high level body bringing together public sector, private sector and international financial institutions within APEC where each can bring its own expertise to bear. Ministers identify priorities, processes and resources; the private sector examines sponsors, contractors, short and long term financiers; and the international financial institutions bring experience, best practice, anti-corruption and other skills. This process is inclusive and has the potential to filter out investments that are unlikely to have desired local benefits. It may offer a useful framework for African, Latin American or even Arctic collaboration, or to give life to pan-Atlantic mechanisms within the Atlantic Basin Initiative.

*Part III*

**Security Issues**

# Chapter Seven
# The Impact of the Pivot on the Alliance

*Robert E. Hunter*

With the scheduled termination to NATO's International Security Assistance Force (ISAF) operation in Afghanistan at the end of 2014, NATO will be approaching its 20th anniversary as an "active" rather than "passive" or "deterrent" alliance. What began as a brief, 20-day air campaign in August-September 1995 to help bring the Bosnia conflict to a close has expanded into a virtually permanent succession of NATO military activities with active or potential combat engagement. The deployment of NATO's first peacekeeping forces in Bosnia, followed by the 86-day air campaign to stop Serbian ethnic cleansing of Kosovo and then deployment of the Kosovo Force, firmly established the Alliance as having assumed responsibilities "outside of area." That was beyond the geographic area formally defined in Article 6 of the Treaty of Washington as potentially applying to the treaty's Article 5, the statement of mutual commitment by NATO allies against external aggression. Since that time, NATO has been constantly engaged: in Afghanistan (the first-ever invocation of Article 5 following September 11, 2001), in counter-terrorism maritime deployments in the Mediterranean, in counter-piracy off the East coast of Africa, and in the 2011 Libyan conflict.

While in Afghanistan at the end of 2014 the "guns" will not "fall silent," NATO will find itself without a major military engagement. This brings with it questioning about the future role(s) of the Alliance. This is not just a matter of bureaucratic nostalgia, i.e. "We have this instrument, what are we to do with it?" Nor will it necessarily lead to significant demobilization after a job completed. Just as NATO did not go out of business at the end of the Cold War, there is no pressure now for it in effect to go out of business, nor even to go into a standby mode.[1]

---

[1] This chapter was completed before the crisis over Crimea led to its incorporation into the Russian Federation and to various Western responses. Commentary by the author

This does not mean that pressures that deeply affect NATO's capabilities to act militarily or to be employed are not there. But they were there even before it was decided that NATO allies would wrap up most of their deployments to Afghanistan at the end of 2014. The conclusion that NATO does not need the same level of military capabilities, measured in terms of manpower, equipment, overall capabilities, and budgets, took place many years ago, beginning with the collapse of East-West confrontation in Europe. Movement in that direction was accelerated only in part by judgments about future potential threats and challenges to the security of allies; there were also fiscal realities—or choices: that both competing uses of funds and the great financial crises beginning in the late 2000s argued for less spending on military power.

There have been several efforts to offset the impact of these budget cuts.[2] NATO has invented a concept called Smart Defense, to emphasize capabilities that are most likely to be in demand in some future, notional conflict or contingency;[3] the European Union (Common Security and Defense Policy—CSDP) has experimented with pooling

---

on NATO's potential role and the impact on the Alliance of developments regarding Ukraine can be found here: http://www.lobelog.com/will-putin-save-nato/. In general, however, the arguments presented in this chapter regarding rebalancing of U.S. strategic perspectives ("pivot") have not been invalidated. Indeed, if anything, there will be increased need for European allies to be responsive to U.S. desires for support in its strategic engagements beyond Europe, given the increased need for NATO allies, especially in Central Europe and the Baltics, to be reassured about the strength, purpose, and potential direct engagement of the basic U.S. political and security commitments, both under NATO's Article 5 and in bilateral relationships.

[2]One effort is the informal expectation that each ally should spend at least 2% of its gross domestic product (GDP) on defense, an expectation that has done less to inspire reluctant governments and parliaments to increase spending than to dramatize publicly that they will not do so. See, for instance, the valedictory speech to a defense ministers' meeting of the North Atlantic Council by Secretary of Defense Robert Gates on June 10, 2011: "What I've sketched out is the real possibility for a dim, if not dismal future for the transatlantic alliance." *The Security and Defense Agenda (Future of NATO)*, as delivered by Secretary of Defense Robert M. Gates, Brussels, Belgium, June 10, 2011, http://www.defense.gov/speeches/speech.aspx?speechid=1581. This reasoning has always contained a basic flaw: U.S. military spending is not just for European contingencies, but world-wide.

[3]See, for example, NATO, "Smart Defence," last updated on April 26, 2012, at http://www.nato.int/cps/tr/natolive/topics_84268.htm.

and sharing capabilities across nationalities;[4] the revolution in CISR (command, control, communications, computers, intelligence, surveillance, and reconnaissance) uses technology to make military capabilities more efficient and, in saving manpower, less expensive.

Budgets are not the only factor that will determine NATO's future role. There is also reluctance on the part of allied governments and peoples, including in the United States, to become involved in other conflicts, short of direct threats to the homeland; this has been particularly evident in the Middle East, notably in regard to Iran and even Syria, with its civil war and major civilian casualties that bring to mind the suffering in Bosnia two decades ago.

Thus there are inherent pressures against the Alliance's looking for new things to do, at least as discretionary acts. The Alliance is now firmly out of area, but both economics and politics raise questions about the "where" and "how"—as well as the "why." The impact of this development on the possibilities of allied engagements in regard to the rebalancing of U.S. security and other attentions to East and South Asia will become obvious.

## Offsetting Factors Shaping the Alliance Future (1)

Nevertheless, nearly 20 years of continuous NATO military engagement, all outside of area, along with the vagaries of the future, argue in the opposite direction: that at least NATO should retain a capacity to act, to be able to meet various contingencies that could call for military and political-military responses to protect the interests of allied states, including in "Article 5 situations" but also in "non-article 5 situations," potentially in the Middle East, Africa, or elsewhere. Where, when, and how such requirements could emerge is inherently unpredictable, as the Alliance has discovered since the end of the Cold War. Having capacities, even if they only prove to be insurance that never has to be invoked, is a wise investment; it also has intangible benefits, including strengthening other aspects of transatlantic relations.

---

[4]See, for example, European Defence Agency, "Factsheet: EDA's Pooling & Sharing," February 6, 2013 at http://www.eda.europa.eu/docs/default-source/eda-factsheets/final-p-s_30012013_factsheet_cs5_gris.

Notably, the NATO Alliance and its integrated military command structure are now in their seventh decade, and this experience has had an extraordinarily positive impact. Indeed, NATO experience has been sharpened by moving from latent to active, through active combat, peacekeeping deployments, and elements of a so-called Comprehensive Approach (i.e., integration of non-military activities). The Alliance has developed skills and capacities unmatched by any other agglomeration of military forces. A vast array of support facilities and capabilities has also been created, including:

- A host of common standards;

- A single command language in allied military engagements (English);

- Forces with a high degree of interoperability across services and nationalities;

- Command and control capabilities and development of head-quarters on land, sea, and air, some rapidly deployable over great distances and which can be configured for different tasks and demands;

- Joint or at least on-call sealift and airlift and ISR (Intelligence, Surveillance and Reconnaissance);

- Extensive common training, educating, and exercising;

- Formal and informal specialization in military tasks across services and nationalities;

- Supportive relationships among (competing) defense companies and industries across the Alliance;

- Burden-sharing and risk-sharing among allied nations;

- A significant number and geographic distribution of partner countries engaged in allied activities and deliberations; and

- A methodology for reaching political decisions on the basis of consensus which has built in a robust, joint-and-several commitment to decisions once taken, even where actual military action has been undertaken by coalitions of the willing and able.

Such capabilities are not lightly to be dispensed with. Even in circumstances when there are no direct threats, real or perceived, on the immediate horizon, these capabilities, practices, and habits have added value by helping to inhibit the emergence of new challenges by outside parties (at least states), an existential deterrent, and to increase the psychological confidence of allied peoples.

The NATO Alliance has also fostered political cohesion among its members, helping to shape the nature, character, and extent of relationships in many areas; developing expectations about behavior of different allies toward one another; and being a critical element in a community of interests and values that would probably not otherwise exist. At the same time, these capabilities, practices, and habits help with dispute resolution among allies. They also help bridge what could otherwise be political if not also strategic divergences among allied countries. Not least, the Alliance has helped to prevent the reemergence of a great divide separating the two sides of the Atlantic, such that, even without the existence of a compelling geopolitical challenge in Europe, the United States (with Canada) has not retreated from Europe but remains a European power, although it has radically reduced its deployed military power on the Continent.

With the difficulties allies face in creating and sustaining military capabilities, the economic pressures, the partial loosening of cohesion, the emergence of different perspectives regarding security, writ large—especially caused by facts of geography and propinquity to new challenges—the Alliance remains an instrument that could be used in new ways, provided that allies can agree on essentials like the nature of threats and challenges, their locus, appropriate responses, sharing of burdens and risks, and other factors critical to decisions to deploy or apply military force and other elements of power and influence.

By contrast, security relationships among European states within the European Union, including the CSDP, do not have the same quality, based on all the structural and experiential elements that help give political strength to the NATO alliance. Nevertheless, the EU's structure, roles, and experience, especially in the context of European political integration, will enlighten its perspective regarding potential roles beyond the Continent, military and non-military, whether in Africa, the Middle East, or possibly even regarding the U.S.-led rebalancing to Asia. The EU and its member states on a bilateral basis have long been involved in peacekeeping and other security-related engagements, both military and non-military, beyond the territories of its member states. Its European Defense Agency (EDA) helps to develop military capacities; and European aid, investment, and other economic projects—government, NGO, and private sector—are essential elements of security-promotion "outside of area."

## Offsetting Factors Shaping the Alliance Future (2)

It is possible that European allies will perceive that they have political, economic, or security interests in other parts of the globe that argue for becoming engaged in the Far East and South Asia, including military involvement, in addition to the more-likely comprehensive approach—which ties in non-military security responses.

A more important motivation for possible European involvement in a U.S.-led rebalancing of strategic engagement is the continuing desire of the allies to preserve the full range of other relationships across the North Atlantic. A critical reason that NATO continued in being following the end of the Cold War was the common perception that the work of the Alliance and of transatlantic security relations was not completed. The creation of a "Europe whole and free" and at peace, in President George H.W. Bush's historically-significant phrase, is still short of completion, especially concerning the future roles of the Russian Federation. It took more than a century to "solve" the "German problem." "Solving" the geopolitical "problem" of the Russian Federation will take be many years and has been vastly complicated by the 2013–2014 crisis over Ukraine, until—if possible—new patterns of behavior and structures integrate Russia in a positive, comprehensive, and more-or-less permanent way into broader international society, within which it will not pose either a real or perceived threat to any European state.

For virtually all central European states, the Russian Federation is at least a latent threat and the actions of its current government under President Vladimir Putin were far from reassuring even before the most recent Ukraine crisis. Hence, a major reason for most of these states' seeking to become NATO members (and, secondarily, in terms of their perceptions of security, EU members) and to gain a strategic commitment from the United States; and hence their desire that the United States remain fully engaged as a European power. Even west European states relatively unconcerned about inherent or incipient Russian power see a continuing U.S. strategic commitment as useful, along with the indispensable role that the United States plays in the functioning of the global economy and international financial system.

More than any other factor, the desire to have the United States strategically committed to Europe led all the NATO allies to send military and other security personnel to Afghanistan, whereas few saw much if any threat to their homelands from either the Taliban or al-Qaeda (or its ilk). The allies went to Afghanistan mainly as part of an implicit bargain with the United States to ensure against the possibility that the shifting of U.S. attention elsewhere, plus a sense among the American people that Europeans were ungrateful (or that European governments were simply lacking in either military capacities or political will), would lead to diminished U.S. attention to European security concerns on the Continent, however residual for many European states.

But as ISAF and European military engagement in Afghanistan come to an end, what will replace them as a means for Europeans to show the United States that they actively support U.S. interests beyond the Continent, in order to curry favor in Washington and with the American people? One answer is to support the United States in some fashion in its rebalancing to Asia; another is to be useful to the United States elsewhere.

Only time can test European willingness to respond to a U.S. search for allied support beyond Europe. In the Far East, so far, there is little indication that having allies involved militarily would be instrumental to keeping the United States strategically engaged in Europe to the degree and in terms that Europeans want, in part because deployable military capabilities of almost all allied states (except for some British and French naval and air power) are not relevant to providing security reassurance to U.S. allies and partners in the Far East in regard, principally, to the rise of Chinese power. Further, the United States has not so far articulated any such desire for European buttressing of its own increasing security presence.

Not so with regard to other geographic areas. Other current and potential U.S. searches for greater roles to be played by European allies and partners, including NATO and the EU, derive from several reasons: to help relieve the United States of always having to take lead responsibility for acting; to show the American government and people that the Europeans are being useful to the United States; to sustain capabilities that might have later application, without knowing now where that could be; and hence to reinforce U.S. willingness to be strategically engaged in Europe, even when the United States is less convinced than European allies of the need to do so. Because of the Ukraine crisis at time of writing, the United States needs no added incentive to be engaged strategically in Europe, but in the future it will likely do so, again.

### Africa

Prior to the onset of the Ukraine crisis in full measure, in recent years the locus of active security threats and challenges to the North Atlantic area had shifted beyond Europe. The threat of terrorism as a phenomenon and of asymmetrical warfare as an instrument has increased in importance, both relative to past conflicts and in terms of the amplifying effect (and hence political impact) of modern media. This has been a central security preoccupation from Pakistan through Afghanistan to the Arabian Peninsula and now into various parts of Africa.

European states, at least on the Continent's southern littoral, are particularly affected, indeed to a greater extent than the United States, by events in North Africa, especially with the so-called Arab Spring and the spread of Islamist political and military activities into parts of Africa south of the Sahara and along the Indian Ocean. The 2011 Libya conflict was instructive. Outside countries most directly affected were those most likely to face an influx of refugees, the further stimulation of Islamist-based terrorism, and the generic (but often ill-defined) quality called instability. The United States, in the phrase often used, "led from behind." In Europe, this was meant as a criticism,[5] but it related more to the fact that the United States had less directly at stake

---

[5]In the United States, this term was used to suggest that Washington was supporting its allies, that it was not abstaining from "leadership," that the relationships built up within NATO had not become irrelevant, but that the United States was keeping out of active

in Libya than did a number of European states and the European Union. European criticisms regarding the limited but still critical U.S. military involvement, along with NATO's formal abstention, derived less from military needs than political expectations: that the premier Western alliance, NATO, "should" have had a role and that the United States "should" have taken the lead. The conduct of the crisis, therefore, was less about interests of allies, taken as a whole, than about the way in which NATO, the EU, and the United States were perceived in terms of being willing to act on behalf of interests, correctly or incorrectly evaluated, as seen by a number of allies.[6]

At the same time, the United States is increasingly not prepared to accept that what it sees as areas and events largely peripheral to its core security concerns must be embraced by the United States and, in the process, formally by NATO. This was a key lesson of the Libyan crisis. However, given that developments in North Africa (West of Egypt, with its importance to peace in the Levant, especially because of the 1979 Egypt-Israel Peace Treaty) affect the United States less than many European states, there is a sense of "the shoe's being on the other foot" in relation to the phenomenon discussed earlier of allies going to Afghanistan largely in order to keep the United States pinned to Europe. U.S. support for interests of greater intrinsic concern to some allies falls into a similar frame. In the interests of allied solidarity and of convincing Europeans that they should be engaged with the United States in areas of lesser interest to them (e.g., the rebalancing

---

participation in yet another war, with "boots on the ground," in line with U.S. public opinion. Even in Bosnia and Kosovo, a major factor for only using air power was to keep U.S. (and allied) casualties to a minimum and in fact there were virtually none.

[6]The partial analogy could be with the Bosnia and Kosovo conflicts, where the United States was seen by European states as having special responsibilities, even though both places are far closer to all of them than to the United States, and there was likely to be little direct impact on the United States of the conflicts' there continuing, including in the flow of refugees. Instead, both conflicts became important because they were close to NATO territory, came to be seen as somehow a test of whether NATO and the EU could be relevant in the post-Cold War world and, hence, whether the United States both would be engaged in that effort and would take the lead. Further, resolving the conflicts in Bosnia and Kosovo was important in major part to show that NATO (and the EU) could be counted upon to play roles in wrapping up the Cold War and "ending history" in the center of Europe. The Bosnia and Kosovo wars were only ancillary geopolitically but critical "geo-psychologically." Not so North Africa or Africa south of the Sahara.

to East Asia), the United States would need to show sensitivity to European concerns. This is also true regarding Africa south of the Sahara, including 2013's French-led intervention in Mali.[7] The opposite argument can also be made: that by taking care of problems in Africa that could have wider ramifications, Europeans like the French who act are doing so not just on behalf, implicitly, of the interests of other European states and of Alliance as a whole, but also on behalf of the United States, which might otherwise need to become more engaged, including militarily.[8] These factors relate to the U.S. rebalancing to Asia and the potential impact on NATO, as will be explored below.

Further, whether NATO would assume a formal role in North Africa—e.g., through the training and arming of security forces—or whether roles would be assumed by individual NATO allies, has also related to activities clustered under the rubric of comprehensive approach. There are three levels: 1) tried-and-true activities in so-called capacity building; 2) roles to be played either by the NATO Mediterranean Dialogue[9] or by non-NATO entities, especially the European Union (e.g., the Barcelona Process and the Mediterranean Union);[10] and 3) whether, among Western allies and partners, there should be a division of labor regarding different regions. For example, Europeans would be expected to carry more of putatively-shared burdens in North Africa and Africa south of the Sahara, while the United States would carry more of the burden in dealing with the future of the Russian Federation, as well as shared security interests elsewhere.

---

[7]The U.S. creation of an African command has increased U.S. involvement in military affairs in that continent even though AFRICOM was supposed to be a true "comprehensive approach" instrument. The United States has also gained increased strategic interest in the Gulf of Guinea because of the substantial rise of oil exports from that region.

[8]This reasoning is similar to that used in support of UN peacekeeping operations and why the United States should support them: that they relieve the United States of potential responsibility for securing its own interests.

[9]Algeria, Egypt, Israel, Jordan, Mauritania, Morocco, and Tunisia.

[10]See the website of the Union for the Mediterranean: http://ufmsecretariat.org/ufm-countries/ and http://europa.eu/legislation_summaries/external_relations/relations_with_third_countries/mediterranean_partner_countries/rx0001_en.htm.

## The Middle East

The Middle East has again intruded itself forcefully upon the United States and European states, though not so far upon NATO or, at least in regard to CSDP, upon the European Union. Several dimensions are important, notably the continued role of al-Qaeda and other terrorist organizations in different parts of the region (e.g., Yemen), the continuing civil war in Syria, chronic uncertainties about Iraq's future, progress (or lack thereof) in diplomacy regarding the Iranian nuclear program, and the ever-lasting peace process between Israel and the Palestinians.

Three recent developments in the Middle East impact most particularly on the Atlantic Alliance.

*Syria*. At time of writing, the civil war in Syria is well into its third year. One key element, relevant to the Western Alliances, was President Barack Obama's drawing a so-called red line regarding the use of chemical weapons, followed by their use, then followed by tangled diplomacy about whether the United States would take the lead in conducting air strikes in Syria. After the House of Commons voted down British participation, Obama asked Congress for authority to use force, air strikes were put on hold, Secretary of State John Kerry worked with Russia to find a way out, and the immediate crisis abated. At the same time, U.S. and Western policy toward the conflict remained unclear, including a lack of shared understanding about the broader implications both for Syria and the region if Syrian president Bashir al-Assad were deposed, as Obama and others had called for.

Further, there has been no clearly-defined and –agreed allied position on Syria or shared analysis of the potential impact of events there on the Alliance and its members' security interests. The crisis has further illustrated that, in the post-Cold War, post-aftermath-period era, there has been some divergence of the interests of different allies, at least in terms of translation into action policies, even in a region close to Europe. This was illustrated by declarations that NATO as an institution would not become involved in Syria.[11] The crisis has also illu-

---

[11]See, for example, Jan M. Olsen, "Secretary General: NATO Will Not Take Part in Syria Strike," *Atlantic Council*, September 2, 2013, at http://www.atlanticcouncil.org/blogs/natosource/secretary-general-nato-will-not-take-part-in-syria-strike.

minated strains and tensions regarding the different roles that allies are prepared to play in such circumstances.[12] The chemical weapons issue also led France to question America's steadfastness and consistency.

Given these strains, tensions, and questions, both about the interests of the Alliance as a whole and the leadership role of the United States in a place so close to Europe, it would surely be much more difficult to gain allied consensus—and potentially even coalitions of the willing and able—to follow a U.S. lead in its rebalancing to Asia, where there is even less of a sense of shared security interests.

*Iran.* The NATO allies' collective interests would be even more directly affected if Western-Iranian relations again soured and if Iran were to move toward acquiring a nuclear weapons capability. Allied states have paid much greater attention to Iran than to Syria; Britain, France, Germany, and the EU's High Representative for Foreign Affairs and Security Policy are directly involved in negotiations with Iran. Yet NATO as an alliance has not been engaged and the issue has rarely been discussed by the North Atlantic Council.[13] Neither the European allies nor the United States and Canada see the crisis over the Iranian nuclear program and ancillary issues to be appropriate for NATO action. Nor has the United States been criticized by its allies for not taking the matter formally to the Alliance, traditionally the locus for transatlantic strategic consultations. Despite the importance of the issue and the potential challenges to the entire Alliance, this matter is too far outside of area, both geographically and in terms of the potential for the Alliance to play an effective role. After Afghanistan and Iraq, it is doubtful that more than a handful of allies, if that, would be prepared to support U.S military operations. Indeed, allies' resistance to the resort to military force would, in the event of US military

---

[12]These problems began as early as the Bosnia crisis, when it took more than two years for the United States to convince all the allies—i.e., to gain a consensus at the North Atlantic Council—that the Alliance needed to use airpower to end the war, which, when the Alliance did act, only took 20 days to achieve.

[13]This is somewhat analogous to the U.S. decision in September 2001 not to involve NATO as an institution in military operations in Afghanistan, although a few highly-capable allied militaries did take part. Indeed, the Alliance's first and only invocation of Article 5 of the Treaty of Washington, on September 12, 2001, was initiated by allies, not by the United States.

action against Iran (perhaps provoked by Israel), likely cause an Alliance crisis even worse than that over the 2003 invasion of Iraq.

*Israel-Palestine.* The third primary area of concern for allied nations in the Middle East[14] is the continuing conflict between Israel and Palestine. Virtually all express concern that this conflict has not been resolved; all, at least verbally, argue that it is one of the most important issues in the Middle East, and some argue that it is key to peace and security throughout the region. There is also widespread expectation in Europe that the United States will press the two parties toward a resolution. Indeed, the United States has taken the lead on this and related issues for decades, even though, beginning in 2002, there has formally been a Quartet of the United States, EU, UN, and Russia with at best a nominal role to play.

The continuing Arab-Israeli conflict and expectations of America's leading role as peacemaker have not led to a reduction within the Alliance in respect for the U.S. role as leader within NATO itself, at least not directly. There has been a tacit agreement to segregate out this particular set of tensions from broader understandings and expectations. At the same time, there is already a proposal for engaging NATO formally if there is a peace treaty between Israel and an independent state of Palestine.[15] The idea of some form of a NATO peacekeeping force in Palestine has been conditionally blessed by at least one NATO Secretary General.[16] The allies have informally acknowledged that the value of ending the Israeli-Palestinian conflict would be so important to the West that even running risks in deploying peacekeeping forces, following a peace settlement and with related prospects of reduced tensions across the region, would be acceptable.

---

[14]This leaves aside places like Yemen, continuing difficulties in Iraq, spill-over effects of Afghanistan, and the low but not non-existent risks of a collapse of the Egypt-Israel Peace Treaty.

[15]See Robert E. Hunter and Seth G. Jones, *Building a Successful Palestinian State: Security* (Santa Monica, CA: RAND Corporation, 2006), downloadable at http://www.rand.org/pubs/monographs/MG146z2.html.

[16]"The Secretary General of NATO has mentioned three *Big Ifs*. If the parties involved came to an agreement and if they requested NATO to help them implement and if there were a UN Security Council Resolution, then NATO member countries would need to discuss it." *NATO Questions & Answers*, at http://www.nato.int/cps/en/natolive/topics_59419.htm.

## Implications for NATO and Rebalancing

This discussion contains a number of implications for the Alliance relevant to the U.S. rebalancing to Asia, including:

1. European allies will continue to want a fundamental U.S. strategic commitment and practical engagement to deal with the future of the Russian Federation, as first priority, plus potential uncertainties about their capacity to cope on their own in response to other challenges on the Continent.[17] While it is impossible to calculate the extent to which the United States, including the Congress and the American people, would require European support for U.S. interests outside of area in order to justify providing the level of engagement on the Continent that allies want, there is risk in allies' testing this proposition. The 2013–2014 crisis in Ukraine is vivid evidence of the continued European need to be confident of wholehearted U.S. commitment.

2. It is doubtful that the European allies, possibly excepting Britain and France, would be prepared to take part in military aspects of U.S. support for allies and partners in the Far East, at least without serious provocation directly impinging on European interests. Post-Cold War divergences of interests among allies in areas much closer to home, notable during the 2011 Libyan conflict, argue against a shared assessment of challenges in the Far East. But if the European allies do need to demonstrate support for the United States ''outside of area,'' where should that be? And would the European allies respond in terms sufficient to satisfy the United States? It was one thing for European allies, along with partners in Europe and elsewhere, to join ISAF, following a direct assault on the United States; it would be quite another to support the United States in other ventures.

---

[17]Two such areas are developments in the Balkans and risks of "backsliding," politically, in some new member states of Central Europe, where today Hungary is most obvious. The latter risk was identified during the initial NATO enlargement process. Efforts by U.S. Senator Kay Bailey Hutchinson in 1998 to create a formal procedure within NATO to help deal with such problems were rebuffed by the Clinton administration.

3. Developments since the December 1995 IFOR deployment in Bosnia and continuing through all other NATO deployments, especially in Afghanistan, have brought to the fore the need for an effective comprehensive approach, with implications both for the availability of non-military instruments of power and influence and their effective integration within a holistic approach to security. It is also now clear that NATO will not itself be able to do all that is needed, but will need to work with other institutions, beginning with the EU and the UN. Hence, the need to resolve promptly the political stalemate involving Turkey, Greece, and Cyprus, which inhibits NATO—EU cooperation.

4. Europeans can thus be useful to the United States in non-military ways, especially economic, as part of an overall comprehensive approach that goes beyond the current limited NATO definition. Individual European states and the European Union have significant interests in the Far East and South Asia that will call for serious foreign policy engagements. The European private sector will be critically important, as well as NGOs. However, cooperation with the United States in economic areas, including providing non-military security reassurance to regional partners and allies in the Far East, can be in tension with European and American economic and commercial interests and competitions, with resulting differences of views and interests, in both public and private sectors. So far, the United States has made no connection between European support for its political, economic, and security policies in the Far East as "compensation" for strategic engagement on the Continent, but it might develop.

5. Two geographic areas where the European allies can be useful to the United States in more classic security terms, in addition to their own inherent interests, are North Africa, Africa south of the Sahara, and the Middle East as far east as Pakistan. Indeed, events in the Middle East, notably the demands of dealing with Iran and the Syrian civil war and the latter's wider implications, call into question the extent to which the United States can rebalance toward Asia, at least anytime soon, even though the trend of economic developments

inevitably argues for a greater focus on that region.[18] The same could prove to be true, at least in the near term, regarding crisis over Ukraine and Russian assertiveness, in general. Further, even if successful, the Obama administration's new diplomatic opening to Iran, designed in part to lessen tensions and facilitate rebalancing to Asia, does not hold out hope of lessening U.S. engagement in the Middle East for the foreseeable future, in part because of the U.S. need to reassure regional partners that it will not cede primacy to Iran.[19]

6. The United States will thus look to European allies and partners to play a greater role, wherever possible, in the Middle East, in addition to North Africa and Africa south of the Sahara. What these roles would be in the Middle East is not yet clear, nor whether the Europeans would be willing to respond. While greater European involvement cannot be a complete substitute for continuing U.S. engagement and for providing reassurances to local partners, it could relieve the United States of some of its current burdens. In the longer term, the United States may look to the Europeans to support U.S. actions in regard to rebalancing, but for the foreseeable future active European roles in Africa and the Middle East are the outer limits in providing a substitute for soon-ending allied ISAF deployments.

7. A role for Europeans can also include joining the United States and regional countries in trying to fashion a regional security structure and patterns of behavior to replace defunct and imperfect security arrangements. This idea is currently premature, but thinking about its value, possible parameters, and means of bringing it about should begin promptly.[20]

---

[18]This is offset somewhat by the promise of the Transatlantic Trade and Investment Partnership, or TTIP, but even if fully successful, TTIP will not have a critical impact on the continuing economic rise of China and the potential geopolitical impact of that rise, along with that of India.

[19]These fears about Iran's gaining regional primacy, much less hegemony, are fantasy, but they are still a fact of regional politics and expectations about the United States.

[20]See, for example, Robert E. Hunter, *Building Security in the Persian Gulf* (Washington, D.C.: RAND Corporation, 2010), http://www.rand.org/content/dam/rand/pubs/monographs/2010/RAND_MG944.pdf.

8. The lack of a central defining threat or challenge to NATO countries and the Alliance as a whole is having a predictable impact on considerations of "What does NATO need?" in terms of capabilities. Recent experience argues for preservation of core capabilities, including those defined at the 2012 Chicago Summit as collective defense (deterrence and Article 5), crisis management, and cooperative security (partnerships).[21] However, these generalities do not provide much guidance about the tools that NATO (much less the EU) will need to be able to respond to challenges and threats as they emerge. This admonition applies even if the Alliance or individual allies do not extend their military reach to the Far East; there will be enough to do in Africa and the Middle East and potentially in "places as yet foreseen" to argue for preserving core capacities.

## Rebalancing and NATO in Practice

The new U.S. predilection to focus more on security issues, writ large, in East and South Asia than on residual security issues in Europe—other than the Russian Federation's future and future behavior abroad—does not immediately point to significant implications for the NATO Alliance. The shift of U.S. attention farther east can be a concern for some European states, especially because of the obvious and extensive diversion of Washington's attention away from NATO. Fortunately, this does not apply to economics and finance, notably the Transatlantic Trade and Investment Partnership (TTIP), which engages the United States with the European Union, but not NATO, and—preoccupation with Russian assertiveness aside, at least for now—TTIP and other economic ties are increasingly becoming the linchpin of transatlantic relations.[22]

---

[21]See Chicago Summit Declaration Issued by the Heads of State and Government participating in the meeting of the North Atlantic Council in Chicago on May 20, 2012, http://www.nato.int/cps/en/natolive/official_texts_87593.htm?mode=pressrelease.

[22]In light of the end of the Cold War—"NATO's most important security business having been completed"—this is a natural reversion to the three-part transatlantic relationship crafted in the late 1940s: political, economic, and military, adding up to a strategic whole.

If differences of viewpoint and strategic locus do cause problems for the cohesion and sense of purpose for the NATO alliance, what ameliorative steps can be undertaken? These should not be designed just to keep the Alliance in being, even though having an insurance policy for the future has its own utility. But parliaments are unlikely to fund capabilities that are just about insurance, other than for psychological security in central Europe (a need enhanced by recent Russian actions), unless there is practical utility—such as we have seen in Africa and counter-piracy operations. But what of East Asia? There are a number of things that NATO and the European Union should be planning for, beginning now, along with efforts by individual countries. The following are among the most important:

1.  NATO should place greater emphasis on partnerships, of various kinds, qualities, and locations. This was probably the most important initiative to come out of the Chicago Summit and one of the most important Alliance-savers for the future.[23] Already, several countries have become valuable assets for NATO and EU deployments, both in military and non-military areas—note the 20+ non-NATO countries involved in ISAF.[24] There are several formal NATO partnerships, including the flagship Partnership for Peace (PFP), the largely political Euro-Atlantic Partnership Council (EAPC), the Mediterranean Dialogue, and the Istanbul Cooperation Initiative (ICI), along with special NATO arrangements with Russia, Ukraine, and a few smaller countries.[25] There are proposals for rationalizing the various partnerships and relating both the capabilities (military and non-military) of different partners, choosing the right institution for cooperation (notably the EU, the UN, and the African Union), and defining areas and conditions where partners are prepared to be engaged.

---

[23]Because of the increased importance in transatlantic relations of economic as opposed to military connections, TTIP is potentially the most important "Atlantic relationship saver."

[24]There are a number of countries—Sweden and Finland are notable in Europe—with a tradition of taking security seriously and backing it up with capabilities and willingness to deploy them.

[25]See "Partnerships: A Cooperative Approach to Security," (last updated October 28, 2013) at http://www.nato.int/cps/en/natolive/topics_84336.htm.

Partnerships exist in the Far East, along with formal alliances, where the United States in particular works with a number of countries. Some regional countries, including Australia, New Zealand, Japan, and South Korea, are already engaged with NATO, notably in Afghan deployments and in consultative and quasi-decision-making arrangements in Brussels for so-called Troop-Contributing Nations (TCNs). These partnerships can be expanded, with direct links to NATO across the board and the inclusion of far more countries than heretofore—e.g., Indonesia, Singapore, and the Philippines. There could eventually be cooperative arrangements between NATO and ASEAN, or subsets of the latter, where there is a shared perspective of regional security interests and requirements.[26]

2. One of NATO's great values is its development of common standards, common training and education, and a common methodology. There would be value in making this NATO package available to friendly countries elsewhere in the world, and some is already being done with U.S. allies and partners in the Far East. This can be systematized, with military and non-military personnel and institutions directly linked to NATO, including with its non-allied partners, to create a common set of standards and practices for all of the key "Western" allies and partners. This methodology might eventually be extended to other countries in the region, including China, if it were engaged productively in the outside world. A good instrument for pursuing these developments is the U.S. European Command, headquartered in Stuttgart.

3. NATO has a wide range of capabilities, institutions, and activities that could usefully engage personnel from allies and partners from East Asia, as well as from the Middle East, Africa, and elsewhere. Training and education facilities, centers of excellence, processes for standardization, and relations among private sector entities (especially armaments industries) could be made available to allies and partners from elsewhere.

---

[26]ASEAN members are Brunei Darussalam, Indonesia, Lao PDR, Malaysia, Myanmar, Philippines, Singapore, Thailand, and Vietnam.

4. Some competition continues between NATO and CSDP; and some NATO allies worry that cooperating with East Asians, especially in response to U.S. rebalancing, could risk their getting dragged into some U.S. military venture as a function of becoming engaged in security arrangements far from areas of their own national interests. Given the difficulties of reaching agreements on common interests and shared engagements even in the Balkans, Africa, and the Middle East, this is not a trivial point.

5. The U.S. rebalancing to East Asia is not just limited to the military and political-military dimensions. Global economic shifts are the prime mover, and here Europe is as engaged as is the United States. Non-governmental sectors, especially in business and economics, will be more engaged than sectors with a security cast. Of course, the aspiration for developing a common transatlantic approach regarding the full range of relationships with China and India is most unlikely to be achieved. There are even some misgivings, not just in China but also in Europe, that TTIP (combined with the Trans-Pacific Partnership—TPP) could be construed as ganging up on China. This is the same reason some East Asian allies and partners of the United States see value in both TTIP and TPP. At the very least, a mechanism would be needed for interaction among European states and North America, with others involved, as appropriate, on the full range of activities and engagements implied by rebalancing.

6. NATO will also need mechanisms for engaging partners from other parts of the globe, not just Troop-Contributing Nations, as at present, but also for other purposes and with other capabilities. These need to include a consultation and decision-making structure either embedded in or paralleling the North Atlantic Council. It could include the creation of an informal consultative mechanism located in the Far East, provided there are protections against European nations' becoming more engaged in regional security than national self-interest might dictate. Ideally, there should be a common consultative and even decision-making mechanism engaging both NATO and the European Union in regard to their activities—just as

there would be value in creating, now, such a mechanism for NATO-EU cooperation closer to home. If there is to be a true comprehensive approach, these two institutions need to stop keeping one another at arm's length. The same applies to the way national bureaucracies are organized and interact at home. In the governments of most European countries and the United States, there is insufficient interaction between those personnel who work on security issues in the narrow sense (e.g., NATO) and those who work on issues that are about security in a broader sense, especially economics. In the US government, notably, the conversation between bureaucrats and even some political leaders who focus on NATO and those who focus on TTIP (EU) remains primitive.

## Conclusions

NATO's future will depend on major transformations not just in the way it does business but also on the political framework within which it operates. "Outside of area" is now a central operating principle, but what that slogan means will vary from ally to ally. Nor can there be a single template for determining what NATO will do in the future: the test will be to preserve the best parts of the Alliance and especially the political, military, and other practices built up over more than six decades. NATO's value as an instrument remains important; but the demands of deciding just what that instrument should be used for and where and how and by whom will be a constant challenge. The effort to shoe-horn activities back into the same old ways of Alliance business is not just doomed to failure, it is not even necessary to preserve the best of the best as an instrument of security-promotion for all NATO members and partners.

Changes and adaptations are taking place more-or-less piecemeal, both within NATO and in its interaction with other institutions, like the EU and the UN, and as between public and private sectors. Whether that piecemeal approach will suffice is doubtful. Of far greater utility would be creating a process for developing a new Transatlantic grand strategy, along with a new Pacific grand strategy, beginning with assessment of changes taking place, the interests of individual countries over time and collective common interests to the extent they can be divined or bargained out, and appropriate responses. Only then should tasks be assigned to individual institutions, notably NATO, EU, NATO-EU, U.S.-Canada-EU, UN, Middle East, African, and Asian partnerships, bilateral relationships, and public and private activities. This process of creating a new transatlantic grand strategy would have to be flexible and ever-adaptable.

Significant progress in developing this new, but essential, approach is almost certainly too much to hope for by the time of the Cardiff NATO summit in September 2014; or in any of the current EU processes; or, as they are currently conducted, in the periodic U.S.-EU summits. But all can start the ball rolling, a continuing, strategically-oriented and rigorous process of assessment and then political leadership needed to create and operate institutions and processes that can serve not just the allies and partners well, but also other countries and institutions, governmental and non-governmental. These efforts would need to be made even if there were no rebalancing to East and South Asia and the Western Pacific. With the rebalancing, these efforts become indispensable for the health and future of the Atlantic Alliance.

## Principal Recommendations Related to NATO

1. **Develop an overarching Transatlantic Framework for engagements with East and South Asia (rebalancing), within which NATO would be a critical sub-element.** Continue breaking down barriers between NATO and various EU institutions, finally ending the impediments imposed by some NATO allies and EU member states. Engage the private sector and NGOs in this overarching and also functional approach;

2. **Relate developments in Allied and partner military structures and budgets to requirements for engagements out of area, including in defining capabilities that would either be necessary or useful,** taking advantage of programs such as Smart Defense and pooling-and-sharing. Continue pursuing lessons learned, in military, political, and economic terms, especially from NATO or NATO-related operations in

Afghanistan and Libya, as well as other operations, especially engaging the EU's Common Security and Defence Policy or national operations, as in Mali.

3. **Create a mechanism within the Alliance, similar to the 2003 Berlin-Plus arrangement with the EU, which would allow individual NATO lead nations to use NATO assets in agreed operations in North Africa and the Middle East.**

4. **Apply the EAPC and PFP models to countries farther outside of area in the direction of East and South Asia;**

5. **Develop a NATO relationship with China, at first informal, drawing upon the (once-and-potentially-future) NATO-Russia relationship and institutions. Do the same with India.**

6. **Create at NATO Headquarters an Assistant Secretary General (ASG) position to deal with these relationships** or bring them directly into the Secretary General's Private Office (PO). Appoint a Senior Civilian Representative (SCR) of the NATO Secretary General for East Asia and another for South and Southwest Asia (broadening the mandate of the current SCR for Afghanistan); and

7. **Use the U.S. European Command as lead agency, also assisting allied and partner countries, in forging practical relationships with East and South Asian countries,** as well as cooperating with NATO military and functional institutions and agencies, including NATO schools and centers of excellence, for purposes of interoperability, training, exercises, and the adaptation and inculcating of the NATO method.

# Chapter 8
# How NATO Can Pivot Towards Asia

*Karl-Heinz Kamp*

Asked about the foreign policy legacy of the Obama presidency, future generations might point to the U.S. strategic shift towards Asia announced in January 2012. Although this move was not as new as it seemed and was really initiated by the George W. Bush administration, it will profoundly affect U.S. long term security and defense policy.

Washington made it clear from the outset that this "pivot"—later renamed "rebalancing"—will be neither an anti-European move nor a mere rearrangement of armed forces on the global strategic chessboard. Instead, it will be as political and economic as it is military. It takes note of the fact that in today's fairly stable Europe there is much less "unfinished business" to deal with. Hence, most European Allies have supported the view that the crisis-prone situation in Asia requires far more attention from the United States—not least because the tendency in Europe is to support the U.S. role as a defender of international order and of the global commons.

If the leading power of the Euro-Atlantic community changes its strategic priorities, the repercussions on the other Allies are bound to be severe. It should, therefore, come as no surprise that many Europeans still have to come to grips with the consequences resulting from the pivot. European NATO members have to address the repercussions of the U.S. shift as they face two other fundamental challenges. First, the financial crisis in Europe goes beyond any of the economic recessions of the past decades and has forced almost all Allies—even the big spenders of the past—to significantly cut their foreign and defense policy expenditures. This painfully strips their options to act forcefully on the international scene. Second, the withdrawal of combat troops from Afghanistan should be finished by December 2014, ending the biggest military mission in NATO's history. That raises the question: how can a political-military institution justify its existence and the consumption of scarce resources if it is no longer committed to a major operation crucial to all member states?

Two opposite extreme conclusions could be drawn from the current tidal change in the Euro-Atlantic security landscape. On the one hand, there could be a case for future downsizing of NATO's tasks and purview, in order to re-focus the Alliance on its core mission of military self-defense. On the other hand, it could also be argued that the whole of NATO should follow the United States with a major gearing of its efforts towards the Asia-Pacific region, where there is much more "unfinished business" to deal with, and where major risks for Alliance security could emerge.

Between these extremes lies a third option: to widen NATO's horizons to the Asia-Pacific region gradually, according to its capabilities, and to support the American pivot by disburdening the United States in other regions closer to Europe. Such a limited re-orientation of priorities would mean a coherent transatlantic approach to the new security requirements of the 21st century. This third way, however, requires clarification of a number of issues. How far will the pivot go, and what does it actually imply? Why do European NATO members need to take developments in Asia into account, and what can NATO's role be in terms of ensuring a consistent transatlantic attitude towards the Asia-Pacific region?

## The Pivot—A Moving Target

Assessing European reactions—inside or outside NATO—would require a clear picture of what the pivot will actually be and how it will ultimately materialize. However, as with many new political concepts or strategies, the idea of a stronger U.S. focus on the Asia-Pacific region still raises a number of questions. Moreover, policy blueprints are not carved in marble but are subject to political developments or sudden changes in the international landscape—and there are a number of factors that are difficult to predict but may have major impact. Rebalancing might look quite different in a couple of years from the situation its architects initially envisaged.

One important factor will be the development of the U.S. defense budget in coming years. This will depend not only on overall economic developments, but also on priorities set by the government. In view of the ongoing sequestration process and U.S. Defense Secretary Hagel's firm intention to assess critically every major defense project, it remains to be seen what kind of activities will actually be implemented in the Asia-Pacific region. Further budgetary cuts and an ongoing battle between Republicans and Democrats could render ambitious policy concepts futile, whereas a lasting economic recovery would widen the leeway of future administrations.

A second policy development likely to have an impact is the changing situation in the Middle East and North Africa. When the pivot was conceptualized in 2011, the prospects for what was then called the "Arab Spring" seemed to be cautiously optimistic. This led to the overall U.S. calculation of a 60/40 ratio of U.S. military resources (60 percent for Asia and 40 percent for Europe).[1] Today, with the Arab world in flames, Libya falling into chaos, Syria in the midst of a humanitarian catastrophe, Egypt returning to more authoritarian rule and Iran working on the technology to develop nuclear weapons, this calculus could change. A future U.S. President might be forced to again pay greater attention to the Middle East and keep sufficient military forces rapidly available to address problems originating there. Such a pivot away from the pivot would once more change the entire geostrategic equation.

A third source of insecurity is the "Russia factor"—i.e. the persistent deterioration of U.S.-Russia and NATO-Russia relations. Despite a number of symbolic resets, there has been a constant worsening of relations with Russia. U.S.-Russia missile defense collaboration has foundered on the apparently irreconcilable positions of the two sides, while NATO-Russia cooperation has been limited. In addition, NATO's eastern European members still harbor concerns about Russia, while Moscow's harsh words and behavior vis-à-vis its neighbors or former allies are hardly calculated to alleviate such worries. The situation culminated with Moscow's annexation of Crimea in March

---

[1]As Secretary of Defense Leon Panetta indicated in his speech at the Shangri La Dialogue in Singapore on June 2, 2012, http://www.defense.gov/transcripts/transcript.aspx?transcriptid=5049.

2014 against international protests.. Small wonder, then, that international political debate features talk of a possible new "Cold War" in which the United States regain the role of hedging Russia's intention to at least partly re-establish its former empire. Should this negative trend continue and lead to a more confrontational relationship with Russia, one of the major justifications of the pivot—i.e. stability and the absence of direct threats in Europe—would become doubtful. Not only the eastern European NATO members will insist on firm American commitments, bolstered by credible military capabilities—thus limiting the possible extent of Washington's rebalancing from the Atlantic to the Pacific.

The situation will be further complicated by a current "wild card" on the international agenda, which has the potential to influence any of the developments mentioned above—the so-called shale gas revolution. The prospects of U.S. energy self-sufficiency will have a significant impact on America's global engagement. It may be too simplistic to argue that, as a result of the shale gas revolution and decreased dependence on oil imports, the United States can afford to reduce its engagement in Europe, North Africa and the Middle East. This would mean underestimating the American role in global stability, the need to safeguard the global commons and the special U.S. responsibility for Israel. Yet, a profound change in the world energy business, with the United States no longer the main buyer but a net exporter, and the major flow of Gulf oil going not to the United States but to Asia, would have far-reaching—and currently unpredictable—consequences. It could result in North America and Europe working much closer together on exploiting their shale gas resources, and thereby paying less attention to North Africa or the Middle East. Alternatively, a stronger engagement by China in the Middle East to secure its energy interests might require counter-balancing efforts by the United States in this region, which again would place a strain on the resources intended for the Asia-Pacific region. Russia might continue to lose weight in international relations and compensate for this weakness by even more assertive behavior, frightening its neighbors in the West and in the East—again Moscow's moves against Ukraine are telling in that respect. Declining oil prices might also mean that Middle Eastern regimes would no longer have the ability to suppress revolutionary change by bribing their elites with petrodollars. Each of these possible developments would require a different approach by the United States, as well as by NATO.

## The United States and NATO: Different Points of Departure

Though the American focus on the Asia-Pacific region has only recently gained prominence, Europe and North America have actually been engaged there for a long time—albeit on different levels and with different aims.

The United States has always been a Pacific power,[2] as a defender not only of order in the region but also of global stability. This stability seems seriously challenged by the almost incredible rise of China—economically, politically and militarily. The pivot in its current incarnation is noticeably anti-Chinese in character and has its roots in the 1996 Taiwan Strait crisis.[3] In fact, Washington perceives China's rising economic power as posing a more profound challenge today than the economically weak Soviet Union at the time of the Cold War. In addition, the economic growth of the entire Asia-Pacific region can be seen as giving China a "choking capability"—i.e. the ability to block important sea lines of communication, which are critical for the entire Euro-Atlantic community. By the same token, however, the same concern with regard to the blocking capability also holds true from Beijing's point of view: China is vitally dependent on freedom of maneuver in the Strait of Malacca and a U.S. blockade of this waterway in a major crisis could hit the Chinese economy at a very sensitive point. Given strong economic interdependence and mutual vulnerability, U.S.-Chinese relations do not, therefore, necessarily have to be confrontational. China has been financing large parts of the American debt and is, at the same time, highly dependent on access to U.S. markets.

NATO has undergone an interesting evolution with regard to engagement in areas far from its geographical boundaries. During its first four decades, NATO saw itself as a truly North Atlantic security

---

[2] Canada is the second Pacific power in NATO, due to its geography and strategic orientation. France claims the same status, due to its overseas territories; however, given the size of the areas concerned, this seems unfounded.

[3] Robert S. Ross, "What the Pivot Means for Transatlantic Relations," *German Marshall Fund of the United States*, GMF Policy Brief, May 2013.

institution and opened its perspectives to the Asia-Pacific region only after the end of the Cold War. In the early 1990s, the first formal high-level consultations started between NATO and Japan. The 9/11 catastrophe forced Alliance members not only to expand their geographical horizons to Asia but also to use military force, together with a large number of countries in the Asia-Pacific region, thousands of kilometers away from their borders. Still, NATO was hesitant to regard the Asia-Pacific region as its area of concern. From 2005 on, Washington pushed NATO to develop close partnerships at least with democracies like Australia, New Zealand, South Korea and Japan—called "Contact Countries" or, later, "Global Partners." European Allies like Germany or France were initially skeptical with regard to possible institutional ties with these nations, as this might lead to a global NATO acting as a world policeman. Washington countered these concerns by pointing out that a global security perspective should not be equated with global membership (the Washington Treaty limits possible new members to European countries), or with an interest in global interventions. This disagreement was then put on hold.

A major leap forward was the approval of NATO's new Strategic Concept of 2010, in which development of partnerships beyond NATO's geographical boundaries—not least on a global scale—was defined as one of the core missions of the Alliance. Even if many Allies still pay only lip service to this global dimension of NATO and tend to stick to their Eurocentric world view, the seeds of a globalized NATO have been sown. This holds all the more true as NATO has, in military terms, long been an actor on the world stage. Currently, NATO forces are present on three continents—in Europe, in Asia and in Africa.

## Why NATO Will Have to Pivot

So far, even major European Allies tend to avoid serious debates on whether they should orient their security policy more strongly towards the Asia-Pacific region. This is partly because Europe in general has not been renowned for a global foreign policy view. Even if Europeans are economically very active in Asia, few regard the region and developments there as a strategic challenge. In addition, most Europeans, even those who regard themselves as putative world powers, have to realize the painful limitations in their capacities to act decisively on the global stage. Lastly, the eurozone crisis has now been dominating European political priorities for half a decade. The fact that European leaders are rushing from one summit to the next to save near-bankrupt economies makes demands on the time and energies of the key players, leaving only limited room for the development of new foreign policy concepts. Given the urgency of the crisis, one can hardly blame European decision makers for remaining much more focused on their own region than on global issues.

The U.S. announcement in early 2012 that it would place greater emphasis on developments in the Asia-Pacific region marked a watershed for the entire Atlantic Alliance and, in particular, for its European members. If NATO's leading power redefines its strategic priorities, European Allies will no longer be able to stick to traditional interpretations of NATO's purview—widespread Eurocentric preferences notwithstanding. Instead, they will have to broaden their security policy horizon to Asia as well. This holds all the more true as pressure on NATO to redefine its geographical horizons emerges not only from Washington's foreign policy shift, but also from a number of other facts or trends which cannot be ignored.

### The Relevance of Asia

Economic growth in the Asia-Pacific region is breathtaking. The 21 economies in the region account for a combined GDP of $39 trillion, or 56 percent of world economic output. Asia is exporting huge quantities of goods to Europe and the United States and is in turn becoming a giant consumer market for U.S./European products. The region also has half of the world's population and some of the largest military forces worldwide. At the same time, the economic and political situation there is extremely volatile. China shows impressive growth rates, but also struggles with severe social and ecological problems. India's economy took off at a startlingly rapid pace, but then became stuck in corruption, nepotism and the incompetence of decision makers. Pakistan has been in decline for years and seems on its way to becoming a failed state—the first with nuclear weapons. Thus, in a globalized world where geographical distance is a decreasing factor in any risk analysis, it becomes increasingly evident that strategic shocks in the crisis-prone Asia-Pacific region will have fundamental repercussions for security and prosperity in Europe. This is not a fundamentally new insight, but one that has gained importance since most European economies have been hit by the financial crisis.

### NATO's Defense Vocation

NATO's core mission of defending the security and the vital interests of its member states, as specified in Article 5 of the Washington Treaty, has undergone a significant evolution that has not been fully embraced by all member states. In the run-up to the adoption of NATO's new Strategic Concept in November 2010, there was intense debate within the Alliance on Article 5 defense missions as opposed to expeditionary operations. The eastern European Allies argued that NATO should focus on the defense of Allied territory, whereas others saw NATO's main task in executing military crisis management missions outside Europe. Today, these discussions on expeditionary forces versus territorial defense seem futile, since Article 5 might not necessarily—as many Allies assume—be equated with the defense of Europe. Instead, a missile attack by North Korea on Alaska (and, given the waywardness of the regime in Pyongyang, this is hardly a far-fetched scenario) would be just as certain as a Syrian attack against Turkish territory to trigger an Article 5 response. Even beyond questions of collective defense regulated by Article 5, immediate action in order to protect vital interests could become necessary. For instance, should a war in the Middle East prompt Iran to block the Strait of Hormuz, NATO could not remain passive for the simple reason of not having suffered a direct attack. The same would hold true for the Strait of Malacca, linking Asia with the Middle East and Europe, which carries more than 50,000 merchant ships every year—equivalent to 40 percent of the world's trade. In both cases NATO interests would be vitally threatened, even without an armed attack against Allied territory as specified in Article 5.

If all Allies agree that NATO is meant to defend the territorial integrity, physical security and vital interest of all member states, then it becomes evident that there can be no implicit limitation of NATO's responsibility to Europe and its neighborhood. Instead, NATO has to be oriented also to distant regions, where regional tensions or crises can have an impact on the security of Alliance members.

*NATO as a Partnership Agency*

In its 2010 Strategic Concept, NATO defined cooperative security through partnerships as one of its three core functions. This was not simply a question of paying lip-service to the *"zeitgeist"* of international cooperation, but an essential prerequisite for NATO's role as a security alliance in the 21st century. A dense network of partnerships with countries or institutions far beyond NATO's borders can provide the Alliance with three key crucial benefits. First, NATO can obtain military, political or financial support from partners in its missions abroad—ISAF, with 21 non-NATO countries involved, is a clear example. Second, through partnerships, NATO can have a say in certain regions and at least try to affect political developments with a view to defusing crisis situations or easing tensions. Even if this influence depends on the situation and cannot be guaranteed, it can be an important element of preventive security policy. Third, through training and military assistance, NATO can enable partner countries to take care of their own regional security and to intervene, if needed, in crisis situations on their doorstep. Empowerment of this kind can reduce the pressure on NATO to use its own forces for out-of-area crises.

All three benefits apply in the case of the Asia-Pacific region. Countries like Australia, New Zealand, Japan, Singapore, South Korea and Malaysia contributed to NATO's mission in Afghanistan. Through partnerships, European NATO members in particular can acquire additional means of influence in the region, complementing the economic ties they have through the European Union. Many Asia-Pacific countries are particularly interested in military cooperation with NATO, to learn standardization and procedures, the Alliance being seen as the "gold standard" of multinational military action.

However, if NATO intends to take its partnerships seriously, it can hardly limit its dealings with partners around the globe to a purely Brussels-centered approach. Instead, common exercises and training missions need to take place in the regions concerned. From this perspective, a coherent partnership policy virtually forces European NATO members to place stronger emphasis on the Asia-Pacific region. Such a logic, however, raises the question of whether European NATO members have the capabilities to operate so far away from their national borders and, if so, which of them.

### The Nuclear Element

NATO defines itself as a "nuclear Alliance"—a term that refers to a number of characteristics:

- the entire Alliance regards nuclear deterrence as a core element in its security policy;

- three of its twenty-eight members are nuclear weapons states: the United States, France and the United Kingdom;

- two of these three—the United States and the United Kingdom—have taken a nuclear commitment for their non-nuclear Allies (so-called "extended deterrence");[4]

- one nuclear state—the United States—has stationed nuclear weapons on the territory of some non-nuclear members.

For a nuclear Alliance like NATO, the Asia-Pacific region is particularly relevant. Asia contains five nuclear players: China, India, Pakistan, Russia and North Korea. All are at odds with each other or other neighbors and all could pose a nuclear challenge to Euro-Atlantic security—whether because of potential aggression, because of the problems of nuclear proliferation, or because of dangers stemming from political instabilities.

In addition, the United States has given nuclear security commitments not only to its European Allies but also to Asian countries like Japan and South Korea. These countries note with great interest that U.S. commitments to Europe are bolstered by three substantiations of credibility: the deployment of nuclear weapons on Allied territory; common nuclear exercises; and nuclear consultations with Allies through a dedicated NATO body, the Nuclear Planning Group (NPG). None of these elements exist in U.S. nuclear relations with its Asian allies—the American commitment is primarily a verbal one, bolstered by appropriate national nuclear planning and the occasional presence of U.S. nuclear submarines or aircraft in Asian-Pacific countries. It is small wonder, then, that there is greater discussion in the Asian region regarding the credibility of U.S. nuclear commitments

---

[4]France rejects the idea of explicit nuclear commitments. However, Paris approved NATO documents which state that the French nuclear posture contributes to NATO's overall deterrence.

without visible and permanent nuclear symbols. On the other hand, not every NATO member state is fully convinced of the need for U.S. nuclear weapons on European soil, and some have shown interest in the Asian model of extended deterrence without nuclear deployment.

## What Can NATO's Role Be?

In light of these factors, it becomes evident that European NATO members should not only passively take note of the U.S. reorientation to Asia-Pacific but actively support it. This imperative remains even if Russia's expansionist policies seem to revitalize NATO's classical role of defending its European members. In a globalized world, the need for granting NATO's territorial integrity does not render developments in regions far beyond Europe less relevant.

Given Europe's limited capabilities, though, the problem is what form active support could take and what Europe could do. In addition, it is worth scrutinizing who benefits from a potential European engagement: the Europeans themselves, the Asian partner countries, or the United States?

From a European point of view, the intention should be to pursue European interests in a region increasingly relevant to those interests. At the same time, Europe is aware that its capabilities for long-range power projection are very limited, and are even continuing to decline, as a consequence of financial cuts in almost all European countries. However, reducing international influence to the level of military capacities is just half the truth. Europe—and particularly the European Union—has certain assets which, while arguably not compensating for a lack of hard power, nevertheless have value as a source of influence on international developments. First, the EU can use its economic influence to support or penalize the behavior of other actors. EU sanctions against China after the Tiananmen Square massacre might not have prevented Beijing from beefing up its military, but they certainly had an effect. Otherwise, China would not have been so keen to have these sanctions lifted. Second, the EU embraces most of the European members in NATO (21 out of 26 European NATO members) but does not include the United States. In terms of power politics, this might make the EU a toothless tiger, but it has advantages in regions where skepticism to Washington's superpower attitudes is strong.

The influence of most European NATO members in the Asia-Pacific region will nevertheless remain limited. Still, Europe could show the flag and demonstrate its interest in the region by some concrete measures. For instance, NATO has Liaison Offices in Moscow and Kiev to show presence in these countries, and to correct misperceptions on NATO among the public and in decision making circles. Cities like Tokyo or Seoul would be ideal locations for Liaison Offices of this kind, as they would bring an important political payoff for a comparably limited price tag. Another strong signal of interest in the region would be the physical presence of NATO representatives on a regular basis. Visits should not be limited to occasional trips by the NATO Secretary General or the Chairman of the Military Committee to individual countries, but should also include the regular participation of these NATO leaders in important regional meetings like the ASEAN Regional Forum (ARF).

From an Asian perspective, partnership with NATO opens another channel for contacts with the Euro-Atlantic community. Having close ties not only with Washington, but also with European NATO members, is regarded as an added value. In this respect, Asia perceives NATO to a large extent as a European organization: it is no coincidence that, in the Japanese Foreign Ministry, it is the "European Affairs Bureau" that deals with NATO.[5]

If NATO wants to fulfill these expectations, it has to urgently improve its capabilities to consult closely with key partners in the Asia-Pacific region. Currently, there is not even a forum or a permanent body in which such consultations could take place. In Europe and in the Middle East, these forums exist: in the "Partnership for Peace" (PfP), for instance, NATO meets with European and Central Asian countries, whereas the Mediterranean Dialogue (MD) gives the Alliance a framework for interaction with its North African partners. In addition, there are bodies like the NATO-Russia Council for permanent bilateral discussions. With Asia-Pacific countries, NATO meets on a permanent basis only with those engaged in Afghanistan—

---

[5]See Michito Tsuruoka, "NATO and Japan as Multifaceted Partners," Research Paper No. 91 (Rome: NATO Defense College, April 2013).

in the so-called ISAF Contributors' Meetings. After NATO's withdrawal from the Hindu Kush in 2014, these meetings will no longer exist. Therefore, NATO has to create a table to sit and consult with its Asian-Pacific partners on a regular basis.

This establishment of a new forum could be done as part of a partnership reform, which is overdue anyway. Current partnerships are still arranged in regional groupings: Europe and Central Asia, Mediterranean, and the Gulf countries. Even if NATO deals with all partners in a flexible and pragmatic way the classification in regions is less and less sustainable. For instance, Sweden and Belarus belong to the same group of PfP countries. In reality, NATO has three categories of partners. The first category includes countries like Austria, Sweden, and Finland that share NATO's values, contribute to NATO operations and are fully developed democracies. This enables NATO to include these countries as far as possible in its internal consultations and deliberations. Another group encompasses Central Asia, the Middle East and Russia and includes countries that cooperate with NATO fruitfully and with mutual benefit but without the close consultations of the first group. The third category includes countries like China that reach out to NATO in a non-obligatory manner to see whether there is common ground for closer cooperation.

Since there four Asian-Pacific countries (Japan, South Korea, Australia and New Zealand) belong to the category of "almost members," NATO should create a new forum to gather these advanced partners, regardless of their geographical origin. Australia and Austria would sit together with South Korea and Sweden.[6] Such a forum would facilitate regular meetings among those countries politically closest to the Alliance and would allow the partners in the Asia-Pacific region to be involved even more deeply in NATO's decision *shaping* (whereas decision *making* would be the preserve of the member states in the North Atlantic Council). Privileged treatment of like-minded countries would not preclude contacts or partnerships with other Asian countries like Pakistan, China or Mongolia, but relations with such countries would involve a much lower level of inclusion in NATO's affairs. The decision as to which countries should belong to the privileged

---

[6]Karl-Heinz Kamp and Heidi Reisinger, "NATO's Partnerships After 2014: Go West!" Research Paper No. 92 (Rome: NATO Defense College, 2013).

forum for advanced partners should be based on Alliance consensus, just as consensus is required to accept new NATO members. If all Allies agree, an interested partner should be able to join the advanced partners' forum.

Potential criticism that this would create a "red carpet lounge" for specific countries, or would re-establish the political "West," hardly applies. There is nothing wrong or offensive in the idea that a democratic and value-based alliance, which emphasizes in its founding document (the Washington Treaty) the principles of democracy, individual liberty and the rule of law, treats politically like-minded partners in a privileged manner. Cooperating closely with like-minded countries does not exclude fruitful partnerships with others on a less binding level.

Another topic on which NATO could be particularly beneficial for many Asia-Pacific countries is nuclear deterrence. Since nuclear weapons remain an important factor in international relations, NATO and most Asia-Pacific partners remain confronted with the nuclear question, which is: how to deter whom with what? As indicated earlier, both the Euro-Atlantic and the Asia-Pacific regions deal with nuclear commitments and extended deterrence differently, and each has a strong interest in the models of the other. Through its Nuclear Planning Group, NATO has long-standing experience in nuclear consultations between nuclear haves and have-nots. In 2012, the Alliance even managed to come up with a new nuclear deterrence concept—the Deterrence and Defense Posture Review (DDPR)—despite different perceptions among Allies of the role of nuclear weapons. Through an intense nuclear dialogue NATO could share its nuclear expertise with Asian-Pacific countries, and in turn non-nuclear European Allies could benefit from access to the experiences and concepts of their Asian counterparts. As a first step, interested Asian-Pacific partners could be offered an observer role in selected NPG meetings.

From the American point of view, Europe's limited but noticeable and—what is more—complementary power could be useful in a number of respects. Europe could show greater engagement in its neighboring regions, particularly the Middle East and North Africa, in order to unburden Washington's military capabilities as they become more strongly oriented towards Asia. Particularly in Arab countries, not being American is even perceived positively. Requests from Iran or

Syria to countries like Germany to act as a mediator in ongoing crises—even if these offers might have a tactical background—show an appreciation of a European role in the region. It is also worth noting that European influence in the Arab world does not stem only from the EU's financial engagement. European money in countries such as Egypt might be easily replaced by funds from the Gulf monarchies like Saudi Arabia. Still, Arab countries understand that they cannot tread the path towards modernity without Europe, and moderate forces in the region at least are fully aware that modernization is the only way out of the current difficulties.

Potential military engagement by Europe will certainly depend on the support of U.S. military assets, but the example of Libya has shown that the Europeans are willing, and at least partly able, to take the lead in military crisis management. As an example, France in its new White Paper explicitly states its readiness to contribute to global peace and security and promises to keep full spectrum forces for this purpose.

Even before sending forces into combat, the Europeans could do more to free American resources for duties in the Asia-Pacific. A number of European NATO members provide naval forces for anti-piracy operations off the Horn of Africa. These forces could be permanently deployed in the Indian Ocean, to show the flag and to function as an immediate response capability.

Beyond military capabilities, Washington still attaches importance to the political support of its Allies to legitimize its own actions—particularly in light of the American public's intervention fatigue. Recent events in Syria have shown how hard the Obama administration has tried to gather European support, although it would have been fully able to execute military strikes against the Assad regime on its own.

Finally, Washington has a vested interest in Europe's economic recovery and notices positively the tremendous efforts of some European Allies to overcome the constructional shortcomings of the Eurozone. By devoting time and energy to this issue, Europe might be partly distracted from global developments, but could ultimately regain its capacity to act forcefully on the international scene—if necessary, with hard power.

## Recommendations for NATO's To-Do List

The U.S. rebalancing to the Asia-Pacific indicates the relevance of the region for the entire Euro-Atlantic community—European NATO members must take note of this fact. Despite the limited and Euro-centered capacities of many Allies and regardless of the new focus on containing Russia, NATO could take a number of steps to cope with the U.S. strategic reorientation and to pursue, in particular, European member interests in the region. Moreover, NATO could demonstrate that the proverbial pivot is not about changing priorities from one region to another but about a trilateral approach to security: Europe, Asia and North America. Specific recommendations are:

1. **To show the flag and to visibly demonstrate its interest in the region, NATO should open Liaison offices—along the lines of the existing ones in Moscow or Kiev—in key Asia-Pacific capitals like Tokyo, Seoul or Canberra.** This would provide information about the Alliance to a broader audience and would symbolize NATO's interest in the region.

2. **To be informed about trends and events in the Asia-Pacific, NATO should send high-level representatives to important regional fora like the ASEAN Regional Forum.** By doing so, NATO could take part in regional debates and would be regularly updated about important developments.

3. **To unburden the United States, NATO should transform its anti-piracy mission into a Standing Maritime Group in the Indian Ocean**—in addition to those two groups which are already cruising in the Atlantic and the Mediterranean. This would provide NATO with another rapid reaction capability and would free U.S. capabilities to focus on the Asian-Pacific region.

4. **To permanently include the advanced partners in the Asia-Pacific in NATO's consultations, the Alliance needs to create a special forum for those countries that are "almost members"—independent from their geographical origin.** With such a forum, countries like Japan or Australia, together with European partners like Finland or Sweden, could closely confer with NATO members on all questions of common interest and could be included into relevant decision shaping processes.

5. **To facilitate a mutually beneficial dialogue on nuclear questions, NATO should give those countries in the Asia-Pacific region that enjoy U.S. nuclear commitments observer status in certain Nuclear Planning Group meetings.** This would help develop the concept of nuclear deterrence in a world where nuclear weapons still pose a fundamental threat and where the number of nuclear players is more likely to increase than to become smaller.

These limited but feasible measures would be a first, but very relevant attempt to react to the new realities of the Asia-Pacific, as this region becomes both a strategic challenge and an opportunity in the 21st century.

## Chapter Nine

# European Crisis Management in Asia: The Case of Aceh

*Pieter Feith*

Many argue that Europe has no role to play in promoting Asian security. This case study demonstrates the opposite. Europe has a very constructive role to play in global crisis management.

It is relatively rare that a window of opportunity opens for successful mediation or conflict management. At least one of the parties to a conflict must have reached the conclusion that the continuation of armed struggle no longer serves its fundamental interests and that the alternative of a negotiated outcome is worth exploring. Manifestation of serious political will on both sides to engage in talks is a further precondition. The sides may find each other without outside assistance, but more often than not, a wise and even-handed mediator will assist and guide the process in a direction where substantial gains can be obtained for both. And, as confidence in the other side's intentions takes root, the implementation of agreed commitments, if carried out in good faith, provides additional reassurance that mutual expectations and calculations will become reality. Here again is where a credible international actor with the necessary leverage can assist to make the process sustainable and irreversible.

It did not need the devastating force of the *tsunami* on Boxing Day 2004 to see all these elements come together in Indonesia's province of Aceh, situated at the northern tip of Sumatra bordering the Malacca straits. Before the massive wall of water swept over the coastlines of Southeast Asia, both the government of Indonesia and the Aceh Independence Movement (known locally as GAM) had established contact with mediators from Finland. And it is certainly true that, while the immediate aftermath of this unprecedented disaster caused delay and uncertainty, the one positive effect was that it galvanized the desire of the two parties to look for a negotiated settlement of the conflict. Beginning in January 2005, the government of Indonesia and GAM affirmed their willingness to extend the cease-fire agreement and to enter into a dialogue.

Was the window opening? Signs were encouraging that indeed it was. The rebels were hard pressed on the battlefield while their political leadership lingered in exile in Sweden. More importantly perhaps, in Jakarta a reform-minded duo had assumed power following the 2004 presidential elections. Former General Susilo Bambang Yudhoyono ("SBY" as he is referred to locally) had gone on record that the armed conflict in Aceh could not be resolved through military means. In addition, he was a prominent advocate of modernizing the armed forces of Indonesia (TNI) by bringing it under democratic control and confining its core mission to external defense. This meant that the legacy of the Suharto years, during which the army had expanded into the areas of law and order and the exploitation of natural resources—in particular in the outer provinces such as Aceh—was drawing to a close. This provided political cover to SBY's running mate, Jusuf Kalla, to pursue energetically the quest for overtures with the Acehnese liberation movement.

In addition, a mediator was ready to assist—former Finnish President Martti Ahtisaari, a trusted and experienced international peace broker and chairman of the Helsinki-based *Crisis Management Initiative*. Ahtisaari was not the kind of person to waste his time on endless deliberations. Was the movement ready to contemplate some form of far-reaching autonomy as part of the Republic's constitutional framework and shelve its aspirations at independence? During the 1980s, GAM fighters had received military training in Libya. Following 9/11 however, the international mood had grown less sympathetic towards attempts at secession by radical Islamic movements at the expense of the stability of friendly and potentially allied states. Next to autonomy rights to be agreed upon, the issue of revenue sharing of Aceh's vast natural resources, including oil and gas, would again be on the agenda. These resources had been part of the ill-fated Cessation of Hostilities Agreement of 2001, which collapsed leading to a resumption of hostilities. Then, as now, 70 percent of the income would be retained by the local authorities.

Another positive development was that in Brussels, ministers of the European Union, next to agreeing substantial programs for emergency and reconstruction aid, took a broad view on the common response by expressing support to processes ending internal conflicts in areas devastated by the *tsunami* disaster. The prospects for achieving peace and reconciliation seemed most promising in Aceh.

## Negotiations

The first three negotiation rounds during the spring of 2005 resulted in substantial progress in exploring the concept of local self-government, improving the human rights situation and the granting of an amnesty to the GAM fighters. Ahtisaari informed the EU in March that he aimed at an agreement that would be comprehensive and sustainable. It would include the decommissioning of GAM weapons, the withdrawal of 30 "non-organic" TNI battalions and the organization of local elections with participation of Acehnese local candidates. An effective monitoring mechanism was to become a key element of the deal. To that end, a small monitoring mission with authority and freedom of movement would be invited to oversee the process. For Jakarta, bearing in mind the painful steps leading to independence of Eastern Timor, the United Nations was not acceptable to play that part. Nor, for different reasons, would the United States or Australia be able to play such a role. The EU could therefore consider itself a likely candidate. Time was of the essence—the mission should be in place by the summer. By the time Ahtisaari came to Brussels to brief the ambassadors in the Political and Security Committee in May, he found cautious interest. A fact-finding mission was agreed as a next step in order to ascertain the conditions for deploying a presence.

Certainly the High Representative for the Common Foreign and Security Policy of the EU, Javier Solana, understood that an opportunity presented itself to demonstrate the EU's ability to become a global player in international crisis management—as it had set out to do in a clear and concise document agreed by ministers in 2003, called the "European Security Strategy."[1] Since 1999, when French President

---

[1] "European Security Strategy—A Secure Europe in a Better World," Council of the European Union (Brussels, 2003), http://www.consilium.europa.eu/uedocs/cmsUpload/78367.pdf.

Chirac and British Prime Minister Tony Blair took the initiative at St. Malo, the European Union was busy developing its European Security and Defense Policy, using its military and civilian crisis management instruments for addressing the assessed key threats of the new millennium—terrorism, proliferation of weapons of mass destruction, regional conflicts, state failure and organized crime. The member states, acting in full support of these ambitious goals, committed themselves to provide dedicated military units, police, judges and prosecutors for operations and missions led by the EU. Rapid deployment, including at the request of the United Nations, and engagement not only in Europe's immediate neighborhood but extending to other parts of the world, were part of this proactive, confident approach. Would not a pivot to faraway Indonesia add credibility to Europe's role in a globalizing world? On the other hand, for immediate planning needs, further clarification was needed with regard to the parties' intentions and their political will to follow through on their agreed commitments. Specifically, did the independence movement have a chain of command with compliant commanders in the field and with the political leadership at the top? And was TNI to follow directions from the President as the commander-in-chief, even if that entailed giving up on material interests and revert to peace-time conditions in accordance with the law? We had to find out. As a first step for doing so and at the invitation of the chief negotiator, in my capacity as Solana's closest advisor for operational matters I attended the next round of talks in Finland. Meeting the two delegations was the point of departure for building confidence—trust in Ahtisaari's commitment that he would find an implementing organization, and in my own person as a potential candidate to assume the lead on the ground. Old friendships count: I met Martti Ahtisaari at the end of the 1970s in New York when he was the UN Commissioner for Namibia; and later on in Brussels in 1999 when he brokered the end of NATO's air campaign against Milosevic and I briefed him on the Alliance's plans to deploy ground forces in Kosovo.

The European Union needed a formal invitation, as the legal base for its mandated activities on Indonesian territory; and a Status of Mission Agreement regulating a host of practical issues like privileges and immunities, security, and the dress code for the unarmed monitors.

The Indonesian side suggested that the mission should be a joint one with nationals from five ASEAN states—Malaysia, Thailand, Philippines, Singapore and Brunei. A regional organization of which Indonesia was a prominent member would shoulder part of the responsibility, and in doing so, absorb most of the nationalistic sensitivities about western interference in the internal affairs of Indonesia. It would also help the Europeans better understand the language and cultural characteristics of an unfamiliar environment. This was as innovative as it proved effective.

In Aceh province, meanwhile, incidents continued to take place, often followed by brutal retaliation from the security forces. Ahtisaari did not hesitate to remind the authorities in Jakarta that a climate of security needed to take hold and that restraint and discipline on both sides was called for. Member states in Brussels accepted my proposal to take further steps in preparing a possible deployment by conducting a reconnaissance in the area. All of this in anticipation that the negotiators would succeed in finalizing a deal and that little time would remain thereafter—a rare sign of confidence and readiness to build on what had been achieved thus far.

The principal aim of my team's visit in June was to ascertain on the ground that the parties were ready to move. A number of the Jakarta-based ambassadors did not conceal their ambivalence, and it was true that the military's record in conflict areas had been dismal in the past. The embassies were registering the views of the Ministry of Foreign Affairs, which traditionally considers itself the guardian of Indonesian sovereignty and territorial integrity. But the Ministry had played no role in the Finland negotiations for a good reason: to underscore the internal nature of the conflict. I hoped to hear from the President in person. SBY asked the EU to trust him. Drawing on his experience as a UN observer in Bosnia, he knew that the conflict in Aceh had to be solved on the basis of negotiations. But clear procedures and timelines were required. What about the weapons surrendered by the rebels, he asked me. I suggested that they be destroyed immediately as part of a public ceremony for all to see. That would convey a powerful message to the population that their security would henceforward be assured by the legitimate authorities and not by the rebels. He liked the idea. Vice-President Kalla explained the government's plans for reintegrating the fighters into society and incentives to help them find income and employment.

The other key player I needed to see was the GAM commander in Aceh, Zakariah Saman. Flying by helicopter and with security forces closing in, we managed to locate him in the bush, standing in an open clearing together with about seventy of his fighters. Was he informed and did he agree to hand in about 840 weapons in good working condition? The answer was affirmative on both counts. Apparently cell phone connections between Aceh and Sweden did function—a chain of command of sorts was in place.

I had previously witnessed the fifth round in Finland when agreement was reached on decommissioning and on a ceiling of residual police and military personnel following the withdrawal of 31,000 security forces. The movement representatives and their Australian adviser initially balked when they learned that 14,700 military and 9,100 police would remain in the province. But they could be persuaded to accept these high figures after Ahtisaari suggested to include a provision in the agreement whereby the military would be tasked with external defense and that the police would receive special training in upholding human rights standards. The significance of these requirements for the government was expected to go well beyond the situation in Aceh and constitute a precedent for other conflict areas in Indonesia's sprawling territory.

The agreement was concluded only a day before the Council of EU Ministers, gathering for their last meeting before the summer break, were in a position to confirm their readiness to assist in its implementation. In order to avoid any semblance of recognition of the GAM independence movement, the agreement is called the Helsinki Memorandum of Understanding. Rigorous timelines were foreseen to prevent the deal from unraveling. Following a formal signing ceremony on August 15, the implementation would start one month later on September 15.

The EU was left facing a challenge to deploy its presence in the shortest possible timeframe. Initial planning foresaw a mission consisting of about 140 monitors and fifty decommissioning experts. In a constructive atmosphere we consulted with ASEAN representatives in Jakarta leading to an understanding that these countries would together provide another ninety monitors as well as the deputy head of the mission. Headquarters and the eleven field offices were to be fully integrated, with officers from both ASEAN and the EU alternating leadership positions. This and the policy of total transparency with regard to decision making and reporting, including in our contacts with the parties, contributed significantly to ultimate mission success.

This was a challenge for the European Security and Defense Policy (ESDP).[2] Despite strong leadership by Javier Solana, the ambition to become a global player in crisis management suffered some initial reverses and brought to light structural weaknesses. While high levels of functional integration have been achieved in certain areas such as the internal market, foreign policy remains firmly under the control of the member states. According to the EU Treaty, the operational activities of the Union are embedded in consensus on a foreign policy framework. Member states, each with their traditional interests and priorities, will therefore have to agree on actions to be taken. And where deep divisions occur (such as over the invasion of Iraq in 2003 or later on over Kosovo's independence), the EU's impact in the world suffers as a consequence. Enlargement of the Union undoubtedly brought many benefits but decision making, often under time constraints, in a committee setting is clearly more cumbersome than similar processes in the capitals of the major powers—inter-agency disputes notwithstanding. Political consensus is a key requirement for EU external success. Such was the case with Indonesia, a country with about 230 million Muslim inhabitants and a developing center of gravity for European trade and investment. No member state had fundamental objections to sending a common mission to Aceh. Here was an opportunity to close the ranks following the disagreement over the 2003 Iraq invasion. Measured in terms of capabilities needed to carry out the monitoring task, the Aceh operation would not seem to present a serious problem, although preparation time was short. Personnel needs were broadly met and Sweden generously provided logistics, communication and medical support normally used for internal emergencies.

A final factor constraining the further development of the ESDP is the lack of coherence between the institutions. Notwithstanding some

---

[2]Under the Lisbon Treaty renamed Common Foreign and Security Policy (CSDP).

improvements under the Lisbon Treaty of 2009, the Commission retains authority over trade and development. The concept of a comprehensive approach aims at drawing together all these instruments in one coherent, effective foreign policy action including in the context of crisis management. However, this aim is a far cry from reality. Also the size of the budget for international crisis management including the procurement of equipment and services is in the Commission's hands and its size at the time amounted to a pittance.

In the Aceh case, there was little room for meeting the expenses for this unforeseen operation, and the shortfall had to be met by member states acting on a voluntary basis. In addition, time was too short to complete the normal procedures for launching the mission before August 15, the date of the signature of the peace accord. In agreement with the Indonesian authorities, an "Initial Monitoring Presence" was therefore established of about fifty personnel whose names were added to the diplomatic list of their embassies in Jakarta, thereby providing the legal base for their presence on Indonesian territory. Although not a mission of the European Security and Defense Policy in the formal sense, this fix (which followed the precedent of the Kosovo Verification Mission in the late nineties) would serve to close the gap on the ground until the "Aceh Monitoring Mission (AMM)" would take over on September 15. To be sure, incidents did occur during that initial period, but their presence helped maintain respect for the cease fire and avoid a general breakdown of the still-fragile process before implementation had properly started.

An information strategy could now be rolled out with messages for different audiences, at the local and Jakarta levels. The aim was to socialize the agreement and to solicit the population's support for efforts to create a safe environment for the authorities to operate in the ravaged area with the support of the international community. Without peace, the post-tsunami reconstruction goals would be much more difficult to attain and, conversely, successful reconstruction and resumption of economic activity would help the reintegration of the former fighters into civilian life. Spoilers on both sides were targeted, including illegal militias acting in support of the security services against the independence movement.

In the Jakarta Parliament, opposition parties and a group of former generals needed to be convinced that the deal was in the national interest and that the mission would not extend beyond the eighteen months mandate as initially foreseen. With regard to possible non-compliant GAM fighters, the message was that the mission, with the authority given by the sending organizations, would be even-handed and scrupulous in dealing with attempts to circumvent the agreement. As part of these efforts I had frequent meetings with civil society including women advocacy groups and *ulemas*, or Islamic teachers, who were expected to help promote reconciliation and respect for customs and traditions. Additionally, I met with the military and police commanders in Aceh, who reassured me of their willingness to cooperate but also produced a long litany of complaints about GAM violations, most recently a firefight on July 25. Clearly mistrust was in plentiful supply—among the Acehnese with regard to Jakarta and among the Indonesians with regard to the international organizations. This needed to be overcome if we were to succeed.

## Implementation

The signing ceremony of the Helsinki Memorandum of Understanding[3] on August 15, 2005 was shown on a big screen before the Beiturrahman Mosque of Banda Aceh for the population to follow. The material damage caused by the disaster was there for all to see, and the mass graves testified to the human suffering. Most families had lost one or more beloved ones. The registration and laying to rest of the deceased had not been completed. Meanwhile, the images from far away Finland, the speeches and the solemnity of the event raised hopes among the people who greeted the signing with loud cheers of approval.

The first fifty members of the initial presence were now going through induction covering code of conduct issues as a matter of continuous attention. The agreement contained clear stipulations for decommissioning and redeployment out of the area. Nonetheless, I concluded that proactive monitoring was called for in order to guide the parties to the agreed end-state. The example of the Joint Military

---

[3]See Aceh Monitoring Mission website http://www.aceh-mm.org.

Commission was adapted, a forum chaired by the commander of NATO forces in Bosnia for the purpose of giving directions to the parties, setting the agenda and imposing timelines. The meetings, with an initial frequency of once or twice a week, invariably ended with an agreed communiqué and a press conference to inform the population of the outcome. Similar consultations were to be organized at the level of the field offices so that problems could be solved locally before they would escalate into major crises.

The sides agreed to participate in what became known as the Committee on Security Arrangements (COSA), each of them organizing themselves to provide continuous connectivity and presence in the capital Banda Aceh. With nearly fifty meetings during the mandate period, the forum served its useful purpose of facilitating dialogue, strengthening confidence and occasionally hosting high-level guests. Jakarta's chief representative was one of the ministers negotiating the Helsinki agreement, underscoring the civilian control over the security forces. The GAM movement was represented by an articulate, moderate activist named Irwandi Youssouf who had managed to wrestle himself out of the roof of the prison building just in time before the tsunami waters engulfed the compound. Increasingly, these men would use the COSA meetings for side chats to settle issues among themselves. The GAM political leadership in exile in Stockholm elected to keep their distance during the first months in the process, and it was only in April 2006, coinciding with a Solana visit, that we managed to persuade them to return and to assume leadership and responsibility. By then, the decommissioning had been completed, and attention turned to the political provisions of the agreement.

Two days after the entry into force of the agreement, on Indonesia's Independence Day, some three hundred Acehnese fighters were released from prison, followed by a presidential decree granting formal amnesty "to all persons who have participated in GAM activities." This was a hopeful beginning. As head of the monitoring mechanism I examined 116 cases, all of whom, with the exception of eleven persons, were given their freedom back. A serious incident clearly instigated by rebels was dealt with firmly—a first test in the eyes of keenly attentive Jakarta of the measure of our evenhandedness and alertness. We ordered an investigation and publicly condemned the attack.

On September 15, the AMM started operations and the first decommissioning event took place. Among the first arms handed in were many unserviceable and antiquated pieces of weaponry. But during the following days the target for the first round was easily reached, to the obvious relief and satisfaction of the Jakarta government and the Brussels hierarchy. As intended, the ceremony on the central square of Banda Aceh and some other collection points took on a festive mood as the population witnessed the sawing of equipment that many had come to regard as a threat to their individual security and well-being. This first step was soon reciprocated by the relocation of 6671 military and 1300 police away from Aceh. We were invited to attend the farewell ceremony at Lokhseumawe Harbor.

All of this bode well for smooth further work, but every day's reality also brought the mission members a steady dose of mistrust from the side of the military and police. We seemed to live in two different worlds, one of growing camaraderie and another one of constant surveillance and observation of our movements. A special police detachment of three hundred men had been sent from Jakarta to ensure the mission's safety and protection, but it soon went a step further to engage in monitoring the monitors. Our local staff, in particular, felt the pressure from casual remarks or unsolicited text messages. In order to be prepared for the worst case assumption, a policy of strict transparency was followed successfully. This was a reminder that the two parties were not placed on an equal footing and that one of them was in a position to withdraw consent to the mission at any given point in time.

The second decommissioning round in October took more effort. The GAM representative struggled to convince his field commanders to give him the required number of weapons. A special collection event had to be organized on Sabang Island facing Banda Aceh, where all of a sudden some fifty brand new weapons turned up—unclear from where they originated, but it closed the gap. This, in turn allowed for another withdrawal of government security forces.

The frequency of local non-compliance and incidents increased. Team leaders were the first to respond but rebel commanders were simply unwilling to enter into contact with the monitors. Nor did the military always follow the rules, for instance by moving units without prior notification to the mission. In a clear instance of excessive use of force a suspected criminal without GAM connections was summarily shot by an army unit. Following investigation, I raised this incident as a matter of utmost concern during the next *COSA* meeting. Not only did the military accept the results of our findings but they also agreed to the inclusion of the following statement in the communiqué of the meeting: "In connection with this the AMM draws attention to the stipulation in the MoU that organic TNI units in Aceh will assume an external defense posture only and that law and order tasks shall be the responsibility of the police."[4] This was significant as it pointed to growing awareness and a beginning of acceptance among policymakers in Jakarta of the need for security sector reform and modernization of the country's armed forces.

A start was made with organizing the payment of reintegration packages in the form of land or cash to three thousand fighters, as foreseen in the agreement. The government disbursed the aid during the Ramadan holiday period in order to show goodwill and assist the beneficiaries in reengaging with society. However, the program stalled as the fighters balked at registering out of fear for reprisals. It also overwhelmed the bureaucracy already overburdened with providing assistance to the victims of tsunami. Despite the creation of a new agency for reintegration, little progress was achieved during the mandate period.

The two final rounds of decommissioning ended successfully, although again not without drama. GAM attendance at the table of the COSA meeting of November 30 suddenly included new faces, Irwandi having been relegated to the second row by a senior activist freshly released from detention in August and by field commander Teungku Ubit. Both men assumed a distinctly uncooperative posture by arguing that all weapons had been handed in and even in excess of what had been agreed. I chose to show a firm hand in the face of this maneuver—a balance of 142 weapons was to be presented if the rebels were to remain in compliance. This cleared the air and after some

---

[4]"Press Statement on the Outcome of the Meeting of the Commission on Security Arrangements (COSA)," Council of the European Union (Banda Aceh, October 19, 2005), https://www.consilium.europa.eu/uedocs/cmsUpload/Press_Statement_COSA-19.10.05-Final.pdf.

internal wrangling, the weapons were delivered, some of them to remote areas of southeastern Aceh that required helicopter transport to collect them. This led to further government withdrawals "in honor and dignity." A final ceremony with the symbolic cutting of weapons was held at the location where it all began—Banda Aceh's central square, the heart of local government.

The conservative press questioned whether all arms had been handed in. The answer frankly was: not sure, but would it matter? The real question was to know if this outcome had yielded enough trust to allow the parties to continue walking the road towards peace together. A statement by GAM confirming their readiness to demobilize and dismantle the organization was helpful in this respect. The President drew a positive conclusion. SBY visited Banda Aceh on December 27 to attend the solemn commemoration of the tsunami disaster. We then moved into a meeting with the Islamic leaders, the *ulemas*, where a positive mood indicated that the people felt safe and wanted to focus on reconstruction and development. The President was visibly pleased, not in the least because the results in Aceh, echoed by the international and pro-government press, would silence his critics back in Jakarta.

The next phase unfolded in the capital, at some distance from our vantage point in Aceh and with less access to information and influence. A new Law on the Governing of Aceh (LOGA) had to be enacted with the approval of the national parliament (DPR). This law was promulgated with some delay on August 1, 2006, and encapsulated the basic principles and provisions of the Helsinki accord. However, some serious discrepancies appeared. Thus, while it confirmed the autonomous status of the province, decisions of the national parliament concerning Aceh were not to be taken in consultation with and with the *consent* of the legislature of Aceh. This was a severe restriction on the autonomy rights. In reply to my request for clarification, Jakarta ministers sought to reassure that the process of consensus building between the national and provincial authorities would be further elaborated by presidential decree. Also with regard to matters like raising taxes by the local authorities, the method of revenue sharing and the mission statement of the armed forces in the province, Jakarta seemed to take a step back in comparison to their previous commitments.

The return of the GAM leadership from exile was long overdue. This finally succeeded when Javier Solana visited Jakarta. When Solana assumed the chairmanship of the COSA meeting in Banda Aceh, he found the Stockholm based leaders Malik Mahmoud and his deputy Zaini Abdullah in front of him. Speaking on behalf of the EU, he reminded them that they should not waste time transitioning into a political movement as part of a democratically elected, multi-party system in Aceh. This touched upon our exit strategy, which was predicated on the readiness of the two parties to enter into direct dialogue on political issues. As part of this exit, the mission was extended with the consent of Jakarta until June 15 and again until September 15 in order to cover the local elections.

During this period of time, the size of the mission shrank to 85 monitors with fresh expertise added in the areas of political analysis, legal affairs including human rights and reintegration. Throughout the mandate period, I continued to press the government on the establishment of a Human Rights Court for Aceh and a Truth and Reconciliation Commission, as foreseen in the Helsinki MOU and in the LOGA. However, these efforts failed to bear fruit. Because of its implications for the rule of law, the mission also spent considerable time and effort clarifying the role of the TNI armed forces, thereby addressing concerns among the people of Aceh dating back to a record of serious human rights violations and impunity during the past decades. In November 2006, the commander in chief TNI, Marshal Suyanto, spoke at my invitation to a town hall meeting of civil society representatives and former GAM fighters clarifying that TNI responsibilities were limited primarily to external defense. During the spring, a program was initiated by UNDP and IOM providing human rights training to the police.

## Exit

President Ahtisaari visited Indonesia in August 2006 to attend the first anniversary of the signing of the Helsinki Memorandum of Understanding. At a conference in Jakarta, SBY spoke movingly about his personal involvement in the various stages of the process. By then the mission had completed its main tasks with only the provincial elections in Aceh remaining. Once the decision was taken to set the date on December 11, the President asked me to recommend a final extension of AMM in order to provide presence during the elections. His request was agreed by Brussels and the participating ASEAN countries. During this final phase the mission was drawn down to a mere 36 monitors with all field offices having been closed. However, at the invitation of the government, an EU Election Observation Mission was deployed under the authority of the European Commission and the European Parliament to observe polling and the final stages of the election campaign. This was a welcome contribution from the other two main institutions of the European Union demonstrating its capacity to use a broad range of instruments in post-crisis situations.

The elections, assessed as "free and honest" by the Observation Mission, resulted in a clear victory for Irwandi Youssouf, the mission's main interlocutor during the past months. He became the first Governor of the autonomous province Aceh. Again this was a positive outcome as he had proven to be committed to the continuation of a constructive dialogue with the national government. And it was not without its significance because during the election campaign the GAM movement had shown signs of splitting up between "young Turks" including Irwandi, and the old guard centered on the exiled leadership in Stockholm. Aware that control was to slip out of their hands, Malik and Zeini returned once again in order to engage more actively in the crucial final stages of the mandate period.

The 44th and final meeting of the Commission on Security Arrangements on December 2 proved to be an important one. From its side, the government was ready to authorize the establishment of local political parties before the end of the year. GAM would then be given six months to register and to dissolve its armed wing as soon as possible thereafter. This offer was accepted and included in the agreed outcome of the meeting. With the elections held, AMM had completed its assigned tasks and disbanded on December 15—the first ESDP mission in Asia had come to an end.

## Final Thoughts

Too often the mediator focuses on closing the deal—leaving the implementation for another day. Not so with Martti Ahtisaari, whose efforts resulted in a quality peace agreement with strong linkages between commitments and implementation.[5] Considering that monitoring the security provisions of the peace agreement constituted one of the core elements of the AMM mandate, the mission was generally considered a success giving a boost to Indonesia's international reputation.[6] Certainly among the member states of the EU, the outcome was welcomed as a highpoint in the evolving European Security and Defense Policy—an example of the EU's *soft power* and ability to use its panoply of instruments for effective international conflict resolution and crisis management. Indeed, the decommissioning and disbandment of the independence movement as well as the relocation of non-organic TNI units out of Aceh unfolded as agreed and within the prescribed time limits. By deploying rapidly to be ready to start monitoring on the day the deal was signed, AMM contributed to making the process irreversible by the time these confidence building measures were fully carried out.

President Ahtisaari's organization, *Crisis Management Initiative*, concluded in 2012 that the security situation in Aceh was perceived by the local population as good and that "the armed forces participation in maintaining internal security has been substantially reduced."[7] Of note, piracy declined in the Malacca straits as peace in Aceh took hold. Also in other respects the record is positive, most importantly that the dialogue between the parties continues. A number of issues have been left unresolved and there are differences in interpretation of what was agreed. This may be due, certainly seen from the movement's perspective, to the sequencing of steps as foreseen in the peace agreement, leaving GAM with little leverage once the weapons had been surrendered. True, decommissioning and relocation were to be undertaken in parallel, but the next phase of implementing the political entitlements left the movement in an asymmetrical position.

---

[5] The 2008 Nobel Peace Prize covered President Ahtisaari's successful efforts in negotiating an end to the conflict in Aceh.

[6] See "A Triumph for Peace," *Frankfurter Allgemeine Zeitung*, December 16, 2006; See also: Roy H. Ginsberg and Susan E. Penksa, *The European Union in Global Security: The Politics of Impact* (London: Palgrave Macmillan, 2012).

[7] "Aceh Peace Process Follow-up Project," Crisis Management Initiative, June 2012, http://www.cmi.fi/images/stories/publications/reports/2012/aceh_report5_web.pdf.

The parties have not used the dispute settlement mechanism contained in the agreement. Maybe that was to be expected in the context of a regional heavy-weight such as Indonesia, keen to preserve its sovereignty and nervous about foreign interference. Accordingly, both sides have an interest in working together on the full range of governance issues. Thus, on the question of the exploitation of Aceh's vast natural resources, both on- and off-shore, it is in everybody's interest that the rules and regulations are clarified to include the exact delineation of competences between the national and local authorities in order to stimulate foreign direct investment on a sustainable basis. Using its development resources in the wake of the monitoring mission, the EU should perhaps have done more to strengthen the capacity of the Acehnese administration to give real content to the complex issues of local self-government. Finally, the agreement contains some important benefits for good governance in Indonesia as a whole by raising awareness for human rights at the operational level and security sector reform. How far this will lead to a real change of mindset among the political elite is unclear. The peace process may have reached the stage of irreversibility, yet it cannot be considered as fully self-sustainable. It will need continuous political will, commitment and effort in order to yield the gains expected by the people of Aceh. It is therefore to be hoped that the general and Presidential elections foreseen for the summer of 2014 will result in national leadership as personally committed to peace and wide-ranging autonomy for Aceh as the duo Yudhoyono—Kalla was.

For the short and medium term, there are concerns related to the transition of GAM from an armed insurgency to a political player in a democratic, multi-party field. Following the departure of AMM, a political party was indeed established by GAM leader Malik Mahmoud, but without broad consultation he decided that its name was to be "Partai GAM." Since the acronym includes the word independence, it predictably led to strong protests from the Jakarta government. As a consequence the party was renamed "Partai Aceh" in 2008. But the group around Malik and Zaini successfully consolidated its power. The former assume the elevated position of *Wali Nanggroe* as a kind of successor to the historic Sultanate of Aceh, while the latter took over the Governorship in 2012 following local elections. Recently these leaders have made a point of using the flag of the former independence movement as the official symbol of the province. This claim is another demonstration of their lack of political sensitivity: it exacerbates a still fragile relationship with Jakarta and is seen by outside observers as step towards a one-party system in Aceh.[8]

Meanwhile, the European Union may have shed some of its global ambitions. European military units will not likely engage on Asian territories, not in the least because of local political sensitivities. Seen from European capitals, priority will be given to operations under the Common Foreign and Defense Policy in areas closer to the European continent where threats originate such as terrorism, failing states, uncontrolled migration and piracy in Northern and Central Africa, the Middle East and the Indian Ocean. Interestingly, Netherlands and Chinese military now operate side by side in Mali as part of a UN-led peacekeeping mission. This is not to say that Europe will be absent in Asia. In a quiet and effective way, significant resources and expertise are spent by the EU, its member states and non-governmental actors on assisting Asian counterparts in the areas of mediation and conflict resolution. This is particularly the case in Myanmar where the window of opportunity is slowly opening. And there is an as yet untapped potential for strengthening the "natural" partnership and cooperation between the Union and ASEAN in the response to natural and man-made disasters.

## Recommendations

There are five specific recommendations that flow from this case study that should apply to a transatlantic pivot to Asia:

1. **The United States and Europe should continue to help mediate peaceful, sustainable solutions to internal conflicts in Asia, based on the rule of law and respect for individual and collective human rights.**

2. **The European Union should enhance the effectiveness of its actions by the coherent and comprehensive use of its**

---

[8]"Asia Briefing 139," International Crisis Group, May 7, 2013, http://www.crisisgroup.org/en/regions/asia/south-east-asia/indonesia/b139-indonesia-tensions-over-acehs-flag.aspx.

crisis management instruments, including military and civilian capabilities, trade and development.

3. The European Union and ASEAN, as norm and treaty based organizations, should engage in structured cooperation, including in dealing with natural and man-made disasters.

4. NATO should stand ready to associate itself where appropriate.

5. With the support of the United States, countries in the region should step up their programs for security sector reform and redirect the mission statement of their armed forces towards external defense as a primary task, taking account of future challenges to the stability of the region.

*Part IV*

# The Broader Pivot

*Chapter Ten*

# Human Rights and the Rule of Law

*Abiodun Williams*

Discussions of the U.S. pivot to Asia have often paid little attention to human rights and the rule of law, even on the practical level of implementation. Scholars and practitioners most animated by the implications of the pivot tend to be those engaged in military analysis or economic diplomacy, relegating human rights considerations—in practice if not in design—to a level of secondary concern.

Such a narrow view of the pivot is ably contested by the essays in this volume and, moreover, misreads the pivot as enunciated by U.S. policymakers. Time and again, the Obama administration has under-lined that the pivot is an all-encompassing enterprise, concerning not just security, whose role has been over-emphasized, but also human rights, democracy and the rule of law. Human rights are an avowed component of the pivot and will be affected by the wider elements of the American "rebalance."

When considering Europe's role, these changes present both opportunities and threats. The European Union—the primary focus of the treatment of Europe in this chapter—constitutes itself inter-nally on a rule of law basis and, in its external relations, emphasizes the primacy of rules, both in inter-state relations and in terms of the social contract at the level of the nation-state. As such, it has a clear stake in changes to the human rights environment in Asia.[1] The pivot also concerns transatlantic relations in the human rights field. One of the clearest achievements of the partnership between Europe and the United States in the post-war era was the construction of the prevail-

---

[1]See for example Gráinnede Búrca, "EU External Relations: The Governance Mode of Foreign Policy" in Bart Van Vooren, Steven Blockmans and Jan Wouters, eds., *The EU's Role in Global Governance: The Legal Dimension* (Oxford: Oxford University Press, 2013), pp. 39–58.

ing international human rights regime. As the United States reorients its attention to Asia, questions may be raised about the sustainability of this transatlantic consensus. Will the United States and Europe maintain a common approach to global human rights issues, or will they engage in a "race to the bottom," substituting human rights concerns for alliance-building and market entry?

The United States and Europe confront a mixed human rights environment in Asia. Over the past decades there have been improvements in terms of individual freedoms, good governance and democracy, with several states making the transition away from authoritarianism. In recent years, signs of an opening in Burma/Myanmar have been particularly welcome. Nevertheless, flagrant abuses in many Asian countries persist. Until recently, Asia had been the only region of the world without an inter-governmental human rights regime, and the system that is slowly being put into place continues to be the target of strident criticism. The need for international engagement is clear.

As the United States implements its pivot, and as Europe considers its response, careful attention will be necessary, from civil society and elected officials, to ensure that the commitment to human rights in policy statements is realized. Both American and European officials must ensure that human rights concerns are not sacrificed for "wider" aims and that requisite support for rule of law initiatives—crucial for individual freedoms as well as inter-state reconciliation—remains strong. As Asia's rise gains momentum, whether the United States and Europe address Asian countries on human rights and rule of law questions in a complementary manner or whether their engagement is divergent, both geographically and in terms of priorities, will have a lasting effect on rights standards at the global level.

This chapter opens with a discussion of the place that human rights and the rule of law have in the pivot as expressed by U.S. officials and the current status of the European response. It then briefly introduces the notion of a "transatlantic values agenda" in this field and the challenges that U.S. and European conceptualizations of human rights face in Asia, where dominant traditions diverge from "universalism." The ends and means of both U.S. and European strategy on human rights and rule of law promotion are subsequently discussed, with a focus on methods of engagement at the domestic, regional and international level. The chapter concludes with concrete recommendations for U.S. and European actors to strengthen existing human rights interventions and to adapt activities to the changing geopolitical context.

## Human Rights and the Pivot: American and European Agendas

As outlined by senior U.S. government officials, the pivot to Asia is a whole-of-government initiative concerning not just enhanced security alliances and a change in military posture, but also diplomacy, human rights, economics, development and inter-societal relations. Introducing the concept in November 2011, then Secretary of State Hillary Rodham Clinton outlined a six-point plan of action, which included democracy and human rights. The inclusion of these priorities, Clinton argued, was a reflection of the United States' core strength: "even more than our military might or the size of our economy, our most potent asset as a nation is the power of our values—in particular, our steadfast support for democracy and human rights." Similarly, referring to 20th century Europe where the United States "recognized that it was not only our moral convictions but our economic and security interests that would be best met by a democratic Europe,"[2] the Administration has emphasized that without progress on human rights or democratic governance, the prospects of attaining the wider strategic objectives of the pivot will be adversely affected.

The inclusion of human rights in the pivot is not an aberration, but demonstrates consistency with American strategic thinking as reflected in the 2010 National Security Strategy, which states that "the United States can more effectively forge consensus to tackle shared challenges when working with governments that reflect the will and respect the rights of their people, rather than just the narrow interests of those in power."[3] In his speech to the Australian Parliament in

[2]Statement of Daniel B. Baer, Deputy Assistant Secretary Bureau of Democracy, Human Rights and Labor, U.S. Department of State, "Rebalance to Asia: What Does It Mean For Democracy, Good Governance And Human Rights?" Hearing before the Subcommittee on East Asian and Pacific Affairs, United States Senate, 113th Congress (2013), p. 2, http://www.foreign.senate.gov/imo/media/doc/Baer_Testimony.pdf.

[3]Office of the President of the United States, *National Security Strategy* (Washington, D.C.: Government Printing Office, 2010), p. 37, http://www.whitehouse.gov/sites/default/files/rss_viewer/national_security_strategy.pdf.

November 2011, President Obama provided the practical corollary to this abstract pronouncement, arguing that human rights were being applied through the pivot in three specific ways: strengthening civil society; advancing the rights of all people, including minorities; and encouraging open government.[4]

Nevertheless, ever since the pivot policy was announced, concern has been expressed that human rights considerations will be sidelined. In hearings of the Senate Foreign Relations Committee in March 2013, East Asia and Pacific Subcommittee Chair Senator Ben Cardin voiced his disappointment with agendas for bilateral meetings between the United States and Asian countries that made good governance and human rights "a footnote rather than a priority."[5] When the views of influential foreign policy experts are surveyed, these fears appear well-founded. Those who hold sway deem trade and investment as the primary interest of both the United States and the EU in Asia, followed by non-proliferation and military build-up, climate change, energy and resources.[6]

It is against this backdrop that Europe must consider its approach. As many other authors in this volume explain, the reorientation of U.S. relations to Asia is not being undertaken in isolation; rather it is an endeavor which the United States is encouraging many of its partners to replicate.[7]

---

[4]Barack Obama, "Remarks by President Obama to the Australian Parliament," The White House (speech, Canberra, Australia, November 17, 2011), http://www.white-house.gov/the-press-office/2011/11/17/remarks-president-obama-australian-parliament.

[5]Statement of Senator Ben Cardin, "Rebalance to Asia: What Does It Mean For Democracy, Good Governance And Human Rights?" Hearing before the Subcommittee on East Asian and Pacific Affairs, United States Senate, 113th Congress (2013). http://www.foreign.senate.gov/imo/media/doc/Cardin%20Opening%20Statement1.pdf.

[6]Based on the results of an online survey of European and American officials and experts conducted by the EU Institute for Security Studies in February-March 2012. Around 100 responses were collected. The results reflect only a small sample of expert opinion. Patryk Pawlak and Eleni Ekmetsioglou, "Transatlantic Strategies in the Asia Pacific: Findings of a Survey Conducted Among EU and US Foreign Policy Experts," *European Union Institute for Security Studies* (June 2012), http://www.iss.europa.eu/uploads/media/analysis_asia_pacific.pdf.

[7]Kurt Campbell and Brian Andrews, "Explaining the US 'Pivot' to Asia," *Chatham House* (2013), p. 2, http://www.chathamhouse.org/sites/default/files/public/Research/Americas/0813pp_pivottoasia.pdf.

Europe does not share U.S. geopolitical advantages in Asia. As the President of the European Council, Herman van Rompuy, declared in 2012, "Europe is clearly not a Pacific power and will not become one."[8] Indeed, European leaders prefer to speak of Europe as a partner for Asian countries. In the Asia-Pacific, Europe has none of the advantages its Neighborhood Policy provides on its own borders; nor can it rely on the lure of potential membership to improve human rights standards in third countries, as it has done in eastern Europe.

Nevertheless, the shift in American emphasis has led to debate about whether and how Europe should follow suit. Despite having, traditionally abstained from the East Asian arena since de-colonization, Europe has stepped up its engagement in the past few years. EU High Representative Catherine Ashton attended the Association of South East Asian Nations (ASEAN) Regional Forum in 2012, building on the EU's membership of the ASEAN Regional Forum and accession to the Treaty of Amity and Cooperation. Commentators on European foreign policy stress that such actions, while late, are essential. Javier Solana, the EU's former High Representative, has called on Europe to recognize "a critical historical juncture, one that demands [Europe's] own pivot eastward—a coherent and decisive Asian strategy that builds on Europe's strengths."[9]

While it is clear that Europe needs to act, its comparative advantage has sometimes been unclear. As the global center of gravity shifts to Asia, it is no longer obvious—as it was at the end of the Cold War—how European countries should adapt to geopolitical change. Moreover, the preferred European *modus operandi*, "effective multilateralism," is no longer as compelling as it was in the 1990s when the United States appeared to many Europeans as an outlier in its preference for unilateralism. Europe now risks being isolated as the United States and Asia converge around a "sovereigntist" approach to interna-

[8]Herman Van Rompuy, "Europe on the World Stage," European Council (speech, London, May 31, 2012), http://europa.eu/rapid/press-release_PRES-12-237_en.htm.

[9]Javier Solana, "Europe's Smart Asian Pivot," Project Syndicate, September 17, 2013, http://www.project-syndicate.org/commentary/the-eu-s-startegic-advantages-in-asia-by-javier-solana.

tional relations, where loose cooperative mechanisms take precedence over rule-based international institutions.[10]

This growing appreciation of the need for European action creates scope for both the European Union and its member states to join the United States as a valued partner and, as Solana suggests, to add much-needed capacity and expertise in areas where Europe has traditionally been a leading actor. This is a role that Europe is already beginning to play, focusing less on military presence than on economic, governance and "non-traditional security" issues.[11] France's Foreign Minister, Laurent Fabius, made such a claim in a speech at ASEAN's Headquarters, distinguishing the U.S. "military" pivot from a French "diplomatic, economic and human one."[12] An effective European pivot, it is argued, will harness European assets as a norm entrepreneur, promote regionalism to guarantee human rights and assist in building the rule of law.

A differential emphasis in European and American implementation of foreign policy rebalances to Asia would be consistent with traditional conceptions of the European Union (and to a lesser extent, its member states) as a different kind of power in international relations. This is reflective in the literature on the EU's distinct role as a "civilian,"[13] "normative,"[14] or "ethical"[15] power, a characterization which has guided European external relations substantively and procedurally.

---

[10]Richard Gowan, "The U.S., Europe and Asia's Rising Multilateralists" in Patryk Pawlak ed., *Look East, Act East: Transatlantic Agenda in the Asia Pacific*, European Union Institute for Security Studies, Report No. 13, December 2012, p. 26; Michael Smith, "Beyond the Comfort Zone: Internal Crisis and External Challenge in the European Union's Response to Rising Powers," *International Affairs* 89:3 (2012), p. 660.

[11]Nicola Casarini, "The European 'Pivot,'" European Union Institute for Security Studies (March 2013), http://www.iss.europa.eu/uploads/media/Alert_Asia.pdf.

[12]Laurent Fabius, "Speech by Laurent Fabius at the ASEAN Headquarters," Embassy of France in Laos (speech, Jakarta, Indonesia, August 2, 2013), http://www.ambafrance-laos.org/Speech-by-Laurent-Fabius-at-the.

[13]François Duchêne, "Europe's Role in World Peace," in Richard Mayne ed., *Europe Tomorrow: Sixteen Europeans Look Ahead* (London: Fontana, 1972), pp. 32–47.

[14]Ian Manners, "Normative Power Europe: A Contradiction in Terms?" *Journal of Common Market Studies* 40 (2002), p. 235.

[15]Lisbeth Aggestam, "Introduction: Ethical Power Europe," *International Affairs* 84 (2008), p. 1.

There is, as Stokes and Whitman write, a "deeply embedded notion that the EU should seek to stress the distinctiveness of its capabilities and aspirations for international relations."[16]

European officials appear open to this approach. In the EU's 2012 East Asia Guidelines, there are references to the EU's "broad approach to security" which includes "the development and consolidation of democracy, the rule of law, and respect for human rights and fundamental freedoms."[17] This reflects broader strategic EU engagement on the issue. "Human rights," High Representative Ashton has stated, "are one of my top priorities and a silver thread that runs through everything we do in external relations."[18] There is also evidence to suggest that U.S. policymakers and analysts believe Europe may be well-positioned to "take a lead" in terms of advancing human rights and good governance policies in Asia.[19]

It should be stressed that, in order to succeed, European and American efforts in the sphere of human rights and good governance must be complementary. Headway has been made in this regard at the policy level, not least in the U.S.-EU Statement on the Asia-Pacific Region in which Secretary Clinton and High Representative Ashton "decided to further cooperate with Asia-Pacific partners in promoting democracy and human rights [...]."[20] U.S. and European experts who saw a potential leadership role for Europe on human rights also determined that the highest level of convergence between European and American interests in Asia was on promoting human rights and the rule of law.[21]

---

[16]Doug Stokes and Richard G. Whitman, "Transatlantic Triage? European and UK 'Grand Strategy' After the US Rebalance to Asia," *International Affairs* 89.5 (2013), p. 1096.

[17]Council of the European Union, "Guidelines on the EU's Foreign and Security Policy in East Asia Policy," June 15, 2012, p. 2, http://eeas.europa.eu/asia/docs/guidelines_eu_foreign_sec_pol_east_asia_en.pdf.

[18]Council of the European Union, "EU Adopts Strategic Framework on Human Rights and Democracy," June 25, 2012, http://www.consilium.europa.eu/uedocs/cms_Data/docs/pressdata/EN/foraff/131173.pdf.

[19]Pawlak and Ekmetsioglou, *op. cit.*

[20]"US-EU Statement on the Asia-Pacific Region," Office of the Spokesperson, U.S. Department of State, July 12, 2012, http://www.state.gov/r/pa/prs/ps/2012/07/194896.htm.

[21]Pawlak and Ekmetsioglou, *op. cit.*

In practice, what must be avoided is the perception that complementary efforts, or even European leadership, amount to one partner in the transatlantic alliance being handed a politically sensitive brief, while the other reaps the rewards. As Antonio Missiroli has written: "The rise of the East should not divide the West."[22] In this sense, in the human rights field as in other areas, the task at hand does not imply a simplistic division of labor, but rather a sophisticated leveraging of the power of European and American networks. Nor does a European "lead" on human rights and the rule of law imply that Europe should set aside other strategic objectives in the economic or military spheres. Instead, the pivot presents Europe with an opportunity to harness its comparative advantage on the world stage to pursue shared U.S.-European aims.

The stakes for both Europe and the United States go beyond the Asian region, where there are clearly human rights issues demanding attention. Both the United States and Europe are major stakeholders in the existing geopolitical order and institutional configuration,[23] as much in the human rights field as in others. As global power shifts, if Europe and the United States are concerned with maintaining the gains of human rights institutions over the past seventy years, the Western powers will have to work to "embed the foundations of the western-oriented international system so deeply that China has overwhelming incentives to integrate into it rather than to oppose and overturn it."[24] This endeavor will require not just concerted action in Asia and with regard to Asian powers, but will also require a greater degree of consensus between the United States and Europe about the role of multilateralism. In the coming decades, shared values alone may not be enough to sustain the primacy of the United States and EU universalist conception of human rights.

---

[22]Antonio Missiroli, "Introduction" in Pawlak, *op. cit.*

[23]Smith, *op. cit.*, p. 659.

[24]G. John Ikenberry, "Liberal Order Building," in Melvyn P. Leffler and Jeffrey W. Legro, eds. *To Lead the World: American Strategy after the Bush Doctrine* (Oxford: Oxford University Press, 2008).

## Transatlantic and Asian Conceptions of Human Rights

Suggestions that the U.S. pivot—and any complementary European action—imply normative impacts on human rights presuppose the existence of a "transatlantic values agenda" at odds with Asian norms. Although comparison of the respective heritages of European and American approaches to human rights identifies divergences as well as commonalities—not least in the long list of economic and social rights which are incorporated into the Charter of Fundamental Rights of the European Union, in contrast to the more parsimonious U.S. Bill of Rights[25]—the construction of the international human rights regime in the post-war era was, by and large, a common endeavor.

Indeed, the debate about whether the Universal Declaration of Human Rights can justifiably bear the name universal, given the extent to which it was inspired by "American and Western European" values and to which it owed its genesis to the European Enlightenment, is a reminder of just how closely the United States and European countries have stood together. Notwithstanding more openness to collective rights in Europe, both sides of the Atlantic stress the sanctity of individual rights and the presumption that the individual should be protected from the arbitrary exercise of state power.

Despite the conclusion of the Cold War, it readily became apparent that the confrontation between the transatlantic approach and a separate tradition, which rejected universalism, would continue. The gulf between the two conceptions of human rights was particularly manifest at the Vienna Conference of 1993, leading U.S. Secretary of State Warren Christopher to argue, in the United States' opening statement, that "we cannot let cultural relativism become the last refuge of repression."[26]

The countries which had—months before the Vienna Conference— set forth their own view of human rights as rooted in national and cultural traditions in the 1993 Bangkok Declaration on human rights, include many which are now the object of the pivot: Singapore,

---

[25]Cass Sunstein, "Why Does the American Constitution Lack Social and Economic Guarantees?" *Syracuse Law Review* 56 (2005), p. 1.

[26]Elaine Sciolino, "U.S. Rejects Notion That Human Rights Vary With Culture," *The New York Times*, June 15, 1993.

Malaysia, Indonesia and Vietnam. These states, through individual pronouncements and preferred methods of engagement in inter-governmental mechanisms, evince a different understanding of universality,
often referred to as "Asian values" pursued through the "ASEAN Way"
of intergovernmental deliberation and consensus.[27] The chasm of
opinion in Vienna was unsurprising when viewed in the context of the
ASEAN Ministerial Meeting (AMM) of the previous year and the
communiqué that resulted, which stated that "basic human rights,
while universal in character, are governed by the distinct culture and
history of, and socio-economic conditions in each country, and that
their expression and application in the national context are within the
competence and responsibility of each country."[28]

   This view of the prerogatives of states is congruent with the founding principles of ASEAN as outlined in the 1967 ASEAN Declaration
and the 1976 Treaty of Amity and Cooperation. These instruments
describe a form of inter-governmental cooperation very different from
the rule-based order of the European Union, stressing mutual respect
for independence, sovereignty, equality of all nations and non-interference in international affairs, human rights included. This system
reflects the colonial history of the region and Asia's preference for
loose affiliations underpinned by non-intervention. It is notable that
the Treaty of Amity and Cooperation does not cover human or fundamental rights, and while the ASEAN Charter, adopted in 2007,
includes references to international standards including International
Humanitarian Law, it does not explicitly reference International
Human Rights Law. Progress from this baseline has been slow. In July
1993, an ASEAN communiqué incorporated a separate section on
human rights for the first time and in 2007, ASEAN committed to the
establishment of a human rights body, the ASEAN Inter-governmental Commission on Human Rights Commission (AICHR), which was
launched in 2009. Notwithstanding these signs of progress, the
AICHR and a subsequent ASEAN Declaration on Human Rights

---

[27] For a definition of the "ASEAN Way" see, for example, Paul J. Davidson, "The Role
of Law in Governing Regionalism in Asia" in Nicholas Thomas, ed., *Governance and
Regionalism in Asia* (London: Routledge, 2009): 224–249.

[28] ASEAN, "Joint Communiqué of the 25th ASEAN Ministerial Meeting," (Manila,
Philippines, July 21–22, 1992), Paragraph 18.

(2012)[29] have been controversial and there is little sign of convergence between the region's sovereigntist preferences and the consent-based conception of sovereignty prevalent in the West.

Indeed, although it is, in reality, problematic to talk of "Asian values" given the recent emphasis on human rights as well as the diversity of opinion which characterizes ASEAN's approach, in many cases East Asian and Pacific countries have tended to link discussion of human rights and democracy to indigenous values which are presented as an alternative to liberal-democratic western norms. The elements of Asian values, as expressed by such states, run counter to the principles of individual liberty and the prioritization of civil and political rights typical of the West. Instead, greater weight is given to duties than to rights, with an emphasis on society rather than the individual. As such, many Asian states tend to stress economic and cultural rights over civil and political concerns. Approaches by external actors such as the United States and the EU to condition relations or assistance on "western" human rights standards directly have therefore been met with strong opposition and led to a deterioration in relations. When Burma/Myanmar acceded to ASEAN in 1997, the EU opposed its membership on human rights grounds. This was viewed by Asian countries as interference in an internal matter and the dispute led to EU-ASEAN ministerial meetings being postponed during the period 1997–2000. ASEAN has asserted that such tactics will undermine the existing global human rights regime.[30]

In reality, although Asian countries stress adherence to morally binding international human rights instruments like the Universal Declaration on Human Rights and the Vienna Declaration, many have not bound themselves to related operational treaties. For example, Singapore, Malaysia, Brunei, Burma/Myanmar and China are among the twenty-five countries internationally that are not parties to the International Covenant on Civil and Political Rights.

---

[29]ASEAN, "ASEAN Declaration on Human Rights," November 19, 2012, http://www.asean.org/news/asean-statement-communiques/item/asean-human-rights-declaration.

[30]ASEAN, "Final Declaration of the Regional Meeting for Asia of the World Conference on Human Rights (Bangkok Declaration)," April 7, 1993.

## Transatlantic Ends and Means

Given the divergence between "transatlantic values" and the Asian approach, the decision to include human rights and democracy as part of the six policy pillars of the U.S. pivot is noteworthy. The statements by President Obama and Secretary Clinton, cited above, attempt to create strategic linkages between human rights and the wider U.S. agenda, though the coherence of the policy is not always clear. Indeed, there has been limited discussion of both U.S. ends and means in terms of promoting and protecting human rights through the pivot.

As the implementation of the pivot has progressed, further insight has been gained, aided by pressure from civil society and legislative oversight. The decision by the U.S. Senate Foreign Relations Subcommittee on East Asian and Pacific Affairs, in March 2013, to open hearings on the "Asia rebalance" by discussing democracy and human rights was a major step forward in this regard. Implicitly referencing concern that as Asian countries hedge against China, the United States might turn a blind eye to human rights abuses, the Subcommittee's Chairman, Senator Ben Cardin, argued that "we must remember as we 'rebalance to Asia' that the fundamental respect for the human rights of every person, every woman, man and child, is the underpinning to security and prosperity. Good governance which includes a respect for human rights is key to economic growth."[31]

This rare hearing provided an opportunity for Obama Administration officials to expand upon the strategic rationale for a focus on human rights. They emphasized that good governance and human rights were priorities not just in support of human dignity, but also to build effective institutions which bring development and intercultural exchange, both of which underwrite peace. "While the rebalance reflects the importance the U.S. government places on our strategic and economic engagement in the Asia-Pacific," asserted Joseph Yun, Acting Assistant Secretary of State for East Asian and Pacific Affairs, "the dimension that binds the entire strategy together is our strong support for advancing democracy and human rights."[32] Daniel Baer,

---

[31]Statement of Senator Ben Cardin, *op. cit.*, p. 2.

[32]Statement of Joseph Y. Yun, Acting Assistant Secretary Bureau of East Asian and Pacific Affairs, U.S. Department of State, "Rebalance to Asia: What Does It Mean for

Deputy Assistant Secretary in the Bureau of Democracy Human Rights and Labor, further argued that "U.S. national interests will be most durably met by a world in which states are part of a stable rules-based order. That stable order can only be grounded on the durable peace that human rights and democratic governance deliver."[33]

Although human rights are codified in the policy aims of the pivot, their pursuit in practice can be problematic, especially when human rights considerations come into apparent conflict with other objectives. As the scholar and commentator Walter Russell Mead has argued:

> There is a fly in the pho, however: human rights. The Obama administration appears to be shifting from the realist and Jeffersonian perspective of its early period to a more activist and Wilsonian policy as time goes on. That causes problems in Southeast Asia where the imperatives of realist thinking lead toward engagement of regimes like Vietnam and an imperfect Myanmar while a more Wilsonian approach would be more aloof. It's likely that some of the administration's ugliest internal fights in the second term will be over the relationship of the two components of the pivot, and at this early stage it is hard to predict which approach will win out.[34]

Such internal debates came to the fore early in President Obama's second term, with disquiet among the human rights community becoming increasingly evident. An opinion piece in *The Atlantic* magazine argued, for example, that "the excitement in Washington over the 'pivot' has overshadowed some serious human rights concerns among many of the United States' new friends,"[35] highlighting the plight of the

---

Democracy, Good Governance and Human Rights?" Hearing before the Subcommittee on East Asian and Pacific Affairs, United States Senate, 113th Congress (2013), p. 2, http://www.foreign.senate.gov/imo/media/doc/Yun_Testimony1.pdf.

[33]Statement of Daniel B. Baer, *op. cit.*, p. 2.

[34]Walter Russell Mead, "Top U.S. Officials Pivoting in Asia, But What about Human Rights?" *The American Interest*, November 17, 2012, http://www.the-american-interest.com/blog/2012/11/17/top-u-s-officials-spend-the-week-pivoting/.

[35]Joshua Kurlantzick, "Dear Obama: Pivoting to Asia Doesn't Mean Abandoning Human Rights," *The Atlantic*, January 23, 2013, http://www.theatlantic.com/interna-

Rohingya minority in Burma/Myanmar, the disappearance of a rights activist in Laos and political assassinations in Cambodia. When the president visited both Burma/Myanmar and Cambodia several months earlier, *The Washington Post* raised questions about his itinerary, wondering whether "in the interest of balancing China the United States [will] be willing to tolerate autocracy and human rights abuses by its Asian allies — as it did the crimes of dictators during the Cold War?"[36]

Although U.S. officials are loath to acknowledge the gap between aspiration and practice, there remains a fundamental tension between pursuing human rights and strengthening political and military ties, particularly when the United States develops military-to-military relations with armed forces which may themselves be responsible for abuses. In this respect, a complementary transatlantic approach has significant value. Although Europe may lack the "strategic purchase" in Asia which the United States enjoys and which it seeks to expand, the very fact that the EU is not a Pacific power is, as Javier Solana has highlighted, a "paradoxical asset... [the EU] does not carry the burden of great-power status in Asia. Far from being a weakness, this is precisely the source of the EU's potential strength in Asia, for it provides a degree of diplomatic agility that the American heavyweight cannot muster."[37] Sharing American ends of a rights-based international order, preventing conflict and enabling equitable growth, the EU may be better posited, geopolitically and institutionally, to make headway in this regard.

### Bilateral Initiatives

In advocating for improved human rights standards at the country-level, the United States and Europe share international credibility and ought to continue to single out abuses in target countries, including through the procedures of the UN Human Rights Council and Third

---

tional/archive/2013/01/dear-obama-pivoting-to-asia-doesnt-mean-abandoning-human-rights/267423/.

[36]"On Asia Trip, Mr. Obama Must Send Clear Signals on Human Rights," *Washington Post*, November 17, 2012, http://www.washingtonpost.com/opinions/on-asia-trip-president-obama-must-send-clear-signals-on-human-rights/2012/11/16/f8a5064a-2e77-11e2-beb2-4b4cf5087636_story.html.

[37]Solana, *op. cit.*

Committee of the General Assembly, regardless of the context of the pivot. It is encouraging, therefore, that the highest level policy statements on the pivot have couched the strengthening of specific ties on progress in this regard. In her initial exposition of the pivot, Secretary Clinton wrote, for example that:

> As we deepen our engagement with partners with whom we disagree on these issues, we will continue to urge them to embrace reforms that would improve governance, protect human rights, and advance political freedoms. We have made it clear, for example, to Vietnam that our ambition to develop a strategic partnership requires that it take steps to further protect human rights and advance political freedoms. Or consider Burma, where we are determined to seek accountability for human rights violations. We are closely following developments in Nay Pyi Taw and the increasing interactions between Aung San Suu Kyi and the government leadership. We have underscored to the government that it must release political prisoners, advance political freedoms and human rights, and break from the policies of the past. As for North Korea, the regime in Pyongyang has shown persistent disregard for the rights of its people, and we continue to speak out forcefully against the threats it poses to the region and beyond.[38]

While "naming and shaming" remains important, and can lend support to domestic civil society activists as well as embarrassing recalcitrant governments on the world stage it is not, of course, the only way of improving standards. Nor, as the Asian rejection of "universalism" and hostility to conditionality in the 1990s suggested, is it necessarily the most effective method. Both the United States and Europe have undertaken important work in incrementally strengthening the rule of law in target countries, for example through USAID's Justice Strengthening To Increase Court Effectiveness (JUSTICE) program which has provided $20 million to improve court efficiency, strengthen contract and intellectual property enforcement and build confidence in the

---

[38]Hillary Rodham Clinton, "America's Pacific Century," *Foreign Policy*, November 2011, http://www.foreignpolicy.com/articles/2011/10/11/americas_pacific_century.

integrity of courts.[39] For the European Union, such technical capacity building projects are particularly appealing because, as development projects, they can be implemented through the supranational "community" method avoiding the contentious inter-governmental process which remains necessary for the EU to take a common position on more forceful human rights advocacy. The EU's European Instrument for Democracy and Human Rights (EIDHR)—which made € 1.1 billion available globally between 2007 and 2013—is a key tool in this regard and is credited, for example, in contributing to the abolition of the death penalty in the Philippines, reducing domestic violence in Cambodia and protecting migrants from violence in Vietnam.[40]

Increasingly, countries in Asia are emerging as strong partners in this regard, a vital development given the primordial importance of national protection systems for human rights. The NGO Freedom House, in its 2013 *Freedom in the World* report, found for example that the Asia-Pacific had made the greatest progress worldwide over the preceding five decades in achieving gains in civil and political rights.[41] Over the last thirty years, the region has become manifestly more democratic with the introduction of democracy in the Philippines, South Korea, Thailand, Mongolia, Taiwan, Indonesia and East Timor. Though the rhetoric of democracy does not imply adherence to its tenets, and while there is no universal agreement on what democracy means in practice, both the EU and the United States have made headway in assisting with the adoption of practical elements of a rule of law culture. Examples of such assistance include helping transitional states like Cambodia and East Timor build institutions for effective governance, as well as providing electoral support, which is another, but by no means the only, piece of the puzzle. The 2015 elections in Burma/Myanmar will be a particular test for the efficacy of external electoral assistance, on which the EU puts particular emphasis and which USAID is also supporting.

---

[39]Statement of Joseph Y. Yun, *op. cit.*, p. 4.

[40]Council of the European Union, "EU Adopts Strategic Framework on Human Rights and Democracy," *op. cit.*

[41]Freedom House, *Freedom in the World 2013* (Washington, D.C.: Freedom House, 2013).

The success of such country-specific initiatives can depend in large part on practical considerations such as capacity and resources. The United States does not currently have designated human rights officers in all missions in the Asia-Pacific region, for example, whereas the European Union has recently established a system of EIDHR focal points in each of its Delegations reflecting, perhaps, Europe's desire for profile in this regard. In implementing such projects, the United States and the EU can share practice and must ensure that their efforts are complementary.

Moreover, although U.S. policy pronouncements on the pivot stress "democracy and the rule of law" in one breath, it is important that specific Western-style systems of governance are not conflated with the rule of law itself. Engagement by western actors has been most successful—as in the case of Germany's Rule of Law Dialogue with China—when the rule of law is addressed in a more technical than ideological way. The importance of such a focus extends beyond the level of individual human rights. Strengthening the rule of law between and within states is also vital if reconciliation between neighboring Asian countries, many of which have suffered from intense rivalries, is to be a realistic prospect. Ongoing disputes over territory, not least relating to claims by China and Southeast Asian states over islands in the South China Sea, and claims by both China and Japan to the Diayou/Senkaku Islands, offer the ever-present risk of escalation. Regional reconciliation dialogues, convened within institutionalized frameworks like those discussed below, are tools that allow Europe and the United States to pursue simultaneous security and human rights objectives, underwritten by an effective rule of law.

### Regional Efforts

Improving the rule of law at a regional level is something that can be addressed with recourse to a 'best fit' model among the network of actors in Europe and the United States. Europe's self-conception as a "normative power" and its success in creating both a regional human rights architecture on the European continent—both within the EU and outside it—as well as myriad other institutional mechanisms, make it well-positioned to improve institutional protections for human rights in Asia and to foster the rule of law.

In its own relations with Asia, the EU has focused on "enmeshing" rising Asian powers through bilateral negotiations and frameworks, with an emphasis on strategic partnerships which seek to create institutionalized links, thereby rendering painful the cost of defection.[42] When moving from commercial briefs to the more contentious area of human rights, however, the EU holds less sway, not only because of sensitivity amongst its partners but also because of an external view of the European Union primarily as a trading actor. As Michael Smith has written, "the lesson appears to be that when efforts are made to go beyond the rhetoric and the comforting general sentiments to negotiate material obligations and commitments—whether these are in the security or the welfare sphere—things become much more difficult."[43]

Rather than tackle issues of human rights and democracy head on, therefore, the EU can further the transatlantic rights agenda more effectively by "modeling" its uniquely successful integration process, without necessarily emphasizing human rights in the first instance, but rather by gradually aiding the emergence of such mechanisms. Both the United States and the EU are in favor of emerging trends towards regionalism in Asia, with former Assistant Secretary of State for East Asia, Kurt Campbell arguing that a "strong and integrated ASEAN is fundamentally in the US national interest."[44] The EU, it is similarly claimed, has "supported regional integration more consistently that any other international player."[45]

The EU's assets in this regard are clear. It has, as is widely recognized, "a preference for procedure"[46] and is guided, from the 2003 European Security Strategy to the Lisbon Treaty by the global pursuit of "effective multilateralism." The EU's East Asia Guidelines further express that "the EU needs, and seeks to promote, multilateral solutions to global challenges... [including] human rights and good governance" and call on the EU to "be willing, if requested, to share lessons drawn from its own experience in post-war reconciliation, and in con-

---

[42]Smith, *op. cit.*, p. 665.

[43]*Ibid.*, p. 666.

[44]Campbell and Andrews, *op. cit.*, p. 6.

[45]Casarini, *op. cit.*

[46]Stokes and Whitman, *op. cit.*, p. 1097.

fidence-building, preventive diplomacy and conflict resolution."[47] Moreover, the EU has previous experience in cultivating regional mechanisms in Asia which have furthered multilateral dialogue. The ASEAN+3 grouping (ASEAN and China, Japan and South Korea) emerged from discussion in the context of the Asia-Europe Meetings (ASEM), which have been held since 1996.

Skeptics sometimes assert that Asia is unlikely to replicate European institutionalization because of underlying differences in history and culture. However, as liberal-institutionalist scholar Andrew Moravcsik argues, rather than being a culturally homogenous entity, the EU is based on bargaining among diverse national interests, not dissimilar from ASEAN; that European multilateralism was driven at the outset by managing economic interests, rather than political matters (the core of Asian sensitivities) and that Asian rejection of formal-hierarchical institutions does not hold sway because the EU is in reality a highly decentralized international institution.[48] Moravcsik's argument is principally economic: "Like nearly every other successful international organization in modern times, the EU is designed to manage globalization through mutually beneficial interstate policy coordination."[49] Yet in his compelling demonstration that there is nothing innately European about the form of integration that Europe has pursued, it follows that through institutionalization ASEAN can also make gains in democracy, the rule of law and human rights.

Saliently, the very act of inter-state bargaining both relies on domestic rule of law and helps to strengthen it. As Moravcsik stresses, high levels of compliance with EU law are the result not of compellence at the European level, but are guaranteed by regulators, judges and domestic politicians. Commitments, he writes, "are only as reliable as far as domestic 'rule of law' institutions in individual European countries are credible."[50] This leads him to doubt whether Asian governments are capable either of negotiation or enforcing international

---

[47]Council of the European Union, "Guidelines on the EU's Foreign and Security Policy in East Asia Policy," *op. cit.*

[48]Andrew Moravcsik, *The Choice for Europe: Social Purpose and State Power from Messina to Maastricht* (Beijing: Chinese edition, 2008), Preface, p. 15.

[49]*Ibid.*, p. 20.

[50]*Ibid.*, p. 19.

agreements on, for example, economic liberalizations. In the context of the pivot, the EU (as well as the United States) therefore ought to increase the volume of assistance to ASEAN countries to develop rule of law institutions, not only for the sake of human rights and development, but also—in the long term—to mitigate the risk of conflict between states.

### Strengthening Existing Human Rights Mechanisms

In terms of an explicit focus on human rights, both the United States and Europe can offer lessons from inter-governmental human rights mechanisms that have been developed in their respective regions, which can be crucial supranational checks on national protection systems. European mechanisms, often described as the most effective such bodies worldwide, offer particular guidance, both as a model and in terms of exchanges of experts and officials.

The institutionalization of human rights mechanisms in Asia has been a slow process, with the formation of an inter-governmental commission (AICHR) in 2009[51] and the subsequent issuance of an ASEAN Human Rights Declaration (ADHR) in 2012. The flaws of the AICHR and AHRD have been widely discussed. The Commission, importantly, lacks any kind of enforcement mechanism, falling back on ASEAN's consensual approach which traditionally leads to a lowest-common-denominator outcome given the effective veto power of authoritarian regimes. Moreover, while individual governments can appoint or remove commissioners as they see fit, individual citizens have no means of approaching the Commission directly to lodge complaints. Western concern was summed up by the *Wall Street Journal* which opined that "the United Nations once boasted the world's most toothless human rights body—until the Association of South East Asian Nations formed one too."[52] The United Nations High Commissioner for Human Rights, Navi Pillay, also expressed concern at the lack of consultation of civil society organizations:

---

[51]Tan Hsien-Li, *The ASEAN Intergovernmental Commission on Human Rights Institutionalising Human Rights in Southeast Asia* (New York: Cambridge University Press, 2011).

[52]"ASEAN's Toothless Council," *Wall Street Journal*, July 22, 2009, http://online. wsj.com/news/articles/SB10001424052970203517304574303592053848748.

> I encouraged AICHR not to react defensively to civil society partners, but to open the doors and harness their energy and contributions. This has been the key to success for similar mechanisms in all other regions of the world.... I remain concerned, therefore, when I hear continued frustration from civil society partners about a lack of transparency and willingness by AICHR to engage with them in taking forward the human rights agenda.[53]

While the AICHR had no mechanism through which to submit complaints and no enforcement procedures, it did have a mandate to develop strategies for the promotion and protection of human rights, including the development of an ASEAN Human Rights Declaration, which was launched in 2012. This document proved even more controversial than the AICHR. Although the Declaration begins by reaffirming international commitments, including "the respect for and promotion and protection of human rights and fundamental freedoms, as well as the principles of democracy, the rule of law and good governance," it subsequently balances individual rights against duties and the prerogatives of states, attaching all-encompassing limitations on the exercise of enumerated rights. ASEAN's approach led to a strong response from a coalition of regional NGOs, led by Human Rights Watch, who declared that "the document is a declaration of government powers disguised as a declaration of human rights."[54] Joining the criticism, the International Commission of Jurists also stated that "it is unfortunate that ASEAN Member States do not realize that they have just adopted a text that is a radical departure from international human rights law."[55] Vocal opposition to the formulations taken by the ADHR flowed not just from human rights organizations, but from

---

[53] "Statement by the High Commissioner for Human Rights at the Bali Democracy Forum," United Nations Office of the High Commissioner for Human Rights (speech, Bali, Indonesia, November 7, 2012), http://www.ohchr.org/EN/NewsEvents/Pages/DisplayNews.aspx?NewsID=12752&LangID=E.

[54] "Civil Society Denounces Adoption of Flawed ASEAN Human Rights Declaration," Human Rights Watch, November 19, 2012, http://www.hrw.org/news/2012/11/19/civil-society-denounces-adoption-flawed-asean-human-rights-declaration.

[55] "ICJ Condemns Fatally Flawed ASEAN Human Rights Declaration," International Commission of Jurists, November 19, 2012, http://www.icj.org/icj-condemns-fatally-flawed-asean-human-rights-declaration/.

western governments, including the United States which expressed "deep [concern] that that many of the ASEAN Declaration's principles and articles could weaken and erode universal human rights and fundamental freedoms as contained in the UDHR."[56]

In this context, there is a clear need for international actors, especially the EU and the United States, to strengthen the capacity of civil society actors to engage in processes to strengthen regional human rights mechanisms, as well as offering direct assistance to develop ASEAN's normative human rights framework. Although the ASEAN Declaration on Human Rights is deeply flawed, its negotiation and adoption do show that ASEAN member states are sensitive to international pressure for attention to be paid to human rights. They have also stressed an "evolutionary approach" in this regard, implying that there is ongoing room for maneuver. Moreover, the process has catalyzed more coordinated inter-Asian civil society advocacy.

Both the AICHR and ADHR therefore provide a tentative opening for further EU and U.S. support for human rights and rule of law in Asia, alongside specific entry points where interests align. Practical methods of engagement include track two dialogue, which the EU has developed given that certain issues continued to be deemed "too sensitive" for formal EU-ASEAN meetings. Although the inter-governmental ASEM process (Asia-Europe Meeting) which is conceived as a "policymaking laboratory," has increased its coverage on human rights, notwithstanding the incorporation of the ASEAN principle of non-interference, more detailed treatment is given by the Asia-Europe Foundation (ASEF), which increases lower-level contacts between officials, civil society and academics. This process includes informal seminars on human rights, thirteen of which have taken place since 1997, covering issues as varied as national human rights mechanisms, political parties and the citizen and perspectives on the International Criminal Court.

The experience of ASEF suggests that it has been more effective to increase the space in which Asian civil society operates, and to promote democracy and the rule of law from within, than to force con-

---

[56]Victoria Nuland, "ASEAN Declaration on Human Rights," U.S. Department of State Press Statement, November 20, 2012, http://www.state.gov/r/pa/prs/ps/2012/11/200915.htm.

tentious issues onto the official ASEM agenda. Nevertheless, given the dominance of proceedings by well-organized European NGOs, the need for capacity-building in Asia is pressing. For this to happen, efforts must be expanded to harness the power of civil society, a key aspect of the "network diplomacy" which Secretary Clinton advanced during her tenure in office. Talk of the need for a "business pivot" could also usefully include a human rights dimension. The business community enjoys influence within ASEAN and integrating corporate social responsibility into human rights and economic and trade relations between ASEAN and third regions is an effective way of furthering a human rights agenda.[57]

Particular traction is likely to be made on the transatlantic rights agenda, and on reinforcing regional cooperation, when the EU and the United States pinpoint areas of mutual concern with Asia-Pacific countries and where track two initiatives can be as effective as high-level pronouncements. Human trafficking is one such case and is an appropriate entry point given the extent to which it is a transnational challenge affecting both human and national security. Increasingly, states are recognizing the negative consequences of allowing "traffickers to cooperate better than governments."[58] It is also an area of acute demand in the region. According to the Trafficking in Persons Report of the U.S. Department of State, although four East Asia Pacific countries were moved off the U.S. government's Tier 2 watch list in 2012, East Asia retains the largest number of human trafficking victims in the world, a rate of 3.3 per 1000 persons.[59] Although many victims are trafficked within Asia itself, many are also trafficked to Europe and the United States (or migrate there and subsequently fall victim to traffickers). Coordinated analysis of "demand and supply" factors in policy design and implementation is therefore a particularly germane area for EU-Asia and U.S.-Asia cooperation.

---

[57]Sriprapha Petcharamesree, "The Human Rights Body: A Test for Democracy Building in ASEAN," International Institution for Democracy and Electoral Assistance (Stockholm, Sweden, 2009).

[58]"Human Trafficking—Challenges to Europe and Asia," EU-Asia Dialogue Conference Report (Vienna, Austria, June 13, 2013).

[59]U.S. Department of State, "Trafficking in Persons Report 2012" (June 2012).

Both the United States and the EU are engaged in high profile initiatives to counter human trafficking in the developing world and have focused on capacity building, whether in terms of legislative assistance or implementation. In the Asia-Pacific Region, there is scope for alignment with the 2004 ASEAN Declaration on Trafficking in Persons, which seeks the establishment of a "regional focal network." The Bali Process on People Smuggling, Trafficking in Persons and Related Transnational Crime, of which the United States is a member, has also recently launched a working group on human trafficking, an issue which has also been integrated into the Bandar Seri Begawan Plan of Action to strengthen the ASEAN-EU Enhanced Partnership (2013–2017). Within the region, efforts such as the United Nations Inter-Agency Project on Human Trafficking in the Greater Mekong Sub-Region (UNIAP), which encourages government-to-government activities, including through inter-agency law enforcement collaboration, demonstrate how the issue has catalyzed transnational cooperation. Further measures, including the use of the ASEAN Regional Forum as the "focal network" called for in 2004 have been suggested as means of increasing coordination and building confidence in the legitimacy and effectiveness of regional fora.[60]

## International Human Rights Commitments

In addition to strengthening regional mechanisms, European actors are particularly well-suited to assist Asian states in adhering to international human rights regimes, including by providing technical support for national incorporation and implementation, as well as educating interlocutors in Asia about international bodies and norms.

All countries now participate in the Universal Periodic Review Process of the UN Human Rights Council. Encouraging Asian countries to cooperate in good faith with human rights treaty bodies and the Human Rights Council is not only in keeping with international obligations, but also emphasizes that protecting human rights and the rule of law is a United Nations agenda, rather than a narrowly western

---

[60]Michael Kingsford, "Can the ASEAN Regional Forum Have a Role in Maintaining Regional Security?" Centre for Defence and Strategic Studies, Australian Defence College (March 2012).

one. Countries with a particular interest in working through multilateral processes—as Thailand has exhibited through the Bangkok Dialogue in the Rule of Law—are potential partners in such fora. [61]

Prevention and punishment of mass atrocities and other international crimes should be a priority for engagement, especially given skepticism in Asia towards both the International Criminal Court and emerging concepts such as the Responsibility to Protect. Europe's comparative advantage with regard to advocating for ICC accession is in its own record: almost all European countries—including all EU member states—are States Party to the Court. In contrast, only 18 Asian states are members of the Court, with a notable absence of regional powers including China, India and Indonesia. The United States, while no longer openly hostile to the Court, is unlikely to be its standard bearer.

Although the tradition of non-interference holds sway, and despite different traditions about individual criminal responsibility, non-adherence to the ICC in the region does not necessarily represent an "Asian perspective" given the differential reasons for non-ratification of the Rome Statute. While certain states are clearly opposed to the Court, others lack the capacity to implement the ratification process. International criminal justice is not an alien concept to Asia as recent procedures in Cambodia, Bangladesh and East Timor have demonstrated.[62] By educating its partners about the role of the Court—particularly in terms of complementarity—and by providing technical assistance to complete ratification and incorporation into domestic law, the EU is well-placed to strengthen regional human rights mechanisms in Asia while simultaneously serving the cause of international criminal justice by combating "impunity gaps."[63]

Without effective action to widen the scope of international human rights mechanisms to Asia, the "transatlantic rights agenda" will face significant obstacles in the coming decades. As the foregoing analysis describes, for much of the post-war era Europe and the United States

---

[61]"Bangkok Dialogue on the Rule of Law," Thailand Institute of Justice (November 15, 2013), http://www.bangkokdialogue.org/.

[62]"Re-emerging Asian Actors and International Law: Asian and European Perspectives on the International Criminal Court," ASEFUAN Dialogues 2012 Conference Report, Clingendael Institute (The Hague, 2012).

[63]*Ibid.*

were at the helm of the development and management of international organizations and regimes. As the EU's East Asia Guidelines make clear, this situation will not persist: "The countries of East Asia, as their international economic and political weight increases internationally, are increasingly influential in the effort to achieve [...] vital global objectives."[64] The leadership of East Timor in the New Deal for Fragile States and the co-chairmanship of Indonesia of the High-Level Panel on the post-2015 Development Agenda are two examples of this trend in practice.

The implications of such developments will be felt not just within Asia, but also in other regions of the world, where competition between the West and Asian powers—particularly China and India—is already noteworthy, especially with regard to the appeal of development assistance which comes without human rights conditionalities. If Europe fails to convince more Asian states of the utility of the International Criminal Court, for example, a consensus with skeptical Africa states may develop, severely undermining recent progress towards international criminal justice.

Even if setbacks to global human rights norms are not felt as a result of direct competition, there may be ramifications as global governance increasingly takes the form of "patchwork multilateralism," whereby regional processes (such as free trade agreements or human rights mechanisms) form a global whole rather than 'central' global bodies such as the WTO or UN remaining pre-eminent. If this is indeed the future course of multilateralism, ensuring high standards at the regional level will become critical.

## Conclusion and Recommendations

The United States and Europe share both a strategic objective in furthering human rights and the rule of law in Asia and consolidating the international human rights regime, which has made steady progress since its inception following the Second World War. Many of their methods, especially at the country-level, are also similar, and the two must strive to act in concert, share best practices and identify

---

[64]Council of the European Union, "Guidelines on the EU's Foreign and Security Policy in East Asia Policy," *op. cit.*

opportunities for engagement. Care must be taken not to undermine the mutual pursuit of human rights through short-sighted positioning. Internally, Europe faces an additional challenge to ensure that EU Member States speak with one voice and do not undercut consistency in EU-ASEAN relations by pursuing bilateral strategies which marginalize human rights issues.

Successfully engaging Asian countries on human rights and the rule of law will not come through rehashing debates about universalism and relativism nor by setting as a strategic objective the explicit adoption by Asian states of the tenets of the transatlantic values agenda. More effective will be strengthening domestic rule of law institutions and civil society to foster a rule of law culture at the national level and to support effective multilateralism by drawing on the less controversial elements of regional integration in Europe.

Appreciating and leveraging the diversity of views *within* Asia will be a critical task for the transatlantic alliance. Notwithstanding "Asian values" and the "ASEAN Way," there is scope for the emergence of human rights champions in the region, even if those states do not directly impose values on their neighbors. Thailand, for example, is asserting itself as a leader in the rule of law field. Indonesia is a leading player in the post-2015 development agenda and East Timor has been at the heart of restoring "ownership" to international engagement in fragile states through the New Deal.

Based on the foregoing analysis, here are some policy recommendations:

### *In terms of domestic policy planning:*

1. **Mainstream human rights in the pivot.** Human rights remain a rhetorical pillar of the pivot, but there is too little to show for this in practice. In addition to increasing financial resources for human rights and rule of law initiatives the United States and the EU should invest in human capacity. The rollout of EIDHR focal points in EU Delegations is a good example of progress in this regard, and should be replicated in the appointment of Human Rights Officers in U.S. missions. To enhance the coherence of the transatlantic rights

agenda at the field level, such personnel must coordinate activities and share best practices.

2. **Encourage scrutiny from civil society and legislators.** Civil society and legislative actors have played an important role in highlighting potential derogations from human rights concerns as the pivot has been implemented, and ensured that the issue retains salience, even as political and security matters dominate the debate. Such dialogue must continue if human rights are to become a genuine pillar of the pivot.

3. **Maintain a common voice.** Although there are divergences in the transatlantic approach—especially in terms of the EU's emphasis on multilateralism—the United States and the EU share a rights agenda, which they ought to pursue in concert. There is a particular challenge for the EU and EU member states in developing foreign policy coherence to ensure the European actors speak with one voice and do not undercut progress on human rights. Where possible, initiatives that use the community method are favored in this regard. In any event and regardless of the policy at stake, EU external action should fully harness the reinforced mandate of the High Representative and the newly established European External Action Service to that end.

*In terms of interventions in Asia:*

1. **Focus on domestic rule of law initiatives**. Fostering the rule of law, in both its "thin" (institutions, codes and procedures) and "thick" form (the emergence of a genuine rule of law culture) creates the enabling environment for the protection of human rights, as well as the ability to negotiate inter-governmentally and implement decisions taken at a transnational level. Such initiatives, which include judicial capacity building, access to justice and legal education, also have the virtue of being less controversial, both domestically and in the target country.

2. **Increase civil society capacity.** Track two initiatives have been successful in building contacts and trust and have provided an important forum for discussion of human rights. For

Asian partners to engage effectively in such processes, domestic civil society capacity must be strengthened, which has further benefits for government accountability. Although informal exchanges can be particularly productive, when the civil society "space" is directly threatened (as in the case of Cambodia proposed 2011 NGO law) the EU and the United States must continue to speak out.

3. **Target mutual wins.** Issues such as human trafficking, which transcend the conceptual boundaries of human rights and transnational security challenges, are useful entry points for international partnerships the encourage dialogue, build trust and demonstrate the success of concerted coordination measures. The United States and the EU should continue to support initiatives in this regard and consider the establishment of new fora to implement such activities.

## Chapter 11

# Asia's Rise and the
# Transatlantic Economic Response

*Jeffrey J. Schott and Cathleen Cimino*

The second half of the 20th century was a period of transatlantic economic hegemony. The United States helped rebuild war-torn economies and was a main driver of the dynamic growth in trade in the postwar era. The United States was the *demandeur* of all eight rounds of multilateral trade negotiations under the General Agreement on Tariffs and Trade (GATT); U.S.-European collaboration set the agenda for and led to the successful conclusion of each of those rounds. This leadership contributed to the strengthening of the trade architecture and the establishment of the World Trade Organization (WTO) in 1995. But unlike the GATT era where a transatlantic compact was sufficient to produce global trade pacts, in the WTO era U.S.-EU agreement is still necessary but no longer sufficient to achieve success.

In the 21st century, many developing countries now play an active role in global economic initiatives. The rise of Asia combined with the new institutional structure of the WTO have been important factors in this regard.

Asia's success story—driven by steady expansion of trade and investment and increasing integration in global value chains—has led some observers to proclaim this new era as the "Asian Century."[1] Projections of Asian economic growth show sharp increases in developing Asia's aggregate share of global GDP: in the first decade of the 21st century, the dynamic growth of China and India, along with the mem-

---

[1]See for example, the speech by Former WTO Director General, Pascal Lamy, "'Asian Century' Means Shared Prosperity, Responsibility and Multilateral Agreements, Lamy Tells Conference," WTO news (speech, Geneva, March 11, 2013), http://www.wto.org/english/news_e/sppl_e/sppl269_e.htm.

bers of the Association of Southeast Asian Nations (ASEAN), more than doubled their combined share of global output and exports, as shown in Table 1. Projections for 2025 suggest that China's GDP will rise to $17 trillion, accounting for 17% of global GDP, compared with GDP of $1.2 trillion and 4% global share in 2000; while India's GDP will reach $5.2 trillion, about the same as Japan. Similarly, China, India and the large ASEAN economies are projected to increase their combined share of world exports from 18% in 2010 to 25% in 2025, while the US and EU combined share will drop from around 43% to 36%. The Asian Development Bank projects that by 2050, Asia could account for more than half of world GDP, trade and investment.[2]

What are the economic consequences of Asia's rise for the transatlantic partners? Do they face a new "Défi Asiatique?" Asia is undoubtedly on the rise. But predictions that the aggregate growth of the region portends the advent of an "Asian Century" seem to exaggerate the potential "défi" for the transatlantic powers, in at least three respects:

First, in an era of accelerating globalization, it is hard to talk about a country or continent dominating the global scene. Interdependence is a fact of economic life; at the same time, it both drives and constrains political action by major economic powers around the globe.

Second, while these economies will become bigger and richer in terms of aggregate GDP, with the exception of Japan, South Korea, and Singapore, they are not "rich." As Table 2 demonstrates, the United Nation's Human Development Index (HDI) ranks China 101 out of 186 countries, India ranks 136, and Indonesia ranks 121—even after decades of rapid growth. Moreover, the inequality-adjusted HDI reveals that income disparities within these societies remain high: taking this factor into account, China's index falls from 0.70 to 0.54 and India's index falls from 0.55 to 0.39 on a scale of 0 to a high of 1, compared to a drop of 0.94 to 0.84 for the United States. To be sure, there has been measured progress of convergence in the developing world

---

[2]Asian Development Bank (ADB) *Asia 2050: Realizing the Asian Century* (Washington, D.C., August 2011), http://www.adb.org/publications/asia-2050-realizing-asian-century.

[3]United Nations Development Programme, *Human Development Report 2013: The Rise of the South Human Progress in a Diverse World* (New York: United Nations, 2013), p. 2, http://hdr.undp.org/sites/default/files/reports/14/hdr2013_en_complete.pdf.

## Table 1. Predicted GDP and trade growth in the next decades for select countries ($ billions)

| Real GDP | 2000 Billions (2000 US$) | % of world GDP | 2010 Billions (2007 US$) | % of world GDP | Est. 2025 Billions (2007 US$) | % of world GDP |
|---|---|---|---|---|---|---|
| European Union[a] | 8,131 | 26 | 16,629 | 29 | 22,714 | 22 |
| China | 1,198 | 4 | 4,850 | 8 | 17,249 | 17 |
| India | 460 | 1 | 1,559 | 3 | 5,233 | 5 |
| Indonesia | 165 | 0 | 550 | 0 | 1,549 | 0 |
| Japan | 4,667 | 14 | 4,250 | 7 | 5,338 | 5 |
| Korea | 553 | 2 | 1,135 | 2 | 2,117 | 2 |
| Malaysia | 93 | 0 | 207 | 0 | 431 | 0 |
| Singapore | 95 | 0 | 202 | 0 | 415 | 0 |
| Thailand | 122 | 0 | 266 | 0 | 558 | 0 |
| United States | 9,898 | 31 | 14,049 | 24 | 20,237 | 20 |

| Exports | Value | % of world exports | Value | % of world exports | Value | % of world exports |
|---|---|---|---|---|---|---|
| European Union[a] | 2,785 | 35 | 4,753 | 33 | 7,431 | 26 |
| China | 279 | 3 | 1,622 | 11 | 4,579 | 16 |
| India | 60 | 1 | 207 | 1 | 869 | 3 |
| Indonesia | 67 | 1 | 172 | 1 | 501 | 2 |
| Japan | 512 | 6 | 833 | 6 | 1,252 | 4 |
| Korea | 205 | 3 | 386 | 3 | 718 | 3 |
| Malaysia | 112 | 1 | 189 | 1 | 328 | 1 |
| Singapore | 184 | 2 | 210 | 1 | 263 | 1 |
| Thailand | 81 | 1 | 203 | 1 | 476 | 2 |
| United States | 1,093 | 14 | 1,536 | 11 | 2,813 | 10 |

| Imports | Value | % of world imports | Value | % of world imports | Value | % of world imports |
|---|---|---|---|---|---|---|
| European Union[a] | 2,992 | 37 | 5,039 | 33 | 8,094 | 27 |
| China | 201 | 3 | 1,332 | 9 | 4,253 | 14 |
| India | 63 | 1 | 267 | 2 | 916 | 3 |
| Indonesia | 40 | 0 | 161 | 1 | 483 | 2 |
| Japan | 407 | 5 | 738 | 5 | 1,238 | 4 |
| Korea | 159 | 2 | 403 | 3 | 792 | 3 |
| Malaysia | 76 | 1 | 162 | 1 | 315 | 1 |
| Singapore | n.a. | n.a. | 194 | 1 | 281 | 1 |
| Thailand | 56 | 1 | 191 | 1 | 468 | 2 |
| United States | 1,304 | 16 | 2,209 | 15 | 3,577 | 12 |

[a]Figures for the European Union include the EU-25 countries and in addition, Iceland and Switzerland. EU trade with the world includes intra-EU trade in addition to extra-EU trade, which overestimates the percentage of world trade represented by these countries.

*Note:* Data for 2000 uses 2000 dollars for base year. Data for 2010 and 2025 estimates use 2007 dollars.

*Source:* Peter A. Petri, Michael Plummer and Fan Zhai, *The Trans-Pacific Partnership and Asia-Pacific Integration: A Quantitative Assessment* (Washington, DC: Peterson Institute for International Economics, 2012); World Bank World Development Indicators database, http://data.worldbank.org/indicator.

**Table 2. Human Development Index (HDI) for select countries, 2012**

| Country | HDI[a] | | Inequality-adjusted HDI[b] | |
|---|---|---|---|---|
| | Value | Rank | Value | Rank |
| China | 0.699 | 101 | 0.543 | 67 |
| India | 0.554 | 136 | 0.392 | 91 |
| Indonesia | 0.629 | 121 | 0.514 | 78 |
| Japan | 0.912 | 10 | - | - |
| Korea | 0.909 | 12 | 0.758 | 28 |
| Malaysia | 0.769 | 64 | - | - |
| Singapore | 0.895 | 18 | - | - |
| Thailand | 0.69 | 103 | 0.543 | 67 |
| United States | 0.937 | 3 | 0.821 | 16 |

[a]The HDI is based on three dimensions (health, education, and income) and four related indicators. The HDI sets a minimum and a maximum for each dimension and calculates where each country stands in relation to these "goalposts," expressed as a value on a scale of 0 to a high of 1.
[b]IHDI is measured as HDI adjusted for inequalities in the distribution of achievements in health, education, and income.
*Note:* A dash indicates index not available.
*Source:* UNDP (2013).

toward higher levels of human development.[3] But persistent development challenges also means that political priorities in these societies will have to continue to focus on managing domestic adjustment through income redistribution, leaving less political capital and resources to devote to economic objectives abroad.[4]

Third, the evolution of powerful Asian economies does not mean that Asia will become a powerful region. While the major economies are integrating, intra-Asian economic integration still lags behind Asia-Pacific and North American arrangements, namely the Trans-Pacific Partnership (TPP) and North American Free Trade Agreement (NAFTA). The Regional Comprehensive Economic Partnership (RCEP)—led by ASEAN plus Australia, China, Japan, South Korea, India, New Zealand—would set a precedent in the region, but it is not the functional equivalent of the TPP. Important challenges remain from accommodating least developed economies like Myanmar and foot-draggers to liberalization like India. Moreover, increasing competition for global investment and export market share has already incited political tensions and protectionist measures directed against

[4]Jeffrey J. Schott, "The Asian Century: Reality or Hype?" *The International Economy*, Summer 2013a, pp. 17–18, http://www.international-economy.com/TIE_Su13_Asia CenturySymposium.pdf.

erstwhile RCEP negotiating partners.[5] Structural shifts in the major Asian economies, in particular the growth of the service sector in India and China, may create additional frictions.[6] This growing friction between regional powers means these countries will continue to depend importantly on trade with the United States and the European Union, and will hesitate to assume major global leadership roles. Combined, these factors will likely place a constraint on the pace of economic growth and intra-Asian integration.

Within this context, this chapter assesses the transatlantic response to Asia's growing economic importance. First, we provide an overview of U.S. and EU trade and investment and the importance of their commercial ties with Asia. Second, we examine the evolving U.S. and European responses to Asia's rise and their differing strategies of economic engagement. The U.S. economic "pivot" to Asia began more than a decade ago and has been amplified by the TPP initiative. The European Union's response has been more limited, but deepening trade ties with Asia became a growing priority during the mid-2000s. Third, we assess the recent convergence of U.S. and EU policy initiatives toward Asia: the transatlantic partners have gone from competitive regionalism in Asia to cooperative transatlantic regionalism through the launch of negotiations on a Transatlantic Trade and Investment Partnership (TTIP). TTIP has the potential to improve U.S. and European competitiveness in the global economy, and thus is an integral component of the transatlantic strategy to address the new commercial challenge from emerging Asian countries. But to achieve that result, both sides will have to revise specific regulatory policies to either align or harmonize with the other TTIP partner.[7] Fourth, we

---

[5]For example, a growing proportion of India's trade defense measures, including antidumping and countervailing measures, have targeted China. Analysis by Tovar (2011) shows that in 1997, 53% of India's total antidumping measures affected developed countries, another 22% affected China, and the rest affected other developing countries. By contrast, by 2009 only 25% of the total stock of Indian measures was imposed against developed countries, 36% against developing countries, namely Malaysia, Thailand, and Japan, while almost 40% were imposed against China alone. Patricia Tovar, "India: The Use of Temporary Trade Barriers," in *The Great Recession and Import Protection: The Role of Temporary Trade Barriers* Chad Bown ed., (London: Centre for Economic Policy Research and World Bank, 2011).

[6]Schott, *op. cit.*, pp. 17–18.

[7]This stands in contrast to most of the Asian initiatives by both sides which focused on enhancing market share and elaborating new trade rules based on U.S. or EU practice.

**Table 3. U.S. trade with select partners in Asia ($ billions)**

| Partner | 2002 | | | 2012 | | |
|---|---|---|---|---|---|---|
| | Exports | Imports | Total two-way trade | Exports | Imports | Total two-way trade |
| ASEAN countries | 39 | 80 | 119 | 71 | 124 | 196 |
| Indonesia | 3 | 10 | 13 | 8 | 19 | 27 |
| Malaysia | 9 | 25 | 34 | 11 | 27 | 38 |
| Philippines | 7 | 11 | 18 | 8 | 10 | 18 |
| Singapore | 15 | 15 | 30 | 31 | 20 | 51 |
| Thailand | 4 | 16 | 20 | 10 | 27 | 37 |
| Vietnam | 1 | 3 | 3 | 4 | 21 | 26 |
| China | 21 | 133 | 154 | 104 | 444 | 548 |
| India | 4 | 12 | 16 | 19 | 42 | 61 |
| Japan | 48 | 125 | 173 | 65 | 150 | 215 |
| Korea | 21 | 37 | 58 | 40 | 61 | 101 |
| Total U.S. trade with select Asia partners | 132 | 387 | 520 | 298 | 822 | 1,120 |
| Total U.S. global trade | 693 | 1,202 | 1,896 | 1,353 | 2,334 | 3,687 |

ASEAN = Association of Southeast Asian Nations
*Note*: Figures rounded to nearest $ billion.
*Source*: World Bank World Integrated Solutions (WITS) Database, http://wits.worldbank.org/wits/.

summarize the findings of key studies to date that have estimated the prospective quantitative impact of the TTIP on trade and income as well as the precedential impact of TTIP on Asia and the world trading system.

## Transatlantic Trade and Investment in Asia

Transatlantic trade and investment in Asia has expanded dramatically over the past decade. U.S. trade with its top partners in Asia—namely, China, Japan, South Korea, India, and the major ASEAN countries (Indonesia, Malaysia, Philippines, Thailand, Vietnam and Singapore)—comprised about 30% of total U.S. global trade on average during the past decade, as outlined in Table 3. From 2002 to 2012, two-way trade (imports plus exports) with these Asian partners more than doubled. U.S.-China and U.S.-India trade has driven this trend with two-way trade expanding more than four times since 2002.

Table 4 shows that U.S. foreign direct investment (FDI) in Asia accounts for about 12% of total U.S. global FDI. Singapore and Japan remain the most important destination markets for U.S. FDI, while Japan accounts for the majority share of Asian FDI in the United States.

**Table 4. U.S. foreign direct investment (FDI) stock for select Asian countries, 2012 ($ billions)**

| Country | Outward FDI stock | Inward FDI stock |
|---|---|---|
| ASEAN countries | 189.6 | 27.5 |
| Indonesia | 13.5 | 0.1 |
| Malaysia | 15.0 | 0.7 |
| Singapore | 138.6 | 26.2 |
| Philippines | 4.6 | 0.2 |
| Thailand | 16.9 | 0.2 |
| Vietnam | 1.1 | 0.0 |
| China | 51.4 | 5.2 |
| India | 28.4 | 5.2 |
| Japan | 134.0 | 308.3 |
| Korea | 35.1 | 24.5 |
| Subtotal | 438.5 | 370.5 |
| % of U.S. global FDI | 9.8 | 14.0 |
| Total U.S. global FDI | 4,453.3 | 2,650.8 |

ASEAN = Association of Southeast Asian Nations
*Source*: U.S. Bureau of Economic Analysis, Direct Investment & Multinational Companies (MNCs) database, http://www.bea.gov/iTable/index_MNC.cfm.

Table 5 indicates that the European Union's two-way trade with top trading partners in Asia averaged about 25% of total EU global trade over the past decade. Trade with Vietnam, China, and India in particular has seen the largest expansion of two-way trade, and the EU is now China's largest trading partner. Notably, EU two-way trade with China, South Korea, India and the ASEAN countries exceeds that of the United States; and in 2012, the EU was the top trading partner of China and India. The European Union is an important source of FDI in Asia with an accumulated total of $620 billion invested in select Asian countries as of 2012. However, Asian investment in Europe remains small. Table 6 shows that the EU's major trading partners only account for 7% of total FDI in the EU, with more than half from Japan. The amount of Asian FDI in the EU is similar to Asian FDI in the United States, namely $377 compared to $371 billion. However, Asia accounts for 14% of total U.S. FDI worldwide (table 4) but only 7% of total EU FDI worldwide (table 6).

As dynamic drivers of the global economy, it is no surprise that trading partners in Asia comprise a growing share of U.S. and EU trade and investment. However, the transatlantic partners still remain each other's most important market for trade and cross-border investment.

## Table 5. EU trade with select partners in Asia ($ billions)

| Partner | 2002 | | | 2012 | | |
|---|---|---|---|---|---|---|
| | Exports | Imports | Total two-way trade | Exports | Imports | Total two-way trade |
| ASEAN countries | 37 | 62 | 99 | 96 | 128 | 224 |
| Indonesia | 4 | 10 | 15 | 11 | 20 | 31 |
| Malaysia | 8 | 15 | 23 | 17 | 26 | 43 |
| Philippines | 3 | 8 | 11 | 6 | 7 | 13 |
| Singapore | 14 | 13 | 27 | 39 | 28 | 67 |
| Thailand | 6 | 11 | 18 | 17 | 24 | 41 |
| Vietnam | 2 | 4 | 6 | 6 | 24 | 30 |
| China | 33 | 83 | 116 | 173 | 381 | 555 |
| India | 12 | 13 | 25 | 45 | 47 | 92 |
| Japan | 40 | 68 | 108 | 64 | 98 | 161 |
| Korea | 16 | 23 | 39 | 44 | 53 | 97 |
| Total EU trade with select Asia partners | 139 | 248 | 387 | 422 | 708 | 1,130 |
| Total EU-27 global trade | 843 | 885 | 1,727 | 2,166 | 2,301 | 4,468 |

ASEAN = Association of Southeast Asian Nations
*Note*: Figures rounded to nearest $ billion.
*Source*: World Bank World Integrated Solutions (WITS) Database, http://wits.worldbank.org/wits/.

## Table 6. EU foreign direct investment (FDI) stock for select Asian countries, 2012 ($ billions)

| Country | Outward FDI stock | Inward FDI stock |
|---|---|---|
| ASEAN countries | 236.3 | 99.5 |
| Indonesia | 31.9 | -2.4 |
| Malaysia | 23.4 | 8.8 |
| Philippines | 9.7 | 1.8 |
| Singapore | 152.5 | 88.1 |
| Thailand | 18.8 | 3.2 |
| Vietnam | n.a. | n.a. |
| China | 151.8 | 34.4 |
| India | 53.8 | 11.3 |
| Japan | 127.0 | 207.5 |
| Korea | 50.7 | 23.7 |
| Subtotal | 619.5 | 376.5 |
| % of extra-EU FDI | 9.3 | 7.4 |
| Total extra-EU FDI | 6,685.5 | 5,068.5 |

n.a. = not available
*Notes*: Original data in billions of euros converted to U.S. dollars using annualized exchange rate of 1.284 for 2012 according to the European Central Bank (ECB), http://sdw.ecb.europa.eu/browse.do?node= 2018794.
*Source*: Eurostat, EU direct investment - main indicators, http://appsso.eurostat.ec.europa.eu/nui/ show.do?dataset=bop_fdi_main&lang=en.

**Table 7. US–EU bilateral trade in goods and services, 2006–2012 ($ billions)**

| Year | US exports to the EU — Total exports | | | | US imports from the EU — Total imports | | | | Two-way goods and services trade[a] | Goods and services trade balance |
|------|-------|----------|------------|---------------------------|-------|----------|------------|---------------------------|------|------|
| | Goods | Services | Billions $ | % of U.S. global exports | Goods | Services | Billions $ | % of U.S. global imports | | |
| 2006 | 216 | 146 | 362 | 24.8 | 333 | 128 | 461 | 20.8 | 822.8 | -99.8 |
| 2007 | 249 | 176 | 425 | 25.7 | 359 | 142 | 501 | 21.3 | 926.0 | -75.9 |
| 2008 | 277 | 194 | 471 | 25.6 | 372 | 153 | 526 | 20.7 | 996.9 | -54.2 |
| 2009 | 225 | 175 | 400 | 25.3 | 284 | 137 | 420 | 21.5 | 820.2 | -20.4 |
| 2010 | 243 | 175 | 418 | 22.7 | 322 | 139 | 461 | 19.7 | 878.8 | -43.2 |
| 2011 | 273 | 190 | 463 | 22.0 | 373 | 150 | 523 | 19.6 | 986.2 | -59.8 |
| 2012 | 269 | 200 | 470 | 21.3 | 387 | 154 | 541 | 19.7 | 1,010.4 | -70.6 |

[a]Two-way trade calculated as the sum of exports and imports of goods and services.

*Note:* Trade figures are revised as of September 2013 and not seasonally adjusted.

*Source:* U.S. Bureau of Economic Analysis, International Transactions database, http://www.bea.gov/iTable/index_ita.cfm.

## Table 8 Foreign direct investment (FDI) stock by industry, 2012 ($ billions and percent)

| Industry | Stock of U.S. FDI in EU-27 | | Stock of EU-27 in U.S. | |
|---|---|---|---|---|
| | % of global US FDI $ billion | by sector | % of FDI in US $ billion | by sector |
| Mining | 16 | 7 | n.a | n.a |
| Manufacturing | 275 | 43 | 605 | 67 |
| Food | 22 | 38 | 9 | 29 |
| Chemicals | 67 | 50 | 188 | 80 |
| Primary and fabricated metals | 10 | 43 | 29 | 62 |
| Machinery | 21 | 41 | 72 | 83 |
| Computers and electronic products | 39 | 39 | 20 | 33 |
| Electrical equipment, appliances, and components | 14 | 63 | 31 | 80 |
| Transportation equipment | 25 | 38 | 56 | 52 |
| Other manufacturing | 78 | 43 | 200 | 69 |
| Wholesale | 69 | 34 | 125 | 43 |
| Retail trade | n.a. | n.a. | 32 | 62 |
| Information | 88 | 60 | 103 | 83 |
| Depository institutions | 65 | 54 | 120 | 60 |
| Finance (except depository) and insurance | 343 | 44 | 237 | 65 |
| Real estate and rental leasing | n.a. | n.a. | 24 | 47 |
| Professional, scientific, and technical services | 51 | 54 | 75 | 70 |
| Holding companies (nonbank) | 1,184 | 61 | n.a. | n.a. |
| Other industries | 150 | 49 | 327 | 58 |
| All industries total | 2,240 | 50 | 1,648 | 62 |

n.a. = not applicable

*Notes*: U.S. direct investment position reported on a historical-cost basis. 2012 preliminary figures revised as of September 2013.

*Source*: U.S. Bureau of Economic Analysis, Direct Investment & Multinational Companies (MNCs) database, http://www.bea.gov/iTable/index_MNC.cfm.

Tables 7 and 8 show that in 2012, U.S.-EU trade in goods and services totaled about $1 trillion annually and the stock of two-way FDI was valued at nearly $4 trillion. The transatlantic markets remain each other's top source and destination for FDI: the United States invests 50% of its global FDI in the European Union, while the European Union invests more than 62% of its global FDI in the United States. While Asia has steadily increased its share of U.S. and EU trade to the extent that the magnitude of trade is comparable to transatlantic levels, Asia's share of transatlantic investment continues to be significantly outpaced by U.S. and EU investment in each other's markets.

Economic engagement with their Asian partners has been to the benefit of the transatlantic economies. But TTIP now represents an opportunity to improve U.S. and European competitiveness vis-à-vis

Asia. Further deepening bilateral trade ties and the integration of U.S.-EU economies through the TTIP comprises an important component of both sides' response to Asia's rise. The following section summarizes the progression of U.S. and EU trade responses to Asia and the potential role of TTIP.

## U.S.-EU Trade Response

The United States and European Union's deepening economic ties in Asia have become a significant driver of the trade policies of both sides. As argued here, TTIP is an important component of U.S.-EU global strategies in the wake of Asia's rise. The progression of economic engagement in Asia by both sides offers an important historical context.

The rise of dynamic Asian economies fundamentally changed the landscape of multilateral trade negotiations. During the latter decades of the GATT era, the "Quad" countries—the United States, European Union, Canada, and Japan—formed the de facto steering committee of multilateral trade initiatives, although in most cases the important decisions were crafted by the transatlantic G-2. But the transatlantic leadership of the global trading system was predictably diluted with the inauguration of the WTO in 1995 and further still as the institution's agenda evolved over nearly two decades. The rise of emerging markets, including the BRICS countries —Brazil, Russia, India, China, and South Africa—among others, and expanded WTO membership meant that achieving consensus on new trade agreements became more complex as WTO initiatives had to balance the interests and priorities of the broader membership: it was not that all members participated actively in WTO deliberations, but their views needed to be represented in the talks and their priorities accommodated in WTO decisions. And the management of the WTO negotiations process has become more cumbersome since more countries now have a vested interest in the negotiating outcomes. The Quad passed into the ether a long time ago and now at least 10–15 countries have to be engaged in the WTO's inside steering group. With increasing economic leverage, China and India became part of informal caucuses that steered

---

[8]No one group of countries is to blame for the current Doha impasse, but as Craig Van Grasstek reflects, "The stalemate in the Doha Round negotiations shows that members

the WTO talks into serious roadblocks.[8] To be sure, this shift under-mined the prospects for successful completion of the Doha Round; transatlantic positions in the WTO did not quickly adjust to that new reality.

Difficulties from the start of the Doha Round diverted attention from comprehensive multilateral initiatives to complementary or alternative regional trade initiatives as means of pursuing more mean-ingful commitments on trade issues both old and new.[9] In recent years, the United States and the European Union turned to mega-regional pacts like the TPP and TTIP. Many other WTO members, especially developing countries, also turned to bilateral and regional trade agreements (RTAs) to address trade problems that were not being fixed through the sluggish Geneva process.[10]

In economic terms, the US "pivot" to Asia started more than 15 years ago when the United States responded to Asia's rise by deepen-ing its economic engagement in the Asia-Pacific region. A crucial component of this policy shift was the intensification of U.S. efforts to negotiate China's WTO accession, which required China to commit to a level of trade liberalization well above that of other developing

---

have yet to work out the proper division of the burdens, with developed countries and emerging economies having very different views of how much each of them should bear." See Craig Van Grasstek, *The History and Future of the World Trade Organization*, (Geneva: World Trade Organization, 2013), p. 561.

[9]The debate over the relationship of regional trade agreements (RTAs) and multilater-alism has a rich history that dates well before Jacob Viner's classic tome. See Jacob Viner, *The Customs Union Issue* (New York: Carnegie Endowment for International Peace, 1950). Some emphasize the constructive nature of RTAs as setting useful prece-dents which can complement and incentivize progress within multilateral trade talks; while others emphasize the growing network of RTAs as substituting or undermining multilateral trade talks. See Washington Trade Report (WTR), "RTAs: From Building Blocks to Stumbling Blocks," *Washington Trade Report* 39.37 (September 2013), pp. 1-7 and Van Grasstek, *op. cit.* The outlook for the relevance of each path could crystallize following the critical outcome of the ninth WTO Ministerial in December 2013. Still, it remains unclear how the major trading partners of mega-regional pacts will attempt, if at all, to find a strategy for using super-regional pacts to re-engage multilateral negotiations—or in other words, a strategy towards gradually "multilateralizing regionalism." See Richard Baldwin and Patrick Low, eds. *Multilateralizing Regionalism: Challenges for the Global Trading System* (Geneva: Cambridge University Press for the World Trade Organization, 2009).

[10]For analysis of these trends see WTR, *op. cit.*

countries in the WTO. Soon after, the United States pursued its most significant integration effort to date, enshrined in the Korea-U.S. or KORUS FTA, which is considered the "gold standard" of FTAs and has established important precedents for U.S. trade talks both with Europe and the Asia-Pacific. U.S. strategic interests regarding the rise of China and North Korea's militarism played an explicit role in pursuing such initiatives. However, U.S. efforts to expand markets have not been confined to Northeast Asia. In 2002, the United States initiated the Enterprise for ASEAN Initiative, which led to the signing of the U.S.-ASEAN Trade and Investment Framework Agreement (TIFA) in 2006—a pre-requisite for U.S. FTA negotiations. The United States concluded an FTA with Singapore in 2004, but U.S. bilateral trade negotiations with Thailand and Malaysia were suspended in 2006 and 2008 respectively; subsequently, talks with individual ASEAN countries were or likely will be restarted under the umbrella of the TPP.[11] Current TPP negotiations comprise 12 countries, including four ASEAN countries (Brunei, Malaysia, Singapore, and Vietnam), Japan, and other important U.S. trading partners (Australia, Canada, Chile, Mexico, New Zealand, and Peru).

The TPP talks represent the culmination of U.S. economic engagement in the region. The TPP-12 account for almost 40% of global GDP and 25% of global exports; when completed, which could take place in 2014 well before TTIP talks move into second gear, the TPP will represent the largest free trade zone in the world. The TPP seeks comprehensive trade liberalization covering goods and services and WTO-plus rulemaking on investment, competition policy, labor and environment, and disciplines on state-owned enterprises, among others.[12]

The TPP deal is important not just for the anticipated economic gains or setting a new standard for trade accords; the TPP also parallels regional integration efforts of the ASEAN+6 (Australia, China,

---

[11]Whether the United States will pursue trade talks with ASEAN in the future is uncertain. But a U.S.-ASEAN FTA would be a prerequisite for U.S. participation in the RCEP.

[12]See Jeffrey J. Schott, Barbara Kotschwar, and Julia Muir, *Understanding the Trans-Pacific Partnership: Policy Analyses in International Economics* (Washington, D.C.: Peterson Institute for International Economics, January 2013).

India, Japan, South Korea, New Zealand) through RCEP launched in May 2013. The overlapping participation in the two integration efforts—7 of 16 RCEP members are in the TPP, plus 4 other interested countries (Indonesia, South Korea, Philippines, Thailand)—could make it easier to link the two in a hybrid arrangement that promotes free trade and investment across the region.[13,14] This approach has also been considered a possible way of deepening the U.S.-China commercial relationship short of a bilateral FTA.[15] To be sure, this long-term vision still faces severe constraints and challenges, and how the United States will manage the relations between the concurrent initiatives will be important. But it indicates a likely foundation for achieving further meaningful economic integration in the Asia-Pacific region.

While the United States pursued wide-ranging FTA initiatives in the Asia-Pacific as a complement and/or hedge against the increasingly evident drift in the Doha Round, the European Union resisted new FTA ventures and stuck to a singular focus on WTO talks in the early years of the Doha Round. The EU began to emulate U.S. initiatives in

---

[13] *Ibid.*, p. 62.

[14] To illustrate the potential economic impact, Petri, Plummer, and Zhai calculate that the TPP and RCEP tracks pursued separately would achieve collective GDP gains of approximately $770 billion and export gains of $1 trillion; however, the consolidation of the two tracks would offer the most significant outcome, with GDP gains of nearly $2 trillion and export gains of $3 trillion. See Peter A. Petri, Michael G. Plummer, and Fan Zhai, *The Trans-Pacific Partnership and Asia-Pacific Integration: A Quantitative Assessment: Policy Analyses 98* (Washington, D.C.: Peterson Institute for International Economics, November 2012).

[15] A "hybrid" approach linking the two agreements may be less essential should China eventually join the TPP. Some viewed the TPP talks as deliberately excluding China from integration efforts via "containment" policy of the United States. Schott, Kotschwar, and Muir (p. 58) argue that three reasons undermine this claim: a trade agreement cannot effectively "contain" an economically and politically large and influential country like China; the US benefits from cooperation with China to mutually address global and regional challenges in both of the realms of economics and security; and no country in Asia exclusively wants to contain China given the trade and investment integration in the region and larger incentives for improving competitiveness. Further, while the consensus is that China is not ready for a comprehensive accord like the TPP, China has indicated less wariness toward the TPP and closer interest in its provisions. Meanwhile, some Chinese political leaders have expressed initial interest in exploring a China-US FTA.

the Asia-Pacific in the mid-2000s when Brussels ended its self-imposed moratorium on new FTA negotiations.[16] However, with the exception of South Korea, where EU policy largely matched the U.S. initiative, the EU has been unable to use its strong market share to achieve substantive trade agreements with ASEAN or China,[17] or pursue broader regional initiatives like the TPP. But the EU is seeking to reverse this trend, especially to mitigate the pending preferential treatment that U.S. firms would enjoy from its TPP partners in Asia. Like the United States, EU efforts to engage ASEAN as a collective unit have been limited, and instead economic engagement has centered on separate bilateral agreements with the larger trading partners.[18] In September 2013, the EU completed a draft FTA with Singapore and is currently in trade talks with Malaysia (initiated September 2010), Vietnam (June 2012) and Thailand (March 2013). By contrast, ongoing FTA talks with India have gone farther than U.S. initiatives, but are on the brink of failure due to intractable differences regarding agricultural subsidies, services, and government procurement, among other issues. Similar bilateral efforts with Indonesia have been unfruitful, suggesting that advancing a comprehensive trade and investment agenda in the region still faces significant obstacles in the medium-term.

To date, the Korea-EU or KOREU FTA remains the EU's most significant economic engagement effort in Asia, because it establishes

---

[16]This accompanied the release of the Global Europe Strategy in 2006, which outlined a vision for renewed FTA talks and trade strategy. See *Global Europe: Competing in the World*, European Commission (Brussels, 2006), http://trade.ec.europa.eu/doclib/docs/2006/october/tradoc_130376.pdf.

[17]However, initiatives with these countries are ongoing. The EU and China began investment negotiations in November 2013. See "EU Investment Negotiations with China and ASEAN," European Commission, October 18, 2013, http://trade.ec.europa.eu/doclib/press/index.cfm?id=975.

[18]The EU and ASEAN initiated FTA negotiations in 2007 but after seven negotiating rounds, the talks were suspended in 2009 "in order to reflect on the appropriate format of future negotiations." The EU blamed economic and political differences among the ASEAN members, namely Myanmar. EU opted to pursue bilateral agreements from which in the future could lead to consolidating into a broader ASEAN regional agreement. See "Free Trade Agreements," European Commission, last update May 2, 2013, http://ec.europa.eu/enterprise/policies/international/facilitating-trade/free-trade/ (accessed on October 10, 2013).

similar comprehensive and high standards as the KORUS FTA as well as ample precedents for the transatlantic talks[19] and possibly for EU trade talks with Japan, which launched in March 2013 but have seen limited progress. Indeed, the negotiations on the KOREU pact started from the KORUS baseline, though the final terms differ from the KORUS FTA in some notable respects.[20] The KOREU talks started when the KORUS talks ended, but because of political obstacles in both the U.S. and Korean legislatures, the KOREU FTA actually entered into force in July 2011 almost a year before the KORUS FTA.

The United States and European Union's deepening economic ties in Asia have become a significant driver of the trade policies of both sides. Just as each side pursued its own Asian strategy, competitive liberalization strategies in Asia have also helped to instigate regional trade integration in the Asia-Pacific as well as integration between Asia and Europe, as shown in Table 9. The transatlantic partners have gone from competitive regionalism in Asia to cooperative regionalism through the TTIP–in other words, to shared trade and investment objectives in Asia based on their high standard trade pacts with South Korea.

Through TTIP, United States and European leaders are now essentially seeking to achieve a transatlantic counterpart to the TPP. However, because membership in the TPP is also a key component of the U.S. strategic response, TTIP may hold an even higher profile in Europe's regional and global strategy. Nevertheless, unlike previous Asian initiatives of the transatlantic partners that focused on enhancing market share and elaborating new trading rules based on U.S. or EU practice, the TTIP may require changes in current U.S. or EU policies; neither has had to face such demands to change current domestic policies in previous FTAs to any great extent. Whether and if so how they conform domestic policies will have important implications for both the bilateral relationship and for the world trading system writ large.

---

[19]Jeffrey J. Schott and Cathleen Cimino, *Crafting a Transatlantic Trade and Investment Partnership: What Can Be Done*, Peterson Institute for International Economics Policy Brief 13-8, March 2013.

[20]For a brief summary see Schott and Cimino, *op. cit.*, table 3.

**Table 9. U.S. and EU bilateral and regional trade agreements in Asia**

| United States | |
|---|---|
| **Partner country** | **Agreement[a]** |
| *Entered into force* | |
| Korea | FTA (2012) |
| Singapore | FTA (2004)/TPP |
| *Under negotiation* | |
| Brunei | TPP (2010) |
| Japan | TPP (2013) |
| Malaysia | TPP (2010) |
| Vietnam | TPP (2010) |

| European Union | |
|---|---|
| **Partner country** | **Agreement[a]** |
| *Entered into force* | |
| Korea | FTA (2011) |
| *Under negotiation* | |
| India | FTA (2007)[b] |
| Japan | FTA (2013) |
| Malaysia | FTA (2010) |
| Singapore | FTA (2010)[c] |
| Thailand | FTA (2013) |
| Vietnam | FTA (2013) |

FTA = free trade agreement; TPP = Trans-Pacific Partnership
[a]Agreement status as of October 2013; date refers to either the agreements entry into force or the start of negotiations.
[b]EU talks with India reportedly stalled in 2013.
[c]EU talks with Singapore concluded in 2012, but the agreement has not yet entered into force.
Sources: U.S. Trade Representative, http://www.ustr.gov/trade-agreements/free-trade-agreements; European Commission, http://ec.europa.eu/trade/policy/countries-and-regions/agreements/.

## Implications of TTIP[21]

Can TTIP give the United States and European Union a competitive edge over China and the rest of Asia? Some argue yes, by setting rules based on transatlantic standards that others would follow. There are reasons to be skeptical as to what extent TTIP can jointly achieve global standards, discussed in more detail below. But doing so should help contribute to better efficiency and productivity growth in the U.S. and EU economies, which in so doing should enhance the competitiveness of transatlantic firms. This section introduces the initial ambitions and potential limitations of the agreement.

---

[21]This section draws heavily on Schott and Cimino, *op. cit.*

Like the TPP, TTIP is a mega-regional initiative involving countries that account for about 46% of global GDP (versus almost 40% for the TPP). The TTIP aims to deepen the world's largest commercial relationship, laying the foundation for greater economic and job growth. Transatlantic leaders also hope to use the bilateral deal to revive stalled WTO talks and contribute to creating a template for global commercial rules that can strengthen the multilateral trading system.[22]

TTIP negotiations were officially launched in July 2013 with an agenda based on the preliminary work of the U.S.-EU High Level Working Group (HLWG) on Jobs and Growth. The HLWG recommended "a comprehensive agreement that addresses a broad range of bilateral trade and investment issues, including regulatory issues" and called for ambitious market access reform beyond what the two sides have achieved in previous trade agreements.[23] Specifically, the TTIP aims to cover commitments in three major areas: (1) market access, including the elimination of tariffs and limited phase-outs for sensitive products, in addition to services commitments, investment reforms and protections, and expanding coverage of government procurement at the federal and sub-federal levels; (2) regulatory issues and non-tariff "behind the border" barriers, such as WTO-plus rules on sanitary and phyto-sanitary measures, technical barriers to trade, and new efforts toward regulatory harmonization or mutual recognition; and (3) new or "WTO-plus" rulemaking in areas like intellectual property rights (IPR), trade facilitation, competition policy, environment and labor, among others.

By endorsing this ambitious agenda, both sides implicitly committed to address basic differences in key policies and regulatory approaches in several difficult areas, from agriculture to cross-border rules on services, investment, and food and health safety regulations. Disagreements over these issues have confounded transatlantic offi-

---

[22]"US, EU Announce Decision to Launch Negotiations on a Transatlantic Trade and Investment Partnership," Office of the United States Trade Representative, February 13, 2013, http://www.ustr.gov/about-us/press-office/press-releases/2013/february/statement-US-EU-Presidents (accessed on October 9, 2013).

[23]"Final Report: High Level Working Group on Jobs and Growth," European Commission, February 11, 2013, http://trade.ec.europa.eu/doclib/docs/2013/february/tradoc_150519.pdf.

cials for decades. However, previous attempts focused on limited "mutual recognition" deals on specific products or sectors, which ultimately failed due to resistance from independent regulatory agencies pressing their own disparate agendas in response to political pressures.[24] U.S. and EU negotiators recognize that trying to reach a more comprehensive deal offers the best prospects for obtaining sufficient political support, and thus have kept almost everything "on the table" at the start of the TTIP talks.[25] This means that hot-button issues like genetically-modified organisms (GMOs), financial services and cross-border data flows—which raise concerns about data access and related privacy issues in light of revelations of NSA collection methods—will be discussed; however in practice, negotiations in these areas will more likely be restricted to regulatory cooperation related to procedures and processes, rather than the formation of common standards. Five rounds of negotiations as of May 2014 have begun to address some of these issues, but as the talks progress, other products or services may not make the final cut or only be subject to partial reforms.

Given the large volume of transatlantic trade and investment flows, it is true that even small cuts in protection can yield significant benefits to both sides. But the more important gains lie in the potential for substantially reducing high cost, non-tariff barriers (NTBs). Indeed, the high end projections of TTIP gains depend on ambitious results in services and on reducing "unnecessary" regulatory costs. But such outcomes will likely be scaled back as the negotiations proceed and both sides' commitments crystallize, lowering the overall economic gains and moderating the precedential impact of the TTIP on the world trading system. The next section contextualizes the prospective impact of TTIP on the transatlantic economies.

---

[24]Schott and Cimino, *op. cit.*

[25]Despite this commitment, EU negotiators excluded the area of audiovisual services up front, while U.S. officials have indicated maritime and air services may to some extent be off limits. See "Froman Pledges to Preserve Jones Act, Criticizes EU Clean Fuel Directive," *Inside US Trade*, September 19, 2013, www.insidetrade.com (accessed on November 15, 2013).

## TTIP's Economic Potential: Understanding the Numbers[26]

U.S. and European officials launched the TTIP negotiations to bolster economic growth and jobs. The objective is to remove barriers to trade and investment and unnecessary regulatory measures that significantly raise production costs, and thereby improve the competitiveness of firms and workers on each side of the Atlantic. Officials understandably want to cite numbers about what their efforts will yield in terms of increased output and jobs. Several studies have already been published on the prospective economic payoff from the TTIP. Those with the most optimistic projections—based on the most tenuous economic assumptions—seem to be cited the most frequently in the policy debate.

Estimates of the potential TTIP impact vary significantly, owning in large measure to their estimation techniques and the underlying assumptions about what the TTIP negotiators will achieve. In some cases, the assumptions essentially predetermine the results. While we can reasonably assume that almost all tariffs will be phased out, the handling of so-called "behind the border" barriers to trade is much more difficult to quantify. This is particularly important in the case of TTIP, as a substantial part of the effort will seek to align or coordinate domestic regulatory policies that have an impact on trade and investment. Indeed, we would expect the gains from removing tariffs to be far smaller than the gains from regulatory harmonization.

We recognize that the estimates are constrained by the nature of the econometric tools available to the researcher, but these efforts provide useful information about the potential overall trade and output effects. We should add a note of caution, however. The more disaggregated the analysis, the more tenuous the findings—so sectoral results from big computable general equilibrium (CGE) models should be viewed with many grains of salt. Estimates that project the TTIP's aggregate effect on U.S.-EU trade are much more robust than those that seek to parse out the aggregate gains sector by sector.

In order to give meaningful estimates, a study must indicate a benchmark scenario with which to compare their FTA scenario. For example, if TTIP were to be signed into law today, it would be several

---

[26]This section was drafted by Peterson Institute research analyst Tyler Moran.

**Table 10. Comparison of gains from TTIP based on four studies**

|                            | ECORYS | EC (CEPR) | BIS (CEPR) | ECIPE |
|----------------------------|--------|-----------|------------|-------|
| Benchmark year             | 2018   | 2027      | 2027       | 2015  |
| Change in U.S. GDP         | 0.3%   | 0.4%      | 0.4%       | 1.3%  |
| Change in EU GDP           | 0.7%   | 0.5%      | 0.7%       | 0.5%  |
| Change in total U.S. exports | 6.1% | 8.0%      | 7.5%       | n.a.  |
| Change in total EU exports | 2.1%   | 5.9%      | n.a.       | n.a.  |

n.a. = not applicable

EC = European Commission; CEPR = Center for Economic Policy and Research; BIS = UK Department for Business, Innovation and Skills; ECIPE = European Center for International Policy Economy.

*Sources*: ECORYS (2009); CEPR (2013a); CEPR (2013b); and ECIPE (2010).

years (perhaps 10 or more) before all of the provisions were implemented, and even longer before markets fully adjusted to the changes. To capture this, authors choose a time horizon, generally 10 or more years in the future, and project the values of the relevant indicators based on current trends and policy. New estimates are then produced which assume that the relevant policy changes have been fully implemented. Comparing the two scenarios provides estimates of the gains from the proposed policy changes.[27]

This section attempts to shed some light on the projections of TTIP's effect on U.S.-EU trade, so that readers might better understand what the results really show. We summarize the main TTIP studies to date and assess their basic assumptions and findings in Table 10. The studies come from ECORYS; the European Commission; the British Department for Business, Innovation and Skills (BIS); and the European Centre for International Political Economy (ECIPE). We then conclude this section with commentary on which studies provide the most useful and reliable estimates.

---

[27]Comparing the estimated gains between studies involves some important factors. First, the TTIP studies report the gains in a variety of currencies and timeframes, so all gains have been converted to 2007 U.S. dollars, although this does not completely harmonize them. Even after converting the gains to a constant unit of currency, it should be expected that, all else equal, a model of bilateral trade in 2015 will produce smaller dollar gains than a model of bilateral trade in 2027. However, an important note is that it is generally better to compare percent of GDP gains rather than compare gains expressed in units of currency in order to fully capture the relative change from a baseline.

### ECORYS Study

The 2009 ECORYS study, titled "Non-Tariff Measures in EU-US Trade and Investment—An Economic Analysis," is the oldest of the studies discussed here and perhaps the most detailed.[28] The study uses a baseline of 2018 projected from 2008 data. ECORYS focuses on the impact of removing trade-chilling non-tariff measures (NTMs) and has little to say on the effects of tariff removal. The most notable contribution of the study is its attempt to list and quantify the costs of NTMs effecting individual sectors for both trade and FDI. In this context, an actionable barrier is one that is "on the table" for negotiators and could potentially be resolved as a part of TTIP. To make this determination for individual NTMs, the authors relied on expert opinion, a literature review, and a business survey. The data also distinguish between sector-specific NTMs, such as differing technical specifications in the automotive industry, and cross-cutting barriers which effect trade in multiple sectors, such as "Buy American" provisions, which hurt non-U.S. businesses across the board. Overall, about half of total NTMs are considered actionable by the study. Separately, the study also analyzes the specific NTMs that expert and members of the business community most strongly want addressed based on survey data.[29]

The estimates cover nine goods sectors and nine services sectors, examining U.S. barriers and EU barriers individually.[30] In the case of differing regulatory structures and specifications, the study does not attempt to address which of the two is "correct:" U.S. automobile standards represent a barrier to EU exporters, while EU automobile standards represent a barrier to U.S. exporters (insofar as the standards are different). Overall, the simple average of trade cost equivalents for U.S. barriers on EU exports was 25.4% for goods and 8.9% for services; EU barriers averaged 21.5% for goods and 8.5% for serv-

---

[28]ECORYS Nederland BV, *Non-Tariff Measures in EU-US Trade and Investment—an Economic Analysis* (Rotterdam: ECORYS, 2009), OJ 2007/S180-219493, http://trade.ec. europa.eu/doclib/docs/2009/december/tradoc_145613.pdf.

[29]The data from the surveys are used to estimate an NTM variable for a gravity model, giving the trade cost estimates that are then used in the CGE model estimates.

[30]The trade cost equivalents are quite high relative to the corresponding tariffs, exceeding 50 percent in some sectors (chemicals, cosmetics, and biotechnology for U.S. exports to the EU, and machinery for EU exports to the United States).

ices. The estimates also cover barriers to FDI in each sector in a similar manner.

Based on these estimates, the study examines several possible agreements with varying levels of liberalization. The broadest of these, dubbed the "ambitious scenario," delivers the largest gains: a 0.3% increase in U.S. GDP and a 0.7% increase in EU GDP. The scenario assumes that all actionable NTMs are removed, corresponding to a decline in bilateral trade costs on the order of 10% for goods and 4% for services. Achieving such cuts would be highly ambitious, but possible. Of course average percent cuts are an imperfect surrogate for NTM and regulatory reform, but at least are instructive in how reduced transaction costs could boost output and trade. The numbers may seem small, but as a practical matter, they entail a lot of extra savings that could be invested in productive activity and creating good jobs.

### European Commission Study

The European Commission study[31] uses a baseline of 2027 projected from GTAP (Global Trade Analysis Project) 2007 data. The study examines the effects of tariff removal, regulatory harmonization between the United States and European Union, as well as their expected "spillover" effects. The study uses the 2009 ECORYS estimates to quantify the tariff equivalent barriers of NTBs, as well as ECORYS determination of actionability in examining how far an agreement might go.

As mentioned, the study assumes that there will be some spillover effects that apply to countries not directly involved in the agreement. These effects come in two flavors: direct and indirect. The direct spillovers reflect benefits to firms in countries that export to both the United States and to the EU. If the United States and the EU were to harmonize their regulatory standards in a given industry, then exporters outside the EU and the United States would find it simpler to meet one joint standard than two disparate ones. These effects reduce one-way trade costs—it becomes easier for Honda to sell in the

---

[31]Joseph Francois, Miriam Manchinm, Hanna Norberg, Olga Pindyuk, and Patrick Tomberger, *Reducing Transatlantic Barriers to Trade and Investment: An Economic Assessment*, Center for Economic Policy Research (CEPR), (London: CEPR, 2013a), http://trade.ec.europa.eu/doclib/docs/2013/march/tradoc_150737.pdf.

United States and in the EU, but Ford and BMW don't get any corresponding benefit in the Japanese market. Indirect spillovers reflect the assumption that other countries might unilaterally adopt some of the standards set out in TTIP. Because the TTIP would cover the world's largest trading bloc, third countries might feel compelled to adopt some of TTIP's standards in order to make it easier for their firms to sell in the U.S. and EU markets. Unlike the direct spillovers, this effect would be reciprocated and trade costs would fall in both directions.

The broadest potential agreement examined by the study, again called the "ambitious" scenario, entails the removal of all tariffs, the removal of half of all actionable NTMs (one quarter of total NTMs), and the removal of half of all NTMs pertaining to government procurement. In that scenario, the United States gains roughly 0.39% of GDP, while the EU gains 0.48% of GDP. The U.S. gains are broken down further in a 2013 study by the Atlantic Council, the Bertelsmann Foundation, and the British Embassy, through CGE modeling using exports on the state level. The study finds that every U.S. state will make gains in terms of exports and jobs based on the EC study's version of TTIP outlined above.[32] Every state is expected see its exports to the EU rise, relative to the baseline scenario, and to see between 0.5% and 0.75% of total overall employment attributed to TTIP.

Overall, we view the EC study to be quite strong from a methodological standpoint. The use of the ECORYS estimates for NTMs adds credibility, and the assumption that half of these NTMs will be removed seems to be well within the realm of possibility. One could, perhaps, dispute the inclusion of the spillover term (particularly indirect spillovers), but the disaggregation of the estimates shows that the spillover effects were not the driving force behind the results. In fact, the United States actually saw a modest negative impact from the direct spillovers in the ambitious scenario.

---

[32]The impact of TTIP on employment assumes the "ambitious" scenario established in the CEPR study, however the Atlantic Council, Bertelsmann Foundation, and British Embassy (2013) estimates do not similarly assume long-run full employment in the baseline year 2027. This was to reflect baseline forecasts by Moody's of "soft" labor markets in 2027 and higher unemployment (Francois et al., p. 58). Further, the study distributes TTIP's employment impact on the national level to the state level based on Moody's baseline projections of both state and sector-level labor forces.

*BIS Study*

The BIS study was also done by the CEPR and is similar to the EC study, although there are notable differences.[33] First, the United Kingdom is not aggregated into the European Union, so the study reports results for the United States, UK, and EU separately. Second, the spillover assumption from the EC study is dropped. Third, the study takes a somewhat different approach in structuring the scenarios examined. In particular, government procurement is not given special treatment, but the study assumes that certain sectors could be subject to more reform than others.

The strongest agreement examined by the study is the "modified ambitious" scenario, in which all tariffs are removed, 50% of all actionable NTMs are removed, except for the chemicals, motor vehicles, and business services sectors, where 75% of actionable NTMs are removed. These sectors are singled out as being targets for greater liberalization because they are particularly important exports for the UK. In that scenario, the United States gains 0.4% of GDP while the EU (including the UK) gains 0.7% of GDP.

The methodological differences between these two studies do not, in our opinion, create a sharp divide between the two in terms of credibility. A more optimistic observer might find this study more credible than the EC study, given its reliance on modestly higher growth projections. However, we wouldn't expect these differences to have a strong impact on the relative effects we have cited here. The spillover effects included in the EC model, while novel, could be seen as overly optimistic by some observers.

*ECIPE Study*

The 2010 study from the ECIPE draws from GTAP 7. The authors extrapolate their data to 2010 and then project those estimates to 2015, which they use as their baseline. Unlike ECORYS and the two CEPR studies which use its estimates, the ECIPE study does not

---

[33]Center for Economic Policy Research (CEPR), *Estimating the Economic Impact on the UK of a Transatlantic Trade and Investment Partnership (TTIP) Agreement between the European Union and the United States*, Report prepared for the Department for Business, Innovation and Skills (BIS), Reference P2BIS120020 (London, 2013b), http://www.mbsportal.bl.uk/taster/subjareas/interbusin/bis/14733213_869_impact_ttip.pdf.

attempt to directly estimate the costs associated with NTMs or the effects of their removal. Instead, the study assumes that NTM reductions will be captured by an increase in labor productivity and a decrease in trade facilitation costs.

In the most optimistic scenario, all tariffs are eliminated, trade costs fall by 3% of the value of trade in non-commodity goods, and labor productivity increased by 3.5% in sectors with high levels of intra-industry trade, and 2% in all other sectors. In this scenario, and in contrast to the other studies, U.S. gains are up to 3 times larger and significantly higher than EU gains than in other models; U.S. GDP increases by 1.33%, while EU GDP increases by 0.47%.

## Assessment of TTIP Studies

In terms of estimating the level of NTMs, ECORYS (2009) is certainly the most thorough and reliable. The distinction between "actionable" and "inactionable" NTMs is also clearly an important one, and estimating the trend of certain NTMs provides valuable nuance. However, the two CEPR studies piggyback off of this strength by using the tariff equivalent estimates in their own studies, as well as the actionability estimates. The ECIPE study takes a less rigorous approach in capturing the NTM liberalization. The exact calculation of estimates for increases in labor productivity and fall in trade facilitation costs is not explicitly justified. While it is clear that TTIP will have some impact on both of these, the methodology behind their estimates would be a valuable tool in interpreting their results.

With that in mind, we believe that the two CEPR studies are generally the most reliable overall. The differences between the two are not insubstantial, but do not make one significantly better than the other in our view. In the EC study (Francois et al.), the assumption that other countries will adopt some fraction of the harmonized regulations arising from TTIP could be seen as generous. In particular, large Asian economies, which represent the largest block of GDP outside of TTIP, might instead move towards adopting their own standards under RCEP. However, the indirect spillovers represent a small fraction of the overall gains. The direct spillovers, which do not assume any harmonization by non TTIP members, are a larger share of gains and stand on firmer theoretical ground. The modified ambitious scenario in the BIS study (CEPR 2013b) relies on greater liberalization in sectors which are prominent in the transatlantic economy, particularly for the UK. However, if one believes this assumption is too generous, the standard version of the ambitious scenario doesn't include differing treatment between sectors.

Though the final estimates vary depending on the assumptions, this section illustrates that the bilateral impact of TTIP will hinge critically on the potential for reducing behind-the-border NTBs and associated regulatory changes that explore, where possible, the potential integration of existing and future regulations. The key question is whether this effort will facilitate new global standards and to what extent TTIP could contribute to strengthening multilateral trade negotiations. The next section explores the prospects and limitations of TTIP's global impact, drawing out implications for Asia.

## TTIP and the World Trading System

One of the avowed goals of TTIP leaders is to reinvigorate multilateral trade negotiations that have drifted for many years.[34] Past FTAs have served as negotiating laboratories producing new trading rights and obligations in areas like services that then became precedents for multilateral initiatives. TTIP architects expect similar developments from their efforts to align regulatory policies, since the transatlantic standard would apply to a market representing almost half of global output and third countries would be compelled to adopt some of TTIP's high standards. Thus, per this rationale, the TTIP provisions would become the de facto global standards.

But whether the U.S.-EU compact can set global standards for new trade rules and regulatory policies will likely be limited for three reasons. First, to do so would require buy-in from the major Asian economies, which together also represent a significant share of global

---

[34]"Final Report of the U.S.-EU High Level Working Group on Jobs and Growth," Office of the US Trade Representative, February 11, 2013, http://www.ustr.gov/about-us/press-office/reports-and-publications/2013/final-report-us-eu-hlwg.

GDP (the RCEP countries total about 30%) and are developing their own rulemaking in WTO-plus areas that differs in terms of coverage and enforcement from the transatlantic standard. By the time TTIP rules are embedded in U.S. and EU laws and regulations, the transatlantic economies weight in global output will likely have been reduced to about 40%, while Asian countries will represent increasingly important and rapidly growing new markets. Likewise, parallel intra-Asian integration initiatives have the potential to both complement, but also limit transatlantic efforts to set the global standard.

Second, it assumes that the United States and European Union will agree on common regulatory requirements across a range of issues on which they hold sharply different positions. But early indications from the TTIP talks suggest that there are different expectations of how TTIP should approach regulatory issues as well as sharp substantive differences over regulatory policies in specific areas.[35] EU Commissioner for Trade Karel De Gucht has argued that from the EU perspective, regulations in TTIP should be based on three key components: cooperating on future regulations; making existing regulations more compatible, in areas like automotive, chemicals, health, and financial services; and creating new institutions, namely the Regulatory Cooperation Council, to "monitor the commitments made and consider new priorities for regulatory cooperation."[36] But transatlantic regulatory cooperation over sectoral issues has been less emphasized by the United States. According to recent statements by U.S. Trade Representative Michael Froman, the U.S. envisions that TTIP should focus on procedural improvements to the rule-making system; in other words, horizontal disciplines related to transparency, stakeholder participation on rulemaking, and accountability should take

---

[35]For example, see Johnson and Schott, *Financial Services in the Transatlantic Trade and Investment Partnership*, Peterson Institute for International Economics, Policy Brief 13-26 (Washington, D.C.: Peterson Institute for International Economics, 2013); See also "Lew Resolute On Excluding Financial Services Regulations From TTIP Talks," *Inside US Trade*, December 19, 2013, www.insidetrade.com (accessed on January 1, 2014).

[36]For detail, see Karel De Gucht, "Transatlantic Trade and Investment Partnership (TTIP)—Solving the Regulatory Puzzle," Speech given at the Aspen Institute Prague Annual Conference, Prague, Czech Republic, October 10, 2013, http://europa.eu/rapid/press-release_SPEECH-13-801_en.htm (accessed on October 11, 2013).

precedent over the compatibility of sectoral standards.[37] We believe TTIP should be able to make progress toward establishing cooperation on future standards and regulations in specific areas, such as the automobile sector, while negotiations in areas like SPS and financial services that involve existing standards will likely remain centered on procedural cooperation.

Third, the likelihood that TTIP will by default set new global standards fails to recognize that in most instances U.S. FTAs establish rulemaking precedents in WTO-plus areas but they don't set new standards; instead, they incorporate standards that have been established by specialized international institutions, such as in the areas of environment and labor, and supplement the enforcement of those obligations by linking them with the FTA's dispute settlement procedures. In many areas, the TTIP result will likely follow this well-worn path. That said, TTIP could break from this common practice in new areas where enhanced multilateral rules and international standards are lacking, such as competition policy and rules on state-owned enterprise, energy and the environment, local content rules, and possibly even exchange rates. Within these areas, TTIP could set precedents that inform new plurilateral agreements that could take shape as part of the WTO trade agenda moving forward from the Doha Round.[38]

In addition to these new issues, TTIP could contribute to several important issues that have long been on the drawing board of multilateral talks, such as GATS-plus services liberalization and disciplines on farm subsidies. In services, transatlantic progress on new market access opportunities and harmonized regulatory policies could help guide ongoing negotiations on the Trade in Services Agreement

---

[37]"De Gucht Proposal for TTIP Regulatory Effort Contrasts With Froman," *Inside US Trade,* October 9, 2013, www.insidetrade.com (accessed on November 28, 2013); and "Froman Calls on EU Regulators to Be More Like Their US Counterparts," *Inside US Trade,* September 30, 2013 www.insidetrade.com (accessed on November 28, 2013).

[38]The Bali Ministerial in December 2013 did facilitate a modest package that salvaged some initiatives from the Doha Round, but stand-alone plurilateral agreements on discrete issues should be the focus of future WTO initiatives. For examples of such plurilaterals, see Simon J. Evenett and Alejandro Jara, eds., *Building on Bali: A Work Programme for the WTO,* VoxEU.org eBook (London: Center for Economic Policy Research, 2013).

(TISA).[39] But it is the area of farm subsidies in particular that suffers from a deficit of transatlantic leadership. U.S. and EU trade officials have been proponents of the conventional wisdom that disciplines on domestic agricultural support can only be pursued through multilateral pacts. However, such a conclusion need not hold when the prospective deal involves the two biggest farm subsidizers in the world. Indeed a U.S.-EU deal on farm subsidies could serve two important goals: mitigate pressures on domestic budgets and set an important benchmark that could help reinvigorate multilateral talks. A transatlantic commitment to cap those subsidies at or near current levels for several years could help encourage other WTO members to work out a comprehensive package of farm reforms. The U.S.-EU cap would not be bound in WTO schedules until that broader deal was done and could "snap back" if WTO talks don't advance. At present, such commitments would not require significant changes in current policies because subsidy disbursements are very low due to high commodity prices. Regrettably, there is little indication the transatlantic partners will seek to make ambitious commitments in this area.

One of the key objectives put forward in the HLWG report and confirmed by transatlantic leaders in launching the TTIP talks, is to use TTIP to create precedents for and reinvigorate WTO negotiations. To date, however, there has been little indication that either side has mapped out strategies for achieving those goals. Rather the current transatlantic strategy seems to be based on the hope and prayer that competitive liberalization pressures will encourage other countries to come to the table for fear of being left behind. To be sure, other countries, and surely the WTO, have been compelled to reassess their own progress relative to the ambitious efforts of mega-regionals to establish "21st century" trade and investment rules. In that regard, managing TTIP's relationship with the current integration efforts of TPP and RCEP will be an important factor. We believe that the successful conclusion of TTIP, along with TPP and RCEP, could establish channels for linking or converging these mega-regional pacts back onto the multilateral stage.

---

[39] To this end, for example, we have already seen the United States and EU facilitate TISA's adoption of a "hybrid approach" to scheduling services commitments, i.e., a positive list approach for market access commitments and a negative list approach for national treatment commitments.

A number of important features distinguishing the mega-regionals will affect this pathway. Those that promote convergence include the overlapping membership between the mega-regionals, coupled with the pacts being interlinked by bilateral FTAs, namely between the United States, European Union, South Korea and Japan on the one hand and China, Japan, and South Korea on the other. But it is worth noting that in practice, membership restrictions etched into these pacts will need to be overcome: currently, the TPP is limited to the Asian-Pacific Economic Cooperation (APEC) countries;[40] RCEP to ASEAN FTA partners; and TTIP to the United States and European Union, pending an "open enrollment" for third parties—which might be extended first to the NAFTA countries and Turkey. Unlike TPP, however, TTIP does not envision increasing membership prior to conclusion, though each side will continue to deepen its own bilateral and regional pacts. Other important challenges to convergence involve both the substance and timeline of the respective initiatives. The mega-regional pacts will have complementary coverage of trade and investment issues, but not common content, and their negotiating timelines for completing the pacts are not aligned. Whether or not this broad vision can be realized will depend on the uncertain progression of the talks and the sequencing of outcomes in regional and multilateral negotiations. In that regard, the TPP—which is likely to conclude in 2014—will have a big advantage over TTIP and WTO initiatives, and thus could have a stronger precedential impact than TTIP on Asia and the world trading system.

## Conclusions

Asia is on the rise but the potential "défi" for the transatlantic powers has been exaggerated in the public debate. Nonetheless, the United States and the European Union have recognized that the growing economic footprint of the Asian countries requires them, for both political and commercial reasons, to deepen their engagement in the region.

---

[40]For more detail on the implications of these issues on economic integration in the Asia-Pacific and the construction of a broader APEC-wide pact, see Jeffrey Schott, "Revisiting APEC's Membership Freeze," *Boao Review*, November 21, 2013, http://www.boaoreview.com/economy/2013/1121/300.html (accessed on December 2, 2013).

The United States and European Union have pursued separate but comparable responses to Asia's economic rise. U.S. economic policy toward Asia focuses heavily on the TPP and its prospective enlargement to the major economies of the Asia-Pacific region; Europe had a later start but has pursued parallel bilateral agreements with South Korea and other Asian countries. These efforts have in large measure helped advance regional trade integration, as well as integration between Asia and Europe. TTIP provides the opportunity to align U.S. and EU policies on trade and investment in goods and services and to shift the strategy from competitive regionalism in Asia to cooperative regionalism—based on their similar and high standard trade pacts with South Korea.

The TTIP thus represents an important component of the transatlantic economic response to the emerging economic powers of Asia. Estimates of the potential economic gains of TTIP are significant, but they depend importantly on the willingness of both sides to make changes to existing regulatory policies. The successful negotiation of the TTIP would enhance the already robust transatlantic partnership, bolster the competitiveness of the transatlantic economies, and provide a common platform for engaging Asia in both regional and multilateral economic institutions.

To facilitate TTIP's precedential impact on Asia and the world trading system, the United States and the European Union need to have a concrete strategy for using TTIP to strengthen multilateral talks; to date, neither side has done so. Properly crafted, TTIP provisions could help advance new initiatives in areas like services, information technology, and energy and the environment where plurilateral negotiations are paving the way toward broader multilateral accords.

The ability to use the TTIP as a template for deeper integration with the Asia region and for new rules for the multilateral trading system will depend heavily on the willingness of both sides to dismantle their own non-tariff barriers, reduce other burdensome transactions costs, and cooperate more closely on regulatory policies. However, as argued here, the TTIP's potential to set global standards for new trade rules and regulatory policies may be limited not only because of the difficulty of crafting U.S.-EU compromises in sensitive areas, but also because doing so will require buy-in from the major Asian economies who are developing their own rules that differ substantially both in coverage and enforcement from the transatlantic standard.

## Recommendations

1. **The United States and the European Union should conclude a comprehensive agreement on a Transatlantic Trade and Investment Partnership or TTIP** to propel economic growth in the two regions and to enhance the competitiveness of U.S. and European firms and workers vis-à-vis their counterparts in Asian and other countries,

2. **As part of the TTIP negotiations, U.S. and EU officials should give special attention to the coordination of policies that promote the liberalization of trade and investment of services, and develop a common approach to services reforms** that could provide precedents for the plurilateral Trade in Services Agreement, or TISA, being negotiated in parallel with the TTIP.

3. **The transatlantic partners should consult each other frequently on progress in other trade negotiations with Asian partners and draw on the best practices from those experiences in crafting the TTIP** to ensure the complementarity of each other's bilateral and regional initiatives in Asia and elsewhere,

4. **Both sides should develop a framework for extending TTIP membership to third countries to help facilitate the convergence of the mega-regional agreements.**

# Chapter 12

# Competition for Resources and Consequences for the Environment

*Tim Boersma and Jaime de Bourbon Parme*

Asia's rise and its impact on the global state of affairs are undisputed.[1] The turbulent growth of the continent, and predominantly China and India, is expected to have major impacts in terms of resources and the environment. Buzzwords in recent studies on resource scarcity have been 'growing consumption, climate change, price volatility, and resource nationalism.' Not surprisingly, these and other developments in turn can have substantial consequences for both the United States and Europe, and can therefore impact transatlantic relations. In this chapter we explore the cases of energy and mineral resources, to see what the rise of Asia means in terms of resources and what it could potentially mean for transatlantic relations.

## Natural Resources in the World: An Overview of Energy and Mineral Resources

Resource scarcity has been a historic problem, yet the topic has received substantial renewed interest from academics and policymakers in recent years. Scarcity in these debates generally does not imply that resources are becoming physically scarce. Rather, effective distribution of resources is prohibited by for instance a lack of infrastructure, legal or geopolitical barriers. The renewed interest in resource scarcity stems from a global demand growth for major resources, e.g.

[1]The authors wish to thank Professor Raimund Bleischwitz of University College London, Dr. Susana Moreira of the School of Advanced International Studies, Johns Hopkins University, and Dr. Erica Downs of the Brookings Institution for their valuable comments and suggestions.

fossil fuels, food, fertilizers, minerals and timber, which is predicted to last until at least 2030.[2] At the epicenter of this demand growth are China and India, as other emerging economies such as Turkey, Iran, Thailand and Vietnam are also seeing continuous demand growth. In the coming decades hundreds of millions of people will join the global middle classes, and are expected to adopt corresponding consumption patterns. Several studies have argued that whether global resource supplies are substantial or not, supply disruptions and price volatility are likely to occur more frequently.[3]

### Abundant Energy Resources in the United States

Technological breakthroughs can bring about the unexpected. Less than one decade ago analysts and businessmen alike were expecting the United States to become a major importer of natural gas and remain the world's leading oil importer. Following the large-scale extraction of unconventional energy resources, today it is expected that the United States will become a net exporter of natural gas by 2020.[4] According to the International Energy Agency (2012), the United States will replace Saudi Arabia as the world's largest oil producer in 2017 and may become a net exporter of crude oil in 2030. U.S. Energy Information Agency estimates even suggested that the United States had become the world's largest producer of petroleum (oil and natural gas) by the end of 2013.[5] Even if the United States does not attain the production levels expected by the EIA and others, due to existing technological and geological considerations,[6] it is

[2]B. Lee, F. Preston, J. Kooroshy, R. Bailey and G. Lahn. *Resources Futures: A Chatham House Report* (London: The Royal Institute of International Affairs, 2012).

[3]Philip Andrews-Speed and Roland Dannreuther, *China, Oil and Global Politics* (London: Routledge Contemporary China Series, 2011); Bernice Lee et al., *Resources Futures: A Chatham House Report* (London: The Royal Institute of International Affairs, December 2012), http://www.chathamhouse.org/sites/default/files/public/Research/Energy,%20Environment%20and%20Development/1212r_resourcesfutures.pdf.

[4]U.S. Energy Information Administration, "Annual Energy Outlook 2013 with Projections to 2040," (2013a), DOE/EIA-0383(2013).

[5]Hannah Breul and Linda Doman, "U.S. Expected to Be Largest Producer of Petroleum and Natural Gas Hydrocarbons in 2013," *U.S. Energy Information Administration*, October 4, 2013, http://www.eia.gov/todayinenergy/detail.cfm?id=13251&src=email.

[6]First, due to their size only a fraction of the most important shale rock formations

poised to become a major hydrocarbons producer, with the potential to export energy resources.

According to some, the United States lacks "an inspiring vision beyond the tired slogan of 'energy independence' in the midst of interdependence."[7] Admittedly, the U.S. administration appears to hesitate between leaving natural gas trade and exports to the market and intervening to ensure that domestic gas wholesale prices stay low to attract manufacturing industries that provide much-needed jobs in the United States. This, despite the fact that, the effect of unrestricted exports of natural gas on domestic gas prices appears to be limited.[8] Fuelled by increased domestic production and infrastructure constraints (refining capacity and transportation bottlenecks), a similar discussion about the pros and cons of lifting the ban on crude oil exports has started in the United States.

At present, only six LNG terminals are allowed to export natural gas to non-Free Trade Agreement countries and the U.S. Department of Energy is examining the 20+ pending LNG export proposals on an individual basis.[9] Meanwhile, it is worth noting that natural gas is cur-

---

(where most of unconventional energy resources in the US are extracted from) have been drill-tested. Second, long-term productivity figures may not be accurate because most wells are new. Also, technological developments may reduce costs and/or increase productivity of the wells. Tim Boersma and Corey Johnson, "Twenty Years of US Experience—Lessons Learned from Europe," in *Shale Gas in Europe: Opportunities, Risks, Challenges; A Multidisciplinary Analysis with a Focus on European Specificities*, ed. Cécile Musialski et al. (Brussels: Claeys & Casteels Law Publishers, 2013).

[7]Albert Bressand, *The Changed Geopolitics of Energy and Climate and the Challenge for Europe–A Geopolitical and European Perspective on the Triple Agenda of Competition, Energy Security and Sustainability* (The Hague: Clingendael International Energy Programme, 2012/04), http://www.clingendaelenergy.com/inc/upload/files/The_changed_geopolitics_of_energy_and_climate_bressand.pdf.

[8]W. Montgomery, R. Baron, P. Bernstein, S. Tuladhar, S. Xiong, M. Yuan, *Macroeconomic Impacts of LNG Exports from the United States* (Washington, D.C.: NERA Economic Consulting, 2012), http://energy.gov/sites/prod/files/2013/04/f0/nera_lng_report.pdf.

[9]According to U.S. legislation, exports of natural gas to FTA-countries are not restricted. Of the FTA-countries however, South Korea is the only one that is a major LNG importer. Legislative proposals to allow for exports to non-FTA countries that are allies (e.g. European Union member states and Japan) have been pending since early 2013. For most recent updates on LNG export: http://energy.gov/fe/downloads/summary-lng-export-applications.

rently so cheap that it is predominantly produced as a by-product of either tight oil or natural gas liquids, though natural gas wholesale prices have been recovering slowly since mid-2012 (with a price spike in late 2013/early 2014 due to the cold winter and infrastructural bottlenecks). Also, the exploration of options to utilize domestic natural gas reserves continues beyond gas-fired electricity generation, to for instance options to use gas for transportation.[10] [11] This may have an additional upward effect on U.S. natural gas prices.

But what do abundant U.S. hydrocarbon resources mean for world energy markets?[12] It would appear that the United States will always have an interest in maintaining stability in the global oil market, because a country that consumes as much oil as the United States consumes is not invulnerable to supply shocks in what is a global market. Furthermore, the U.S. administration has adopted its newfound hydrocarbon wealth as a key tool in 21st century diplomacy.[13] To give an example, in 2010 the State Department launched the Unconventional Gas Technical Engagement Program (UGTEP) to help countries develop their unconventional natural gas resources safely and economically.[14] When visiting Poland, President Obama explicitly discussed the potential bilateral energy cooperation, including the environmentally responsible development of natural gas and supporting Poland's nuclear power ambitions (which are heavily opposed by Germany, which has moved away from nuclear energy).[15] In late 2012,

---

[10]Bruce Kaufmann, "Natural Gas Vehicles: Driving America to a More Prosperous, Secure, and Sustainable Future," *Progressive Policy Institute* (April 2013), http://www.progressivepolicy.org/wp-content/uploads/2013/04/4.2013-Kauffmann_Natural-Gas-Vehicles_Driving-America-to-a-More-Prosperous-Secure-and-Sustainable-Future.pdf

[11]Note that the IEA predicts that natural gas is going to be used increasingly for transportation, not just in the United States: http://www.forbes.com/sites/michaelkanellos/2013/06/20/natural-gas-to-play-a-bigger-role-in-transportation-iea-predicts/

[12]This online debate gives an impression: http://online.wsj.com/article/SB10001424127887324105204578382690249436084.html.

[13]For an elaborate speech on energy diplomacy in the 21st century by former State Secretary Clinton, visit http://www.state.gov/secretary/rm/2012/10/199330.htm.

[14]U.S. Department of State, "Unconventional Gas Technical Engagement Program," http://www.state.gov/s/ciea/ugtep/index.htm.

[15]The full speech is found here: http://www.whitehouse.gov/the-press-office/2011/05/28/remarks-president-obama-and-prime-minister-tusk-poland-joint-press-confe.

together with the APEC chair of 2013 and the ASEAN chair of 2013, President Obama announced, the establishment of the U.S.–Asia Pacific Comprehensive Partnership for a Sustainable Energy Future. It aims to address energy poverty and energy access issues in the region, with one of the regional priorities being the promotion of the use of natural gas.[16] Additionally, it is worth noting that energy resources are part of the ongoing trade negotiations under the Transatlantic Trade and Investment Partnership (TTIP). The EU has expressed its interest in removing trade barriers in the field of energy, as it seeks to diversify its supplies.[17] To date however it seems that both sides only agree that increasing transparency would be in the general interest. In parallel, U.S. self-sufficiency could eventually mean that the United States becomes less engaged with Gulf affairs.[18]

In sum, even though domestic interests are not always aligned, the U.S. administration seems to have embraced its new position in global energy markets as a means of diplomacy, cooperating with countries where welcomed and promoting U.S. private energy company interests where possible.

### Europe's Fragmented Energy Landscape

In contrast to the United States, the European Union is increasingly dependent on energy imports. In 2010 over 54% of the consumed energy in the 27 member states came from external sources. Domestic production came from a variety of energy resources, most importantly nuclear energy (28.5%), renewable (20.1%), solid fuels (mostly coal, 19.6%), natural gas (18.8%) and crude oil (11.7%). Renewable sources showed the only growth in primary energy production, with its share increasing by 70.9% between 2002 and 2010.[19]

---

[16]U.S. Department of State, "U.S.–Asia Pacific Comprehensive Energy Partnership," http://www.state.gov/e/enr/c56576.htm.

[17]European Commission, "EU-US Transatlantic Trade and Investment Partnership. Raw Material and Energy. Initial EU Position Paper," http://trade.ec.europa.eu/doclib/html/151624.htm.

[18]For the latest information on the TTIP negotiations, visit http://trade.ec.europa.eu/doclib/press/index.cfm?id=988.

[19]European Commission, "Eurostat: Energy Production and Imports," Data from August 2012, http://epp.eurostat.ec.europa.eu/statistics_explained/index.php/Energy_production_and_imports.

Currently a boom in unconventional energy resource production is unlikely in Europe. In Poland, one of the few member states where policymakers have in fact passionately supported unconventional gas extraction, it remains to be seen whether commercial extraction will in fact take place because of issues related to geology, infrastructure, market development, and regulation.[20] To date, several private companies have—after completing exploratory drills and core analysis—left the country to invest their money elsewhere.[21] In July 2013, the U.S. EIA reduced its estimate of technically recoverable shale gas resources from 187 tcf to 148 tcf, based on companies' 'disappointing results' and newly acquired data.[22] Some other countries in the EU are interested in developing their shale gas potential, such as the United Kingdom, but public opposition has been substantial to date. Others are undertaking further studies to address the environmental concerns that have been linked to shale gas (e.g. Netherlands), or have outright banned the technology of hydraulic fracturing (France, Bulgaria, parts of Spain).

In 2012 the Joint Research Center estimated that even if the unconventional natural gas potential in the EU were to be developed, this would only be sufficient to halt European import dependence at around 60% in the future.[23] In addition most of the imports of primary energy resources come from only a few sources. In 2012 almost 55% of crude oil imports came from Russia, Norway, and Libya.[24] Most of the coal consumed in the EU comes from just three suppliers: Russia (26.7%), Colombia (24.9%) and the United States (19%).[25]

---

[20]Corey Johnson and Tim Boersma, "Energy (in)Security in Poland, the Case of Shale Gas," *Energy Policy* 53 (2009) pp. 389–399.

[21]In July 2012 Exxon Mobil was the first company to leave Poland, and later Talisman Energy and Marathon Oil followed that example.

[22]U.S. Energy Information Administration, "Technically Recoverable Shale Oil and Shale Gas Resources: An Assessment of 137 Shale Formations in 41 Countries Outside the United States," (2013b).

[23]I. Pearson, P. Zeniewski, F. Gracceva, P. Zastera, C. McGlade, S. Sorrell, J. Speirs, G. Thonhauser, C. Alecu, A. Eriksson, P. Toft and M. Schuetz (2012) *Unconventional Gas: Potential Energy Market Impacts in the European Union* (Brussels: JRC Scientific and Policy Reports, European Commission, 2012), doi: 10.2790/52499.

[24]European Commission, "Market Observatory and Statistics: EU Crude Oil Imports," http://ec.europa.eu/energy/observatory/oil/import_export_en.htm.

[25]European Commission, "Eurostat: Coal Consumption Statistics," data from May 2013, http://epp.eurostat.ec.europa.eu/statistics_explained/index.php/Coal_consumption_statistics.

Coal consumption in the EU has actually been on the rise since 2009, as it became the preferred feedstock for electricity generation over more expensive natural gas, as a direct consequence of the downturn in international coal prices, following a drop in U.S. demand tied to the shale gas boom.

With the increasing importance of liquefied natural gas however, natural gas too is, albeit slowly, becoming a global commodity.[26] Currently however price differences around the industrialized world are substantial, with natural gas prices in the United States being one third of those in Europe and one fifth of those in Japan. Although this price differential is expected to narrow, IEA forecasts suggest that in 2035 natural gas and industrial electricity prices in the EU and Japan will remain around twice the level of the United States, potentially having substantial knock-on effects for energy-intensive industries.[27] Unsurprisingly (since prices dictate that most LNG flows to Asia and Latin America), the EU has been less successful in attracting LNG supplies, despite making substantial investments in re-gasification terminals.[28] As a result in 2012, 83% of natural gas imports into the EU27 came from just three suppliers, i.e. Norway (35%), Russia (34%) and Algeria (14%).[29] The EU's dependence on external suppliers, in particular regarding natural gas, has also been a key concern of several U.S. administrations.[30]

Considering these developments and the enormous amounts of fossil fuel resources that are being found around the globe, the main challenges in terms of energy security for Europe seem to be to create an attractive market for energy suppliers, to construct long-term

---

[26]John Deutsch, "The Good News about Gas—The Natural Gas Revolution and Its Consequences," *Foreign Affairs* 90 (2011), pp. 82-93.

[27]International Energy Agency, *World Energy Outlook 2013* (Paris: OECD, 2013), p. 261 and further.

[28]Tim Boersma and Geert Greving, "Why Russian Natural Gas Will Dominate European Markets," *The Brookings Institution*, February 24, 2014, http://www.brookings.edu/research/opinions/2014/02/24-russian-natural-gas-european-markets-boersma-greving.

[29]M. Ratner, P. Belkin, J. Nichol and S. Woehrel, *Europe's Energy Security: Options and Challenges to Natural Gas Supply Diversification* (Washington, D.C.: Congressional Research Service, 2013).

[30]*Ibid.*

renewable energy targets to facilitate the transition to a low-carbon economy, to create more ambitious energy efficiency targets. Achieving these goals will not be easy since energy policy and energy resources continue to be the responsibility of the national member states. As a result, member states have designed their own regulatory regimes and made their own choices regarding their energy mix, which are not always compatible. Furthermore, investments in energy infrastructure are lagging: The European Commission estimates that in the period up to 2020 roughly €200 billion of investments are required but will not take place under business as usual conditions.[31]

For instance, the EU has experienced great difficulty in completing the internal energy market for electricity and natural gas. A lack of interconnection capacity, reverse flow facilities, and contractual congestion, has prevented natural gas to continuously flow throughout the continent. In addition, renewable transitions in one country such as Germany have had undesired effects in neighboring countries such as Poland and the Netherlands. With its large installed renewable capacity, on windy and/or sunny days Germany produces an overload of electricity. Since the German grid is not equipped to transport this electricity to the south of the country, there are days that Polish and Dutch consumers can profit from basically free electricity. For Dutch or Polish investors in electricity generation however, this means that they cannot produce electricity and thus lose profits.[32] There is substantial evidence that similar internal market issues and a lack of interconnections pose a greater risk in terms of European energy security than the reliability of external suppliers.[33]

In this process of continuous European integration and institutional development, Europe and Russia are drifting apart.[34] In the EU,

---

[31]European Commission, "Proposal for a Regulation on Guidelines for Trans-European Energy Infrastructure and Repealing Decision Number 1364/2006/EC.2011," Brussels, October 19, 2011, http://eur-lex.europa.eu/LexUriServ/LexUriServ.do?uri=COM: 2011:0658:FIN:EN:PDF.

[32]At the time of writing negotiations for new emissions reductions targets and renewable energy shares for the period up to 2030/2040 were underway in Europe.

[33]Tim Boersma, "Dealing with Energy Security in Europe—A Comparison of Gas Market Policies in the European Union and the United States" (PhD thesis, University of Groningen, 2013), http://irs.ub.rug.nl/ppn/364270020.

[34]Sadek Boussena and Catherine Locatelli, "Energy Institutional and Organizational

policy makers often criticize the EU's dependence on Russia for natural gas. The Clingendael International Energy Programme has warned that the EU cannot afford to experiment with market designs and should focus on attracting sufficient supplies.[35] Still, in 2013 the EU was Russia's only large and reliable client, with Russian Gazprom posting record sales.[36]

Some argue that Russia will eventually move away from Europe and look to its east, predominantly China.[37] Others, like Hill and Lo, disagree. They argue that Russia's pivot is mostly 'talk' and that Russian authorities lack the presence, capabilities, or even the degree of interest to make this move to the east a strategic or economic reality.[38] Furthermore, shifting towards China brings political risks and may also not be realistic because the economic conditions are currently not favorable (enormous investments in infrastructure required, substantially lower profits to be made in China, not creating any geopolitical leverage for Russia).

On the other hand, even though Russian–Chinese relations with regard to natural gas have not been very successful so far, this may change over time and examples from the oil market seem to confirm this. During the 2013 Saint Petersburg International Economic Forum for example, it was announced that Rosneft signed a $270 billion deal to supply crude oil to China.[39] For China, Russia is essential in terms of support for its expanding role in Central Asia, and to some degree Russia also offers political cover to build relations with countries with which Europe and the United States have difficult relations,

Changes in EU and Russia: Revisiting Gas Relations," *Energy Policy* 55 (2013), pp. 180–189.

[35]Clingendael International Energy Programme, *Vision on the Gas Target Model— ASCOS (Ample, Secure and Competitive Supply)*, (The Hague, 2011), http://www.clingendaelenergy.com/inc/upload/files/Gas_Target_Model.pdf.

[36]Boersma and Greving, *op. cit.*

[37]Six agreements between China and Russia have been signed in the period between 2004 and 2013; to date no actual gas has been delivered.

[38]Fiona Hill and Bobo Lo, "Putin's Pivot. Why Russia is Looking East," *Foreign Affairs* 92 (2013).

[39]Denis Pinchuk, "Rosneft to double oil flows to China in $270 billion deal," *Reuters*, June 21, 2013, http://www.reuters.com/article/2013/06/21/us-rosneft-china-idUS-BRE95K08820130621.

such as Iran.[40] Hill and Lo note that Russian oil exports to China to date only comprise 6% of Chinese imports, and there is not much potential for growth in the foreseeable future.[41] Others argue, however, that China's imports of oil have grown substantially over the past decade, and that there may be room for more growth. In 2003, China imported 5,254,800 tons (105,528 b/d) of crude oil from Russia, accounting for 5.8% of China's total crude oil imports. In 2012, China imported 24,329,437 tons (487,253 b/d) of crude oil, accounting for 9% of China's total crude oil imports and ranking Russia as China's third largest supplier of crude oil behind Saudi Arabia and Angola. Hence, even though effective Russian—Chinese natural gas cooperation may not seem plausible in the foreseeable future, the case of oil shows that may well change in the coming years.[42]

### Mineral Resources in the United States

The United States is one of the largest producers of minerals and metals in the world. Yet it has been dependent on imports because it is one of the largest consumers of resources and also because the domestic production of some of these resources has not been economical for many years due to the low labor costs and less strict environmental standards in China.[43] Still, in 2010 the United States was the world's largest producer of minerals such as bentonite, diatomite, and sulfur, and the second largest producer of molybdenum, phosphate and salt. In addition, 12% of the global reserves of rare earth materials are in the United States, ranking second after China.[44]

In 2010 the Department of Energy published its first Critical Materials Strategy, which was updated one year later. It was based on

---

[40]*Ibid.*

[41]Hill and Lo, *op. cit.*

[42]See also: http://www.brookings.edu/blogs/up-front/posts/2013/11/07-shale-energy-revolution-china-downs.

[43]Valerie Bailey Grasso, *Rare Earth Elements in National Defense: Background, Oversight Issues, and Options for Congress* (Washington, D.C.: Congressional Research Service, 2013).

[44]Stormy-Annika Mildner and Julia Howald in Hanns Günther Hilpert and Stormy-Annika Mildner, eds., *Fragmentation or Cooperation in Global Resource Governance? A Comparative Analysis of the Raw Materials Strategies of the G20* (Berlin: SWP and BGR, 2013).

three pillars, i.e. diversification of supplies, substitution of materials and technology, and the promotion of recycling and efficiency. The agency has participated in several bilateral and trilateral meetings on the usage of minerals, efficiency, and substitution, with the EU, Japan, and Australia.[45] That same year, the Government Accountability Office reported that although Mountain Pass holds the largest rare earths deposits outside China, the mine did not have the facilities in place to process rare earth ore into finished components.[46] Even though more rare earth reserves are located in other parts of the United States, it was estimated that rebuilding a U.S. supply chain of rare earths would take up to 15 years, due to a complex set of factors such as capital investment, state and federal regulations, investor concerns over Chinese competition, environmental concerns, technology catch-up, and patent-related issues. Also in 2010, the Department of Defense was summoned by the U.S. Congress to produce an assessment of rare earth supply chains and U.S. vulnerabilities, following China's export restrictions of rare earths in 2010. Shortly before, the Government Accountability Office had presented its initial findings of a rare earth study and concluded that these materials are widely used in defense systems and that effective substitutes do not exist.[47]

In 2012 the Mountain Pass Mine in California, where most of these reserves of rare earth minerals are found, was reopened. The most important rare earth minerals extracted in this mine are cerium, lanthanum, neodymium, and praseodymium. The operator of the mine, Molycorp, also announced the purchase of Neo Material Technologies, which makes specialty materials from rare earths in China and Thailand.[48] In 2012 prices for most rare earth products declined sharply due to the sluggish economy, but also because new supplies

---

[45]http://energy.gov/pi/office-policy-and-international-affairs/initiatives/department-energy-s-critical-materials.

[46]U.S. Government Accountability Office, "Briefing for Congressional Committees: Rare Earth Materials in the Defense Supply Chain," April 1, 2010, http://www.gao.gov/new.items/d10617r.pdf.

[47]*Ibid.*

[48]"MCP News Release: Neo Material Technologies Shareholders Overwhelmingly Approve Acquisition by Molycorp," Mocorp, May 30, 2012, http://www.molycorp.com/neo-material-technologies-shareholders-overwhelmingly-approve-acquisition-by-molycorp.

entered the market and China increased exports. In late 2012 Molycorp CEO Mark Smith resigned, one month after the company
revealed that it was under investigation of the SEC over the accuracy
of its public disclosures.[49]

Restarting the entire minerals supply chain takes time. To date it is
not clear how exactly U.S. authorities are going address concerns over
critical and strategic materials in the short and medium term.[50] On a
case-to-case basis there is some coordination between the United
States and other countries. In 2011 the United States, the EU and
Mexico won a WTO case against China over export quotas regarding
industrial raw materials. In 2013 the United States, the EU and Japan
won another WTO case against China, which had imposed export
restrictions on rare earth minerals.[51] Other initiatives include a
renewed Critical Minerals Program (a 1980s warning system, addressing for example potential supply shortages, and protecting strategic
minerals) and develop partnerships with allies to diversify, as more
countries are seeking options to reduce near complete dependence on
China for rare earth materials processing.[52]

In spring 2013 the U.S. Congress passed new rare earth related legislation giving the U.S. President greater authority to stockpile critical
minerals and directing the Secretary of Defense to report on diversification options and develop mitigation strategies.[53] Furthermore, in
early 2013 legislation was introduced that would require both the Secretary of the Interior and the Secretary of Agriculture to more efficiently develop domestic sources of the minerals and materials of
strategic and critical importance to the U.S. economy, national security, and manufacturing competitiveness.[54] This legislation has been

---

[49]"Update 2—Molycorp CEO Quits Amid SEC Investigation," *Reuters*, December 11,
2012, http://www.reuters.com/article/2012/12/11/molycorp-ceoresignation-idUSL4N
09L65R20121211.

[50]Mildner and Howald, *op. cit.*

[51]"WTO Rules Against China on Rare Earths Export Quotas," *Financial Times*, October
29, 2013, http://www.ft.com/intl/cms/s/0/486d5c68-40b5-11e3-ae19-00144feabdc0.
html#axzz2mALiIgkQ.

[52]*Ibid.*

[53]Bailey Grasso, *op. cit.*

[54]The relevant legislation (H.R. 1960: National Defense Authorization Act) was intro-

referred to the House Committee on Energy and Resources and is generally referred to as the Critical Minerals Policy Act of 2013.[55] Also in early 2013 the Secretary of Defense presented the biannual report on stockpiling requirements for strategic and critical materials. Of the 76 materials evaluated for potential shortfalls, 23 materials presented a potential shortfall. These included six rare earth minerals: yttrium, dysprosium, erbium, terbium, thulium, and scandium, that can be used in for example naval sonar, sensor systems, laser surgery, or television applications.[56] In 2013 the U.S. Department of Energy established the Critical Materials Institute, which carries out research on critical materials and engineering.[57] The institute aims to avoid the impact of materials criticality on the United States by focusing on diversifying supplies, developing substitutes, developing tools for recycling, and forecasting future criticality of materials.[58]

### Mineral Resources in the European Union

Europe's industry is heavily dependent on external suppliers for its raw materials. According to European Commission figures, 100% of primary platinum, cobalt, rare earths and natural rubber come from outside the EU. Important suppliers are China, South Africa, Brazil, and the Democratic Republic of Congo. As an illustration of Europe's dependence on imports of raw materials, the table below presents data on import dependence for several of these materials in 2013.

---

duced in May 2013, passed the House subsequently, and was received by the Senate on July 8, 2013. Bailey Grasso, *op. cit.*

[55]U.S. Senate Committee on Energy and Natural Resources, "Senators Introduce Bipartisan Critical Minerals Legislation," October 29, 2013, http://www.energy.senate.gov/public/index.cfm/2013/10/senators-introduce-bipartisan-critical-minerals-legislation.

[56]For the biannual report from the Secretary of Defense, visit http://mineralsmakelife.org/assets/images/content/resources/Strategic_and_Critical_Materials_2013_Report_on_Stockpile_Requirements.pdf.

[57]"Ames Laboratory to Lead New Research Effort to Address Shortages in Rare Earth and Other Critical Materials," *Energy.gov*, January 9, 2013, http://energy.gov/articles/ames-laboratory-lead-new-research-effort-address-shortages-rare-earth-and-other-critical.

[58]http://cmi.ameslab.gov/.

**Table 1. European Union Import Dependence of Raw Materials**

| | |
|---|---|
| Natural rubber | 100% |
| High-tech metals | 96% |
| Iron ore | 85% |
| Critical raw materials | 77% |
| Bulk metals | 57% |
| Industrial minerals | 46% |

*Source*: Data derived from 2013 EC MEMO-13-92_EN on the European Innovation Partnership.

Dependence on increasingly volatile international markets has made European manufacturing industries vulnerable to price fluctuations and supply disruptions. In order to address the dependence on external suppliers, the EU in February 2013 launched the European Innovation Partnership, which brings together relevant stakeholders to work in several pilot projects in the period to 2020. The European Commission aims to reduce import dependence by promoting domestic mining (estimates suggest that the European soils contain critical raw materials worth €100 billion) and recycling (of for instance rare earths in computers and telephones and platinum in cars). One of the targets of the pilot projects is to find substitutes for identified critical minerals. This is not the first initiative from European policy makers regarding mineral resources. In 2008 the European Commission launched the Raw Materials Initiative, a strategy aimed at responding to different challenges related to access to non-energy and non-agricultural raw materials.[59] It aims to make progress along three pillars: ensuring a level-playing-field in access to resources in third countries, fostering sustainable domestic supply, and boosting efficiency and recycling. The Commission in 2010 presented a list of 14 critical raw materials, to be updated at least every three years (the next update was scheduled for late 2013).[60] A McKinsey report laid out the enormous potential of innovation in material usage and resource efficiency.[61]

---

[59]Commission of the European Communities, "The Raw Materials Initiative—Meeting Our Critical Needs for Growth and Jobs in Europe," November 4, 2008, http://eur-lex.europa.eu/LexUriServ/LexUriServ.do?uri=COM:2008:0699: FIN:en:PDF.

[60]In 2010, the expert report put forth the following critical materials: antimony, beryllium, cobalt, fluorspar, gallium, germanium, graphite, indium, magnesium, niobium, platinum group metals, rare earth elements, tantalum and tungsten.

[61]R. Dobbs, J. Oppenheim, F. Thompson, M. Brinkman, and M. Zornes, *Resource Revolution: Meeting the World's Energy, Materials, Food, and Water Needs* (McKinsey Global

Next to domestic mining and recycling, the European Union is looking for substantial rare earth minerals in its 'vicinity.' Since 2010, there has been an increased interest in Greenland, which is now believed to potentially hold over 50% of the rare earth metals in the world as well as vast reserves of iron, gold, zinc, platinum, diamonds and nickel. Europe's interest is tangible to the extent that the European Commission's Vice President Antonio Tajani has called for 'raw materials diplomacy' to make sure that the EU develops solid relations with Greenland.[62] In 2012 the European Commission and the Greenland government signed a letter of intent to enhance cooperation in mineral extraction.[63]

Politicians in Greenland, however, want to move away from 'colonial Denmark,' opening the way for other interested investors. Since 2005 London Mining owns the Isua iron-ore deposit, and it leads a joint venture with Chinese Sichuan Xinye Mining Investment Co, which aims to bring in 3,000 Chinese workers to prepare the mine for extraction.[64] Foreign interference in Greenland's resource extraction is a contentious issue and the newly elected government in spring 2013 has made clear it wants to safeguard local interests, in the form of regulations and taxes.[65] Recent reports suggest that Greenland— Chinese business cooperation has been slow as a result of distance, cultural differences, environmental concerns and poor local infrastructure.[66]

---

Institute, 2011), http://www.mckinsey.com/insights/energy_resources_materials/resource_revolution.

[62]Fiona Harvey, "Europe Looks to Open up Greenland for Natural Resources Extraction," *The Guardian*, July 31, 2012, http://www.theguardian.com/environment/2012/jul/31/europe-greenland-natural-resources.

[63]European Commission, IP/12/600, http://europa.eu/rapid/press-release_IP-12-600_en.htm.

[64]Will Hickey, "China Targets Greenland for Mining," *Yale Global*, April 18, 2013, http://yaleglobal.yale.edu/content/china-targets-greenland-mining.

[65]"Chinese Business Delegation Visits Greenland," *Nora Region Trends*, July 8, 2013, http://www.noraregiontrends.org/internationalpoliticsnews/article/chinese-business-delegation-visits-greenland/87/.

[66]Pu Jun, "China's Arctic Mining Adventure Left Out in the Cold," *Caixin Online*, November 26, 2013, http://english.caixin.com/2013-11-26/100609820.html.

European institutions, too, have attempted to intensify international cooperation, predominantly but not exclusively with the United States and Japan. Since the 2011 Transatlantic Economic Council the EU and the U.S. cooperate on data sharing and joint analysis regarding raw materials. In 2012 this initiative was expanded, following the exchange of data and the declared ambition of future collective data inventory and analysis. Also, in 2012 a conference on 'Best Practices in Management and Stewardship of Used Electronics' brought together public and private representatives from both sides of the Atlantic Ocean to explore transatlantic cooperation in the field of electronic waste management.[67] The EU, United States and Japan have organized annual trilateral workshops since 2011 focusing predominantly on research of critical materials, particularly substitution.[68] During the most recent of this so-called Critical Materials Initiative in 2013 the EC and the Japan Science and Technology Agency launched a joint initiative on novel substitutes for critical metals.[69] Finally, the EU is engaging with China bilaterally in two dialogues: with a metals working group of the National Development and Reform Commission and with the Ministry of Industry and Information Technology. The initiatives sound promising and there may indeed be substantial room for transatlantic—or broader—cooperation. Yet most of the initiatives so far are unilateral despite opportunity to collaborate.[70] While international governance frameworks to address issues such as price volatility and import dependence are present, they are fragmented and insufficient to address these new challenges.[71] Though U.S.-EU cooperation

---

[67] For an elaborate update on the implementation of the Raw Materials Initiative, see COM (2013) 442 final.

[68] This US-EU-JP collaboration was initiated because several materials that are increasingly used in new technologies in clean energy, transportation and telecommunication are at risk of supply disruption.

[69] European Commission, "Conclusions of the Third EU-US-JP Conference on Critical Materials," http://ec.europa.eu/research/industrial_technologies/pdf/trilateral-conclusions_en.pdf.

[70] Raimund Bleischwitz, "It's a Material World: Managing Metals and Critical Materials against All Odds," *American Institute for Contemporary German Studies*, June 27, 2013, http://www.aicgs.org/publication/its-a-material-world-managing-metals-and-critical-materials-against-all-odds/.

[71] Roderick Kefferpütz and Stormy-Annika Mildner, "From the West to the Rest—Changing Patterns on Global Metals and Minerals Markets: A Need for a Global Dia-

seems crucial in this respect, it is imperative to have large producer countries on board early on. Currently none of the emerging economies is participating in collaborative attempts to increase transparency such as the Extractive Industries Transparency Initiative (EITI). It is worth noting that some emerging economies are implementing EITI at the moment, such as Indonesia.[72] Both the United States and the EU have been taking important steps to increase transparency. The U.S. initiated the Dodd-Frank Act to improve financial transparency. Europe followed with comparable legislation that obliged full disclosure of payment details to governments regarding oil, gas, and mineral transactions, in June 2013.[73]

To advance innovative thinking and changing the status quo, Chatham House has suggested forming the R30, an informal gathering of the world's leading resource producing and consuming countries to fill existing governance gaps.[74] Industry has also tried to respond through mechanisms such as the German Raw Materials Alliance, or *Rohstoff Allianz*.[75] This collaboration of industrial companies combines purchasing power in order to safeguard stable and affordable resource and raw materials flows. This is an example of how private actors can find new ways of cooperation to address future resource challenges. It underlines that access to resources is often not about geology, but more about limits to market functioning and geopolitical challenges.

## The Rise of Asia and 'Resource Pragmatism'

Resource consumption in Asia has been rising at an unprecedented pace, fuelled by economic growth, population growth, urbanization and subsidized prices. With regard to energy resources, Asian govern-

---

logue on Raw Materials in a Changing World," *American Institute for Contemporary German Studies* 56 (2013).

[72]For the Extractive Industries Transparency Initiative visit http://eiti.org/countries.

[73]"Press Release: Oil, Gas, Mineral And Loggies Firms Obliged To Disclose Payments To Governments," European Parliament, June 12, 2013, http://www.europarl.europa.eu/news/en/news-room/content/20130607IPR11387/html/Oil-gas-mineral-and-logging-firms-obliged-to-disclose-payments-to-governments.

[74]Lee et al., *op. cit.*

[75]Website of Rohstoff Allianz: http://rohstoffallianz.com/.

ments have been struggling to manage rising energy demand, in particular because oil and natural gas reserves are relatively modest and the large coal reserves are often of poor quality.[76] Thus Asia's growth increasingly depends on imports and effective trade. Between 2002 and 2012 resource trade has grown nearly 50%, e.g. oil, iron, steel, coal, oilseeds and cereal, which are all feedstock for China.[77] Resource extraction remains concentrated in a handful of countries. Across 19 resources (crops, timber, fish and meat, metals, fossil fuels and fertilizers) the three largest producers on average account for 56% of global production.[78] On the other hand, availability of these resources is not just about global reserves. Increasingly accessibility, transportation routes, environmental considerations, technology and rising costs of production are important. In addition, trade is often prohibited by export controls. Between May 2012 and May 2013, 154 new trade-restrictive measures were adopted and only 18 measures were lifted.[79] Most of these restrictions were initiated in emerging economies such as Argentina, Brazil, India, Indonesia, Russia, China, South Africa and Ukraine.

### Production and Consumption of Energy and Mineral Resources in Asia

China is now the world's largest net importer of oil.[80] Asia's consumption of crude oil surpassed that of North America in 2008.[81] China's domestic production of oil was sufficient to export the com-

---

[76]Charles K. Ebinger, *Energy and Security in South Asia—Cooperation or Conflict?* (Washington, D.C.: Brookings Institution Press, 2011).

[77]Lee et al., *op. cit.*, 2012.

[78]*Ibid.*

[79]"Tenth Report on Potentially Trade-Restrictive Measures Identified in the Context of the Financial and Economic Crisis," European Commission Directorate-General for Trade, 2013, p. 3, http://trade.ec.europa.eu/doclib/docs/2013/september/tradoc_151703.pdf.

[80]"China Poised To Become the World's Largest Net Oil Importer Later This Year," U.S. Energy Information Administration, August 9, 2013, http://www.eia.gov/todayinenergy/detail.cfm?id=12471.

[81]"Asia Is the World's Largest Petroleum Consumer," U.S. Energy Information Administration, February 24, 2012, http://www.eia.gov/todayinenergy/detail.cfm?id=5130 &ampsrc=email.

modity until 1993, yet since then imports have risen dramatically and are expected to continue to do so.[82]

Traditionally, natural gas has not been a dominant fuel source in Asia, though its share as a percentage of primary energy resources has been rising and current projections indicate that Asia's gas market demand is going to be the world's second largest by 2015 (with 790 bcm of demand), after North America.[83] Currently the most pressing limits to Asian gas market growth are the lack of integration of national and/or regional markets, and the continued use of oil-indexation in long-term contracts, which keeps prices higher than in other parts of the world.[84] Following the U.S. shale gas boom and reports from the U.S. EIA about the enormous potential of shale gas in China (holding the world's largest technically recoverable resources, estimated at 1.115 tcf), Beijing has been exploring its options to extract natural gas from shale rock layers. According to the EIA, initial drilling has confirmed the potential, but rapid extraction is hindered by the complex geological structure, restricted access to geologic data and the high costs of in-country service industry activities.[85] Moreover, there may be above-surface concerns such as the lack of a functioning market, industry structure, availability of infrastructure, and availability of water for extraction. In September 2013, Chinese officials acknowledged that the initial targets for commercial exploration have been too optimistic and that shale gas extraction in China is realistically a 'resource that needs a long process to unlock.'[86]

Though coal has received predominantly negative attention because of high carbon emissions and malpractices in mining operations, its days seem far from over. As the IEA predicted in late 2012,

---

[82]Andrews-Speed and Dannreuther, *op. cit.*

[83]International Energy Agency, *Developing a Natural Gas Trading Hub in Asia—Obstacles and Opportunities* (Paris: OECD, 2013).

[84]U.S. Energy Information Administration. "IEA Report Sees Scope for Transformation of Asia-Pacific Gas Market," February 26, 2013, http://www.iea.org/newsroomandevents/pressreleases/2013/february/name,36043,en.html.

[85]U.S. Energy Information Administration, 2013b, *op. cit.*

[86]Chen Aizhu, "China Back To Drawing Board As Shale Gas Fails To Flow," *Reuters*, September 5, 2013, http://www.reuters.com/article/2013/09/05/china-shale-idUSL4N0GY23420130905.

coal could rival oil as the world's top energy resource by 2017, the bulk of which would be consumed in Asia, particularly China (the largest consumer and producer), with India poised to surpass the United States as the second largest consumer.[87] While oil and natural gas imports receive substantial attention in recent studies, coal still provides almost 70% of China's energy needs.[88]

Energy demand continues to increase dramatically in other parts of Asia as well. In October 2013 IEA forecasts suggest that Southeast Asia's energy demand is expected to rise by more than 80% by 2035. As a result, the share of coal in electricity generation is expected to increase to 50% of total production, compared to roughly 35% today. This contributes to the expected doubling of carbon emissions in the region.[89]

In addition to consuming coal, Asia is also becoming a major consumer of mineral resources as it seeks to meet its growing energy demands. China's share of global consumption is expected to increase from 40% today to about 50% in 2020.[90] China's domestic ore production is less than 6% of total global production. Thus between 2002 and 2008 China's has increased substantially its imports of iron ore (+61%), nickel ore (31%), lead ore (45%) and copper ore (29%).[91] Many mining countries have witnessed a rise in the share of minerals exports to China. Australia, for example, has now become a major supplier of iron ore (53% of all exports) and zinc ore and concentrates (30% of all exports) to China, though it is worth noting that Japan remains the largest export market for Australian mineral resources.[92]

---

[87]International Energy Agency, "Coal's Share Of Global Energy Mix To Continue Rising," December 17, 2012, http://www.iea.org/newsroomandevents/pressreleases/2012/december/name,34441,en.html.

[88]Andrews-Speed and Dannreuther, *op. cit.*

[89]Florence Tan, "Southeast Asia's Net Oil Imports to More Than Double By 2035-IEA," *Reuters*, October 1, 2013, http://www.reuters.com/article/2013/10/02/iea-asia-oil-idUSL4N0HR0AV20131002.

[90]Lee et al., *op. cit.*, p. 18.

[91]Masuma Farooki, *China and Mineral Demand—More Opportunities than Risks?* (Brussels: Polinares, 2012).

[92]"Production and Trade Minerals," Australian Bureau of Statistics, last updated January 21, 2013, http://www.abs.gov.au/AUSSTATS/abs@.nsf/0/12D42ED59A2793D8CA25773700169CC4?opendocument.

## Table 2. China Possesses More than Half the Global Supply of These Minerals.

| Commodity | % of global production | Commodity | % of global production |
|---|---|---|---|
| Rare earth minerals | 99 | Magnesite | 57 |
| Antimony (mine) | 90 | Arsenic | 56 |
| Graphite | 85 | Mercury | 55 |
| Magnesium metal (primary) | 83 | Wollastonite | 55 |
| Strontium minerals | 80 | Fluorspar | 54 |
| Tungsten (mine) | 75 | Barytes | 51 |

*Source*: Pitfield, P.E.J., Brown, T.J., Idoine, N.E., 2010. *Mineral Information and Statistics for the BRIC Countries—1999–2008*. British Geological Survey, Keyworth, Nottingham.

Chile over the past years has become a major copper supplier to China, and the two countries have signed a free trade agreement to facilitate bilateral trade.[93] These trends have generated large investments in countries like Chile, Peru, and Bolivia on the one hand, but also bring risks when the weight of resource exports on the national economy becomes large, such as recently reported in Peru.[94] In parallel, China has become a key producer of rare minerals: Table 2 lists the twelve minerals of which China possesses more than 50% of global supplies.[95]

Chinese dominance in the markets for rare earth minerals reflects to a substantial degree its minerals processing capacities, not necessarily the physical availability of global reserves. Nevertheless, dominance in this crucial part of the rare earth supply chain has given the Chinese authorities substantial geopolitical leverage, as illustrated by the often quoted dispute over rare earth export restrictions and rising export quotas. In 2010, prices for rare earth minerals spiked after China, citing environmental reasons, halted shipments of some of these minerals to Japan. The ensuing WTO rare earth minerals dispute has sparked considerable efforts to find alternative sources in

---

[93]"Chile Undermines China's Minerals Market," *China Daily*, September 13, 2012, http://www.chinadaily.com.cn/business/2012-09/13/content_15755862.htm.

[94]William Neuman, "As A Boom Slows, Peru Grows Uneasy," *New York Times*, August 19, 2013, http://www.nytimes.com/2013/08/20/world/americas/as-a-boom-slows-peru-grows-uneasy.html?pagewanted=all&_r=0.

[95]In total, according to the British Geological Survey, China is the world's largest producer of 37 minerals and metals.

other parts of the world, such as the aforementioned reopening of the Mountain Pass mine in the United States, the potential reopening of a mine in South Africa, and exploration for rare earth minerals in Australia and in Canada's Northwestern Territories and Quebec.[96] Chinese activities in Greenland underscore China's need for external suppliers as well. Its raw materials policies may change in the future, as its dominance over the rare minerals market declines. Moreover, as Economy and Levi note, Chinese resource consumption growth is not unlimited, as the Chinese economy continues to transform as well.[97]

### Resource Pragmatism and Strategy

In February 2012, then Chinese President-in-waiting Xi Jinping visited U.S. President Obama and was told that a rising China is expected to play by the same trade rules as other major world powers.[98] However, in many instances it is unclear what those rules are, or even whether everybody is playing the same game.[99] Moreover, it is safe to state that both the United States and the European Union apply 'the rules' to their best advantage, and have a solid track record of protecting their own interests at the expense of free trade. Examples are continued barriers to agricultural imports from outside the European Union (including the United States), or decades-old U.S. levies on ethanol that prevented Brazilian ethanol to be imported into the United States, which was resolved only in January 2012 because the U.S. Congress cut domestic subsidies for corn and Brazilian ethanol production is the only option to meet U.S blending targets.

In order to satisfy its demand growth, Chinese authorities have implemented a pragmatic long-term strategy, including the acquisition of mines, share in mines, and the purchase of trade platforms, which

---

[96]Farooki, *op. cit.*

[97]E. C. Economy, M.A. Levi, *By All Means Necessary—How China's Resource Quest Is Changing the World* (Oxford: Oxford University Press, 2014).

[98]"Barack Obama Tells Xi Jinping China Must Improve Its Human Rights Record," *The Telegraph*, February 15, 2012, http://www.telegraph.co.uk/news/worldnews/barack-obama/9083333/Barack-Obama-tells-Xi-Jinping-China-must-improve-its-human-rights-record.html.

[99]Clyde Prestowitz, "China's Not Breaking the Rules. It's Playing a Different Game," *Foreign Policy*, February 17, 2012, http://prestowitz.foreignpolicy.com/posts/2012/02/17/chinas_not_breaking_the_rules_its_playing_a_different_game?wp_login_redirect=0

seems to be designed to enlarge the country's influence on global minerals markets. The examples are manifold, such as the purchase of shares in copper, gold, and lithium mines in countries like Peru, Chile, and Bolivia, or the acquisition of Canadian energy company Nexen by Chinese CNOOC, which was valued at $15.1 billion.[100] Since 2008, Chinese-backed companies have spent over $175 billion acquiring mineral and petroleum assets around the world, the bulk of these investments being made in Canada ($51.5 billion) and Australia ($25.6 billion).[101] Perhaps as a symbol of the shifting resource balance, in late 2012 Hong Kong Exchanges & Clearing Ltd. bought the London Metal Exchange.[102]

China's pragmatic approach at times has also caused issues. Chinese oil companies were able to purchase oil fields in Sudan, where international oil companies were not interested in buying because of the high political risk.[103] Chinese national oil companies have accepted higher levels of political risk, in part because they have less experience than international oil companies in evaluating these risks, and also because initially there was a perception that 'Beijing' could protect investments abroad.[104] Chinese oil companies have struggled to manage some of these political risks, and their behavior in the international arena has been evolving over time. Spurred by a set of factors such as international market developments and less successful experiences in the Middle East and Africa, Chinese oil companies have increased investments in other parts of the world. In the period from 2008 Chinese oil com-

---

[100]Euan Rocha, "CNOOC Closes $15.1 Billion Acquisition of Canada's Nexen," *Reuters*, February 25, 2013, http://www.reuters.com/article/2013/02/25/us-nexen-cnooc-idUSBRE91O1A420130225.

[101]"China Leads in Resources Buy-Ups," *The Australian*, August 31, 2013, http://www.theaustralian.com.au/business/mining-energy/chinese-leads-the-way-in-resources-buy-ups/story-e6frg9df-1226707883067#.

[102]Kana Nishizawa and Chanyaporn Chanjaroen, "Hong Kong's LME Purchase Helps in Bargaining with China," *Bloomberg*, March 20, 2013, http://www.bloomberg.com/news/2013-03-20/hong-kong-s-lme-purchase-helps-in-bargaining-with-china-li-says.html.

[103]Susana Moreira, "Learning from Failure: China's Overseas Oil Investments," *Journal of Current Chinese Affairs* 42 (2013), pp. 131–165.

[104]Erica Downs, "Who's Afraid of China's Oil Companies," in Carlos Pascual and Jonathan Elkind eds., *Energy Security—Economics, Politics, Strategies, and Implications* (Washington, D.C.: Brookings Institution Press, 2009).

panies have spent $44.2 billion to acquire U.S. and Canadian energy companies.[105] The motives for these purchases are said to be stable access to resources and learning the latest technologies, though anecdotal evidence suggests that Chinese oil companies are also eager to learn the managerial side of natural gas and oil extraction. It is worth noting that these investments too are not always successful. There is, for example, a widely held view that CNOOC overpaid for Canadian Nexen, partly as a consequence of the U.S. oil and gas boom.[106]

China's overseas forays have resulted in controversy, and sometimes even in accusations of not playing by 'the rules of the game.' The emergence of a commercial relationship with Sudan probably contributed to China's watering down of U.N. Security Council sanctions against the country concerning the slaughter of innocent people in Darfur in 2007.[107] In a comparable case, China has vetoed sanctions against Zimbabwe, a country that owns more than 50% of the world's chromium reserves, which China (the world's largest steel producer) uses in making stainless steel. Following a ban on exports of raw chromium from Zimbabwe, in 2013 chrome-processor Afro-Chine Smelting agreed to build six chrome smelters in Zimbabwe to safeguard 'pre-export beneficiation.'[108] Finally, Chinese attempts to build affordable solar panels were so successful that it allowed the country to sell large quantities on European markets, allegedly putting European producers of solar panels out of business. After weeks of tough negotiations, Chinese and European policy makers solved the issue by compromise in July 2013.[109] Similarly, the United States in October

---

[105]Russell Gold and Chester Dawson, "Chinese Energy Deals Focus on North America," *The Wall Street Journal*, October 25, 2013, http://online.wsj.com/news/articles/SB10001424052702304682504579153350379089082.

[106]Charlie Zhu and Bill Powell, "Special Report: The Education of China's Oil Company," *Reuters*, October 6, 2013, http://www.reuters.com/article/2013/10/07/us-cnooc-nexen-specialreport-idUSBRE99600720131007.

[107]For a detailed account of Chinese voting behavior regarding the Darfur case in the UN Security Council, see Medeiros, *op. cit.*, pp. 178 and further.

[108]Oscar Nkala, "Chinese Group Earmarks $20m For Zim Ferrochrome Smelter Acquisitions," *Mining Weekly*, April 12, 2013, http://www.miningweekly.com/article/chinese-group-to-spend-20m-in-zim-chrome-smelter-push-2013-04-12.

[109]Robin Emmott and Ben Blanchard, "EU, China resolve solar dispute," *Reuters*, July 27, 2013, http://uk.reuters.com/article/2013/07/27/uk-eu-china-solar-idUKBRE96Q04120130727.

2012 imposed a levy on Chinese solar panels, in order to halt dumping of the products, which would put U.S. producers out of business.[110]

Has China changed the rules of the game? It seems a hard case to make, though China may play the game differently. Compared to 'Western' companies, Chinese state-owned enterprises appear to apply longer-term perspectives, to accept higher risks in some of their investments, and to strive for strategic integration of supply chains. In China's search for resources in Africa, it seems to have adopted a model that in the 1970s and 1980s was applied by Japan in China. When China started looking outward after the Cultural Revolution in the early 1970s, energy dependent Japan was the first to acknowledge the importance of China's substantial oil and enormous coal reserves.[111] The Chinese, looking to modernize their economy, were interested in modern Japanese plants, industrial technologies, and hard currency. Thus, by the end of 1978, seventy-four contracts between the countries had been signed to finance projects in China, all to be repaid in oil.[112] Applying this model to African states has brought additional challenges, and prompted Chinese oil companies abroad to adapt.[113]

Has nothing changed then? That seems implausible as well. The rise of Asia, and in particular China, may have ended the decades of global leadership by the United States and the transatlantic alliance. In this new world order it is economic muscle, instead of military power, that determines the international balance of power.[114] Foreign access to companies, consumers and natural resources increasingly become valuable instruments at governments' disposal. And in times of volatility, an increase in protectionist behavior is a likely result. State-owned companies initially may be open to foreign investment, in order to get hold of

---

[110]Charles Ebinger and John Banks in Jan Kalicki and David Goldwyn, eds., *Energy and Security—Strategies for a World in Transition*, (Washington, D.C.: Woodrow Wilson Center Press, 2013).

[111]Deborah Brautigam, *The Dragon's Gift—The Real Story of China in Africa* (London: Oxford University Press, 2009).

[112]*Ibid.*, P. 47.

[113]Moreira, *op. cit.*

[114]Ian Bremmer, *Every Nation for Itself—Winners and Losers in a G-Zero World* (United Kingdom: Portfolio Publishers, 2012).

good ideas and technology, but eventually these companies may be more likely to shield their domestic markets from foreign investment, with political, financial and diplomatic backing that Western companies cannot match.[115] Chinese oil companies may receive financial backing that international oil companies do not receive.[116] Yet there is no evidence to support the notion that this financial support has given Chinese oil companies the upper hand in the race for exploration or production assets, simply because the companies rarely operate in direct competition. This may change over the course of time, however, and state financial support should be part of ongoing empirical analysis.[117]

## Are There Environmental Limits to Asia's Growth?

It seems unlikely that resource consumption is going to decline any time soon. That does not just apply to Asia. Despite numerous well-intended efforts to move away from hydrocarbons, for example, both Europe and the United States continue to overuse fossil fuels, and the recent oil and gas boom in North America may well prolong that trend. Yet we also expect the bulk of future resource consumption to take place in Asia. It raises the question whether there may be a limit to this growth. There may be, in the form of environmental limits.

Small pieces of evidence to support this notion have been accumulating over the past years. In July 2013 local authorities reported that a massive water diversion project (aimed to divert water resources to the northeast of the country, where the resource is typically scarce) was at risk because the downstream water quality is increasingly poor and the water was no longer suitable for public use.[118] In September 2013 the *New York Times* reported the death of thousands of fish in a river in central China, following the emission of pollutants by a local chemical plant.[119] Finally, anyone who has visited Beijing recently knows that

---

[115]*Ibid.*, p. 77 and further.

[116]Downs in Pascual and Elkind, *op. cit.*

[117]*Ibid.*, p. 97.

[118]"Pollution Plagues China's Mega Water Diversion Project," *United Press International*, July 30, 2013, http://www.upi.com/Business_News/Energy-Resources/2013/07/30/Pollution-plagues-Chinas-mega-water-diversion-project/UPI-65621375204793/.

[119]Neil Gough, "Pollutants from Plants Killed Fish in China," *New York Times*, Septem-

the air quality in the city is suboptimal, at best. A study published in August 2013 even suggested that the life expectancy in Northern China is currently 5.5 years lower than it would be if the air were not so polluted.[120]

These could all be incidents, and may seem insignificant given the magnitude of the country. Yet it appears that pollution in China has led to increased public opposition.[121] In 2007 a public campaign—notably supported by hundreds of thousands of text messages—halted the construction of a $1.4 billion paraxylene plant in Xiamen, because people feared pollution and hazardous materials in their surroundings.[122] In July 2013, civil protests helped alter plans to construct a uranium enrichment plant in Guangdong province, not far from Hong Kong.[123] Increasingly, media and state officials report about problems related to air quality in Chinese cities.[124]

As China develops and its middle class grows, so will its desire for a cleaner environment, including water resources and air quality. Given the magnitude of its population, Chinese authorities at some point will have to adhere to these desires. That moment may provide a new opportunity to revive collective global ambitions to address climate change and global pollution. A prerequisite, however, would be that by that time the United States and the European Union each have ambitious, explicit and committed ambitions regarding climate change,

---

ber 4, 2013, http://www.nytimes.com/2013/09/05/world/asia/thousands-of-fish-killed-by-waste-from-chinese-plant.html?_r=0.

[120]Y. Chen, A. Ebenstein, M. Greenstone and H. Li, "Evidence on the Impact of Sustained Exposure to Air Pollution on Life Expectancy from China's Huai River Policy," *Proceedings of the National Academy of Sciences* 110 (2013): pp. 12936–12941.

[121]Ebinger and Banks in Kalicki and Goldwyn, *op. cit.*

[122]Edward Cody, "Text Messages Giving Voice to Chinese," *Washington Post*, June 28, 2007, http://www.washingtonpost.com/wp-dyn/content/article/2007/06/27/AR2007062702962.html.

[123]Andrew Jacobs, "Rare Protest in China Against Uranium Plant Draws Hundreds," *New York Times*, July 12, 2013, http://www.nytimes.com/2013/07/13/world/asia/rare-china-protest-against-uranium-plant-draws-hundreds.html?_r=0.

[124]Edward Wong, "Beijing Takes Steps to Fight Pollution as Problem Worsens," *New York Times*, January 30, 2013, http://www.nytimes.com/2013/01/31/world/asia/beijing-takes-emergency-steps-to-fight-smog.html?_r=0.

global pollution, and reduction of resource consumption, something that is currently not the case.

## Conclusion and Recommendations

Asia's influence on global resource markets, from energy to mineral resources, has been increasing substantially, due in large part to unprecedented growth in demand and consumption. At the same time, the United States and the EU may be heading in different directions. The United States is rapidly becoming self-sufficient with regard to energy resources, and efforts are underway to resurrect domestic minerals extraction. The EU is expected to remain import dependent into the future, and has invested significantly in renewable alternatives as well as energy and materials efficiency. Despite these differences, the transatlantic partners are searching for ways to facilitate more trade and increase transparency. That does not guarantee effective transatlantic cooperation in the future, but it is a start. More effective transatlantic efforts should consider the following recommendations.

*Energy Resources*

1. **Stimulate development of technologies to enhance more responsible extraction of unconventional energy resources.** Continuous concerns over water availability and methane emissions for example have to be addressed if unconventional energy resource development is to be deployed in Asia, predominantly China.

2. **Continue investments in renewable energy and energy efficiency.** Recent evidence again confirms that these investments pay off.[125] The EU needs clarity on post-2020 targets for renewable energy and carbon reduction and the EU emissions trading scheme needs structural improvement. At a minimum the proposals that the European Commission published in January 2014 should be adopted and implemented as soon as possible.

---

[125]International Energy Agency, 2013.

3. **Make energy part of U.S.-EU TTIP negotiations.** Currently energy and mineral resources are on the agenda, but many issues have to be addressed first, e.g. the structural wholesale price difference for energy between the United States and the EU. A prerequisite is that the U.S. solves domestic debates about limits on exports of natural gas and oil. Discussion has to include the future of coal, and usage of CCS (Carbon Capture and Sequestration) technologies worldwide.

4. **Orchestrate a broad debate with industry representatives, national governments, and NGOs about reducing energy consumption drastically.** Simultaneously these governments should fund more research on how to achieve this fundamental shift in consumption behavior. It is unlikely that we can continue current trends without at some stage running into a brick wall, whether environmental catastrophe or conflict over access to resources.

5. **Increase and better coordinate efforts to improve energy efficiency and exchange best technologies.** For example, Europe has not realized binding targets for energy efficiency, yet these are urgently needed. Next to substantial savings in Europe this would generate knowledge that can be transferred to other parts of the world. There are enormous efficiency gains to be made as the megacities of the future are designed, in China and other booming countries.

6. **Fund more research on the role of national oil companies and state-backed financing of resource extraction (state capitalism).**

### *Mineral Resources*

1. **Move beyond scaremongering of China investing abroad.** It is rather implausible to lecture others over 'rules of the game' when those rules are not always clear, and even if they are, they are applied in the own interests of those involved. U.S. and European authorities should collectively clarify the rules (e.g. following the R30 recommendation of Chatham House), and subsequently stick to them (lead by example). In

addition, governments should fund more research into the structurally different long-term perspective that Chinese state-owned companies apply, compared to their U.S. and EU peers.

2. **Policy makers on both sides of the Atlantic should facilitate private investments in alternatives for critical minerals, for example by financial or tax stimuli.** Current search for minerals in other locations brings risk that real alternatives are not developed, which is also the largest looming risk of unconventional energy resource extraction.

3. **EU member states must better coordinate their approaches toward both mineral and energy resources in Europe.** Following the example of the U.S. special envoy for energy resources, the European External Action Service should appoint special envoys to direct more coordinated approaches to efficient usage and to safeguard access to both energy and mineral resources. The WTO case on rare earth minerals shows that the United States and EU can cooperate when the occasion arises, but in other cases collaboration may not be evident or U.S. and EU interests may not collide; in such cases a single coordinating figure would be helpful.

4. **Private companies have to come up with innovative mechanisms to safeguard security of supply.** Some examples have been touched upon in this chapter, such as enlargement of purchasing power in the German Rohstoff Allianz. U.S. and EU policy makers should be in constant dialogue with the private sector to recognize these opportunities early on and take away possible regulatory hurdles wherever required.

*Environmental Concerns*

1. **Substantial efforts are required to curb resource consumption, dramatically increase recycling, reduce waste, etc.** Stimulate private sector investments in technology and alternatives. Share best practices. Following EU initiatives on for instance renewable energy, both U.S. and EU policy makers have to develop binding targets curbing resource consumption and increasing mineral recycling rates. Acknowledg-

ing the necessity to drastically reduce energy and mineral resource consumption, U.S. and EU authorities can together establish and finance a Next Generation Commodities Fund, to stimulate the development of innovative energy and minerals technologies and share best practices.

2. **Global initiatives are needed to curb greenhouse gas emissions and move beyond 'we-vs.-they' discussions.** In the run-up to the next climate conference in Paris, 2015, U.S. and EU leaders should together embrace the binding 40% carbon emissions reduction target for 2030 as suggested in recent EU policy proposals. We hypothesize that China and other developing nations sooner than later will run into environmental walls, by which time it would be helpful if the U.S. and EU have adopted binding targets for carbon reduction, in order to start a credible debate.

# Chapter 13
# The New Silk Road

*Mircea Geoana*

## The Geostrategic Setting

The world's economic center of gravity is shifting to Asia. Its strategic focus may also well move to the South China Sea. The United States is currently in the midst of its rebalancing to Asia and is partially disengaging from Europe and the Mediterranean. Europe shows little appetite to follow. But strengthening of new commercial routes that follow the old Silk Road can contribute to a European pivot to Asia, provide economic growth for some of Asia's poorer areas, and enhance stability in an increasingly unstable Southeastern Europe.

Other actors are busy in the region. Russia has annexed Crimea and has effectively stopped NATO and EU enlargement, creating a de facto zone of Russian influence. It also plays spoiler to the West in the Mediterranean. From a Russian perspective, this serves the dual purpose of engaging and supporting Russian allies in the region while bogging down Europe and the United States in a series of local but relevant crisis.

At the same time, Russia carefully calibrates this with its significant role in supporting the U.S. in Afghanistan mainly via the Northern Distribution Network and offering diplomatic solutions to issues like Syrian chemical weapons. In parallel with its increasingly visible propaganda efforts, Russia plays a fairly sophisticated game, despite the limitations of its export base. The Russian dynamism is matched by other actors, and certainly is superbly played by China.

For now the Asian pivot remains mainly an American objective. While the West is hesitant about the extent, implications and commitment to the rebalancing, Asian powers are looking to Central Asia, the Levant, Eastern Europe and Africa as areas of economic and strategic opportunity.

Asia's geography plays out in both directions. While the United States views the Asian continent from its Pacific Ocean shores, it is Europe that should deeply understand the tectonic movement underneath the continent, as both Europe and Asia ultimately share the Eurasian plateau. Asia is part of Eurasia with its western shores on the Atlantic. It is always a reality check for Europeans and Americans to hear Chinese diplomats referring to the Middle East as West Asia. While the U.S. is looking at the Asian East, Europe should build a western pillar for America's Asian pivot.

Southeastern Europe is important to this effort not only because it physically connects Europe with Central Asia and the Levant but also because it can become a trade and investment gateway between east and west. The region needs a new engagement from both the EU and the United States. A New Silk Road can help provide that engagement.

It is telling that for China, the U.S. rebalancing is seen as part of a containment strategy against its economic and strategic interests. China's response is in part an economic and investment offensive towards Central Asia and southeastern Europe. To break the "encirclement" heralded by the U.S. rebalancing, China is developing a pivot of its own. China is building new East-West corridors for its new Silk Road with incredible speed. While projecting hard military power in the South China Sea, China is projecting investments, trade and lucrative deals towards Central Asia, Russia, the Caucasus, Turkey and Southeastern Europe. Its investments in Europe's ports and roads complete an iron Silk Road linking transport infrastructure networks in the near future all across Eurasia.

These very practical moves by China will have an impact on ideological values. If the West is to retain primacy as a social, political and economic model globally, it needs to be a major actor across Eurasia, including active participation in this New Silk Road. Ideology may be obsolete, but differences in perception and objectives are certainly not. This becomes again apparent in Southeastern Europe, and nowhere more visible than around the Black Sea.

## Southeastern Europe as the Anchor of the New Silk Road

Southeastern Europe is the western anchor of the New Silk Road and potentially the channel for a significant part of the world's energy and trade flows. To make the region stable and prosperous, the West has as many potential partners as competitors. If it is to succeed, the West has to avoid the zero sum games that shaped the region for centuries. This is a monumental task that neither the United States nor Europe can undertake alone. A New Silk Road anchored in Southeastern Europe can both help to stabilize that region and serve as an important element in a transatlantic pivot to Asia.

Southeastern Europe is also the West's soft underbelly. For years its strategic importance was dimming. With the Cold War over, Southeastern Europe was becoming a strategic backwater. With the major strategic competition moving elsewhere and the emergence of BRICS as relevant economic players, the region has lost its centrality to Western interests. Except for the Balkan wars of the 1990s, Eastern Europe was largely peaceful. EU and NATO expansion kept both those countries but also the West and Russia locked in a limited competition for influence. Frozen conflicts still flared up from time to time around political processes. From Moldova and Transnistria to Nagorno-Karabakh and through the South Ossetia and Abkhazia in Georgia, there were plenty of reminders of the rift but no major challenge for the West.

Then energy and Afghanistan brought the region back in focus. Repeated gas crises took place as Russia or Ukraine blocked or threatened to block natural gas flows. Now the Russian annexation of Crimea has brought Southeastern Europe back into even sharper focus. Southeastern Europe has again become the competitive ground for ominous forces that shaped its history and still impact its present. In the context of its new role as energy and trade hub between Asia and Europe the region is as critical for the West as is for Russia and China. In a way it is also the region where a new set of rules of engagement needs to be negotiated and asserted between Russia and the West.

Southeastern Europe is important not only because it physically connects Europe with Central Asia and the Levant, but also because it

338 A TRANSATLANTIC PIVOT TO ASIA: TOWARDS NEW TRILATERAL PARTNERSHIPS

can become a trade and investment gateway or a strategic gap between east and west. In both cases the region needs renewed engagement from the both the EU and the United States in both economic and strategic terms.

## A Joint Pivot to Eurasia

The pivot may be an athletic term but its military implications have not escaped China. The same way the pivot towards a certain direction creates opportunity, it leaves the opposite angle undefended. This was noticed by the West's ideological and economic challengers. With Europe unprepared to step in vigorously and the United States busy elsewhere, these emerging powers have started plotting a new reality economically and strategically around Europe. The West is not complete without the significant military and security umbrella provided by the United States. The United States cannot complete its pivot without the other shore of Asia being taken care of.

A recent German Marshall Fund Transatlantic Trends survey indicated that 45% of Americans consider Asia (China, Japan and South Korea) as very important to the United States in comparison with only 44% considering Europe (UK, France, Germany) as key to America's future. The American public (and establishment) see China as a growing security concern while Europeans relate to China more as an economic opportunity.

The "rise of the rest" is a reality, and no hand-wringing or excuses in Europe will hide or stop that. It is a geo-economic reality that will continue to define the geo-political contours of the world in the 21st century. This new reality will inevitably make the United States adjust its global posture to cope, influence, and eventually contain the consequences of this new landscape. It is clear that the saga of the euro zone crisis, accompanied by never-ending mass rallies and staggering unemployment figures in Greece and Spain, has created a perception of Europe's structural weakness and accelerated decline. Debilitating defense reductions and strategic complacency create the impression that the European Union and even NATO may become more like collateral victims rather than significant actors in this new global equation.

This should not be the case. Europe has strategic, economic and soft power resources to continue to be a global player in the 21st century, not as a competitor to the United States but more as the indispensable partner. If Europeans want to stay relevant in this structural shift, the EU should not shy away from this new world, it should deliberately accompany the United States, Canada and other like-minded democracies in pivoting together towards Asia, the Eurasian middle corridor and the Greater Middle East. At the same time, the United States should find a way to include Europe in the logic of its pivot and establish a new, shared division of labor. Developing this New Silk Road can be part of Europe's contribution.

If the pivot is a strictly military concept, there is limited role for the EU. However, if it is part of a grander strategic policy, then the EU's role as a western interface in Eurasia may be critical. Providing willing and capable partners for Western policies from Iran to Central Asia makes the rebalancing to Asia a complete and safe move. The United States cannot face effectively the multiple and growing challenges in Asia with vulnerable hot spots all across Eurasia. It is no wonder that many Chinese experts saw the Ukrainian crisis as an opportunity for China, despite the country's allergy to all sovereignty and autonomy issues. To address the many hot spots in Eurasia, the West needs a strong Europe and a more stable arrangement with Russia. A new Cold War is not a great basis for that.

## Meeting Challenges along the New Silk Road

The first challenge is time. The pivot came as a response to existing and rapidly evolving conditions. The United States, realigning from a decade of costly and grinding wars in Iraq and Afghanistan, needs to partner more effectively with others. Finding ways to do this is a challenge for current leaderships in both the EU and the United States.

With a new European Parliament after the May 2014 elections, and a new EU leadership for the European Commission in October 2014, this should constitute one of the main strategic directions for the EU and a catalyst for the revival of the European project with all its members, especially the United Kingdom. The Ukraine crises should be an incentive for both Europe and the United States.

NATO should review partnership and membership options for countries in the region as part of an effort to secure the western anchor of the New Silk Road. NATO needs to be a sufficiently strong deterrent so that Europe and the Mediterranean are secure even with a less robust U.S. presence. In turn, it is clear that NATO will be sufficiently strong if it is perceived as still relevant to American security. Projects like ballistic missile defense are a critical link between the old and the new NATO, and will help secure a New Silk Road.

The New Silk Road is challenged by instability in Afghanistan, but it also provides some solutions. The redeployment of most U.S. and allied troops from Afghanistan in 2014 makes things more complex. The New Silk Road provides an alternative to the Northern Distribution Network and the Pakistan route for extracting forces and materiel from Afghanistan. It also offers concrete solutions for economic investment of a nature and scale that potentially makes it interesting for otherwise competing actors to have a common stake in the area.

After withdrawal from major operations in Afghanistan, NATO will continue to play a role in the region. The Eurasian landmass will continue to be the critical nexus of world stability and global competition: where America, China, Russia, India, Central Asian powers, Iran, Pakistan and Turkey will simultaneously collide, cooperate and compete. The stability of this middle corridor connecting the two engines of the global economy, the (re)emerging Asian powers and the promising TTIP between the United States and the EU, will be important to economic growth and peace in the world.

The EU cannot and should not be absent from this New Silk Road. Its current limited engagement of the region needs to be stepped up. After the successful completion of the association and free trade agreements with Eastern Partners like Georgia and Moldova, the EU must launch a new and more ambitious strategy for the New Silk Road. The Ukraine crisis should not stop this but on the contrary accelerate it. Georgia and the Black Sea become even more important as a link between Europe and Central Asia.

This new strategy should go beyond what the United States has originally defined as a limited regional exercise in the post-Afghanistan context. Going beyond Central Asia, across the Caucasus towards Europe, the New Silk Road would give European economies much needed oxygen for recovery, exports and jobs creation. In turn this would give Europe a renewed global posture that its citizens and business require.

## Completing the New Silk Road

This "joint pivot" should become an essential part of the new transatlantic narrative. Working together to ensure the stability of the Greater Middle East and Eurasia can become the bedrock of a renewed EU/US/NATO "raison d'être." Sharing the burden and influence together with the United States is the grand game of this century and should be Europe's new Asian project. The New Silk Road is an important element of this broader effort.

In the new financial perspective of the EU 2014–2020, funding should be provided for the continuation of the existing Trans European Networks (TENs) towards the Caucasus and Central Asia, including multimodal transportation, grids, pipelines, and highway.

At a Bucharest Forum conference on the New Silk Road,[1] an e-New Silk Road was proposed. This would make innovation and digital cooperation a part of the connecting forces in the region. It would allow the region's economies to leapfrog and accelerate their convergent path. Border and custom cooperation should be increased, as suggested by the Atlantic Council in Istanbul. The fight against organized crime, trafficking and smuggling should be reinforced. The regional center in Bucharest, where police and customs officers from 12 countries in the region work jointly with Europol and the FBI, should serve as a model that could be extended across the Black Sea.

Effort among international financial institutions and multilateral and regional donors should be better coordinated. The World Bank, the Asian Development Bank, the EBRD, and diverse wealth funds are financing a multitude of infrastructure projects in Eurasia along the New Silk route. Russia is investing in Central Asian and South Asian energy projects. The United States is funding electricity projects in

---

[1]Sponsored by the Aspen Institute Romania and the German Marshall Fund of the United States.

the region. The European Investment Bank should be encouraged to lend to projects along this route, as it recently did for Ukraine.

This coordinated effort between the United States, Canada and the EU needs to be better organized. As a next step, the two sides of the Atlantic should create a permanent coordination mechanism for Transatlantic Diplomacy, Development and Defense (TAD3). A joint inventory of hard and soft power instruments on both sides of the Atlantic needs to be assembled and assessed. This should include the relevant national structures in the EU, the United States, and NATO.

The southern corridor of the New Silk Road connecting Asia to Europe through Turkey and Southeastern Europe should be completed. And the Northern route, used to move military and civilian equipment to and from Afghanistan, should be made permanent. This depends on Russia's future willingness to cooperate with the West. Based on current realities this is highly uncertain, but it could serve as an eventual incentive for greater Russian cooperation.

This effort also requires changes in NATO's Black Sea presence. In addition to reinforcing ballistic missile defenses, NATO must now plan to deal with unmarked military forces and rogue military operations. For the Alliance's eastern members, recent events in Crimea are a stark reminder of NATO's importance. It is also a sign that its clout should not be taken for granted. A renewed investment in peace and security in the region is needed.

Not just NATO but also the EU needs to reassess its answers to the strategic challenges of the future. A mix of security and economic dimensions is at play and these are not limited to the geography of Eastern Europe. Overcoming the differences in perspective that sometimes block and render ineffective Europe's foreign policy capabilities is a precondition for a dynamic Western presence in Eurasia.

Equally essential is a host of policies designed to reverse over-reliance on Russian energy. A European energy revolution is not only possible but is in the making. Already the Ukrainian crisis is changing things. EU's steps towards creating effective European natural gas markets, its energy efficiency policies and its Agenda 20/20/20 all play a role. Countries like Poland are also betting on their shale gas reserves as insurance policy. Offshore exploration in the Black Sea and new discoveries in eastern Mediterranean are also game changers together with the recent opening of U.S. energy exports to Europe. While reducing dependence, these efforts also create more opportunity for an active engagement of Eurasian markets including Russia.

Individual countries are already preparing for this new geo-economic reality. Romania has launched the East-West Gateway national strategic program aimed at connecting the Black Sea port of Constanta and the Danube to Western markets. The port of Piraeus in Greece tripled its volume of transiting merchandise in the last three years since the Chinese takeover.

China is continuing to invest in its policy of energy and multimodal infrastructures, including in Southeastern and central Europe, giving shape to this modern version of the traditional Silk Road. There is a bevy of Chinese-funded and developed infrastructure projects linking its western border to Central Asia, the Caspian and the Mediterranean including the Trans-Asian Railway, also called the Iron Silk Road. China is also using its clout to engage its competitors. It recently invited India to join in the Maritime Silk Road.

China is not alone. HP is shipping all its production from western China by rail all the way to Rotterdam. The Chinese Prime Minister has an annual meeting with 12 of his counterparts in the eastern European region. This format covers all three land corridors that make up the New Silk Road. After Warsaw, Bucharest hosted this meeting with the participation of some 1000 business leaders from both sides. The U.S. Business and European Industrialists Roundtables might follow suit in the key emerging economies along the New Silk Road.

### Conclusion and Recommendations

The region connecting Europe, Asia and the Levant is the very point where the geopolitical tectonic plates of the world meet. It has often been said that the region has suffered from too much history. And we can see it resurface now in Crimea.

The response to the annexation of Crimea needs to be carefully crafted so as to create incentives for a new narrative and not risk rekindling of an old one. Creating a New Silk Road connecting

Europe and Asia can be part of this narrative. It can create both stability along the route and create incentives for Russia to re-engage with the West.

**Europe should adopt a New Silk Road Strategy as a central element of its long-term engagement of Eurasian countries moving ambitiously beyond its Eastern Partnership Policy.** This should cover the Caucasus but also central Asia and the Levant. In fact it would be a European pivot to Asia.

The subject should be on the agenda of EU-U.S. summits as a policy coordination instrument, and it should be discussed at NATO summits.

The joint European-American pivot to Asia is ambitious and comprehensive enough to allow policymakers on both sides of the Atlantic to find it accommodating for a diverse and sometimes competing set of agendas.

The only way the U.S. pivot to Asia will actually work as a long-term strategy is if its flanks and rear are covered. This requires that Europe play a significant part and makes southeastern Europe a critical gateway. Instead of giving in to a new Cold War, this is a vision that eschews a simple containment strategy and replaces it with an ambitious bridge over troubled waters: the Adriatic, the Black and the Caspian seas.

*Part V*

# Implementation

# Chapter 14
# A New Diplomacy for the Pivot

*Christopher R. Hill and Michael Schaefer*

## Incongruent U.S. and EU Interests in Asia

A new transatlantic diplomacy towards Asia is possible, even overdue. But it needs to build on a clear understanding of the starting positions of the United States and the European Union, as well as their respective interests at stake.

In the United States, the pivot was originally envisioned by President Obama as a transfer of strategic focus from wars in the Middle East to opportunities in East Asia. Later rechristened as a rebalancing, the policy shift sought to reflect underlying shifts in strategic emphasis.

Although the "Pacific Century" has not yet materialized, the traditional gravitational alignments of the United States toward the east have begun to adjust due to several factors. U.S. trade flows have begun to move more to the Pacific basin countries (including in Latin America), while in the U.S. the industrial base has similarly moved southward and westward. With the end of the Cold War and reduced tensions in traditional strategic theatres in Europe (an analysis which needs to be revisited in view of the ongoing Ukrainian crisis), established ties with East Asian partners like Japan, the ASEAN countries, and with South Korea especially due to the continuing and very real North Korean threat have gained in relative strategic importance for the United States. While these relationships are longstanding (indeed the United States has defense treaties with five East Asian/Pacific states including South Korea, Japan, the Philippines, Australia, and Thailand) some of them remain limited as long term platforms of cooperation. This is because the United States has been reluctant to be drawn into ongoing and unstable disputes with neighbors.

Meanwhile, new partnerships with China and India are evolving, but contain a host of uncertainties. While China has become one of the drivers of global economy, it will remain a continued challenge to the United States due to its political system, unresolved maritime issues, and its complex relationship with Taiwan. Nonetheless, the institutionalization of the partnership has grown enormously in recent years. The U.S. partnership with China is symbolized by the growth of the mechanism known as the Strategic and Economic Dialogue (the S&ED). It is typically attended by over 200 senior officials from each country representing a broad range of government agencies.

The U.S. partnership with India has also grown exponentially, covering a broad range of issues in economy, energy, defense and strategic issues that have helped make the United States one of India's most important global partners. India, however, remains a country for the medium term perspective that is primarily focused on domestic issues and the challenges that have impeded its development as a modern society and economy.

At the same time, the transatlantic partnership has experienced some difficult times. Transatlantic trust has suffered severe setbacks in the past decade, starting with discord over the Iraq war and deepening as a result of Guantanamo, Abu Ghraib and the recent conflict over NSA data collection in Europe. An increasing number of Europeans do not look at the United States anymore as a role model in terms of values and best practice in society. Notwithstanding these differences, Europe remains the group of countries with which the United States shares relatively more values and interests than with any other region. As a result, the United States, despite its declared willingness to implement its "pivot to Asia" policy for strategic as well as economic reasons, is not likely to pit Atlantic ties against those in the Pacific.

As to the Middle East, the reliance of the United States on its raw material base, specifically hydrocarbons, is fading as a result of new energy technologies, in particular shale gas. These new energy resources have created vast new paradigms in the United States as it is about to take its place as the world's biggest energy producer. It is looking to become an exporter of energy, especially of LNG to the energy-starved countries of the western Pacific basin. Developments in Iran and the worsening civil war in Syria that is now threatening neighboring countries including Iraq make it difficult for the U.S. government to shift attention away from the region.

Furthermore, while the logic of a U.S. rebalancing towards Asia continues to be strong, the execution of the first steps of this pivot, which followed President Obama's announcement at the Honolulu APEC Summit, has created unintended reactions which must be addressed:

- Middle Eastern countries were taken by surprise and saw the pivot as a U.S. strategic withdrawal from the region. The fact that the president's speech came only months before the Arab Spring exacerbated the perception that the United States was abandoning the Arab world precisely at a time of its historic need.

- Within China there is a broad perception that the pivot represents an effort by the United States to challenge its rise and implement a new containment strategy. This perception was strengthened by the way President Obama and his Secretary of State rolled out the new pivot in China's neighborhood. In particular, China was concerned about the rollout in the Philippines, Vietnam and Australia, where maritime issues dominate. There was also the President's important, but misunderstood, opening toward Myanmar, which was perceived as an effort to further encircle China.

Nevertheless, renewed U.S. attention to Asia is a recognition of the underlying realities of the long term importance of the Pacific rim, and should be welcomed by all in the region, including China. It can prove to be a strategic realignment and rebalancing helpful to the region's security and economic prospects, provided it is not seen as a unilateral move by the United States, nor as a withdrawal from the challenges of the Middle East, nor, most importantly as a strategy to contain China.

The EU has no formal policy of a pivot to Asia. Brussels and EU member states have been absorbed by the sovereign debt crisis in Europe, and more dramatically, by a crisis of identity in the European Union. In addition, the EU is facing serious challenges in its immediate eastern neighborhood, namely in its relationship with Ukraine and the Russian Federation. Triggered by the denial of the Ukrainian gov-ernment to sign an Association Agreement with the EU, the majority of the Ukrainian population took to the streets and the Kiev Maidan resulting in the ousting of the Yanukovych government. As an immedi-ate reaction, Russia, in flagrant violation of international law, annexed the Crimea, thus heightening the conflict potential in Eastern Europe and forcing European foreign policy makers to re-prioritize.

All of these processes have absorbed and continue to absorb enor-mous energy and resources, and prevented the EU from designing and carrying out a more active policy both within the transatlantic alliance and with Asia. Nonetheless, the EU and some EU member states have started to engage more substantially in Asia, in particular in East Asia. But contrary to the United States, the European road to Asia is driven less by strategic factors than by economic interests. Volatile European markets and a U.S. market still under reconstruction have redirected trade flows and investments towards Asian markets, especially the booming Chinese economy.

Nonetheless, tensions with Russia which have the distinct prospect of becoming a long term fixture in Euro-Atlantic geo-strategy, also argue for the need for a more comprehensive and stepped up engage-ment with China.

On the fortieth anniversary of the Shanghai Accords in 2012, China and Russia joined together to veto a UN Security Council resolution on Syria. Coming on the day of the anniversary the joint veto was a bitter reminder that what happened in Shanghai some forty years ago was the end of the Sino-Soviet de facto alliance, the beginning of the end of the Soviet threat. Now, as Russia is inevitably pushed away from key Euro-Atlantic institutions, the de facto political and security (though clearly not economic) alliance between China and Russia may be back, especially if the Russia issue causes us not to pay attention to China.

Over the past 10 years, the EU has built a "strategic partnership" with China, as have some EU member states. In the 10 years since the country's accession to the World Trade Organization, China has become the EU's major trading partner. The introduction of the euro has had a profound impact on the Chinese leadership, business com-munity and public opinion. Bilaterally, Sino-German relations have grown into a broad-based strategic partnership going well beyond economic relations. China and Germany, being for each other by far the most important trading partners in Asia and Europe, have instituted a political framework of "Sino-German Inter-governmental Consultations," chaired by the two Prime Ministers, extending cooperation to new areas as urbanization, energy, climate change and rule of law. The Sino-German rule of law dialogue has become one of the most important bilateral dialogue frameworks. Other European nations, such as the UK or France, are following at considerable distance.

EU ties with India are increasing, albeit time consuming and small compared to the exchange with China. Although the EU has a long-standing economic and political relationship with ASEAN, it has been perceived by ASEAN members as neglecting the region, not least because of the continued absence of high-level EU leaders from important regional conferences. Ties with Japan and South Korea are free of tensions and friendly, but mainly economic and not really dynamic in nature.

In sum, the EU has understood the importance of the Asian game, but has not been able to develop a strategic engagement in Asia. Its presence is primarily prompted by the dynamic Chinese economy. Few EU member states have started to develop a long-term, broad-based relationship addressing national, regional and global areas of cooperation.

All in all, Europe follows the rationale of the U.S. pivot to Asia, however not in the context of a formal strategic policy, and mainly driven by economic interests.

## Transatlantic Partnership and Pivot to Asia: No "Zero Sum Game"

For both the United States and the EU, a pivot to Asia is warranted by their strategic and economic interests, different as they are. A shift of attention to the Pacific by the United States should, therefore, not be interpreted by the EU as questioning the value of transatlantic partnership, which remains a cornerstone of U.S./EU foreign, security and foreign economic policy.

The United States and the EU could and should try to better coordinate or even unify their policies towards Asia. A number of parameters seem to be essential in doing so:

- As China is the most important player in Asia, a successful common approach to Asia has to start with a joint understanding as to China's development and its role in the region as well as at the global level. Unlike Western containment strategies toward the Soviet Union during the Cold War, the pivot should be guided by the objective of fully integrating China into the international system. It is a concept too big and important to fail.

- A key to transatlantic cooperation in Asia is to replace the squabbles of the past about security burden-sharing and the values agenda with strong and replicable patterns of cooperation and an enhanced deployment of institutions which have served to tie the Atlantic community and the European community together.

- Another precondition for successful cooperation is a common or at least a comparable philosophical starting point in addressing Asia. This will not be an easy task.

Since World War II, the United States has played a broad and essential role in ensuring stability in Asia and helping to create the conditions for Asia's rise and its growing self-awareness as a significant center of global development. Beyond its economic stakes in Asian markets, which often make it a commercial competitor with the Europeans, the United States perceives its continued presence in Asia as an important element in safeguarding Pacific security and has sometimes been at odds with the Europeans on arms sales, especially to China. The United States continues to encourage the growth of democracy and free markets in Asia. The focus on democratic development among Asian countries has often run contrary to Asia's own culture of noninterference, an approach enshrined in ASEAN's founding documents. Meanwhile, in the context of its often challenging relationship with China, the ongoing enormous U.S. trade deficit with China is a particular burden on the relationship, an issue that not all European countries face in similar terms.

The EU, or at least the majority of EU members, looks at Asia primarily as an increasingly important market. China, India and gradually Indonesia are also seen as essential partners in solving global issues like climate change or energy security. Apart from Germany, most EU member states have a significant trade deficit with China, and all need reciprocity in key areas of trade and investment. Issues of Asian regional security gain priority for the EU if they have a negative impact on the economy, i.e. conflicts over islands or the free passage of waterways. Value issues, i.e. the absence of rule of law and human rights deficits in many Asian societies, have become a strong domestic driver of policy in the EU.

U.S. and EU interests do converge on one important point: both need stability in Asia, if for partially different reasons.

Maintaining stability in the region will require continued stable development processes within all Asian societies, in particular in great countries like China, India, Pakistan, Indonesia and the entire ASEAN community. An extended period of stable growth is needed in the region, as the national development processes will be asymmetric in nature. China needs at least two more generations of stable growth, India and others much longer.

## Joint Interest: Stability in Asia

Working together for stability in Asia will require a comprehensive concept. Ensuring stable domestic development in all Asian countries, keeping regional hotspots under control, enabling reconciliation between historic enemies, and integrating emerging economies into institutional structures are important objectives to which the United States and the EU could contribute, both individually and in some areas by jointly working with Asian partners. From the Asian perspective, the United States continues to be in the lead, with the EU having a comparative advantage where soft power is of the essence.

In looking for areas of engagement, the following will be of prime importance:

### Stable Domestic Development

Elements of the Chinese experience have made it a role model for other Asian societies, both in positive and negative ways. The process of urbanization has been fast, possibly too fast, too uncoordinated and not sustainable in terms of creating a cohesive and stable social system. Unprecedented economic development in parts of the country has opened a huge gap between rich and poor, between the affluent east coast regions and the inland western provinces lagging far behind, as well as between urban and rural areas. The cost of environmental damage throughout the country threatens to upset the dynamism of the economic success. Endemic corruption stirs feelings of frustration, as does the lack of a broad-based system of social security in China's aging society. Increasing protests in the street and a rising vocal and critical internet community puts pressure on local, provincial and central governments. The new leadership in Beijing is reacting with a mixture of reforms, i.e. of the *hukou* system or the one-child-policy, and repression against political critics. While the range of individual freedom for ordinary people has expanded significantly over the past decade, intellectuals and other activists criticizing the autocratic one-party system are being silenced by means of repression. Building the rule of law seems to be the most important single project necessary to ensure social stability in China. Most of these problems are familiar in other Asian, in particular East Asian, societies. Ensuring good governance is a widespread challenge in Asia.

The new Chinese leadership has decided to initiate reforms in most of the areas in question. Rather than antagonizing the Chinese government by public criticism on deficits, in particular in the field of human rights, the EU and the United States should engage in working with the Chinese leadership in key areas of urbanization, of providing clean and efficient energy, and of building a system of social security for all, in particular for people in rural areas. The EU, with its enormous experience in legal integration, should concentrate on rule of law development, building on the 10-year-process between Germany and China. Building rule of law is key to stability in each Asian society and thus for the entire region; therefore, we should concentrate our resources towards that goal rather than building "democratic alliances" which will again be received as containment by those left out. The approach should be result-oriented, not ideological. We should encourage good governance, no matter if we are dealing with democratic or autocratic systems. There should not be double standards in pursuing respect for fundamental human rights.

### Integration of Asian Economies into the Global Economy

While Korea and Japan have successfully integrated into existing international legal frameworks (WTO, IFIs, regional institutions), emerging economies like China, India, and Indonesia are in very different phases of their integrative processes. China's economy, despite efforts by the new leadership to strengthen the domestic market, will remain export-oriented for a long period of time. In the context of its "going-out" policy, it engages more actively in foreign investment activities. It therefore needs a fair and open framework for trade and investment, as do most of the European economies, in particular Germany and the UK. China, as well as other emerging economies, should be vigorously encouraged to take part in intra- and inter-regional trade agreements.

The United States, in working with the EU (TTIP) and Asia (TPP) on broad trade and investment agreements, should take an inclusive rather than an exclusive approach. China already perceives the TPP/TTIP process as an element of containment, as—for similar reasons—do India and other BRICS economies. If these agreements result in regional frameworks undermining the WTO system of global trade and upsetting the progress made in integrating the emerging economies, it would be counterproductive. The Asian countries' legitimate interests and perceptions should be taken on board in designing new trade and investment agreements. China should be offered participation in U.S. cooperation frameworks with Asia, not only in TPP.

Beyond the legal economic frameworks, Asian countries should be included in the process of developing new rules and standards in general. As China and other emerging economies must accept the present rules as the basis for global governance, the United States and EU should resist negotiating new legal frameworks among themselves and offering their product to BRICS partners on a "take-it-or-leave-it" basis. Global governance should become an integrative process, not a zero-sum assumption.

An important area of global governance is the fight against climate change. China, for example, is ready to take decisive national legal action to stop the increase of $CO^2$ emissions and to save energy by more efficient ways of energy consumption or to invest in more alternative and reproductive sources of energy. But, it is reluctant to accept international legal obligations at this point in time, due to concern that some of these obligations would adversely impact its economic growth at a time when hundreds of millions of Chinese remain mired in poverty. Western countries should recognize these national efforts and offer assistance in the implementation and verification of these steps, rather than insist on international legal rules which most of the developing countries are unwilling or incapable of shouldering. The principle of common but differentiated responsibility should remain key, but should be implemented on the understanding that every party to the agreement should do the maximum possible to reach the agreed objectives.

### Assisting Reconciliation as a Precondition for Regional Security

A host of unresolved historical issues stands in the way of resolving open territorial and other security conflicts in the region, namely the island disputes between Japan and China (Diaoyu/Senkaku) or the maritime dispute between China and the Philippines as well as Vietnam over islands in the South China Sea. A politically assertive China, which has become the economic powerhouse of Asia, and provocative actions by conservative forces in Japan such as the nationalization of the Senkaku Islands, have prompted a wave of nationalism in both countries that should be a source of concern to the entire region and beyond.

In view of the complex legal situation underlying the territorial disputes, the United States and the EU should continue to refrain from taking a position on the legal arguments and continue to encourage both sides to use peaceful means, in particular, processes of arbitration, to prevent these disputes from developing into open conflict, which both sides seem to want to avoid. For the United States it is essential to balance carefully its responsibilities arising from the Treaty of Mutual Cooperation and Security with Japan and keeping stability in the Asia Pacific region as a whole on the basis of legitimate interests of all countries in the region.

It is important to understand, however, that ensuring stability in the region will require improved relations between China and its much smaller neighbors. Nationalism is not only a phenomenon in Chinese and Japanese societies; it is very much latent in others as well. As historic roots like the Nanjing massacre are very much at the bottom of Chinese nationalism against Japan, it is inconceivable that the territorial conflicts will be solved without prior progress in reconciling both societies. There is no visible readiness on either side to engage in a serious process of reconciliation, neither between China and Japan, nor between Japan and the Republic of Korea.

This phenomenon needs to be addressed urgently. The Europeans can and should bring in their unprecedented experience of post-World War II reconciliation. We should pool our resources in assisting Asian civil society and science (Japan/South Korea, China/Japan, etc.) to start working on realistic concepts for reconciliation processes. Some of these bilateral disputes could be ameliorated by the creation of regional structures where they can be discussed without the urgency and pressure often applied by restive public opinion on bilateral mechanisms.

### Regional Security

Most Asian countries (i.e. Japan, Vietnam, Malaysia, Philippines, and Indonesia) welcome the U.S. security umbrella, but do not want to be put into a position to ally against China. Beijing will accept continued U.S. military and political presence in the Asia Pacific region if it is not perceived as a means of undermining the rise of China. The pivot to Asia should therefore avoid building communities of "like-minded," i.e. democratic, alliances but rather aim at including all Asian nations in the building multilateral frameworks in Asia.

Europe has particular experience in regional integration and should introduce it much more actively in Asia than in the past. We should examine whether or not models and patterns of cooperation developed in Europe and, with the United States, can work in the Pacific. This should be a coordinated and cooperative strategy, not a unified plan, as the United States and the EU will continue to have partially different interests in the region and are being perceived by countries in the region of pursuing different objectives.

## Asia Must Develop its Own Asian Way of Integration into Global Society

The United States and the EU should work on the premise that Asian societies, not only China, must find their own way both in driving their domestic development and in assuming more regional and global responsibility. They all will be reluctant to accept prescriptions of what has worked in the Atlantic. The approach must be based on the interests of each country, and not be one which is perceived as serving U.S. or EU or "Western" needs or interests above those of the Asians.

A coordinated transatlantic effort should, in general, aim at broadening the Asian role in international fora and negotiations, in standard-setting processes or multilateral negotiation, taking on board legitimate interests of the region or countries concerned. It might involve efforts at more inclusivity of international financial institutions (a process already underway), or in supporting United Nations reforms, in particular Security Council enlargement (although opposition to Japanese Security Council membership has come mainly from China).

There are numerous intra-Asian structures working towards stronger regionalism, such as ASEAN or the ASEAN Regional Forum. The most important framework for intra-regional cooperation is ASEAN plus 3 (China, Japan, South Korea), enlarged by "observers" like India, Australia and New Zealand. Furthermore, the trilateral cooperation between the "Big Three" in East Asia—China, Japan, and South Korea—has developed into a regular summit framework for cooperation. These processes should be encouraged to be more than they have been in the past. However, in view of the recent waves of nationalism between these three societies, a medium or long-term effort rather than a short-term is more realistic.

A transatlantic joint policy towards the East Asian region should build on these existing structures. The United States and the EU may want to try to establish a format in working together with ASEAN plus 3. TPP should be an open architecture, allowing for Chinese and Indian participation. This could also be achieved by a Trilateral trade agreement between the EU, the United States and the "Big Three" (China, Japan, and South Korea).

East Asia is in desperate need of multilateral structures that can help countries to manage bilateral disputes. So far, most of the maritime disputes have gone immediately into bilateral channels with predictable results. Multilateral structures—such as ASEAN—should be encouraged to deal with such conflicts with greater substance, albeit China continues to be reluctant because of its higher leverage in bilateral approaches. The envisaged Code of Conduct seems to be a good avenue to build on.

There is no easy one-fits-all concept to build regional structures. But we can draw from transatlantic experience and from building European institutions. Some aspects of building an EU legal framework, or of NATO coordination, may be applicable to Asia.

Last but certainly not least, Europeans and Americans need to be careful about tone, about "face." We must avoid the perception of imposed standards and values. We must speak clearly about value issues, and not succumb to any self-censorship, but we must be careful that they do not become wedge issues that divide us and the countries of East Asia. Supporting good governance and rule of law should be joint objectives, human rights issues should be addressed in the relevant official channels and not (mis)used for domestic public policy.

## Recommendations for Western Diplomacy with Asia

1. The United States and the EU both have increasing interests in Asia. A U.S. pivot to Asia does not automatically entail a downgrading of the transatlantic relationship, but it will require a more regular and sophisticated coordination of U.S. and EU policies towards Asia. A joint understanding about the areas of common—or at least coordinated—action is possible, but would be facilitated by the development of common principles and parameters for action:

- **The common objective of U.S. and EU engagement in Asia is stable development in the entire region, fair framework conditions for trade and investment in Asia,** and integrating Asian countries into a global network of institutions based on common legal and social standards.

- As China is the most important new actor in Asia, **the United States and the EU should develop a realistic analysis of China's rise, its intentions, and its challenges.** This analysis should be independent of perceptions of China's neighbors, which are naturally driven by anxieties stemming from the size of China's population, economy and power. It is indispensable to arrive at an objective threat perception, taking into account the respective legitimate interests of China and its neighbors (i.e. territorial integrity). It necessitates a common analysis of China's strategic intentions and, in that context, of its objectives in its military build-up (Taiwan, Diaoyu/Senkaku, securing waterways).

2. On the basis of a clear understanding about the key parameters of transatlantic cooperation in Asia, the United States and EU should work together more systematically to develop a common strategic approach to Asia. This might include the following:

- In designing and executing a complementary pivot to Asia, the US and the EU should use existing frameworks more efficiently, and, where necessary, create lean new frameworks. **Our policy towards China/Asia should be a regular agenda item at EU-U.S. summits and at U.S. summit meetings with national European leaders.** While NATO could continue to develop informal frameworks of consultation and cooperation with Asian partners (inclusive process is necessary), regional Asian security issues are unlikely to be accepted as agenda items for Asian-NATO dialogues. We should aim for early cooperation with Asian partners on regional and global issues instead of confronting them with Western "take-it-or-leave-it" options.

- **At the inter-governmental level, the United States and the EU should develop a practice of smaller working parties**: the EU, represented by the Commission and/or the External Action Service, should always be included. Preference should be for informal settings and a mixture of decision-making power and expert knowledge.

- **Beyond the inter-governmental level there is a need for new track II initiatives**. We should think about creating a Trilateral EU-U.S.-Asia Framework, preferably organized by a group of private foundations from Asia, the EU and the United States, tackling relevant issues of global importance (urbanization, resource security, climate change, and regional conflicts). The framework should include important "emerging economies" (China, India, Indonesia and others); it could consist of a bi-annual conference (rotating between Europe, Asia and the United States) as well as of smaller dialogue formats with trans-sectoral participation reflecting a broader range of ideas.

- **ASEAN could be the first group of countries in Asia following the European way of a more integrated multilateralism**. However, we need to understand that integration in ASEAN will meet very different social and political framework conditions, not least prompted by the role of religion in some of ASEAN's member states. Building a sustainable process of institutionalized cooperation continues to be a key to stability. Myanmar needs to be guided into this long-term process.

3. Key issue areas in which the United States and EU might cooperate and coordinate their policies towards Asia include the following:

- A key priority of a coordinated transatlantic policy towards Asia should be support for stable domestic and regional development. This needs to be strictly on the basis of Asian countries defining their own interests, priorities and ways to build their regional structures. **Rule of law development is a key priority, as is the building of sustainable systems of social security**. In this area of urbanization and "building society," the EU and the United States should share information and best practices, but not attempt to develop a common policy.

- **Transatlantic partners should better coordinate economic development policies**, maximizing impact in times of declining funds, and try to develop a strategy of burden sharing in view of the vast challenges ahead.

- In trade and investment, the United States should take an inclusive approach, in particular with regard to China and other BRICS economies. Alternatively, the **United States and EU could envisage trade and investment agreements with the "Big East-Asian Three"** (China/Japan/South Korea). Regional agreements, both by the United States or the EU, must be negotiated carefully so as not to undermine the global WTO framework.

- **The ever more important issue of energy security could be addressed by a cooperative framework with U.S., EU and Asian participation,** reflecting the interests of energy-producing countries, countries of passage, and consumer economies. The objective should be to develop a fair framework for all.

- Reconciliation is a priority in view of solving regional disputes and conflicts. **The EU, with its specific experience in post-World War II reconciliation, should engage more actively with the societies in the region in addressing historic traumas as the source of old and new nationalism.**

- **Solving regional conflicts, like those in the East and South China Seas, requires an even-handed approach.** The United States, as the most important guarantor of stability in the Asia-Pacific, is in the lead, and can contribute significantly if it is perceived as a fair partner and honest broker between the conflicting interests, notwithstanding its vested treaty obligations, which it will continue to honor.

- **The United States and the EU can assist in building national and regional security structures and processes.** While NATO may not be perceived by some countries in the region as a role model, informal partnerships may be welcomed by some Asian partners. The OSCE process may have relevance for understanding how countries with different political systems can work together; but they need to be adapted to the specific requirements of the Asian continent. The EU, with its unique experience in multilateral institution-building and in rule of law development, can contribute to the building of intra-regional institutions.

- **Patience is required as to the readiness of Asian govern-ments to take on global responsibility**. As the China case proves, countries start shouldering responsibility first when their own vital interests are at stake (North Korea, Iran, reform of international financial institutions, and climate change). It is important for the United States and the EU to harmonize their expectation management and to refrain from overburdening countries whose main priority will remain their domestic development for a long period to come. A gradual process of global integration is warranted. Climate change, cyber security, and Arctic issues should be matters of shared concern and be given priority in working with Asian partners.

# About the Authors

**Hans Binnendijk** is a Senior Fellow at the Center for Transatlantic Relations at Johns Hopkins University's School of Advanced International Studies (SAIS), and at RAND. Until July 4, 2012 he was the Vice President for Research and Applied Learning at the National Defense University and Theodore Roosevelt Chair in National Security Policy. He previously served on the National Security Council staff as Special Assistant to the President and Senior Director for Defense Policy and Arms Control. He also served as Principal Deputy Director of the State Department's Policy Planning Staff and Legislative Director of the Senate Foreign Relations Committee. He has received three Distinguished Public Service Awards. In academia, he was Director of the Institute for the Study of Diplomacy at Georgetown University and Deputy Director at London's International Institute for Strategic Studies. He has written widely on U.S. national security issues, on NATO and on Asia. He serves as Vice Chairman of the Board of the Fletcher School and as Chairman of the Board of Humanity in Action.

**Tim Boersma** is a fellow in the Energy Security Initiative at The Brookings Institution. His research focuses on energy policy coordination, energy security, gas infrastructure and regulation, resource scarcity, and unconventional natural gas extraction. He holds a PhD in international relations from the University of Groningen. In 2011–2012 he was a Transatlantic Academy fellow in Washington, D.C. Before becoming a full time academic, he spent five years as a corporate counsel to the electricity production sector in the Netherlands. He is currently finishing a monograph with colleagues titled *Want, Waste, or War? The Global Resource Nexus and the Struggle for Land, Energy, Food, Water, and Minerals*, to be published by Earthscan in 2014. At Brookings he is involved in projects about energy and mineral resources in Greenland, hydrocarbon finds in the Eastern Mediterranean, renewable energy in the United Arab Emirates, and the role of natural gas in European Union energy markets. He is also working on a manuscript entitled *Energy Security and Natural Gas*

*Markets in Europe: Lessons from the EU and the United States*, which is scheduled to be published in the Routledge Studies in Energy Policy series in 2015.

**Jaime de Bourbon Parme** is Special Envoy on Natural Resources at the Netherlands Ministry of Foreign Affairs. His main focus is long-term and durable security of supply of metals and minerals. He also looks at the social and environmental impacts of the extractive indus-try. At the Ministry of Foreign Affairs these topics are approached from a geopolitical, development and security perspective. H.R.H. Prince Jaime de Bourbon Parme has been named a Young Global Leader by the World Economic Forum. Prior to his current position he was responsible for peacekeeping operations in Africa at the Netherlands Ministry of Foreign Affairs. He was also a member of the Cabinet and Political Advisor to Neelie Kroes, European Commis-sioner for Competition; a Political Advisor to the Dutch Commander of the NATO Peacekeeping Mission in Northern Afghanistan; and he helped to set up the Netherlands Embassy in Baghdad. He served as an interviewer for a documentary series on war economies in Sierra Leone, Liberia and Congo; and as an analyst for ABN AMRO Bank in Latin America. He holds a BA from Brown University and an MA from Johns Hopkins University's Paul H. Nitze School of Advanced International Studies (SAIS).

**Cathleen Cimino** is a research analyst at the Peterson Institute for International Economics. She works with Senior Fellows Gary Clyde Hufbauer and Jeffrey J. Schott on economic issues relating to interna-tional trade policy, free trade agreement negotiations, and the future of the World Trade Organization. She is coauthor of *Local Content Requirements: A global Problem* (2013). She has an MA focused in inter-national economics from the School of International Relations and Pacific Studies at the University of California, San Diego and a BA in East Asian Studies and Political Science from Columbia University. Her research background is on the East Asian region. Ms. Cimino's past experience includes stints at the Asia Society and the Center for Strategic and International Studies working on development and eco-nomic recovery issues. She is fluent in Japanese.

**Patrick M. Cronin** is Senior Director of the Asia-Pacific Security Program at the Center for a New American Security (CNAS). Previously he directed the Institute for National Strategic Studies (INSS), including its Center for the Study of Chinese Military Affairs. He has a diverse background in both Asian-Pacific security and U.S. defense, foreign and development policy. He directed research at the International Institute for Strategic Studies in London, CSIS, USIP, and INSS (where he managed a major futures' study for the Vice Chairman of the Joint Chiefs of Staff). In 2001, he was confirmed by the U.S. Senate to the third-ranking position at the U.S. Agency for International Development (USAID). He has taught at Georgetown University's Security Studies Program, Johns Hopkins University's SAIS, and the University of Virginia's Woodrow Wilson Department of Government. He received both his M.Phil. and D.Phil. degrees from St. Antony's College, University of Oxford. In addition to many CNAS reports and numerous articles, his major publications include *Global Strategic Assessment, America's Security Role in a Changing World* (2009); *Civilian Surge: Key to Complex Operations* (co-editor, 2009) and *The Impenetrable Fog of War: Reflections on Modern Warfare and Strategic Surprise* (2008).

**Pieter Feith** was Head of the EU-led Aceh Monitoring Mission (AMM) in Indonesia in 2005–2006 to implement a peace plan negotiated by President Ahtisaari between the Government and the Aceh independence movement. Earlier, he served as Deputy Director General for politico-military affairs at the European Union Council Secretariat and as Director for crisis management in the NATO International Staff. Acting as the Personal Representative of the Secretary General of NATO Lord Robertson in 2001, he engaged in preventive diplomacy in Southern Serbia and in Macedonia. From 2008 to 2012 he was the International Civilian Representative for Kosovo, where he had wide-ranging authority based on a settlement to oversee and assist Kosovo's independence. In parallel, he held the post of the European Union Special Representative mandated to provide EU advice and to promote overall coordination in Kosovo. In the service of the Netherlands Ministry of Foreign Affairs he was posted in Damascus, Bonn, New York (United Nations), Khartoum and Brussels (NATO). He studied Political Science at the University of Lausanne and holds an MA from the Fletcher School of Law and Diplomacy in Medford, Massachusetts. He is a Visiting Scholar at the SAIS Center for Transatlantic Relations.

**Mircea Geoana** is a Senator, Chairman of the Joint Committee of the Romanian Senate and Chamber of Deputies regarding Romania's Accession to the Schengen Area. He serves as High Representative of the Romanian Government for economic strategic projects and public diplomacy. He is the founding member and President of the Aspen Institute Romania and member of the board of the Aspen Institute in the United States. He ran for the Presidency of Romania in 2009. Prior to his political career, he served as Romania's Ambassador to the United States from 1996 to 2000 and as Minister of Foreign Affairs from 2000 to 2004. In this capacity, he also served as OSCE Chairman in office for Georgia in 2001. He is an alumnus of the Polytechnic Institute and the Law School of the University of Bucharest. He graduated in 1992 from the École Nationale d'Administration in Paris, France and in 1999 from the World Bank Executive Development Program of Harvard Business School. He holds a PhD in world economy at the Economic Studies Academy of Bucharest.

**Daniel S. Hamilton** is the Austrian Marshall Plan Foundation Professor and Executive Director of the Center for Transatlantic Relations at Johns Hopkins University's Paul H. Nitze School of Advanced International Studies (SAIS). He also serves as Executive Director of the American Consortium for EU Studies (ACES), the EU Center of Excellence in Washington, D.C., and as Director of the Atlantic Basin Initiative of Eminent Persons and research institutes across the four Atlantic continents. He previously served as U.S. Deputy Assistant Secretary of State for European Affairs; Associate Director of the Policy Planning Staff for two U.S. Secretaries of State; U.S. Special Coordinator for Southeast European Stabilization; and Policy Director for the Bureau of European Affairs. He also served as the first Robert Bosch Foundation Senior Diplomatic Fellow in the German Foreign Office. He has taught at a number of U.S. and European universities; been a consultant to the U.S. Business Roundtable, the Transatlantic Business Dialogue, Microsoft, and advisory board member to many European think tanks and foundations. Recent publications include *The Transatlantic Economy 2014*; *Open Ukraine: Towards a European Future*; *Atlantic Rising: Changing Commercial Dynamics in the Atlantic Basin*; *Dark Networks in the Atlantic Basin: Emerging Trends and Implications for Human Security*; *Transatlantic 2020: A Tale of Four Futures*; and *Europe 2020: Competitive or Complacent?*

**Christopher R. Hill** is the Dean of the Josef Korbel School of International Studies at the University of Denver, a position he has held since September 2010. He is a former career diplomat, a four-time ambassador, nominated by three presidents; His last post was as Ambassador to Iraq from April 2009 until August 2010. Prior to Iraq, he served as U.S. Assistant Secretary of State for East Asian and Pacific Affairs from 2005 until 2009, during which time he was also the head of the U.S. delegation to the Six Party Talks on the North Korean nuclear issue. Earlier, he was the U.S. Ambassador to the Republic of Korea. Previously he served as U.S. Ambassador to Poland (2000–2004), Ambassador to the Republic of Macedonia (1996–1999) and Special Envoy to Kosovo (1998–1999). He also served as a Special Assistant to the President and a Senior Director on the staff of the National Security Council from 1999–2000.

**Robert E. Hunter** is a Senior Fellow at the Center for Transatlantic Relations, and also serves on the U.S. Secretary of State's International Security Advisory Board. He was U.S. ambassador to NATO (1993–1998), Director of West European and then Middle East Affairs (1977–1981) on the National Security Council staff, and Senior Advisor at the RAND Corporation (1998–2011). At NATO, he played a leading role in both crafting and negotiating the post-Cold War transformation of NATO and negotiated NATO's air strike decisions that ended the Bosnia War. At the NSC, he was White House representative for the Autonomy Talks on the West Bank and Gaza and developed the Carter Doctrine. He was a Fulbright Scholar at the London School of Economics (PhD-1969), worked in nine presidential campaigns, written speeches for three presidents and three vice presidents, has more than 900 publications, taught at five universities, and has been decorated by eight European governments and twice with the Pentagon's highest civilian award.

**Karl-Heinz Kamp** is the Academic Director of the German Federal Academy for Security Policy in Berlin. He studied History and Political Sciences in Bonn and holds a PhD from the University of the German Armed Forces in Hamburg with a dissertation on NATO's nuclear planning procedures. Dr. Kamp has been a Research Fellow at the John F. Kennedy School, Harvard University. He served at the Konrad Adenauer Foundation in Bonn and Berlin and on the Planning Staff of the German Foreign Ministry. From 2007 to 2013 he served as the Research Director of the NATO Defense College in Rome to build up NATO's research division. Dr. Kamp is a member of numerous international institutions and academic bodies. In 2009, former U.S. Secretary of State Madeleine Albright selected him as one of the Advisors for the NATO Expert Group on the New Strategic Concept. He has published more than 330 articles on security policy issues in books and journals including *Foreign Policy*, the *International Herald Tribune* and *Washington Quarterly*.

**Rem Korteweg** is a senior research fellow on foreign and security policy at the Centre for European Reform in London. He works on strategic issues including transatlantic relations, security in the European neighborhood, geopolitics of energy, and how Europe pursues its interests amid the rise of non-Western powers. Before joining CER, Mr. Korteweg worked as a strategic analyst at The Hague Center for Strategic Studies (HCSS). In 2012 he had a placement within the Ministry of Foreign Affairs of the Netherlands. In 2006–2007 he was a Fulbright scholar at the SAIS Center for Transatlantic Relations. He has a PhD in International Relations from Leiden University. He is a committee-member of the Netherlands' Advisory Council on International Affairs (AIV), which advises government and parliament on foreign policy issues.

**Michael Schaefer** studied law in Munich, Geneva, and Heidelberg where he passed his Second State Examination in Law in 1978. In the same year, he joined the German Foreign Service. After postings at the United Nations in New York he served as Permanent Representative at the German Embassy in Singapore from 1987 to 1991 and as head of the Political Affairs Section at the German Permanent Mission in Geneva from 1995 to 1999. From 1999 to 2002, he headed the Western Balkans Task Force and subsequently was Deputy Political Director and Special Envoy for Southeast Europe at the Federal Foreign Office in Berlin. From 2002 to 2007, he was Political Director of the Federal Foreign Office, before being appointed Ambassador to the People's Republic of China, a post he held until June 2013. Since July 1, 2013, he has been Chairman of the Board of Directors of the BMW Stiftung Herbert Quandt. He is also honorary professor at the China University of Political Science and Law in Beijing, member of the German Group of the Trilateral Commission, member of the Advisory Board of the Mercator Institute for China Studies (MERICS) and board member of the United Nations Association of Germany (DGVN).

**Jeffrey J. Schott** joined the Peterson Institute for International Economics in 1983 and is a senior fellow working on trade and economic sanctions. During his tenure at the Institute, Schott also has taught at Princeton University (1994) and Georgetown University (1986–1988). He was formerly a senior associate at the Carnegie Endowment for International Peace (1982–1983) and an official of the U.S. Treasury Department (1974–1982) in international trade and energy policy. He is a member of the Trade and Environment Policy Advisory Committee of the U.S. Trade Representative's office and a member of the Advisory Committee on International Economic Policy of the U.S. Department of State. He is the author, coauthor, or editor of numerous books on trade, including most recently *Local Content Requirements: A Global Problem* (2013), *Understanding the Trans-Pacific Partnership* (2013) and *Payoff from the World Trade Agenda* (2013). He holds a BA degree magna cum laude from Washington University, St. Louis (1971) and an MA degree with distinction in international relations from the School of Advanced International Studies of Johns Hopkins University (1973).

**Julianne Smith** is Senior Fellow and Director of the Strategy and Statecraft Program at the Center for a New American Security. She also serves as a Senior Vice President at Beacon Global Strategies LLC. Prior to joining Beacon, she served as the Deputy National Security Advisor to the Vice President of the United States from April 2012 to June 2013. Prior to her posting at the White House, she served as the Principal Director for European and NATO Policy in the Office of the Secretary of Defense in the Pentagon. Prior to joining the Obama administration, she served as the director of the CSIS Europe Program and the Initiative for a Renewed Transatlantic Partnership. She worked as a senior analyst on the European security desk of the British American Security Information Council and in Germany at the Stiftung Wissenschaft und Politik as a Robert Bosch Foundation Fellow in 1996–1997. She is a recipient of the American Academy in Berlin Public Policy Fellowship and the Fredin Memorial Scholarship for study at the Sorbonne in Paris. She received her BA from Xavier University and her MA from American University.

**Alexander Sullivan** is a Research Associate in the Asia-Pacific Security Program and a former Joseph S. Nye, Jr. National Security Research Intern at the Center for a New American Security (CNAS). Prior to joining CNAS, Mr. Sullivan was an independent writer and researcher working on diverse topics ranging from Asian geopolitics and international relations to corporate history. In addition to CNAS publications, his writing has appeared in *Foreign Policy*, *The Diplomat*, and *China-US Focus*. He holds an MA in Chinese History from Columbia University and graduated magna cum laude from Columbia College with an AB in East Asian Languages and Cultures.

**Simon Tay** is a public intellectual as well as private advisor to major corporations and policy makers. He is Chairman of the Singapore Institute of International Affairs, the country's oldest think tank and rated in 2014 as the best in Southeast Asia and the Pacific. He served as a non-elected Nominated Member of Parliament from 1997 to 2001. From 2002 to 2008, he chaired the National Environment Agency of Singapore. He is concurrently an Associate Professor, teaching international law at the National University of Singapore. He was a visiting professor at Harvard Law School, Yale and the Fletcher School of Tufts University. His book *Asia Alone* (2010), about regionalism and the role of America, was well received in the international press. His commentaries feature regularly in newspapers across Asia and he also frequently appears on international television.

**Abiodun Williams** is President of The Hague Institute for Global Justice. Previously, he was Senior Vice President of the Center for Conflict Management at the United States Institute for Peace, and Director of Strategic Planning for United Nations Secretaries-General Ban Ki-moon and Kofi Annan. He served in senior policy positions in UN peacekeeping operations in the Balkans and Haiti. He has held faculty appointments at National Defense University, Georgetown University, the University of Rochester, and Tufts University. He has published widely on conflict prevention, conflict management, international peacekeeping and multilateral negotiations. Dr. Williams holds an MA (Honors) in English Language and Literature from Edinburgh University, as well as a Master of Arts in Law and Diplomacy (MALD) and a PhD in International Relations from The Fletcher School of Law and Diplomacy.

**Reuben Wong** holds the Jean Monnet Chair at the National University of Singapore and is Director of Studies at the College of Alice & Peter Tan (CAPT). He earned an M.Phil in European Politics at Oxford, and a PhD in International Relations at the London School of Economics (LSE). He is the author of *The Europeanization of French Foreign Policy* (2006); *National and European foreign policies* (co-edited with Christopher Hill, 2011); and refereed articles in the *Cambridge Review of International Affairs*, *Politique Européenne*, *Asia Europe Journal*, and *EU External Affairs Review*. Mr. Wong has held visiting positions at Cambridge, the London School of Economics, the Stimson Center (Washington, D.C.), and the East Asian Institute (Singapore). He currently researches the construction of Chinese identity *vis-à-vis* the West, integration theory, EU relations with ASEAN and China, and the politics of disability rights. A Fulbright scholar (2009), he serves on the Singapore Institute of International Affairs (SIIA) Council, and the EU Centre in Singapore. He raises four children to help arrest Singapore's declining birth rate.